Development Drowned and Reborn

Development Drowned and Reborn

THE BLUES AND BOURBON RESTORATIONS IN POST-KATRINA NEW ORLEANS

CLYDE WOODS

EDITED BY JORDAN T. CAMP
AND LAURA PULIDO

THE UNIVERSITY OF GEORGIA PRESS
Athens

© 2017 by the University of Georgia Press
Athens, Georgia 30602
www.ugapress.org
All rights reserved
Set in Minion Pro and Proxima Nova by Graphic Composition, Inc.

Most University of Georgia Press titles are
available from popular e-book vendors.

Printed digitally

Library of Congress Control Number: 2017941819

ISBN: 9780820350912 (hardcover : alk. paper)
ISBN: 9780820350929 (paperback : alk. paper)
ISBN: 9780820350905 (ebook)

For Clyde, with gratitude
    —Jordan T. Camp and Laura Pulido

CONTENTS

We Made It

SUNNI PATTERSON

I'm from a stock that pitch cocktail bombs and hand grenades
We pour cayenne pepper around the perimeter of a building to keep the
    police dogs at bay
I'm the Panther Party in the Desire Housing Projects of New Orleans
I'm a nigga turning the gun on the national guards
Take a long, long look!

I'm a cook in the kitchen asking the misses to taste the dinner
Take a long, long sip!
Cause Death ain't always this good

It's eyes popping out their sockets
It's a lifeless body rocking backwards and forwards
It's a boy stabbed 47 times in front of the church-house
It's a man 43 years old stuffing his penis in a 9 year old girl's mouth . . .
Nah, Death don't always taste good!
Just don't sound like something I wanna eat
Often, I hear them say it was a train came through the room
Left Mama so depressed she was unable to move

Until one day . . .

It was a few months after the Hurricane
Husband and child found the trinity bloody in bed
His wife, his son, his other daughter—DEAD!
And on the end table there was a letter that read . . . it said,

"I couldn't stay here . . . not for one minute longer, and it made no sense for me
to leave here alone, cause who would take care of my babies with their mama
    gone?"

I'm telling you . . . Death ain't always good
It'll leave you fending for water and food
It'll riddle up your body in an Audubon Ballroom
They'll El Hajj Malik El Shabazz you
Crown you King, and then dethrone you in a Lorraine Hotel

They'll disfigure your body where folk can't tell if you Emmett Till or not
Tell them, Mama, "Keep that casket open!"
Let all the world see, it ain't just burning in Mississippi
Hell is hot wherever you be
From the rooftop to the cell block
Step on up to the auction block
And bend over
Touch your toes
Show your teeth
Lift her titties
Examine his balls
Now, this damn near sounds like a hip hop song
But it's slavery at its peak!
It's a circus for all the freaks
They'll warn you caution when you speak
Can't afford the truth to leak.
But we'll say blessed are the meek
And all the ones who make peace
And all the ones who are persecuted for the sake of righteousness
For theirs is the Kingdom
Earth is their inheritance
So, no matter how treacherous . . .
They'll try to trap us in them trenches
They'll dig deeper ditches, but all that matters is this:
Which side will we pick?
Which path will we choose?
It's either win or lose
Cause death don't come in vain.
Not for us to remain enslaved
Or our spirits to remain in cages
It comes so we might be courageous
To fulfill our obligation to our God and all creation
To stand in determination, able to look Death straight in the face and say . . .

We made it!
We made it!
We made it!
We made it!

FIGURES

ABBREVIATIONS

BCVL	Bogalusa Civic and Voters' League
BNOB	Bring New Orleans Back Commission
BOLD	Black Organization for Leadership Development
BPP	Black Panther Party
BRASS	Black Revolutionary Action among Soul Students
CIO	Congress of Industrial Organizations
CORE	Congress of Racial Equality
COUP	Community Organization for Urban Politics
DLC	Democratic Leadership Council
FEMA	Federal Emergency Management Agency
FHA	Federal Housing Administration
HANO	Housing Authority of New Orleans
HUAC	House Un-American Activities Committee
HUD	U.S. Department of Housing and Urban Development
LCRC	Louisiana Civil Rights Congress
LFU	Louisiana Farmers' Union
LIFE	Louisiana Independent Federation of Electors, Inc.
LMDDC	Lower Mississippi Delta Development Commission
MR-GO	Mississippi River–Gulf Outlet
NAACP	National Association for the Advancement of Colored People
NFU	National Farmers Union
NOD	New Orleans Division, Universal Negro Improvement Association
NOPD	New Orleans Police Department
OPEC	Organization of Petroleum Exporting Countries
OPSB	Orleans Public School Board
RNC	Republican National Committee
RSD	Recovery School District
SCU	Sharecroppers Union
SNCC	Student Nonviolent Coordinating Committee
SOUL	Southern Organization for Unified Leadership
TCA	Total Community Action
UNIA	Universal Negro Improvement Association
VA	Veterans Administration
WPA	Works Progress Administration

ABOUT CLYDE WOODS

Clyde Woods was an associate professor of Black Studies at the University of California, Santa Barbara. He died July 6, 2011. A native of Baltimore, Woods received his PhD in urban planning from the University of California, Los Angeles. The bulk of his scholarship focused on the historical geography of the U.S. South and the political influence that the region exerted on the national and global political economy. Woods is the author of *Development Arrested: The Blues and Plantation Power in the Mississippi Delta* (Verso, 1998); coeditor (with Katherine McKittrick) of *Black Geographies and the Politics of Place* (South End Press, 2007); editor of a special issue of *American Quarterly* (61, no. 3, September 2009) that was reprinted as *In the Wake of Hurricane Katrina: New Paradigms and Social Visions* (Johns Hopkins University Press, 2010); and author of "Do You Know What It Means to Miss New Orleans?: Katrina, Trap Economics, and the Rebirth of the Blues," *American Quarterly* 57, no. 4 (2005). His work also has appeared in venues such as the *Professional Geographer*; *Kalfou: A Journal of Comparative and Relational Ethnic Studies*; *American Studies: An Anthology*, edited by Janice A. Radway, Kevin K. Gaines, Barry Shank, and Penny Von Eschen (Malden, Mass.: Wiley-Blackwell, 2009); and *Downtown Blues: A Skid Row Reader*, edited by Christina Heatherton (Los Angeles: Freedom Now Books, 2011).

FOREWORD

Clyde Woods had been working on *Development Drowned and Reborn* for a number of years at the time of his premature death. Toward the end of his life he asked Laura Pulido to ensure that the book was completed and published. Laura and Clyde met in 1987 while graduate students in urban planning at the University of California, Los Angeles. They remained friends and colleagues throughout the rest of Clyde's life. After Clyde's death Laura invited Jordan T. Camp to work with her on completing the book project. Clyde was a member of Jordan's dissertation committee at the University of California, Santa Barbara, they had worked together along with George Lipsitz and others in the collaborative research group School of Unlimited Learning (SOUL) and on the special issue of the *American Quarterly* edited by Clyde entitled "In the Wake of Katrina: New Paradigms and Social Visions," and they had co-organized a number of events, including a session on poetic visions in post-Katrina New Orleans at the American Studies Association meetings in Washington, D.C., in November 2009 with New Orleans artists and activists Shana Griffin, Brenda Marie Osbey, Sunni Patterson, and Kalamu ya Salaam.

Our first step was to edit the latest version of the manuscript that we could locate. Upon reading the manuscript it was clear that the first five chapters were more complete and polished than the last four. As a result, we decided to consolidate the final chapters. This is the biggest change that we introduced to the extant text. In addition, in response to the reviewers' comments, we wrote the introduction and conclusion to help situate both Clyde and the book. Aside from these changes, we checked facts and verified sources, copyedited the manuscript, removed and reworked unfinished passages, added transitions, and, in a few cases, clarified phrases and completed citations to sources. We also selected text from Clyde's article "Les Misérables of New Orleans: Trap Economics and the Asset Stripping Blues, Part 1," *American Quarterly* (2009), that we thought was fitting to use as an ending for the substantive chapters. We added the additional maps except for two that Clyde had envisioned for chapter 1.

Completing a posthumous book is no easy task—intellectually, emotionally, or logistically. Our goal has been to preserve the integrity of the manuscript as the brilliant and inimitable Clyde Woods wrote it, rather than submit it to extensive revision. Our job was to act as midwives, so to speak, giving birth to this nearly completed project. As a result, the reader will see in the latter chapters that we were not able to locate sources for all of the quotes and facts, given that this was the material that Clyde was working on at the time of his death. Some sections of the final chapters are not as fully developed as they would have been, but we included them because we wanted the reader to see what Clyde was thinking and where he might have been going. To be sure, there is an incredible amount of material here and Clyde's voice is clear and consistent throughout. One can see that there is a conviction, a political and intellectual project, and penetrating prose that is in keeping with his first book, *Development Arrested*. We know that this is a book the world needs to read.

We are delighted to be publishing this book with the University of Georgia in the Geographies of Justice and Social Transformation series. Many thanks to our editor Mick Gusinde-Duffy for his encouragement and support throughout, to John Joerschke and Thomas Roche for guiding us through the production process, to Joy Margheim for the expert copyediting, and to Nik Heynen for making the initial connections with the press. We owe special thanks to Jordan Aiken, who verified all the endnotes for the entire manuscript. She was meticulous and enthusiastic and crucial to this project. Many thanks as well to Deshonay Dozier for completing the permission requests. These were major undertakings that neither one of us could have completed given our schedules. Steven Osuna also provided valuable research assistance. Emily Tumpson Molina provided key assistance early in the project. We are grateful to Malik Woods for his support of our efforts, as well as Sonya Baker for her encouragement. Our deepest thanks to Paul Ortiz and Nikhil Pal Singh for reading the manuscript in its entirety and for their generative recommended revisions.

In addition, we wish to acknowledge the support of the Department of Black Studies and the Center for Black Studies Research at the University of California, Santa Barbara, especially Mahsheed Ayoub, Ingrid Banks, Stephanie Batiste, Diane Fujino, Claudine Michel, Jeffrey Stewart, and Roberto Strongman. Both units provided funding, space, and staff support to make this book happen. Melvin Oliver, the former dean of social sciences at the University of California, Santa Barbara, arranged for Laura to come and spend some time at UCSB, which was crucial in preparing the manuscript for publication. We would like to acknowledge the financial support of Ruth Wilson Gilmore, Gaye Theresa Johnson, Charles Nicholson, and Jeffrey Stewart. Many thanks to Sunni Patterson for allowing us to use her poem "We Made It" to open the book, and Ayo Scott and the John T. Scott Family Estate Trust and the Arthur Roger Gallery for graciously allowing us to use "Storm's Coming" for the cover. In addition, we would like to thank Greg Palast and Menaka Mohan for generously sharing figures 5 and 7 with us, respectively. We also wish to acknowledge the Louisiana State Museum's permission to use figures 1 and 2; the Birmingham Public Library for figure 3; and Richard Campanella's permission to use figure 6.

Jordan would like to express gratitude to the Institute of American Cultures and Bunche Center for African American Studies at the University of California, Los Angeles, the Department of Sociology at the University of Massachusetts, Lowell, the Department of African American Studies at Princeton University, and the Center for the Study of Race and Ethnicity in America (CSREA) and Watson Institute for International and Public Affairs at Brown University for the research support and space that allowed him to complete the project. He also benefited from the opportunity to present the book's arguments and engage in discussions at the State University of New York at Purchase. He owes a great deal to Anthony Bogues, Courtney Bryan, Thulani Davis, Ruth Wilson Gilmore, Craig Gilmore, Eddie Glaude, Shana Griffin, Andy Hsiao, Robin D. G. Kelley, George Lipsitz, Brian Meeks, Naomi Murakawa, John Munro, S. Ani Mukherji, Sunni Patterson, Kalamu ya Salaam, David Roediger, and Tricia Rose for providing material, personal, and scholarly support. Jordan owes a particular debt to Christina Heatherton, whose love for Clyde and encouragement to get it right have been essential to the book's completion.

Laura would like to acknowledge the financial resources of the University of Southern California in helping to make this book a reality, the administrative support of the staff in American Studies and Ethnicity, especially Jujuana Lakes Preston; the Ethnic Studies Department at the University of California, Riverside; and the Department of Ethnic Studies at the University of Oregon, which provided both financial and administrative support, especially Donella-Elizabeth Alston. Deep gratitude to Corrine Oishi and Lindley Morton for allowing Laura to hide out and complete the copyediting at their beautiful home. Many thanks to Ruth Wilson Gilmore and Gaye Johnson for love and encouragement along the way, and finally, thanks to Mike for holding down the fort while Laura worked on the manuscript.

Jordan T. Camp and Laura Pulido

INTRODUCTION

The Dialectics of Bourbonism and the Blues

JORDAN T. CAMP AND LAURA PULIDO

> The specific antiracist, democratic, internationalist, African American, and
> working-class pillars of the sustainable Blues development tradition and the Blues
> epistemology gave Jazz its aesthetic, freedom ethic, flexibility, and social vision,
> as well as its political agenda. This allowed the tradition to become central to the
> efforts of working-class Blacks, Asian Americans, Latinos, whites, and colonized
> communities to organize newly imagined and real alliances.
>
> Clyde Woods, *Development Drowned and Reborn*, chapter 3

The death of Clyde Woods in the summer of 2011 robbed the world of one of its most impassioned scholar-activists. While only fifty-four years old when he passed, Woods had earned the respect and admiration of activists, artists, and academics alike for his scholarship on the Blues tradition and political economy, as well as his engagement with antiracist social movements. This dedication and commitment should have earned him a reputation as one of the preeminent Black radical intellectuals of his generation.[1] This study, *Development Drowned and Reborn: The Blues and Bourbon Restorations in Post-Katrina New Orleans*, his final major work, represents one of his most distinctive and urgent contributions. Covering over two centuries of political, cultural, and economic development in New Orleans and the region, the bulk of the book focuses on the period between the overthrow of Radical Reconstruction during the 1870s and the Katrina crisis in the 2000s. In doing so, it provides a unique optic for analyzing the historical geography of New Orleans.

The *longue durée* of resistance is a key theme not only in this book but in Woods's larger corpus of scholarship. He sees it as central to the social vision of the Black freedom movement and as a gift to the larger world. In this book Woods takes an especially long view of freedom struggles, which requires the telling of a deep history. *Development Drowned and Reborn* demonstrates that the study of racism and white supremacy cannot be separated from the study of political and economic development, specifically the roles of enclosures, militarism, and policing in containing working-class communities within particular geographical boundaries in order to facilitate the exploitation of labor and the accumulation of capital and power. Indeed, the present study not only provides what Woods calls a "Blues geography" of New Orleans and the region but also illustrates the dialectical relationship between the regional, national, and global political economies. In doing so, it compels us to reckon with the unfinished business of freedom struggles.[2]

Reading contemporary policies of abandonment against the grain, this Blues geography explores how long-standing structures of racism and class rule were brought into view during the Katrina events. There are several distinct dimensions to Woods's Blues geography. First, Woods renders vivid the centrality of New Orleans for understanding the U.S. political economy, reminding us how it has played a major role as a port city in the world capitalist system for centuries. New Orleans was critical to the development not only of the United States but also the larger Caribbean and global capitalism. This brings us to the second dimension of Woods's Blues geography. He argues that to understand the political, economic, ideological, and geographical relationships between the United States, Latin America, Africa, Asia, and the rest of the Global South, one needs to analyze the historical geography of New Orleans and the region. In doing so, Woods suggests that the expressive cultures of Black New Orleans have been critical to U.S. and global popular culture. He draws out a distinct Blues epistemology to powerfully reframe the historical geography of the region. Woods demonstrates that Hurricane Katrina and its aftermath were not a natural disaster. In no uncertain terms, he shows that Katrina was a human-made disaster.[3]

Though hurricanes have historically been endemic to the city and the region, to call Katrina a "natural disaster" is to relieve ourselves of serious scrutiny regarding the social causes and consequences of the drowning of New Orleans.[4] Woods argues that the organized abandonment of New Orleans was a planned response to the crisis by elites. While the Mississippi River–Gulf Outlet (a shipping channel), the state of the levees, and the concentration of poor Black people in the Lower Ninth Ward evince varying levels of intentionality, the fact is none were accidental. To understand how these material conditions came into being, Woods encourages us to examine "the disastrous choices that were made to create community, racial, class, and gender destitution in the region" (chapter 7).

Development Drowned and Reborn also makes a distinct contribution to the study of environmental justice, a focus that to this point has been less well appreciated in Woods's work. Though it is not foregrounded in the text, environmental justice runs as a theme throughout *Development Drowned and Reborn*. While some social scientists continue to debate whether or not racism is actually responsible for the disproportionate burden people of color bear in terms of environmental hazards, the response to Hurricane Katrina provided a whole new level of evidence regarding the salience not only of racism but also of the deliberate and planned nature of vulnerabilities experienced by poor and working-class people of color.[5] Most centrally, Woods argues that elites have been and continue to be unrelenting in their efforts to justify impoverishment and immiseration. They do so by consistently organizing to undo whatever political and economic advances labor and social movements may have won. To sustain this argument, Woods traces a deeply rooted racist and authoritarian political project to roll back the redistributive agenda of the state implemented by freedom struggles. By weaving this tight analysis of white supremacy and political economy together Woods provides a historical and geographical analysis of the origins and development of contemporary racial capitalism.

Written in dialogue with urban social movements, *Development Drowned and Reborn* offers tools for comprehending the racist dynamics of political culture and economy in New Orleans and beyond. Here, as in all of his works, Woods turns to organic intellectuals, Blues musicians, and poor and working people to instruct readers in this future-oriented history of struggle. Through this unique optic, Woods delineates a history, methodology, and epistemology to grasp alternative visions of development.[6]

◻ ◻ ◻

That Clyde Woods wrote about New Orleans and Louisiana is hardly surprising. Clyde had been a student of the South for decades—not only did he think it was key to understanding the experience of Black working people but he also believed that the South was a pivotal region that in many ways drove the United States. In his first book, *Development Arrested: The Blues and Plantation Power in the Mississippi Delta* (2008), Woods analyzed competing visions of development that were offered for the Mississippi Delta region. Researching these struggles put New Orleans on his radar. Then, after attending Oral History Association meetings and a 2003 Critical Resistance South conference in New Orleans, Woods began developing this study. In 2005 Woods penned a distinct intervention with the publication of "Do You Know What It Means to Miss New Orleans? Katrina, Trap Economics, and the Rebirth of the Blues" in the *American Quarterly* (2005), the flagship journal of the American Studies Association. In reflecting on these experiences Woods concluded,

> I really felt that I did not know much about Louisiana history. . . . It is sort of a problem we all have with trying to explain U.S. history just from the national perspective, or international flows of capital, or world governance, or national governance, or national flows of capital. . . . It's like the tail wagging the dog. Despite what people think there are big dogs in Louisiana that have been hunting for a long time, and when you get to Mississippi or Louisiana you're talking about the storm center of U.S. cultural, economic, and political institutions and transformation at least since the 1830s, and probably before then.[7]

Another reason Woods felt compelled to write this book was because he wanted to offer a longer historical analysis than the concept of "disaster capitalism" allowed. In the wake of Katrina, the concept, deployed by Naomi Klein, became a popular tool to describe the exploitation of crises or "disasters" in order to gut social programs and implement neoliberal agendas.[8] While sympathetic to the radical politics of such a position, Woods felt that as a theory it was limited by a neglect of the history of plantation capitalism. He observed, "Activists in New Orleans were very insistent that there was not just a disaster and people were taking advantage of it, there was a disaster *before* Katrina." Woods clarified, "New Orleans was the most impoverished metropolitan area in the country. . . . There were disasters throughout Louisiana history that really transformed the United States repeatedly." His second disagreement with the disaster capitalism thesis was that it places too much emphasis on disasters, rather than the imperatives of regional blocs with deep historical roots. As many scholars have pointed out, it is in the nature of capitalism to produce crisis. It is partly because of Woods's take on these issues that *Development Drowned and Reborn* begins more than two centuries before Katrina and focuses on the reinvention of spatial and economic dominance in New Orleans and the region well before the storm hit.[9]

It is fitting that *Development Drowned and Reborn* appears in the wake of the 150th anniversary of the Emancipation Proclamation in the United States, since it is a book about multifaceted struggles for freedom. It is a historical geography of racial capitalism and the arts of Black and working-class resistance in New Orleans. For Woods, capitalism is a deeply racialized and spatial system. As in his first book, Woods is extremely attentive to regions. Woods is not only interested in the distinctive nature of New Orleans but also argues that the region's uneven development agenda contributed to the rise of U.S. neoliberalism. He partly builds this argument by focusing on the role of "regional blocs" in shaping the political economy. By regional blocs Woods means dynamic regional power structures that consist of diverse segments but are united in their efforts to "gain control over resources and over the ideological and distributive institutions governing their allocation."[10]

Development Drowned and Reborn foregrounds a dialectic of Bourbonism and the Blues, by which Woods means a clash between antagonistic social visions of development with opposing material interests. The term *Bourbonism*, which originally referred to an authoritarian regime in France, was later applied to the plantation blocs in several southern states, and the Louisiana cotton and sugar blocs in particular. Following the lead of W. E. B. Du Bois in *Black Reconstruction in America* (1935), Woods illustrates how the overthrow of Radical Reconstruction in the 1870s led to the restoration of power for the "Bourbon bloc." In Woods's hands the concept refers to "the extremely hierarchical social philosophy of the dominant regional blocs," that "led the violent movement to overthrow Reconstruction, disenfranchise Blacks and impoverished whites, and create the institutions of debt peonage and prison slavery" (chapter 2).

The Bourbon bloc in New Orleans—made up of representatives of banks, law firms, and major shipping interests, as well as cotton merchants and financiers—sought to legitimate the accumulation of wealth, the evisceration of civil and human rights, and the consolidation of an authoritarian carceral regime in order to maintain its rule. Woods deploys this concept to help us understand how Black, poor, and working-class communities had been deleteriously impacted by Bourbon political and economic policy well before Katrina hit.[11]

Through this approach he describes the roots of policies of abandonment and planned shrinkage deployed in the wake of Hurricane Katrina. "What the failure of the levees in 2005 revealed," Woods writes, "was doubly shocking: the restoration of Bourbonism locally; its restoration nationally under the guise of Reaganism, devolution, starve the beast, and so on; and its restoration internationally under the guise of structural adjustment and neoliberalism. These elite responses to social and economic crises have led to a broken region, a broken nation, and a broken world system" (chapter 7). *Development Drowned and Reborn* observes how theories of neoliberalism have tended to overlook New Orleans as an epicenter where racial, class, gender, and regional hierarchies have persisted for centuries. After all, New Orleans was once considered the "Wall Street of the Confederacy," and as Woods so powerfully put it, "was to become the central shipping, trade, and financial center of a plantation empire encompassing the western territories, the state of California, the Caribbean, Central America, Mexico, and Brazil. . . . This movement reflected a dynamic still central to the political economy of the United States: competing regional imperialisms" (chapter 2).[12]

The book, in turn, is attentive to the development of imperial Bourbonism at the national and global scale. It explores how the Bourbon ruling class consolidated a new historical bloc in the wake of the Civil War and Reconstruction. This bloc produced historically and geographically specific forms of racist social control and labor exploitation such as prisons and sharecropping, which made the region an epicenter of Jim Crow. It sought to win consent to the violent exploitation of labor through appeals to white supremacy. The success of white supremacist ideology and racist practices at both urban and regional scales, Woods contends, provided justification for the expansion of capitalist practices at the national and international scale. These policies were exported around the United States and the world. He traces the circulation of imperial Bourbonism in places such as Central America, South America, the Caribbean, and Africa. As such, this book provides a materialist methodology for interrogating social conflicts between working people and elites across the planet. It offers a model for analyzing antagonistic contradictions between the working-class struggle to redistribute wealth and dominant historical blocs bent on seizing state power, expanding militarism, and accumulating capital.[13]

Woods insists that we wrestle with the long-term structural dynamics of racism and capitalist development in the region. At the same time, however, he wants us to grapple with neoliberalism as a turning point in the history of capitalism. As such, he contributes an original methodological framework for analyzing the rise of neoliberalism. The book suggests that the prevailing focus on the impacts of neoliberalism at national and global scales has led to a neglect of the regional scale. Specifically, he draws our attention to the formation of a "neo-Bourbon bloc," which he argues has been planning "a new era of enclosures, traps, and accelerated asset stripping." He contends that neoliberals consciously sought to roll back the advances of labor and freedom struggles from the civil rights era. This has occurred despite the presence of what he described as "a complex legal regime in the United States to enforce laws against racial discrimination." He powerfully shows how neoliberals have engaged in the stripping away of social and economic rights by constructing "asset stripping enclosure institutions." These enclosure institutions have led to historic levels of racial inequality, structural unemployment, and poverty, and have made New Orleans the most carceral city in the state, with the highest rates of incarceration in the country and the world. According to Woods, the formation of this carceral apparatus was a key feature of a neoliberal enclosure movement, which maintained "a system of militarized regulation, physical boundaries, and social, political, and economic traps." This form of what he called "trap economics" extracts wealth from the racially subordinated poor and working class by privatizing social goods formerly held in common, such as public schools, hospitals, housing, transit, and parks, and increasing expenditures for policing and prisons.[14]

Finally, the book explores the ethical possibilities for a new society articulated in the "Blues epistemology." Here Woods means the philosophy of development that has been expressed in the cultural productions of Black working-class organic intellectuals since at least the Civil War and Reconstruction. According to Woods, the Blues epistemology is a way of knowing rooted in the historic redistributive agenda of freedom and labor struggles. He argues that this epistemology has inspired the efforts of the Black, Native American, Asian American, Latina/o, and white working-class communities in the city to organize multiracial political alliances in a broad struggle for social and economic justice.[15]

As Woods demonstrated in *Development Arrested*, Blues traditions have provided epistemological, philosophical, theoretical, and political alternatives to the dominant ideologies of development. His original and generative contribution to scholarship shifted how we understand the role of Blues music, literature, and poetry in social movements. He explored how the development of the Blues occurred in the context of the violent overthrow of Radical Reconstruction. In turn, he examined how Blues music became a key terrain of ideological struggle. He conceptualized Blues artists, performers, and musicians as "organic intellectuals," that is, intellectuals who articulate the values and interests of their class. In this way, Woods suggests that the Blues should be read not as "mechanistic responses to oppression" but instead as an ethical vision that can be drawn upon in a struggle for a multiracial working-class democracy. This is what Woods means by his concept of the Blues tradition, which he defines as "the break-up of racial and economic monopolies; the economic redistribution of monopolized resources to oppressed and working-class communities; the creation of sustainable communities; the full recognition of human rights; and the affirmation of Black culture and intellectual traditions" (chapter 8). The Blues tradition refers to the countless ways that the working-class has struggled to survive while making its communities and the larger world more livable and just.[16]

As Woods explains in his first book, the concept of the Blues epistemology was grasped by the essayist, artist, and organic intellectual Richard Wright in a famous essay entitled "Blueprint for Negro Writing," which was first published in New Challenge (1937), a communist literary publication of the Popular Front era. Born in Mississippi, Wright was part of the great migration of Black workers to Chicago during the early twentieth century. It was there that he became one of the most influential writers on the Black Left during the Great Depression. In particular, he first achieved literary influence as a member of the Communist Party, where he was an active member in Chicago's John Reed Clubs and had published his work in communist outlets since the early 1930s. During this period Black artists, activists, and intellectuals including Wright, Langston Hughes, Margaret Walker, and others were influenced by the Communist Party's thesis on the right to self-determination for the Black Belt. The Communist Party had also garnered respect for its organizing among the Black working-class defendants known as the "Scottsboro boys" in Alabama, industrial workers in factories, and the unemployed and homeless in cities during the early years of the Great Depression. The Communist Party earned a reputation for militancy by combining an antiracist struggle against the Jim Crow police state with a Marxist commitment to organizing the working class. In "Blueprint" Wright argued that Black writers should tap Black working-class vernacular traditions in their expressive work, as working people provided a distinct social vision that challenged the ideology of leadership articulated by the petty bourgeoisie. The task for writers on the Black Left was to engage with expressive culture, such as Blues and Jazz, which articulate the perspective of the working class in a struggle against racism, capitalism, and U.S. imperialism.[17]

Following this lead, Woods explores the foundations of the Blues epistemology. In his analysis the Blues epistemology was revitalized during the radical 1930s to insist on working-class consciousness and union-based leadership in the freedom struggle. While many analyses of the civil rights movement begin in the aftermath of World War II, Woods traces its roots in campaigns waged by organizations including the Southern Negro Youth Congress, the Congress of Industrial Organizations (CIO), and the National Maritime Union in the 1930s. The formation of these unions "signaled the rise of union-based working-class leadership at the expense of the old-line Black commercial and professional elite." By linking directly with the struggles of the industrial working class, these organizations addressed "voting rights, police brutality, racial discrimination, and labor organizing." In doing so, Woods suggests, they revived a Blues agenda that challenged "elite Black leadership organizations" and demonstrated how "the ability of the middle class to symbolically claim leadership was rapidly diminishing" (chapter 5).

As Woods explains in the epigraph, the Blues epistemology provided Jazz with its politics and aesthetics. By the Great Depression of the 1930s the Blues had achieved a global audience and influenced the "jazz revolution in New Orleans." Woods shows how these cultural practices have been tapped in mobilizing many different working-class and colonized communities. Indeed, a central insight of the book is based on the lessons that can be learned from the history of internationalism and multiethnic alliances in the present. This is especially true, as the reader will see, in terms of the history of indigenous people's struggle. Woods spends considerable energy examining the *longue durée* of resistance and affirmation among African American and indigenous peoples. Not only are they central to the history of New Orleans, but they also illuminate the breadth of white supremacy.[18] Woods was deeply committed to interracial cooperation among people of color and was always alert to moments of working-class solidarity.[19] As Woods noted, Dr. Martin Luther King came to understand this dynamic in the last year of his life as he called for a "general strike" of workers and for the building of the Poor People's Campaign to redistribute wealth to African Americans, Mexican Americans, Native Americans, Puerto Ricans, and poor whites.[20]

Woods shows how organic intellectuals in New Orleans have promoted "working class leadership, social vision, sustainable communities, social justice, and the construction of a new commons."[21] "The Blues," Woods writes, "is an encyclopedia of the multiple forms of traps experienced by African Americans . . . and of how they challenged these practices."[22] He traces a continuity in the Blues tradition from musicians like the Mardi Gras Indians, Buddy Bolden, Louis Armstrong, Mahalia Jackson, Professor Longhair, Jelly Roll Morton, "Blind" Willie Johnson, and Kidd Jordan to radical intellectuals and artists, including W. E. B. Du Bois and Paul Robeson, to social movement organizations, including the radical National Negro Congress, the Southern Negro Youth Congress, and the Civil Rights Congress between the 1930s and the 1950s, to the Deacons for Defense and the Student Nonviolent Coordinating Committee in the 1960s and 1970s, to struggles in the wake of Hurricane Katrina in 2005. In developing this tradition these organic intellectuals, artists, and activists have, according to Woods, articulated the "global significance of the working-class, multiethnic alliance created on the streets of New Orleans" (chapter 2).

Woods instructs his readers to regard the current monograph in the tradition of his earlier book. "Some students considered my first book, *Develop-*

ment Arrested, as an obituary for forgotten African American communities and movements that expired at the hands of an ever-expanding plantation regime," Woods writes. "Many also accepted this historic collapse as inevitable and almost natural. They felt defenseless before political and economic forces that were enclosing their communities, and they imagined rural Black communities to be either more passive than they were or more heroic than they could become." The crises unleashed by neoliberalism in poor and Black communities across the country, he explains, led some to cynically believe that "since class was the determinant of success, as future members of the middle class they had no inherent responsibility to improve conditions faced by the Black working class." Yet he believed in the moral and ethical responsibility to confront the pervasive and persistent problems of racism and poverty in rural and urban spaces. He argues that a "cynical reading" of *Development Arrested* "ignores the most important arguments undergirding the work. First, hegemonic blocs face crises, both short-term and prolonged, more commonly than is typically understood. Second, the African American working-class traditions of resistance, affirmation, and development were also expanding" (chapter 8). In Woods's own words, "reports of the death of African American communities were premature."[23]

We believe *Development Drowned and Reborn* can help us in the search for new theoretical and methodological approaches for analyzing the past, historicizing the present, and articulating different futures. It conveys the politics of such scholarly work in the present neoliberal moment and articulates its relationship to the struggle for global justice.[24] While there will certainly be resistance from above to social movements, this book shows that there is also a memory of the Reconstruction agenda to draw upon in the struggle for a new society. As Clyde Woods put it, "We stand at the dawn of a new era of ethnic and social justice. The voices straining to be heard are legion, and our potential contribution is immense."[25]

Development Drowned and Reborn

I Thought I Heard Samba Bambara Say

The Social Construction of New Orleans

The New Orleans region became a national and international center for social schism and social vision due to the historic movements launched by its people. The origins of this expansive geographical imagination were the product of the continental and global vision of the First Nations and of the European and African settlers. Spanning more than ten thousand years, Native Americans repeatedly transformed the regions that make up present-day Louisiana. Their traditions of development and social organization continue to resonate within Native American, African American, and white communities. During the first one hundred years of European colonization and settlement, various African ethnic groups were able to preserve and share their intellectual traditions in the French and Spanish colony of Louisiana. By the 1830s these multiple social, cultural, and development traditions contributed to the formation of the Blues tradition of ontology, epistemology, and development. This comprehensive development tradition was birthed by the creation of slavery within slavery. The birth of industrial capitalism and the manic demand for cotton from the Deep South by British manufacturers led to the brutal expulsion of Native Americans from the region, resulting in the Trail of Tears. At the same time, tens of thousands of African Americans were ripped from the brutal confines of Upper South slavery and "sold down the river" to the lawless cotton and sugar kingdoms of Louisiana, Mississippi, Alabama, Texas, Arkansas, and Tennessee, the heartland of the Blues. In these troubled lands the Blues would soon become constitutional.

The Blues philosophical system fully emerged from the region after the Civil War. It was used to craft a common identity amid crisis and to investigate and transform regional realities. The first pillars of the Blues tradition were the philosophical discourse and social imperatives central to the Spirituals song movement as it moved westward. The second pillar was the multiple philosophies that informed the numerous freedom movements of the southeastern United States. The third pillar was crafted from the first two: an ethical development agenda that opposed slavery, racism, and monopoly in all of their manifestations. This agenda supported the realization of social justice and sustainable human, community, and cultural development.

The sections below examine the emergence of the Blues development agenda, its African and Native American predecessors, and its work to bring social justice to a region dominated by a powerful planter bloc during five distinctive regional regimes from 1699 to 1860. Native Americans in what became Louisiana established multiple traditions of community-development planning along with peaceful trading networks that stretched from Mexico City to Maine. The development traditions of the Natchez and other indigenous nations remained influential after the initial French colonization in 1699. Native American and African plans to create sustainable societies constantly undermined the imperial designs of the French Crown. This ongoing resistance and imperial war led to the transfer of the colony to Spain in 1765. The Haitian Revolution thwarted the reassertion of French control over Louisiana. The sale of the territory to the United States made Louisiana the center of numerous colonial projects and national schisms. By the 1850s, southern leaders were imagining New Orleans as the economic center of a separate nation. Throughout this tortured history, African Americans built a multidimensional culture in which the desire for freedom was expressed in thousands of different ways. To begin to comprehend the meaning of New Orleans and the gifts it will bring in the future, we must first turn to this history.

Mississippian Civilizations and Planning

The indigenous peoples of the region now known as New Orleans have witnessed the rise and fall of many civilizations. As the region considers its future, we must reflect on the First Nations' contributions to regional consciousness. Louisiana has the second-largest Native American population in the eastern United States. The desperate circumstances in which many Native Americans find themselves today belie their contributions to world civilization. Their history is replete with social, cultural, economic, and intellectual innovations that have shaped the region's material and conscious worlds. Rather than viewing indigenous traditions and peoples as relics of the past, we can understand them as manifesting many of the core principles necessary to construct a new North American commons based on social justice and sustainability.

Archeological evidence suggests that Native American settlements were present in southern Louisiana twelve thousand years ago. The recently discovered fifty-four-hundred-year-old Watson Brake site in northeast Louisiana is considered to be the oldest mound complex in North America. Between 2,000 B.C. and 600 B.C., a major civilization arose at a place now referred to as Poverty

Point, in West Carroll Parish in northeast Louisiana. This religious, cultural, and trade center was organized around the largest earthen works in the Western Hemisphere. The complex provides evidence of the extension of Mexican and Central American social, cultural, technological, and planning innovations into the Lower Mississippi Valley. This year-round settlement centered on an octagonal mound complex, geometrically organized villages, strong religious and civil organizations, solar and stellar orientations, and a highly developed agricultural system whose staple crops were beans, maize, and squash. Radiating from this hub were more than 150 settlements, stretching from the Gulf Coast to the river valleys of Louisiana, Arkansas, and Mississippi. Several villages were within, and near, the present-day boundaries of New Orleans. This civilization influenced the theory and practice of governance, religion, culture, and economics in an area extending from Tennessee to Mexico and from Wisconsin to Florida.[1]

The dissolution of the Poverty Point civilization around 600 B.C. resulted in a return to smaller regional complexes organized around seasonal movements. Transcontinental trade and multinational alliances were reestablished during the Mississippian Period, 800 A.D. to 1550 A.D. The first center of this new civilization was Cahokia, a city of ten thousand to forty thousand persons located a few miles east of present-day East St. Louis, Illinois. The city's inhabitants introduced a new model of social organization: the intensive cultivation of staples, the production and storage of agricultural surpluses, craft specialization, urbanized year-round settlements, and a centralized social system organized around autonomous community, political, and religious institutions. Its central plaza was surrounded by large pyramidal mounds and by large towns with specialized religious and state functions. These innovations first spread southward to the Mississippi and Louisiana nations (Alabama, Caddo, Chitimacha, Houma, Natchez, Taensas, and Tunica) before moving eastward to the Cherokee, Chickasaw, Choctaw, and Creek. Eventually the Mississippian political, cultural, and economic networks stretched from the Rocky Mountains to the Atlantic Ocean and from the Great Lakes to deep inside present-day Mexico. Cahokia was designated a World Heritage Cultural Site by the United Nations Educational, Scientific, and Cultural Organization in 1982.[2]

Numerous explanations have been offered for the collapse of this civilization in the 1500s: resource conflicts, warfare, overpopulation, and the spread of Spanish-introduced diseases such as smallpox, influenza, measles, and typhus. Others cite the four-year quest for gold by Hernando de Soto and his six hundred soldiers between the years of 1539 and 1542. This party of mercenaries left a path of war, destruction, slavery, and disease throughout the Southeast. In 1541 Quigualtam, the Great Sun of the Natchez, ridiculed de Soto's claim of being a deity prior to leading the Natchez and other nations in a successful campaign to expel the Spaniards. Disease, war, and colonization began a long era of social collapse and migrations. Yet the Africans who entered the region after 1700 did not meet a defeated people. They learned many lessons from the indigenous nations in subjects they too had mastered on the other side of the Atlantic: regional planning, sustainable relations with nature, and sustainable social relations. They also shared an encyclopedic knowledge of the forms of resistance, cultural preservation, and intellectual mobilizations necessary to build continental-scale multiethnic alliances. All of this indigenous knowledge and these development traditions entered into the Blues development tradition.[3]

The Plans of the Great Sun, the Sun King, and Samba Bambara, 1699–1765

The clash of competing development traditions in what was to become the New Orleans region began again in the late seventeenth century. Although the trade in beaver fur made Quebec a highly profitable colony for France, by the 1630s overhunting and the rising demand for beaver hats in Europe had begun to set the conditions for the French conquest of the Great Lakes region during the early 1670s. Yet the growth of British colonies along the Atlantic Seaboard and the new Spanish settlements in Florida and Texas were viewed as threats to both the fur trade and to France's vastly more profitable sugar plantation colonies of the Caribbean: Haiti, Martinique, and Guadeloupe. In order to expand the French Empire while blocking the imperial designs of the British and Spanish, King Louis XIV, the Sun King, financed the exploration of the Mississippi Valley. In 1682 René-Robert Cavalier, the Sieur de La Salle, surveyed an arc of regions extending from Quebec to the Great Lakes and then down the Mississippi Valley to the Gulf of Mexico. Without consulting any of the indigenous nations, La Salle claimed the entire ten-million-acre Mississippi basin for France and named it Louisiana, or Louis's land.

The new French approach to colonization and social regulation was developed by Louis XIV and his finance minister Jean Baptiste-Colbert during the 1660s. Jerah Johnson argues that they eventually realized that the English policies of enforcing conformity, limiting mobility, demonizing cultural differences, and maintaining rigid parallel hierarchies were impossible "in a realm as large and diverse as France." Derived from the ancient Roman model of colonization, a "multicultural" assimilationist policy and plan was designed to unite ethnic, regional, economic, and feudal power centers under a single French state.

In its Augustan age the tiny city-state of Rome controlled the world less by military might than by making Rome and things Roman so grand, attractive, and easily accessible that subject peoples everywhere, though they retained their individual identities and traditions, including their own legal codes, willingly accepted, indeed vied for, participation in the glory of being Roman. Colbert and Louis XIV developed a similar program to make the glory of France such that no subject or group of subjects could resist its lure.[4]

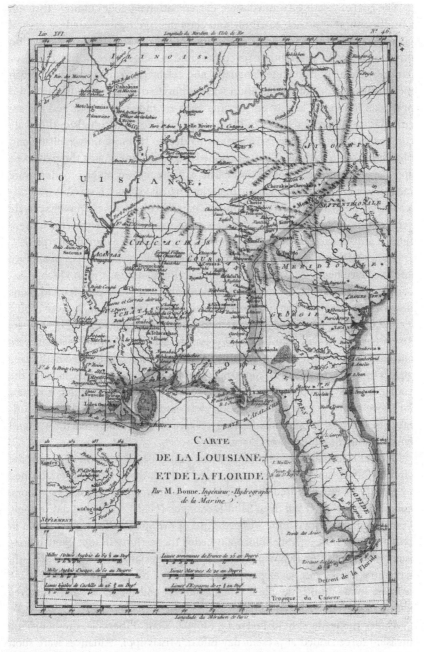

FIGURE 1. Louisiana, 1780 ("Carte de la Louisiane, et de la Floride"), Charles Marie Rigobert Bonne. Courtesy of the Louisiana Historical Center, Louisiana State Museum.

The goal of creating a unified, state-driven national public culture—through a multicultural approach to ethnic and class management—rested on several pillars that continue to resonate in the present period: large-scale construction projects, festivals, galas, other spectacles, and an almost occult-like preoccupation with fashion, cuisine, language, and celebrity. Conversely, the English mercantilist theory of colonization was corporate driven, particularistic, and practical. It focused largely on specifics such as trade regulations and the accumulation of savings that would ensure profits for individuals and private companies. French mercantilist writers tended to be more universalistic and philosophical in outlook. They developed a colonization policy thought to be applicable to all societies at all times. The plan's focus was much broader, more inclusive, and far more systematic than the English version. It was not insignificant that English New World explorations and colonies were mostly private ventures funded by trading companies, whereas similar French efforts were funded almost exclusively by the Crown as extensions of national enterprise.[5]

France's colonization polices were also shaped by its experiences in Quebec and the Caribbean. To prevent rebellions, colonial authorities in Quebec encouraged intermarriage, integrated settlements, and other policies and plans designed to "gently polish" indigenous people into Frenchmen. A more robust assimilation program was developed in the 1630s by a Jesuit superior in Quebec. To protect the heavily outnumbered colonists, select indigenous nations were alienated from their holistic traditions. Catholic missionaries learned native languages to support a policy of "capturing their minds" that involved educating the young, publicly and privately displaying concern and pity, providing hospitals for those dying of European-introduced diseases, encouraging the abandonment of seasonal migrations, moving villages closer to the French forts, and encouraging the adoption of Christianity.[6]

Several historians suggest that Louisiana must be understood as part of the circum-Caribbean plantation social order. Indeed, the colony was established by a party of one hundred French hunters, farmers, pirates, soldiers, sailors, and laborers who set sail from Saint Domingue (Haiti) on the last day of 1698. France began occupying the western third of the Spanish-controlled island of Hispaniola in 1625, and Spain formally ceded the territory in 1697. French Louisiana would eventually prosper and fall due to its status as a satellite of Haiti, a country whose vast sugar plantations and large numbers of enslaved Black workers made it both the most valuable colony and the most dangerous free nation in the Western Hemisphere.

Under the leadership of Pierre Le Moyne, Sieur d'Iberville, the Louisiana invasion force landed at present-day Biloxi, Mississippi.[7] Alliances were soon formed with the Natchez and Chickasaw chiefs in Louisiana and Mississippi. After Iberville left the colony in 1702, his brother, Jean-Baptiste de Bienville, assumed leadership, serving as the colony's commandant or governor during four separate periods between 1701 and 1743.[8] The Ibervilles closely followed the multicultural colonization policy, peacefully coexisting with native people willing to become allies, constructing forts near native settlements, occupying the most fertile and sacred land (economic and cultural imposition), and resettling natives who suddenly found themselves living too close to French "installations" (displacement and enclosure). Students of history who choose to romanticize the colonial assimilation policies of the French simultaneously choose to ignore the foundations of these regimes: enclosure, genocide, and slavery. Those who resisted or allied with the British faced genocide. For example, to secure land for commercial and trade purposes, in 1706 Bienville launched a twelve-year war of extermination and enslavement against former French allies, the three thousand members of the Chitimacha nation residing southwest of New Orleans.[9]

Although the Louisiana colony was governed by the Crown from 1699 to 1712, its disorganization and destitution led Louis XIV to grant control over governance, imports, exports, Native lands, raw materials, the slave trade, and Native American relations to the merchant Antoine Crozat in 1712. Antoine Cadillac was appointed governor and soon he launched several initiatives designed to stabilize the colony: the creation of the Superior Council or city council; the adoption of a legal code; the establishment of trade links; the production of beef, corn, and other foodstuffs; and the production tobacco, indigo, and other crops for export.[10] Only sporadic shipments of goods from France meant that most "of the white population went hungry and naked." As the colonists became increasingly dependent upon the assistance and agricultural production of Native Americans, they soon dispersed throughout the countryside. This period was characterized by hunger, warfare, disease, the growth of the fur trade, and an ever-increasing French burden upon Native American nations. As indigenous agriculture declined, war and exploitation increased. Women from defeated nations were enslaved by the French and forced to both grow food and endure a lifetime of sexual exploitation.[11]

In response to this collapse, in 1717 the Crown awarded a twenty-five-year monopoly over the colony to the Compagnie d'Occident, or Compagnie du Mississippi. Led by banker John Law, the firm grew rapidly and renamed itself Compagnie des Indes after it acquired trading firms operating in India, the Pacific, China, Santa Domingo, Guinea, and Senegal. It played a central role in creating a horrifically violent incarnation of the global economy, linking markets and merchants; fostering war; creating plantation-dominated regions; establishing a global system of dependent port cities, manufacturers, and financial houses; and enslaving and transporting hundreds of thousands, if not millions, of Africans to the Americas.

A new city was needed to fully integrate Louisiana into this global regime. Named after the ruling regent of France, the Duc d'Orleans, New Orleans was

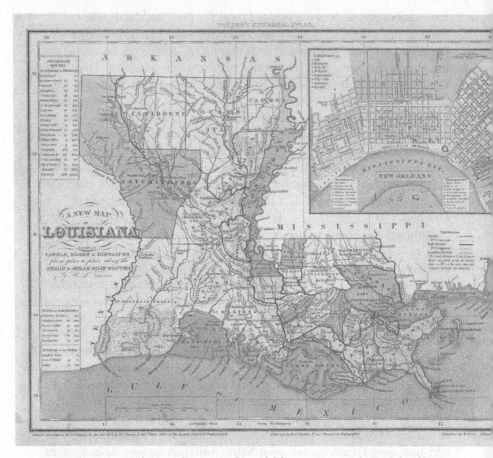

FIGURE 2. Louisiana and New Orleans, 1769 ("Grondvlakte van Nieuw Orleans, de hoofdstad van Louisiana"), Isaac Tirian. Courtesy of the Louisiana Historical Center at the Louisiana State Museum.

founded in 1718 on a Native American trading center. It became the capital of the colony in 1721. The Vieux Carré district (the French Quarter) was built in the 1720s and levees were soon constructed to protect the town from floods and hurricanes. Plantations abutted the district, and their long, narrow rectangular lots stretched from the natural high ground back into the swamps.[12] Several factors contributed to the town's rapid growth. First, Bienville attempted to halt the exploitation of indigenous nations by the colonists because their degradation was thought to undermine social cohesion, thus rendering indigenous people unfit for battle on behalf of the French against the British. After unauthorized residency on Native lands was prohibited, colonists flooded back into town. Native Americans entered the town as enslaved persons, concubines, the displaced, or as traders. To spur population growth and assimilation, the Catholic Church encouraged intermarriage between the French and free native women.

The second engine of growth was the immigration schemes of the Company of the Indies. Class, regional, and ethnic conflicts in Europe swelled the population of the town from four hundred people in 1717 to fifty-four hundred people by 1722. From Germany came refugees from the Thirty Years' War and from France came soldiers, army deserters, smugglers, prostitutes, vagabonds, libertines, those condemned to the galleys, indentured workers, residents of poorhouses, beggars, incorrigible sons and daughters, and those "arrested for acts of violence, murder, debauchery, and drunkenness." Each of these transgressors was considered by the French police to be deportable.[13]

Although the needs of the colony increased, many of the new immigrants avoided agricultural labor in the fetid, humid, and dangerous bayous. To solve the plantation and farm labor shortages, the Company of the Indies directed the African slave trade toward New Orleans in 1719. Most of the enslaved Africans who entered the colony between 1717 and 1731 were transported directly from Senegambia, a West African region then in the process of being disassembled by the company. According to Gwendolyn Midlo Hall, two-thirds of the Africans in the colony, 3,947 out of 5,987 persons, came from this region between 1726 and 1731. Many of the captive workers were from the Bambara nation. After 1729 the African population grew through natural reproduction; only 330 additional Africans arrived during the remainder of French rule, which ended in 1767. Consequently, the Bambara and smaller African ethnic groups were able to preserve their cultures to a remarkable degree. Simultaneously, the European population was declining due to falling immigration rates, rising emigration rates, and death. Of the seven thousand European colonists who arrived in Louisiana between 1712 and 1730, approximately two-thirds succumbed to hunger, disease, and warfare. By 1731 Africans outnumbered Europeans two to one.[14]

Bambara, Wolof, and other Senegambian intellectual traditions continue to influence Afro-Creole, white Creole, Cajun, and Louisiana culture. For example, a large body of received wisdom and forms of social investigation were preserved in the regional orature. Stories of the famed duo of Compere Bouki and Compere Lapin also became part of national culture. In Wolof the name Bouki means hyena. In the orature of Louisiana, Missouri, and Haiti, this character is constantly being outmaneuvered by his friend and enemy Lapin, a hare or rabbit. While the latter is considered a sometimes honorable and clever trickster, the former is associated with foolishness and shame. The two Senegambian characters were also central figures in the oral tradition of the Sea Islands of South Carolina and Georgia, where they evolved into the national icons Brer' Fox and Brer' Rabbit. The two were invoked to engage in an ongoing dialogue on relationships, local social conditions, ethics, and social transformation. Marcia

Guadet argues that the Bouki orature is designed to demonstrate the danger of alliances and the necessity of mental agility.

> [Bouki] attempts to imitate the trickster, but lacking the wit and perspective, ends up getting caught. . . . The duped trickster is an example and a warning that although Trickster can be admired for his wits, one must be careful not to be taken in by him or to attempt to copy his behavior—one must be cautious of the behavior of others, even those considered "friends," or risk being a fool or a dupe oneself. . . . Whereas Rabbit/Lapin sees his enemies realistically and trusts no one, Bouki accepts and trusts the advice of his "friend" and forgets the real dangers of his situation.[15]

A series of these episodes were collected on Louisiana plantations by Alcee Fortier and published in 1895. "Bouqui asked Rabbit if he didn't know that everyone was selling their mothers so as to have something to eat. Rabbit said yes, and that he was going to sell his mother for hominy and gumbo. When they were ready to go, Bouqui tied his mother with a rope and rabbit tied his mother with a cobweb, telling her to jump down from the cart when they reached the briers and run home. She did so, Bouqui sold his mother for hominy and gumbo."[16]

The large system of African cautionary folktales surrounding the duo was transported into Blues music and its extensions. This historic transference of this African archive and its discourses on betrayal and mimicry was recognized by the Senegalese scholar Ibrahim Seck, the director of two "Bouki Blues Festivals" held in Senegal during 2003 and 2005:

> Why the name "Bouki Blues Festival"? What musical form symbolizes human sufferance better than the blues? The blues is a way of life, a synthesis of African culture in America. Its most typical melodic features came from the Sahel and the savannah of West Africa just like Bouki and Lapin, the famous folktale characters that one still finds today in Louisiana. Compere Lapin is nothing else but the American survival of Leuk-le-lievre, the West African hare, who eventually evolved into the cartoon character Bugs Bunny. . . . Bouki symbolizes the persistence of African culture in America, and African wisdom at large. The way West Africans have depicted his character traits summarizes eloquently their mostly dramatic experience with the rest of the world.[17]

During the first half of the eighteenth century, enslavement and horrific brutality resulted in the creation of a seemingly permanent state of rebellion in Louisiana. Founded upon the unification of Native American and African resistance movements, this campaign lasted for nearly a century and a half, from 1731 to 1874. The antebellum tradition of Native American, African, Afro-Creole, and African American rebellion and fugitivism shaped Louisiana, French, and U.S. history in ways not yet fully understood. Yet incorporating this *longue durée* of resistance and affirmation into our understanding of present-day New Orleans allows us to see the continued operation of centuries-old institutions, theories, and practices.

Conversely, reading the current policies of abandonment backward makes the plantation bloc's policies associated with the Katrina tragedy comprehensible.[18]

The unification of Native American and African resistance led Bienville and the Company of the Indies to hurriedly introduce a version of the Code Noir in 1724. It would remain in force until 1803. Using Spanish legal precedents, Louis XIV had introduced the Code Noir of 1685 to defeat African rebellions in the French colonies in the Caribbean. Along with similar Black codes, the Code Noir of 1724 must be viewed as a foundational document in U.S. history. It is an enduring source of legislative innovation designed to socially, physically, culturally, intellectually, psychologically, and spiritually regulate Black behavior, communities, initiative, and movements from the seventeenth century to the present. One of the goals of this racial policy and plan was to halt the use of physical forms of torture such as the rack, mutilation, and dismemberment in favor of "more humane" instruments such as rods, ropes, and shackles. It also attempted to stop abuses that relied on hunger, the denial of clothes, induced alcoholism, the denial of medical care, the sale of spouses and children, and the disposal of the elderly.

The fifty-five articles of the Code Noir governed life, marriage, religion, resistance, and death. The enslaved were also required to receive instruction in Catholicism. The baptized were buried in consecrated ground while the unbaptized were buried in isolated fields at night. Work on Sundays was prohibited in order to allow the enslaved to grow crops or sell the goods necessary to feed their families. Unlike the code of 1685, which created an intermediary caste in the Caribbean, the Code Noir of 1724 banned marriages between persons of African and European ancestry in Louisiana, as well as concubinage. Unlike the British and American practices, no person in bondage could be forced to marry, and marriages between enslaved persons were recognized by the state. There was also a prohibition against separating families through the sale of husbands, wives, or children under the age of fourteen.[19] In addition, the code forbade Africans and their children from carrying offensive weapons, congregating with others enslaved by different slaveholders, or selling commodities without permission. Manumitted persons were subject to either corporal or capital punishment for the theft of goats or poultry. Additionally, those who escaped for over a month had their ears cut off and New Orleans's present-day emblem, the fleur-de-lys, branded on their shoulder. A second similar "offense" resulted in the individual being hamstrung and branded. Execution followed the third escape and capture. Finally, another article held that any "slave who shall have struck his master, his mistress, or the husband of his mistress, or their children, so as to produce a bruise or shedding of blood in the face, shall be put to death."[20]

Although they were heavily dependent upon the Native American nations and the growing enslaved African community, the French intensified the exploitation of both. In 1729 the French attempted to create tobacco plantations on land seized from their Natchez allies. The Natchez chose to confront the French plantation bloc's institution of ethnic and racial disposability. The Natchez Rebellion resulted in the death of 237 French soldiers and settlers, along with the capture of 300 enslaved Africans. The French attempted to annihilate the entire Natchez nation over the course of the next three years with armed forces composed of whites, Blacks, and the Choctaw. Determined to complete this genocide, Bienville waged war on the neighboring Chickasaw and Choctaw nations until they finally surrendered all remaining Natchez citizens in 1740.[21] Not only had Africans participated in the Natchez revolt, but Johnson notes that for "a decade the slave population and the Indian population had intermarried. Enslaved Africans, mostly males, had taken wives from among the enslaved Indian population, and runaway African slaves often moved into Indian communities or formed mixed Indian-African maroon settlements hidden away in the swamps on the outskirts of New Orleans."[22] To resolve this crisis of resistance both groups were given informal corporate status and the alliance with the Choctaw was restored.

The French increasingly used African soldiers to fight the Natchez, destroy the small nation of Chaouchas south of New Orleans, and protect the city against daily Native American attacks. Yet this alliance also proved problematic. As Midlo Hall puts it, "French authorities were indeed walking a thin line between Africans and Indians, creating enmity between the groups but trying to avoid excessive military dependence on either." She concludes that "the weakness of the dwindling French population, especially after the Natchez uprising, and the heavy reliance on slaves for skilled labor as well as for defense and warfare in this vast frontier region enhanced the bargaining power and self-confidence of the slaves."[23]

The line was broken when the Bambara Conspiracy or Bambara Plan emerged from an anti-French confederation composed of Africans and several indigenous nations: the Natchez, the Chickasaw, the Illinois, the Arkansas, and the Miami. This new bloc represented a historic inversion of the French model of ethnic division and assimilation. Although they were discovered before their strategy was launched, the alliance planned major revolts in 1731. Patricia Galloway notes that the resoluteness of the rebels led to many experiments in the burgeoning field of African management, an old Louisiana tradition. "A Swiss citizen who had lived in Natchez, Antoine Le Page du Pratz, investigated the incident and would later describe it in his history of Louisiana. He learned that his trusted first officer and interpreter, a slave named Samba Bambara, was the mastermind. . . . Because of Le Page du Pratz's efforts, French authorities tortured and killed the conspirators, even breaking the female slave on the wheel. . . . Though tortured by fire, the slaves refused to confess."[24]

Native and African resistance led to the withdrawal of the Company of the Indies in 1733 and the return of the colony to the Crown. To quell the rebellions, Bienville and the Superior Council enacted new African social policies designed to promote both assimilation and population growth: slave baptisms, godparenting by whites, marriage, the preservation of family units, the protection of women from rape, wage labor, craft production, vending, hiring out, and the recognition of African, Christian, and worker holidays. In 1746 there were three thousand Africans and Afro-Creoles in New Orleans, compared to sixteen hundred Europeans and French Creoles, Creole meaning born in the Western Hemisphere. Consequently, Bienville's policy produced the most heavily Africanized European-descended population in North America.[25]

African identity was also being transformed during this period. Although the Bambara and other ethnic groups maintained distinct societies, new pan-African institutions were being created through resistance and affirmation. Not only did escape become commonplace during this period, but sometimes French soldiers participated in successful flights to Havana where runaways lived as free persons. In one song from the Spanish period an escapee taunts the attorney general: "O Zeneral Florido! C'est vrai ye pas ca-pab' pren mom!" (Oh General Florido! It's true they cannot catch me!).[26] The act of escape was increasingly transformed into fugitivism: a way of life, a permanent state of being, and an institution with its own sites and networks.

The twin goals of escaping slavery and establishing new communal societies led to the creation of numerous small and highly organized maroon settlements in the region. Comprising Black and Native American members, these communities emerged along the Mississippi River from Point Coupee to Gentilly. Midlo Hall concludes that the maroons "surrounded and infiltrated the French settlement with a network extending through New Orleans, the countryside, and into the cipriere" (cypress swamps). A large proportion of the residents of these utopian communal colonies were women, children, and families who possessed guns for hunting and self-defense. Although perpetually pursued by planters and militias, the maroons remained in constant contact with those who lived on the plantations. They also openly traded in the city, selling logs, fish, birds, berries, corn, sweet potatoes, squash, and game. A number of the colonies evolved into permanent settlements by the end of the French era. Their numbers were replenished when enslaved workers escaped en masse while clearing cypress forests in the bayous.[27]

Although maroons operated outside of French law, their secret places, religious practices, songs, ethics, and social vision became the pillars of a parallel social order. Moluron escaped so many times that a song was created to celebrate his attitude toward bondage and the planter bloc.

> Moluron! He! Moluron He!
> I wasn't born yesterday
> If you treat me well, I'll stay
> If you treat me bad, I'll escape.

This song was still sung openly in Louisiana by Afro-Creoles on the eve of emancipation.[28]

The beginnings of a parallel regional political economy, the Blues political economy, emerged from the interaction of the maroon colonies (freedom villages), small gardeners, traders, artisans and craftswomen, fugitives, religious communities, and social organizations through music, language, marriage, and alliances with parallel Native American institutions and traditions. All of these relationships were central to the life and movements of Samba Bambara. Galloway notes that he "had been the author of two revolts, first at Fort d'Arguin in West Africa and second aboard L'Annibal, when as a result of the first revolt he was sent as a slave to Louisiana." After working for the Superior Council as a translator and as a plantation manager in Natchez, he participated in the Natchez Rebellion and was at the center of the Bambara Conspiracy of 1731. While the plantation tradition of historiography reduces his accomplishments to a desire to kill whites, a long overdue reexamination of his life would reveal his role in promoting a new social vision organized around the desperate quest for freedom, dignity, and the development of new communities, institutions, forms of governance, alliances, and leadership. All of these quests were incorporated into the Blues epistemology.[29]

The French regime entered a state of crisis in the 1750s. It reeled from Chickasaw raids on plantations as far south as New Orleans and from the entry of British traders into the Mississippi Valley.[30] In 1754 the "Clash of Empires" began and what followed is alternatively referred to as the French and Indian War, the War of Conquest, the Seven Years' War, and the First World War. It could just as easily be known as "the plantation slavery wars." Not only did the French surrender Quebec but their colonies in the Caribbean, West Africa, and India were attacked. In addition, the British seized Havana and Manila from the Spanish. Signed in 1763, the Treaty of Paris required France to transfer all of its lands east of the Mississippi River to Britain and its lands west of the Mississippi to Spain.[31]

The Spanish Colonial Plan and Saint Malo, 1765–1800

The Spanish Crown governed the colony from 1765 to 1800. Although this regime introduced several economic and political innovations, it could not isolate the colony from the revolts against the plantation bloc occurring in Louisiana, France, and Haiti. Spain's imperial strategy was organized around preventing British incursions into the sugar plantation regions of Cuba and the mining regions of Mexico and Peru. Upon his arrival in 1765, Governor Antonio de Ulloa reoriented Louisiana's trade relations by banning exchanges with French and British ports in the Caribbean and North America. In response, he was expelled from the colony by a mob of hostile French Creoles in 1768. The regime was restored after the arrival of more than one thousand Spanish soldiers in 1769. Although the Superior Council was replaced by the Cabildo, a governing body and law court, French Creole planters dominated the new body as they had the old.[32]

At the beginning of the 1760s the Louisiana colony had just 8,000 inhabitants. The population of New Orleans stood at 3,190 persons in 1767; 1,288 were enslaved and 99 were free people of color. In an attempt to buffer the colony from British, and later American, incursions, Governors Galvez and Miro encouraged immigration. By 1784 the population had grown to 25,000, with 5,000 persons residing in New Orleans. Among the recent immigrants were 600 to 1,000 Spanish soldiers and administrators. After the Seven Years' War more than 4,000 Acadians or Cajuns also immigrated after a British ethnic cleansing campaign in the French Canadian province of Acadia (Nova Scotia). During the 1780s the Spanish provided these immigrants with Native American land on the southwestern prairie. Another 2,000 immigrants from the Canary Islands, the Islefio, arrived in 1777. Most would eventually settle in St. Bernard and Plaquemines Parishes. Another colony, from the southern Spanish region of Malaga, settled in New Iberia. Anglo-American settlers were accepted and given land grants if they agreed to adopt Catholicism and obey the laws of Spain. As thousands of Americans began pouring into the colony, U.S. secretary of state Thomas Jefferson wrote President George Washington that the United States should take advantage of the Spanish immigration policies. "I wish a hundred thousand of our inhabitants would accept this invitation. It may be the means of delivering to us peaceably what may otherwise cost war."[33]

Germans and Cajuns produced many of the crops and livestock consumed by the domestic market, including the staples of seafood and rice. Yet the plantation-export orientation of the colony was firmly established during the Spanish period, as was the emphasis on new levee construction, increased plantation production, port expansion, and increased trade with Mexico. By the late 1700s sugar and cotton production were expanding rapidly, and these crops became significant exports, along with tobacco, indigo, rice, timber, furs, hides, and fish. Rising export earnings were used to purchase textiles, furniture, manufactured goods, food, and Africans.[34]

The Roman Catholic Church remained a key component of the colony's power structure. The Crown paid the salaries of the priests, who worked closely with political and military officials to maintain order. In addition, Catholic orders such as the Ursulines, Capuchins, and Jesuits all owned plantations, property in New Orleans, and enslaved Africans and Afro-Creoles. Although Africans and Afro-Creoles were the most avid churchgoers, many also continued to practice African religions overtly, covertly, and syncretically.[35]

The number of free persons of color in Louisiana grew to fifteen hundred by the end of the eighteenth century, the largest such population in the United States. A majority lived as farm tenants, while others worked in trades. A number of free women were explicitly and implicitly forced into plaçage, a formalized institution of concubinage.[36] The practice continues to be defined by a racial industry dedicated to romanticizing the exploitation of these women and their families by the plantation regime. Conveniently forgotten is the fact that many of the same French planters who participated in this system were also engaged in acts of brutality against enslaved persons that shocked the Spanish. In order to reduce the intensity of the brutality they witnessed, and to limit the growth of maroon colonies, two militia companies composed of free people of color were formed to monitor the brutality of the planters and, according to Johnson, to "police slaves, pursue runaways, and attack maroon infestations." The militias were also used to defend the city from the ideology of republicanism spreading outward from the French and Haitian Revolutions of the 1790s. Other free people of color and enslaved Afro-Creoles participated with Native Americans in planning a 1795 rebellion in Point Coupee and later with French Creoles in a plan to overthrow Spanish rule. Even after dozens were deported, punished, or executed, free persons of color participated in another plot in 1796.[37]

The numerous revolts in Louisiana and Haiti undermined French, Spanish, and British colonialism in the Western Hemisphere. According to Caryn Cossé Bell, the Spanish government of Louisiana took the threat seriously. "In futile attempts to isolate their Louisiana possession from the spread of revolutionary republicanism, they suppressed seditious activities and banned subversive reading materials. In May 1790, they responded to mounting racial tensions in Saint Domingue [Haiti] by issuing a decree ordering royal officials to prohibit the entry into Louisiana of slaves and free blacks from the French West Indies." In August 1791 a rebellion by more than fifteen thousand enslaved men, women, and children in the northern provinces marked the beginning of the Haitian Revolution. Due to the Spanish fear of Haitian immigrants, only several hundred French Creoles and free Afro-Creoles were able to enter New Orleans from the island before 1793. In that year, a fire destroyed most of the city of Cap-Haïtien, leaving ten thousand people as refugees. Many migrated throughout the Caribbean and to various cities in the United States before reassembling in New Orleans. According to one estimate, between 1791 and 1803 approximately thirteen hundred refugees arrived in New Orleans, including French Creole planter families, enslaved Afro-Creole families, and free Afro-Creole families, some of whom were slaveholders themselves. The Spanish watched in horror as the perpetual rebellion of Afro-Creole and indigenous Louisianans was joined with the perpetual Haitian Revolution. According to Cossé Bell, Louisiana officials were preoccupied with the movement to simultaneously overthrow both plantation regimes and to create new societies. "In 1800, during debates about reopening the African slave trade, Louisiana officials agreed to exclude Saint Domingan blacks and noted the presence of black and white insurgents from the French West Indies who were 'propagating dangerous doctrines among our Negroes.' One angry participant noted 'the insolent anger of slaves toward their masters and other white people,' and another observed that the slaves seemed more 'insolent,' 'ungovernable,' and 'insubordinate' than in 1795."[38]

In addition, Midlo Hall argues that a re-Africanization of Black culture occurred during the Spanish period after the arrival of a large number of African captives from the Bight of Benin. Many were victims of ethnic cleansing campaigns associated with the European slave trade: the Fon, the Mina, the Ado, the Chamba, the Kongo, the Mandinka, and the Yoruba nations. The Vodou religion that accompanied the first Haitian exodus was dramatically reinforced by the arrival of Haitians ethnically cleansed from Cuba after Napoleon invaded Spain in 1809. Midlo Hall further suggests that the ethic of universalism in the colony enabled the rapid socialization of these refugees. "The openness and inter-racialism of the frontier society in which this distinctive culture was born has been remarkably influential among people of all classes, colors, and nations." Midlo Hall attributes this phenomenon to African traditions rather than to romanticized French practices. "Senegambia had long been a crossroads of the world where people and cultures were amalgamated in the crucible of warfare and the rise and fall of far-flung trading empires. An essential feature of the cultural materials brought from Senegambia, as well as from other parts of Africa was a willingness to add and incorporate useful aspects of new cultures encountered."[39] This universal social vision along with similar indigenous Mississippian traditions in the region became central pillars of the Blues ontology and contributed immensely to its later globalizations.

A final tradition present in the region that flowed into the Blues epistemology was the elevation of Afro-Creole heroes to sainthood. Saint Juan Malo was the leader of a network of maroon settlements that controlled bayous between the Mississippi River and Lake Borgne, located southeast of New Orleans. Among these settlements was the village of Chef Menteur (chief liar), so named for the Choctaw chief exiled there for lying to his people. St. Malo resided in Ville Gaillard, a town in St. Bernard Parish described by Governor Miro as a rich village defended by five hundred men. Extensive kin, commercial, and military ties were at the foundation of this manifestation of the parallel Blues political economy. Among the several possible interpretations of St. Malo's name, Charles Bird suggests that "the Bambara term *malo* means 'shame' and is attached to the Mande hero because he is shameless and thus capable of acting when social conventions paralyze others." This "Bad Man" and "Wild Woman" ethic is preserved in the Blues and all of its extensions. Also preserved in the remembrance of the maroon tradition and the continued reality of fugitivism is the constant crossing of boundaries between the formal plantation political economy and the parallel, yet often ephemeral, Blues political economy. Sometimes communities and individuals existed in both and could embody the sacred in both simultaneously. Although he was captured in a 1784 raid, a song celebrating

St. Malo became a foundational part of the region's organic musical and intellectual traditions:

> Alas, young men, come make lament
> For poor St. Malo in distress
> They dragged him up into town
> Before those grand Cabildo men
> They charged that he had made a plot
> To cut the throats of all the white
> They asked who his comrades were
> poor St. Malo said not a word![40]

Freedom to the Afro-Creole population had come to mean more than just the abolition of slavery; it meant planning for and creating a new society. This meant governance by a working-class democracy resolutely opposed to all forms of monopoly. Also, they envisioned and enacted the freedom to honor their religions, sacred spaces, nature, their ancestors, and the growing pantheon of New World saints. Another element of this plan was the establishment of permanent democratic communities on lands that were free from the violent racial and economic enclosures that so far had defined their lives. This Blues agenda necessitated an internationalism among Afro-Louisianans, Haitians, and their allies that imagined, and planned, the end of plantation-bloc domination and of the empires that fostered it.

Retrocession and the Napoleonic Plan, 1800–1803

The coup led by General Napoleon Bonaparte on November 19, 1799, effectively ended the French Revolution. The new government immediately sought to re-establish its plantation slavery empire in the Western Hemisphere. In 1800 a nearly bankrupt Spanish Empire was forced to yield Louisiana and many other territories in the Treaty of Ildefonso. Louisiana was returned to the French, who now considered reoccupying the massive Louisiana Territory. However, all of France's machinations were dependent upon the reconquest of Haiti. Once restored, slavery and sugar production on the island would be used to finance the French regime, its military, and the proslavery mercantile capitalists who were dependent upon oceanic trade. Napoleon was further encouraged by the ongoing conflicts that plagued Haiti. Franklin Knight notes that between 1792 and 1802 "as many as six warring factions were in the field simultaneously: slaves, free persons of color, petit blancs, grand blancs, and invading Spanish and English troops, as well as the French vainly trying to restore order and control." Beginning in 1793, partisans allied with Pierre-Dominique Toussaint L'Ouverture began to transform the island by expelling foreign forces, creating a democratic constitution, partially suppressing a revolt by a free people of color caste, and emancipating the enslaved population in the neighboring Spanish colony of Santo Domingo.[41]

Additionally, according to Anthony Maingot, a free Haiti created a "terrified consciousness" among the rest of the plantation blocs in the Americas and Europe. Consequently, for all these reasons, Bonaparte made the reconquest of Haiti one of his highest priorities. In 1802 he sent his brother-in-law, General Charles Victor Emmanuel Leclerc, and ten thousand elite French troops into battle. Bonaparte ultimately lost the colony, his brother-in-law, and more than forty thousand troops. In 1803 U.S. envoy James Monroe was sent to Paris to negotiate the American purchase of New Orleans and secure navigation rights on the Mississippi River. Instead, Bonaparte sold the entire 828,000 square miles of the Louisiana Territory for $15 million. The treaty was signed on May 2, 1803, and Haiti declared its independence on January 1, 1804.[42] Two hundred years later, Haiti is still the epicenter of the global movement to abolish the plantation and neoplantation development models and the devastating forms of racism, impoverishment, and social chaos they produce.

The Louisiana Purchase in 1803 was followed by the rapid entry of Anglo-American southerners into the new U.S. territory and the city of New Orleans. When the newly appointed governor William C. C. Claiborne rode into the city with an army contingent the year of the sale, he encountered a region defined by multiple forms of governance, citizenship rights, ethnic and racial compacts, autonomous zones, and nationalisms. American rule was contested by enslaved Afro-Creoles, African Americans, free people of color, Native Americans, French and Spanish Creoles, rebellious U.S. citizens, and adventurers from numerous nations who had fought for, and obtained, specific rights under the French and Spanish regimes. The approach to this dilemma taken by U.S. authorities was to block the immediate extension of representative democracy and other rights guaranteed in the Constitution. The Governance Act of 1804 established a state without elected offices. This tactic was soon denounced for its "colonial" structure by John Quincy Adams. Seeking citizenship rights within the District of Louisiana, white Creole Louisianans issued the "Remonstrance of the People of Louisiana Against the Political System Adopted by Congress for Them" in the same year. Some of the free Afro-Creoles in New Orleans also sought to preserve their special status, derived in part from their participation in the city militia that had fought to defend slavery for the previous seventy-five years. The Choctaw, Caddo, and other Native American nations sought to preserve their "collective autonomy" while simultaneously creating a regional governance partnership. Encompassing sections of present-day Louisiana, Mississippi, and Alabama, the Spanish-controlled West Florida region was viewed as a continual threat to economic integration, and Anglo settlers living in this area began to constantly push for a war of conquest.[43]

The Anglo-American Plan that emerged rested on at least four pillars. According to Peter Kastor, "With the federal administration in Louisiana under assault, federal policy makers renewed their efforts to co-opt white Louisianans, contain American troublemakers, reinforce racial supremacy, and promote national security." Although Jefferson's administration was unsuccessful in securing a West Florida treaty, it did create an international trade blockade around Haiti in 1806. The principal reasons given for the adoption of this starvation policy were the historically intertwined goals of preserving both national security and racial supremacy. As Kastor notes, "Haiti constituted an obvious model for slaves who hoped to overturn the racial supremacy of American Louisiana." The Governance Act of 1805 provided new rights for whites, including an elected House of Representatives, a nonvoting congressional delegate, territorial status, and a path to statehood. In terms of boundaries, the Territory of Orleans included much of present-day Louisiana while the Territory of Louisiana consisted of segments of fifteen present-day states.[44]

Kastor also notes that historians of slavery generally ignore the central role Black consciousness and Black movements played in defining diplomacy, whiteness, and national security throughout the Old Southwest. Daily forms of resistance, escape, maroonage, new alliances, rebellions, and the formation of multiethnic and multiracial groups of bandits, pirates, and refugees defined regional life. The escape of enslaved Afro-Creoles to the Spanish territories of Texas and West Florida was so common that the New Orleans City Council passed an ordinance requiring those hired out for work to wear a collar with the slaveholder's name on it. Since "servile insurrection . . . had been a driving force in both the United States and colonial Louisiana," it was not surprising that the first act of the territorial legislature was to create the Black Code of 1806. The code defined enslaved Afro-Creoles as real estate incapable of legally owning or selling anything without permission. Since they could no longer own property, as they did under Spanish rule, the right of self-purchase was also extinguished. According to the new code, "[an enslaved person] owes to his master, and to all his family, a respect without bounds, and an absolute obedience, and he is consequently to execute all the orders which he receives from him, his said master, or from them."[45] The Black Code was a form of militarization that replaced the limited autonomy present in the French and Spanish colonization schemes with the caste-like English system of extreme conformity, social immobility, and hypodescent (the one-drop rule).[46]

By 1810 New Orleans was the nation's fifth-largest city and was becoming central to the global economy. It became both a supply center for western migration and the main shipping point for cotton destined for the textile mills of New England and Europe. The city was also the preeminent financial and trade center of the booming Lower Mississippi Valley. By 1820 thousands of steamboats and other vessels clogged its waterways.[47] New Orleans was also rapidly becoming an unparalleled center for mercenaries, assassins, filibusterers, and coup plotters planning the seizure of power in New Spain (Mexico), Latin America, Central America, and the Caribbean. For example, as early as 1805 President Thomas Jefferson's former vice president, Aaron Burr, arrived in the city in order to launch a secessionist movement that would create a new empire with British assistance. If successful, the Burr Conspiracy would have both created an empire encompassing the Louisiana Territory and much of northern Mexico and blocked Jefferson and the plantation bloc's plan to extend slavery westward.[48]

Despite the fear of the Haitian "contagion," white Creoles in Louisiana successfully lobbied for the entry of white Creoles from Haiti and the people they enslaved. In addition, according to Kastor, special provisions were soon made for the Afro-Creole and African American mistresses, concubines, and children of plantation owners and other white males. For example, the statutes of the new Louisiana Civil Code of 1825 "legally recognized concubinage between white men and enslaved black women, expressly provided limited property rights to enslaved black women (and their miscegenational children) in concubinage relationships, and treated manumission and free blacks favorably." The state also recognized the right of the enslaved to enter into contracts to secure their freedom and to sue for their liberty if the contract was violated.[49]

Cossé Bell suggests that American authorities also failed in their attempts to limit and criminalize the immigration of free people of color to New Orleans:

> The multiracial influx nearly doubled the size of the city's urban population. With the entry of 2,731 whites, 3,102 free persons of African descent, and 3,226 enslaved refugees in the 1809 migration, the city's total population jumped from 8,475 in 1805 to 17,242 in 1810 with 6,331 whites, 4,950 free people of color, and 5,961 slaves. The in-migration of over six thousand free persons of color and enslaved refugees increased the city's black majority from 56.8 percent of the total population in 1805 to 63.3 percent in 1810. Of all the major American cities, only Charleston, South Carolina, possessed a comparable proportion of African-American residents, with a 53 percent black majority.[50]

Many Haitian free Afro-Creoles had to enter the city surreptitiously. Of the group of more than eight hundred, approximately two hundred were veterans of the Haitian Revolution who refused to recognize the authority of Toussaint L'Ouverture. Led by former lieutenant colonel Joseph Savary, this force would reassemble and then fight as a unit in the Mexican war of independence from Spain and in the defense of the city from British attacks during the War of 1812. Settling in the First Municipality (the French Quarter) and the Third Municipality (the Faubourg Marigny), Haitian immigrants, Kastor notes, reinforced the city's tripartite racial structure, which was distinct from the usual Anglo-American biracial one.[51]

The rapid changes occurring in Louisiana did not deter the enslaved Afro-Creole, African American, and Haitian immigrant communities from their campaign to simultaneously demolish plantation slavery and create a new, equitable society. On January 8, 1811, Haitian-born Charles Deslondes and his compatriots launched the largest revolt of the enslaved in U.S. history. Departing from St. John the Baptist Parish, drummers led a military formation of five hundred who liberated and burned plantations as they marched toward New Orleans, thirty-five miles to the southeast. According to Pierre, many of the participants "had heard, seen, or experienced such cruelties as being thrown into cauldrons of boiling sugar or being buried from the neck down and having their faces smeared with syrup to whet the appetites of the ants."[52] They were met and defeated by U.S. troops deployed to put down the rebellion. Reportedly, sixty-six rebels and two whites died during the battle. Another twenty-two rebels were executed and their decapitated heads were placed on polls along the River Road as a warning. The increased militarization of Black and Native American life led to the intensification of their campaigns for autonomy. Consequently, when the British attacked New Orleans in 1814, enslaved Afro-Louisianans engaged in a mass exodus from the plantations toward the British lines.[53]

Along with the creation of new political, religious, and economic institutions, statehood in 1812 led to a degree of stability for the new planter regime. Yet plantation-bloc opposition to strong civil institutions resulted in the institutionalization of privatized social services. The desire to maintain racial, class, and gender supremacy meant that demands for the common good and a socially responsible public sector were viewed as threats to the social order. Then as now, churches, entrepreneurs, and philanthropists delivered fragmented forms of educational and social services. This "starve the beast" view of the welfare state would be adopted nationally and globally during the 1980s. The failure of this plantation policy tradition was so monumental that nearly two centuries later Louisiana ranked at the bottom in educational achievement when compared to the other forty-nine states.[54]

The national panic of 1819 and the declining availability of land in the Southeast sparked a massive movement to Louisiana and the Old Southwest by Anglo-American whites. They brought tens of thousands of enslaved African Americans with them to populate the new plantations of Louisiana, Mississippi, and Texas. Free Blacks throughout the nation also migrated to New Orleans. The growth in the population of enslaved, free, and Haitian-born Blacks once again led to fears of rebellion. These fears were realized in March 1829 with the launching of another revolt in St. John the Baptist Parish. By 1830 the Lower Mississippi Valley was poised on the precipice of a globally defining economic boom and New Orleans was on the verge of becoming the largest slave market in the world. Yet few anticipated the birth of a cultural renaissance among Afro-Louisianans that has yet to end.[55]

The Cotton Empire Plan and the Second Trail of Tears, 1830–1860

During the 1830s New Orleans became an international center of trade, production, conquest, and slavery. Louisiana financiers, slave traders, shippers, bankers, and cotton and sugar planters occupied a central role in the development of the nation. During the cotton boom, Arkansas, Louisiana, Mississippi, Tennessee, and Texas planters heavily relied upon the New Orleans complex to secure labor, financing, and shipping. The city also emerged as an imperial city, a financial and military staging ground for coups and colonization projects aimed at Mexico, Texas, Central America, and the Caribbean. The New Orleans plantation bloc also played a central role in orchestrating one of the most monumental human disasters in North American history, the Second Trail of Tears or the Second Slavery.[56]

First, by the 1840s New Orleans was the country's second-largest city. Its river-adjacent plantations were quickly being converted to faubourgs, or suburbs. The ongoing Anglo and Creole conflict resulted in the creation of three self-governing municipalities in 1836. The First Municipality was the Creole-dominated French Quarter and its suburbs that expanded northward toward Esplanade Ridge. Part of the district was the Afro-Creole Faubourg Tremé, one of the central sites of African American history. Upriver from the French Quarter and across Canal Street was the Second Municipality, the new American city in Faubourg St. Mary. The American sector grew rapidly due to the concentration of commercial activity and shipping. The construction of the New Basin Canal, which linked the municipality to Lake Pontchartrain and major rail lines, transformed this sector into a trade and transportation hub. During this period the New Orleans plantation bloc's ethnic, racial, and class disposability institution also victimized the Irish. The American elite preferred to use desperate Irish laborers for the dangerous project rather than highly valued enslaved Blacks. "Laboring in water up to their hips, canal diggers were very susceptible to yellow fever, malaria, and cholera. Estimates of the number of Irishmen buried along the New Basin Canal ranged from 3,000 to 30,000. Behind the canal a huge warehouse district sprung up in Mid-City, which Pierce Lewis has described as a "dangerous Irish ghetto on the site of the present day Superdome." The American elite moved further uptown into the Garden District. Downriver from the French Quarter was the Third Municipality, Faubourg Marigny. This working-class district was populated by Creoles in addition to recent Irish and German immigrants. According to Lewis, the "third was of little importance to the city's decision-makers and has remained so since. In modern times, its heart is the Ninth Ward, a blue collar area for whites and blacks which is terra incognito to the city's elite, and noticed mainly as the butt of bad jokes." The plantation bloc's disposable neighborhood ethic contributed directly to the uneven investment in infrastructure and social services. It also

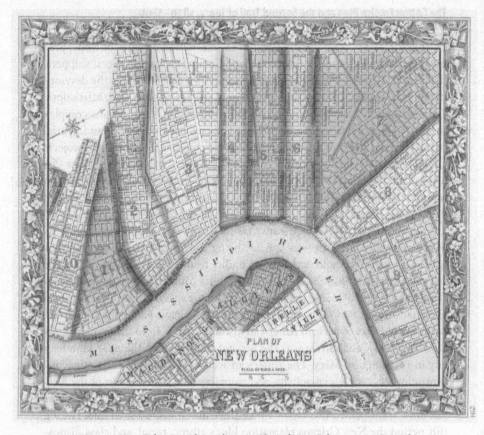

FIGURE 3. Historic New Orleans, with wards, 1860/Plan of New Orleans, 1860, Samuel Augustus Mitchell. Courtesy of the Birmingham Public Library.

repeatedly led to the construction and collapse of inferior levees in the Ninth Ward prior to 2005.[57]

The stability of the land deteriorated the further one moved inland away from the natural river levee. The practice of dividing property into long rectangular lots meant that each plantation parcel had several features: river access for transport, a natural levee on which to build homes, drained land for growing crops, and swampland. As the faubourgs grew, the canals separating plantations were drained to create the city's famous wide boulevards. The boulevards met at a massive swamp, the bottom of the bowl, referred to today as Mid-City.[58] In the Vieux Carré Creole sector, enslaved and free Blacks lived in the same neighborhoods as white residents and slaveholders. The American sector was defined by long superblocks with the large houses of wealthy whites facing the boulevards while Blacks and poor whites resided on the small interior streets.

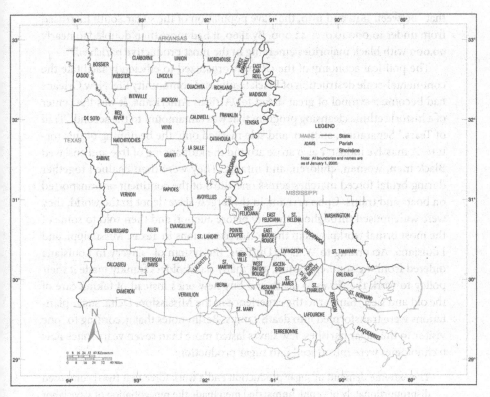

FIGURE 4. Louisiana parishes. U.S. Census Bureau, Census 2000.

Other Blacks in search of housing lived along the battures and riverbanks and in the bayous without flood protection or landownership. Although storms and floods regularly destroyed these settlements, the fate of the inhabitants was of little concern to city leaders. The settlement pattern became part of the larger ethnic and class spatial enclosure institution that forced Black working-class residents into dilapidated homes in the most disaster-prone districts over the course of two centuries.[59]

New Orleans became the epicenter of African American suffering during the "Second Middle Passage" between 1830 and 1860. During the cotton boom, production in the United States increased from three hundred thousand to four million bales a year between 1812 and 1850. Hundreds of thousands of persons were separated from their families in the Upper South and resold on the auction blocks of New Orleans. Approximately 120,000 enslaved African Americans were transported from the Eastern Seaboard to the territories of Alabama, Georgia, Louisiana, and Tennessee during the 1820s and another 300,000 were rendered during the 1830s, primarily to Mississippi and Alabama. Ira Berlin notes that "between 1810 and 1830, the slave population of the sugar South increased from under 10,000 to over 42,000. By 1860, it had more than doubled to nearly 90,000 with black majorities emerging in the most productive parishes."[60]

The political economy of the city was organized to efficiently facilitate the continental-scale destruction of Black family and community life. New Orleans had become a symbol of great dread for African Americans. It was the center of a historic ethnic cleansing program that was tantamount to the second "Trail of Tears." Separation, auction, and sale marked only the beginning of this torture. A massive industry also arose around the kidnapping of free and enslaved Black men, women, children, and infants. They were then chained together during brutal forced marches across one-third of the continent or transported on boats and trains. Upon arriving in the largest slave depot in the world, they were warehoused throughout the city before auction and then sold to some of the most brutal workplaces in the world, plantations in Texas, Mississippi, and Louisiana. According to W. E. B. Du Bois, the system of "slavery in Louisiana differed from the southern South, and many slaveholders frankly made it their policy to work the slaves to death and buy new ones instead of taking care of the old and sick." Similar to the experience in the Mississippi Delta, sugar plantations were transformed into death camps. Berlin notes that according to "one visitor to the sugar parishes, few slaves lasted more than seven years" once new technologies were introduced into sugar production:

> The extreme demand of sugar production and a work force that [was] composed disproportionately of young unmarried men made the renegotiation of slave labor particularly contentious, and the violence that accompanied it particularly savage. Few Southern slaves were accustomed to working at the murderous pace sugar production demanded. . . . "From the time of the commencement of sugar making to the close, the grinding and boiling does not cease day or night," recalled Northrup. "The whip was given to me with directions to use it upon anyone who was caught standing idle." . . . [Also,] deaths in the sugar parishes outnumbered births. At mid-century, the fertility rate of slave women in St. Bernard and St. James parishes was only 60 percent of that of slave women in the cotton south. . . . With high mortality and low fertility, sugar planters sustained their workforce only by importation.[61]

The disposability of Black life became New Orleans's signal philosophy and business. One of the central chroniclers of this tragedy was *DeBow's Review*. Published in New Orleans by James DeBow beginning in 1846, the *Commercial Review of the South and West* was both a business journal and the national voice of southern plantation capitalism. It discussed everything from commodity prices, tools, and financing, to the effective management of enslaved Black communities. According to Berlin, "the internal slave trade became the largest enterprise in the South outside the plantation itself, and probably the most advanced in its employment of modern transportation, finance, and publicity. It developed its own language: prime hands, bucks, breeding wenches, and fancy girls. . . . They demeaned as 'refuse' those whom they believed could not withstand the rigors of the transcontinental journey—the aged and the broken." William Chenault and Robert Reinders argue that despite claims of superior morality, northern migrants and industries participated fully in this bloody political economy:

> Non-Louisiana control of shipping and banking was accompanied, quite natu-
> rally, by out-of-state ownership of most of the city's insurance companies in 1850.
> Though state and city taxes were leveled during the decade upon such firms, in
> 1860 a majority of the twenty insurance companies listed in the city directory were
> northern or English concerns. The northern-born community . . . formed a sub-
> stantial segment of the city's population and provided a strong element of economic
> and middle-class leadership. Certainly the businessmen from New England and
> Middle Atlantic states were entrenched in commercial and financial circles. . . . The
> president of the New Orleans Chamber of Commerce through most of the decade
> was a New Yorker. . . . The Yankees residing in New Orleans were prominent ex-
> ponents of the dominant political persuasions in the city. Two of the five mayors in
> the 1850s were born in the free states, and the Whiggery that pervaded New Orleans
> commercial interests was as typical of northerners as of wealthy southerners and
> nearby sugar planters.[62]

Abolitionist Visions in New Orleans

It was no coincidence that abolitionist Harriet Beecher Stowe set the key por-
tions of *Uncle Tom's Cabin* in New Orleans and rural Louisiana. It was also
no coincidence that the most brutal character in the 1852 best-selling novel is
Yankee planter Simon Legree. In her defense of the novel published in 1854, she
reviews the brutal laws of the state governing slavery and denounces the widespread acceptance among whites of torture as a way of life:

> It is true that the civil code of Louisiana thus expresses its humane intentions:—'The
> slave is entirely subject to the will of his master, who may correct and chastise him,
> though not with unusual rigour, nor so as to maim or mutilate him, or to expose
> him to the danger of loss of life, or to cause his death . . .' The expression 'unusual
> rigour' is suggestive again. It will afford large latitude for a jury, in States where
> slaves are in the habit of dying under moderate correction; where outlawed slaves
> may be killed by any means which any person thinks fit; and where laws have to be
> specifically made against scalding, burning, cutting out the tongue, putting out the
> eye, etc. What will be thought unusual rigour?[63]

Stowe then turns her attention to a Code Noir provision that was still present in
the state's criminal code. Although Black testimony was excluded, the defend-

ers of slavery cited the following law as proof of the enlightened treatment the enslaved received in Louisiana:

> If any slave be mutilated, beaten, or ill-treated, contrary to the true intent and meaning of this section, when no one shall be present, in such case the owner or other person having the charge or management of said slave thus mutilated, shall be deemed responsible and guilty of the said offence, and shall be prosecuted without further evidence, unless the said owner, or other person so as aforesaid, can prove the contrary by means of good and sufficient evidence, or can clear himself by his own oath, which said oath every Court under the cognizance of which such offence shall have been examined and tried is by this Act authorised to administer. Code Noir. Crimes and Offences, 56, xvii. Rev. Stat. 1852, p.550. s. 141.[64]

Stowe then proceeds to ridicule the tortured logic of the provision:

> Would one have supposed that sensible people could ever publish as a law such a specimen of utter legislative nonsense—so ridiculous on the very face of it! The object is to bring to justice those fiendish people who burn, scald, mutilate, etc. How is this done? Why, it is enacted that the fact of finding the slave in this con- dition shall be held presumption against the owner or overseer, unless—unless what? Why, unless he will prove to the contrary—or swear to the contrary, it is no matter which. . . . The question is, If a man is bad enough to do these things, will he not be bad enough to swear falsely? As if men who are the incarnation of cru- elty, as supposed by the deeds in question, would not have sufficient intrepidity of conscience to compass a false oath! What was this law ever made for? Can any one imagine?[65]

Finally, Stowe indicts the plantation bloc and its allies for creating a form of profit-driven despotism which was arrayed against the human spirit. She con- demns it as the worst form of society possible and destructive to the country as a whole:

> Slavery, then, is absolute despotism, of the most unmitigated form. It would, how- ever, be doing injustice to the absolutism of any civilised country to liken American slavery to it. . . . Is the slave suspected of a crime? His master has the power to examine him by torture. . . . His master has, in fact, in most cases, the power of life and death, owing to the exclusion of the slave's evidence. . . . These are all abuses for which despotic governments are blamed. They are powers which good men who are despotic rulers are beginning to disuse; but, under the flag of every slaveholding State, and under the flag of the whole United States . . . they are committed indis- criminately to men of any character. . . . But the worst kind of despotism has been said to be that which extends alike over the body and over the soul; which can bind the liberty of the conscience, and deprive a man of all right of choice in respect to the manner in which he shall learn the will of God, and worship him.

Yet this power to control the conscience . . . [is] placed in the hands of any men of any character who can afford to pay for it. . . . It is a most awful and most solemn truth that the greatest republic in the world does sustain under her national flag the worst system of despotism which can possibly exist.[66]

The Second Slavery

In New Orleans, according to John Blassingame, enslaved Blacks worked as "draymen, porters, carpenters, masons, bricklayers, painters, plasterers, tinners, coopers, wheelwrights, cabinet makers, blacksmiths, shoemakers, millers, bakers and barbers. Most, however, were unskilled laborers owned by brickyards, iron foundries, hospitals, distilleries, railroad companies, and Catholic convents." Many of the men and boys worked as stevedores on the city's docks or as municipal laborers, jockeys, and vendors. In addition to enduring the never-ending exploitation of domestic servitude, women and girls worked as street vendors, flower girls, seamstresses, nurses, and sex workers. Still others worked on the farms and sugar plantations in the city and adjacent parishes.[67]

Interracial sexual relationships were constructed amid multiple forms of institutional racial violence: enforced prostitution, the auction block, concubinage, domestic exploitation, rape, threats, and scarcity. Not only did the number of Black women far exceed the number of Black men, the number of white men far exceeded the number of white women. For Blassingame, among the forms of psychological torture experienced by Black women was extreme social isolation. Enslaved women and girls "who lived with their owners frequently had a difficult time developing normal conjugal or filial relations: they were often prohibited from even using the ordinary names which indicate family relationships." In addition, New Orleans was a port city, a center for white leisure and sex tourism, and a national marketplace for enslaved concubines classed as "fancy girls." Blassingame notes that these "beautiful Negro women" were purchased for as much as $8,000. Walter Johnson's interrogation of this term reveals that "fancy" meant fantasy. It was not an adjective but "a transitive verb made noun, a slaveholder's desire made material in the shape of a '13 years' old Girl, Bright Color, nearly a fancy for $1135." Plaçage also continued and has been alternatively depicted as a common-law marriage between a white man and a free woman of color with implicit financial and child-rearing responsibilities, on the one hand, and by Floyd Cheung and others as "a ritualized system of prostitution" and sexual slavery, on the other.[68]

The possessive investment in whiteness among some Blacks in Louisiana intensified as the new American regime leveled the French and Spanish multicultural system of racial assimilation and the American frontier system of multiracial alliances. Increasingly, Native Americans faced further marginalization, displacement, and genocide while the status of free Blacks became tenuous.[69] Considered a threat to the preservation of slavery, the free Black population was composed of several elements: those who purchased their freedom or the freedom of friends and family; those manumitted for a variety of reasons; the manumitted concubines and children of white men; those who obtained their freedom based on service in the French and Spanish militias; those who sued for their freedom; and others who migrated from other parts of the United States or who immigrated from Haiti, other parts of the Caribbean, Europe, and Mexico. Included within their ranks were architects, bookbinders, engineers, doctors, jewelers, merchants, musicians, moneylenders, real estate brokers, grocers, tailors, merchandising agents, undertakers, importers, and slaveholders. By 1830, 735 free Blacks owned 2,351 enslaved Blacks, over half of whom were family members soon to be manumitted. Increasingly during this period, free Blacks were subject to arrest and abuse. In 1849 the legislature decreed that masters freeing enslaved persons must send them to Liberia, and by 1857 Governor Wickliffe was preparing plans for the mass deportation of free people to Haiti.[70] The threat of expulsion resulted in a panic. Many free Blacks fled the state, and their population declined from 19,226 persons in 1840 to 10,939 persons by 1860.[71]

As the Civil War neared, the conflict between contending cultural movements intensified. According to Blassingame, increased racial regulation associated with the new auction-block regime of the "Second Slavery," or the regime of disenfranchisement, debt peonage, and state-sanctioned and extralegal terrorism, led some enslaved and free Blacks to accept the "concept of the goodness, purity, and sanctity of whiteness and the degradation of blackness." Conversely, others chose to more fully incorporate rebellion into their daily life. There were "numerous accounts of slaves having insulted or struck whites; and sometimes slaves stole, drank, and caroused almost at will. . . . The white man was the enemy from whom it was justified to steal and with whom one dissembled." One of the epicenters of cultural conflict within the U.S. Black community, New Orleans soon became a center for a new alliance among Blacks trapped in the confines of the Second Slavery. This unity movement served as a pillar of the Blues movement and its various manifestations continues to resonate throughout the world.[72]

We Built This City: The Sacred New Orleans Renaissance

During the years leading up to the Civil War, New Orleans became the Rome of the new American empire of slavery. In this new capital of the Second Slavery, many of the foundations of the Blues emerged from the fusion of five distinct and simultaneous cultural revolutions. Not only did New Orleans become a religious doctrinal center, but the cultural movements that emerged during this renaissance fundamentally reorganized African American culture, spirituality, ethics, and social vision. These globally significant movements also prepared African Americans for the coming war. Consequently, the possessive investment of all African Americans in New Orleans became transcendent.

First, the African communities arriving in Louisiana prior to the nineteenth century continued to project their intellectual movements onto the region after the 1830s. Hall concludes that the majority of the founding African population of Louisiana, 1719–1726, came from the Bight of Benin. The Ewe, Mina, Ado, and Fon from Dahomey shared many cultural and religious practices, including Vodou. This highly democratic theology emphasized respect for the manifestation of the divine in all forms of nature and the use of divination, and it held out the possibility that every individual could become an oracle. These traditions, along with Legba, the deity governing uncertainty, all flowed into the Blues. As previously noted, between 1726 and 1746 the majority of Africans arriving in Louisiana were from Senegambia, primarily the Bambara. The latter's "profound knowledge" system stressed decades-long apprenticeships, the transmigration of souls from one person to another, the unity of all life, a sensitivity to the pain of the earth, and governance based on multiple, democratic, and life-long associations or schools. Often referred to as griots, families of musicians served as historians, educators, social observers, and political analysts. These performers were both celebrated and denigrated in the Bambara social order. Additionally, musical performances were also viewed as a religious activity, the equivalent of a prayer. All of these elements entered the Blues. Both Michael Gomez and Hall note the presence of enslaved Muslims in Louisiana. While several scholars have suggested that Blues song styles, vocal techniques, and instrumentation exhibit Arab-Islamic influences, Sylviane Diouf views the "Levee Camp Holler," recorded in the 1930s, as being structurally identical to the traditional Muslim call to prayer.[73]

The free Afro-Haitians who fled during the revolution had become increasingly embittered by their treatment in Louisiana, which included the denigration of their soldiers after the War of 1812, subjection to the new slave codes, prohibitions on their immigration, and daily terrorism. Consequently, they led and influenced four social-cultural revolutions involving benevolent societies, literature, voodoo, and shotgun houses. Afro-Haitians and free Afro-Creoles developed several benevolent societies that also served as cultural organizations. Writers associated with La Societe des Artisans condemned the betrayal of veterans, slavery, poverty, police brutality, the legal system, the use of cages, and the plantation bloc. This literary movement was part of a larger movement that included Haitians in Haiti and France whose works celebrated the maroons, Africa, and pan-African visions of social justice. Many of the works ran afoul of an 1830 Louisiana law prohibiting the possession of written material likely to produce "discontent" among free Blacks and "insubordination" among the enslaved. The penalty for this offense was "from three to twenty-one years of imprisonment at hard labor, or death."[74]

Inspired by the Haitian and French Revolutions, the movement shared the holistic African approach to the arts and French Romanticism's concern with using the arts for social change. Consequently, the New Orleans group supported several projects, including the Sisters of the Holy Family, an order of African American nuns dedicated to improving the plight of impoverished free persons and the enslaved, and La Societe Catholique pour L'instruction des Orphelins dans L'indigence (Catholic Society for the Instruction of Indigent Orphans). One of the prominent members of this movement, Armand Lanusse, published *L'Albuin Literaire: Journal des Jeunesens, Amateurs de Litterature* (The literary album: A journal of young men, lovers of literature) in 1843. After he was accused of advocating revolt, he edited and published *Les cenelles: Choix de poesies indigenes* in 1845. Containing eighty-five poems by seventeen authors, this work is considered the first literary anthology published by an African American in the United States. Cheung has described it as "an important, politically charged document. . . . These poems anticipate another African-American genre of social complaint: the blues."[75]

Enslaved Afro-Haitians torn from their nation on the eve of freedom now found themselves trapped in the brutal confines of Louisiana. Still, they launched several renaissances. First, they united with the Afro-Creole, Native American, and African American enslaved population to launch many abolition movements against the region's plantation bloc. Second, the Vodou community was revitalized by their arrival and the establishment of their secret societies. Their variant of the religion had strong Kongo theological influences. One of the *Les cenelles* poets, Nelson Desbrosses, left New Orleans to study Vodou in Haiti with a famous *houngan* (priest), J. B. Valmour. Both returned to the city and contributed to the revitalization of the religion.[76] Various accounts suggest that during a 1791 ceremony Vodou *houngan* Dutty Boukman and a priestess launched the Haitian Revolution with the following words:

> The god who created the sun which gives us light, who rouses the waves and rules the storm, though hidden in the clouds, he watches us. He sees all that the white man does. The god of the white man inspires him with crime, but our god calls upon us to do good works. Our god who is good to us orders us to revenge our wrongs. He will direct our arms and aid us. Throw away the symbol of the god of the whites who has so often caused us to weep, and listen to the voice of liberty, which speaks in the hearts of us all.[77]

Many believed that a movement based on this religion could play a transformational role in the South. It did revitalize the existing healing traditions with the addition of queens and doctors and through the expansion of the pantheon of Afro-Creole and African American saints and deities. During the 1850s Marie Laveau became the most well-known exponent of this knowledge system. She led a large multiethnic and multiracial movement that celebrated Black religious leadership, women's leadership, political power, cultural autonomy, and the sacredness of Black people, places, and nature in the very epicenter of North American slavery. Many of the theological and organizational elements of Vodou entered the Blues.[78]

Finally, the shotgun house, a Dahomean architectural style preserved in Haiti, was firmly established in New Orleans during this period. Often described as an icon of African American poverty, this African technology has been celebrated by a growing number of communities, scholars, and builders. Artist John Biggers notes that although "often people say these are called shotgun houses because a bullet fired through the front door would go right out the backdoor without hitting a wall, evidence suggests that this name is actually a corruption of the word shogon. In West Africa, 'shogon' means 'God's House.'" Painted with cosmograms in Haiti, the shotgun design kept houses cool in the summer and warm in the winter. As they spread throughout the South and beyond, shotgun porches, parlors, and rows became iconic, foundational, and sacred communal spaces instrumental in the reproduction of family, community, and the Blues.[79]

The Kongolese Renaissance was sparked by the enslavement and transport of nearly two million men, women, and children from that region to the Western Hemisphere between 1760 and 1830. From the 1770s onward, the vast majority of Africans who came to Orleans Parish came from the Kongo (Bakongo, Cabinda, and northern Angola). The French were heavily involved in the trade of enslaved Africans between Cabinda and Haiti in the three decades before the revolution. Joseph Miller notes that in "New Orleans, the combination of slaves brought from the French Caribbean and from British shipments from Cabinda in the last years of slaving added an influential cohort of Congo to the complex slave populations of nineteenth-century Louisiana."[80] These captives brought with them their civil traditions, organizations, cultural practices, and theologies. Although the original Kongolese theology was slowly transformed after the arrival of the Portuguese and the introduction of Catholicism beginning in 1482, many of its preinvasion traditions would go on to influence African American theology and culture in Louisiana, South Carolina, Haiti, Cuba, and Brazil.[81]

What Ina Fandrich has called the "Kongolization of New Orleans" revolved around the preservation of several specific traditions that survived the Atlantic passage: the resurrection of the dead, the transmigration of souls, a theology "formed by a constant stream of revelation that was not under the control of a priesthood," the constant presence of a parallel world populated by ancestors and deities, the sun as a personal being, cosmograms, and the centrality of the crossroads or cross—expressed as birth, life, death, and rebirth. The practice of honoring universal and regional deities, male and female, along with honoring family ancestors in special houses or shrines also traveled to New Orleans. John Thornton suggests that conversion to Roman Catholicism among the Bakongo elite of the Kongo Kingdom during the sixteenth century "rarely involved any fundamental religious change."[82] Other Kongo cultural traditions were also preserved. Robert Farris Thompson argues, "Important Ki-Kongo words and concepts influenced black English, especially the lexicons of jazz and blues, as well of lovemaking and herbalism." He goes on to cite several other contributions to "black American metaphysical traditions of conjuring and healing" that entered the Blues: the words *jazz* and *funk*; sacred medicine such as mojo bags, goofer dust, and toby charms; and the use of High John the Conqueror roots. "The influences and improvisations upon Kongo art and religion in the western hemisphere are most readily discernable in four major forms of expression: cosmograms marked on the ground for the purposes of initiation and mediation of spiritual power between worlds; the sacred Kongo medicines, or minkisi; the use of graves of the recently deceased as charms of ancestral vigilance and spiritual return and the related supernatural uses of trees, staff branches, and roots." Complex cosmograms have thousands of levels of meaning. On the one hand, the crossroads as a portal between worlds occupies a central place in Blues ontology and defines the tradition. Yet it simultaneously possesses a seemingly endless metaphorical elasticity.[83]

In addition to sacred arts traditions organized around the assemblage of natural and found objects, the Kongolese Renaissance helped transform New Orleans into the "land of a thousand dances." The nationalities of greater Kongo brought with them numerous dances (the mambo, the rumba, the samba, and the tango), their distinctive rhythms, and their dance societies. On the eve of the Civil War, at community gatherings on Congo Square and on plantations throughout Louisiana, people danced the Bamboula, *pile chactas, carabine, babouille, conjaille,* and *calinda* of the Ewe to the accompaniment of the violin and African drums, rhythms, and rituals. The lyrics of the songs accompanying the *calinda* consisted of withering critiques of the plantation bloc. In his essay "The Dance in Place Congo," George Washington Cable notes that the song was a "grossly personal satirical ballad . . . that well-known song of derision, in whose ever multiplying stanzas the helpless satire of a feeble race still continues to celebrate the personal failings of each newly prominent figure among the dominant caste."[84] Gavin Jones argues that the use of this tradition by white Creoles and Cajuns from the late eighteenth century onward represented both "the white adaptation of African-American satire as an artistic genre" and a "surreptitious transmission of African-American culture" that is simultaneously subversive. The emphasis upon seduction, social and racial transgression, endless ridicule, and combat found in the *calinda* aesthetic tradition remains central to cultural practices in Haiti and Trinidad, just as it has remained central to the Blues and its extensions: Zydeco, Jazz, Rhythm and Blues, Soul, Funk, and Hip Hop.[85]

Finally, in the several decades prior to the Civil War, the new pan-African, Afro-Creole, and Afro-Haitian institutions established in Louisiana during the previous century collided with the powerful African American institutions brought into the region during the massive internal slave trade. The Second Slavery and the Second Trail of Tears drew hundreds of thousands of African Americans, and the entire nation, into the vortex that was the New Orleans slave market. Many of the African Americans sold on the city's auction blocks were exposed to the sights and sounds of the multiple renaissances occurring in the city, the region, and the rural plantation communities. However, they also brought their traditions to the region, particularly the revolutionary Black Christian social gospel of Nat Turner, David Walker, and Harriet Tubman. Chained together, they traveled the long road from communal and familial death to social rebirth. Johnson documents the shock experienced by those who encountered them on their journey:

> Many observers were struck by the fact that as slaves departed for the South they were often singing. Former slave Peter Bruner remembered that the slave traders whipped the slaves to make them sing as they left, and Sella Martin explained that the songs were meant to 'prevent among the crowd of Negroes who usually gather on such occasions, any expressions of sorrow for those who are being torn away from them.' But, Martin continued, 'the Negroes, who have very little hope of seeing those again who are dearer to them than life, and who are weeping and wailing over separation, often turn the song thus demanded into a farewell dirge.' . . . These songs, then, were memorials for the communities the trade had destroyed.[86]

They entered the city singing old songs in a new way:

> As they sang songs they knew in common, slaves in the trade came to know one another. Songs could remind Christian slaves of transcendence and resistance and secular slaves of the deep structure of culture and community they shared with the slaves they met in the coffle. Indeed, many of the songs slaves in the conk must have sung—"Bound to Go," "Good-Bye, Brother," "Lay This Body Down," for example— were themselves accounts of imagined journeys which spun together temporal and spiritual imagery of loss and travel. Moreover, even as their content helped to prepare slaves for the journey ahead, their meaning was not exhausted by that content: in singing these songs, slaves began to transform the coffle into a community.[87]

New communal bonds were built by a song movement that traveled in both directions over the fifteen-foot walls of the auction houses. Crafted from the deepest imaginable psychological pain, the auction-block renaissance gave to the Blues its irrepressible will, its indestructibility, and its malleability. This new, profound working-class knowledge system became the lifeblood of the people imprisoned on the plantations outside the city. The new ontology, epistemology, and praxis that emerged among them is the Blues. Although there are hundreds of dialectics and dozens of regional, religious, ethnic, and gender identities embedded in the Blues pantheon and its extensions, the central ethical core is the creation of a socially just and sustainable society in the bosom of a social structure dedicated to economic monopoly and the exploitation of Black working-class communities, families, individuals, and traditions. In the Rome that was New Orleans, a new doctrinal center emerged. The destruction of slavery was prophesied by the spirituals and all of the above traditions. The eschatological dilemma posed by the end of slavery times fused these traditions together. Multiculturalism and internationalism defined its very existence. Consequently, the Blues became constitutional, transformative, and perpetually expansive.

In addition to these multiple cultural revolutions, the New Orleans plantation bloc was also beset by other crises on the eve of the Civil War. By 1846 the new Democratic governor and legislature, representing the growing number of small white farmers, had crafted a constitution that eliminated property restrictions on white male voters. Although there was white unity on the question of the extension of slavery to the territories, Mexico, and Central America, conflicts among whites over class, ethnicity, religion, and immigration led to a prolonged period of chaos. According to the *New Orleans Delta* of May 6, 1860, thuggery prevailed: "For seven years the world knows that this city, in all its departments, Judicial, Legislative and Executive, has been at the absolute disposal of the most godless, brutal, ignorant, and ruthless ruffianism the world has ever heard of since the days of the great Roman conspirator. . . . The ministers of the law . . . shed innocent blood on the most public thoroughfares with impunity. . . . The electoral system is a farce and fraud; [in addition to] the knife, the sling-shot, the brass knuckles determining . . . who shall occupy and administer the offices."[88] Additionally, handbills seized in New Orleans during the 1830s contradict the southern "happy slave" propaganda. Blassingame notes that several handbills told "slaves to rise and massacre the whites; that Hannibal was a Negro, and why should not they also get great leaders among their numbers to lead them on to revenge?; that in the eyes of God all men were equal; that they ought instantly to rouse themselves, break their chains and not leave one white slave proprietor alive; and, in short, that they ought to retaliate by murder for the bondage in which they were held."[89] The legacy of multiple insurrections also haunted the city. After Nat Turner's 1831 revolt in Southampton, Virginia, plots in Louisiana were reported in 1837, 1840, 1841, and 1842 before a significant uprising was launched in New Iberia Parish in 1856. These events along with other plots, revolts, and similar attempts to create autonomous communities kept the region and the entire South in a state of perpetual panic: the abolition of slavery in Mexico (1829); the constitutional ban on slavery in California (1850); the clashes in "Bloody Kansas" during the 1850s; and John Brown's Harper's Ferry raid in 1859. Then, in July 1860, hundreds of fires were simultaneously set throughout the state of Texas by Black, white, and Mexican abolitionists. From one end of the South to the other, African Americans and their allies were launching movements to secure abolition, democracy, and multiple forms of autonomy. Louisiana, Mississippi, Texas, and other lands touched by the New Orleans renaissance were at the center of the conflict between the plantation development tradition and the emerging Blues tradition. In response, the southern plantation regime declared its independence, created a region-wide army, and launched a war to defend and expand African American enslavement.[90]

CHAPTER 2

I Thought I Heard Buddy Bolden Say

*Reconstruction, Bourbonism, and the Jazz
Renaissance Blues as Planning*

On the eve of the Civil War New Orleans was the "emporium of the South" and key to the prosperity of the now globally significant Mississippi Valley. A large percentage of the goods produced in the upper valley flowed through its port. In addition, the cotton grown in the Lower Mississippi Valley was considered "white gold" by the planters, merchants, shippers, and financiers who amassed vast fortunes. The wealth generated by slavery and cotton soon fueled the demand for a separate southern empire. Yet almost half of the residents of Louisiana were African American, 350,000 of 708,000 persons. In 1860 the 332,000 enslaved persons in the state were the inheritors of a tradition of resistance unparalleled in the United States. Despite numerous personal, social, cultural, and economic ties, relations between the 25,423 Blacks and the 122,601 whites residing in New Orleans were completely permeated by the rural and urban African American movement for abolition, sustainable development, civil rights, and social and cultural justice. Consequently, the plantation bloc's decision to continue its war against the Blues freedom agenda while simultaneously waging war against the North signaled the demise of slavery.[1]

Immediately after Abraham Lincoln won the presidential election of 1860, Louisiana governor R. C. Wickliffe called the legislature into emergency session. Before the assembly he declared Lincoln's ascendance a mortal threat to the institution of slavery: "By a purely sectional vote, and in contempt of the earnest protest of the other section. . . . [The election was] to be considered as evidence of a deliberate design to pervert the powers of the Government to the immediate injury and ultimate destruction of the peculiar institution of the South."[2]

Five states seceded prior to the opening of the Louisiana secession convention on January 23, 1861. Three days later the ordinance of secession passed by a vote of 113 to 17. The representatives also voted 84 to 45 against sending the ordinance for ratification by a statewide popular vote for fear of its defeat. Louisiana's senators, John Slidell and Judah Benjamin, immediately resigned from the U.S. Senate and joined the Southern Congress, whose first meeting was held on February 4, 1861. The Civil War officially began when troops under the command of the white Creole New Orleans native General Pierre Gustave Toutant-Beauregard shelled Fort Sumter in Charleston harbor on April 12, 1861. In the imagined Confederate world, the new cotton and sugar lands of Mississippi, Arkansas, Louisiana, and Texas were to be the economic heartland of the "Velvet Empire." The largest city in the Confederacy, New Orleans was to become the central shipping, trade, and financial center of a plantation empire encompassing the western territories, the state of California, the Caribbean, Central America, Mexico, and Brazil. Although masked by the term *sectionalism*, this movement reflected a dynamic still central to the political economy of the United States: competing regional imperialisms. New Orleans had become one of the centers of southern plantation bloc imperialism and one of the centers of its opposite, the Blues vision of global community.

Sensing the coming peril, over one hundred free Blacks from the rural parishes emigrated to Haiti in January 1860. According to Karen Battle, many free Blacks decided to remain in New Orleans: "Possessing a combined estimated value of about $20 million . . . the Creoles of color decided to stick it out and prepare themselves for the long and arduous struggle for what they felt was theirs by right of birth."[3] Yet many soon found themselves forced into military service. At the beginning of the war, Confederate officials organized free men of color into the Louisiana Native Guards. Those who didn't join "voluntarily" were threatened with the seizure of their property and lynching.

In an attempt to decapitate New Orleans, the Union army sailed up the Mississippi River and captured the city on April 25, 1862. The occupation sparked a wave of major and minor insurrections by whites and Blacks. A general rebellion in the city by whites against the Union troops subsided only after Commodore David Farragut threatened to level the city with artillery. Military governor Major General Benjamin Butler moved quickly to suppress resistance and transform the social order. Among his initiatives was the enlisting of free Blacks into the reorganized Louisiana Native Guards and other regiments. Ten months after the occupation began, 29 percent of those enslaved on Orleans Parish plantations had escaped. For Blassingame, these men, women, and children brought a new sense of justice to the city, and they rapidly transformed daily life:

> Most slaves gloried in their owners' bitter defeat. They gave vent to their pent-up hatred, regularly insulted whites, and generally refused to stay in "their place." No longer would they stand when whites entered a room, move off the street to let whites pass, allow their owners to control their families, work when they were ordered to do so, cower before a white man's frown, or stand passively by while they were slapped, kicked, or flogged.[4]

When Union troops marched through the parishes during the fall and winter of 1862, more than two hundred African Americans per day joined their ranks, "singing, dancing, and praying." After liberating themselves, many of the "fugi-tives" joined the Union regiments in order to liberate their families, Louisiana, and the entire South. The number of Blacks in the Union army quickly swelled to fifteen thousand. Others found refuge in New Orleans only after subverting, compromising, and avoiding the blockades established by Confederate troops and the city police. The monumental nature of this exodus was captured in the pages of the *New Orleans Black Republican*: "Our people came naked, starving, sick, frightened, hunted, and filled with doubt and fear. . . . They came poor— they came with hardly a pillow on which the aching head might rest—they came with sad and sorrowing faces—they came cut, scarred, mangled. . . . History furnishes no such intensity of determination, on the part of any race, as that exhibited by these people to be free. . . . Nobly did many thousands die in the swamps, or give their bodies to the black waters of the bayou, rather than go back to their worse than Egyptian bondage."[5]

Still, the refugees from the countryside were met with unending duplicity and massive resistance to Black emancipation and to the recognition of their civil and human rights. Union troops controlled only twelve parishes in south-ern Louisiana, while the other thirty-five remained under Confederate control. In addition, as noted by W. E. B. Du Bois, Lincoln was not the resolute oppo-nent of slavery often imagined: "Lincoln had never been an Abolitionist; he had never believed in full Negro citizenship; he had tried desperately to win the war without Negro soldiers, and he had emancipated the slaves only on account of military necessity." Lincoln's Emancipation Proclamation of September 22, 1862, declared the abolition of slavery in those states that did not rejoin the Union by January 1, 1863. It covered only territories held by the Confederacy and, conse-quently, Blacks who lived in Louisiana parishes under Union control officially remained in slavery. Furthermore, while white Unionists in the state were di-vided on the question of Black suffrage, the secessionist Democrat majority re-mained violently opposed to voting rights. In order to placate the Confederates and the proslavery Unionists, Lincoln replaced Butler with General Nathaniel Banks in December 1862. The latter immediately launched a campaign designed to forcibly push Blacks out of the city and back onto the plantations as laborers, expand trade with the North, and deny Black suffrage.[6]

For Du Bois, powerful economic blocs outside the South viewed the Eman-cipation Proclamation as a positive signal. "Northern capital and Southern sym-pathizers in the North hailed the message because it carried no note of revenge or punishment, and contemplated speedy restoration of political independence in the South and normal industry." Southeastern Louisiana became the test case for Lincoln's Southern Reconstruction Plan in 1864 when the region became the first Deep South territory to hold a federally organized election. Although the state constitution of 1852 banned Black suffrage, it was used as the foundational document. Union strategists hoped to create a loyal class of white male Louisianans who were willing to swear an oath of allegiance to the United States. Excluded were several classes of rebels: high-ranking Confederate civil and military officials, those who had resigned from federal positions to aid the rebellion, and those who massacred Black soldiers rather than treat them as prisoners of war. Radical Unionists in the state refused to participate in the election due to the ban on Black suffrage. One Radical congressman suggested that Lincoln and Banks had organized a state doomed to fail: "another hermaphrodite government . . . half military and half republican, representing the alligators and frogs of Louisiana."[7]

Divisions also arose within the Black community around the question of suffrage. The previously free Afro-Creoles joined the Republican Party and demanded enfranchisement. During a meeting at Economy Hall on November 5, 1863, several based their demand on their military service during the Battle of New Orleans in 1815. Others cited their property ownership, businesses, professions, and literacy as reasons for enfranchisement. While some elements within the free Afro-Creole community were arguing for Afro-Creole male enfranchisement, others supported universal Black male suffrage. For example, the bilingual newspaper *L'Union*, the first Black Republican newspaper, founded in 1863 by wealthy Afro-Creoles, advocated for both universal suffrage and universal education.[8]

What African Americans actually obtained from the constitutional convention of 1864 was partial victories and new disasters. Michael Hahn was elected governor in February 1864 and, despite another boycott by the Radicals, a second election was held on March 28 to select delegates to the constitutional convention. After a mass meeting, free Blacks sent two representatives to Washington to see Lincoln and present him with a petition with one thousand signatures favoring Black suffrage. After the meeting, Lincoln wrote Hahn a letter in support of a very limited form of enfranchisement for the Creole elite and Union veterans: "I barely suggest, for your private consideration, whether some of the colored people may not be let in, as for instance, the very intelligent and especially those who have fought gallantly in our ranks. . . . But this is only [a] suggestion, not to the public, but to you alone."[9]

The constitutional convention was called to order on April 6, 1864. In addition to abolishing slavery, it gave the legislature the power to extend suffrage to Blacks based on taxation, military service, and intelligence. In addition, it created segregated public schools and a minimum wage for public works employment. However, the proposal to designate all who had less than one-fourth Black blood as white, the quadroon bill, was defeated and, later in the year, the new legislature banned both Black suffrage and interracial marriage. As Du Bois notes, the Shreveport-based Confederate government issued its own proclamations in 1864: it "recognized the right of all whites to vote; voted $500,000 to pay for slaves lost by death or . . . while impressed for public works of the state; and decreed the death penalty for any slave bearing arms against the Confederate states."[10] A large number of Blacks bore arms against the Confederacy in Louisiana. Over one thousand free men of color in New Orleans joined the Union's Louisiana Native Guards under the command of Butler in 1862. Fourteen thousand more came from the ranks of the enslaved. It was these men, along with the many Black women who rebelled against the Confederacy, who were being threatened with death.[11]

Several congressmen crafted an alternative to Lincoln's Louisiana Reconstruction Plan in the Wade-Davis bill. U.S. senator Charles Sumner of Massachusetts referred to Lincoln's Louisiana Plan as "a mere seven months' abortion, begotten by the bayonet, in criminal conjunction with the spirit of caste, and born before its time, rickety, unformed, unfinished whose continued existence will be a burden, a reproach, and a wrong." Although the legislation passed both houses of the Republican-dominated Congress, Lincoln refused to sign the bill in July 1864. U.S. senator Wendell Phillips of Massachusetts described Lincoln's refusal as an invitation to massacre: "Gentlemen, you know very well that this nation called 4,000,000 of Negroes into citizenship to save itself. . . . It never called them for their own sakes. It called them to save itself. . . . What more contemptible object than a nation, which for its own selfish purpose summons four millions of Negroes to such a position of peril, and then leaves them defenseless."[12]

As the war was concluding African Americans faced the dawn of the age of assassinations and massacres. Lincoln appealed to Congress to recognize Louisiana as a restored state in February 1865. This act was denounced by African Americans and white abolitionists alike as a betrayal of the promise of suffrage and human rights. Two months later, on April 9, 1865, after four years of Civil War, 630,000 deaths, and more than one million casualties, General Robert E. Lee surrendered the Confederate Army of Northern Virginia to Lieutenant General Ulysses S. Grant at the Appomattox Court House. In his last speech, April 11, 1865, Lincoln's defense of his Louisiana Plan was succinct: "We shall sooner have the fowl by hatching the egg than by smashing it."[13] He would witness neither. Four days later Lincoln was assassinated in the Capitol, and the plan to create a Third Slavery gained momentum. Thrust into the swirling crucible of emancipation, Black Louisianans were forced to remain perpetually vigilant. This necessity gave the Black southern working-class organic intellectuals who created the Blues epistemology, an enduring sadness for the human condition, an unmatched precision in the field of social observation and critique, and an imperative to intensify their movement to transform the region.[14]

The Presidential Reconstruction Plan and the Mechanics' Institute Massacre

Immediately after Lincoln's death a movement was launched to restore political and economic power to the Confederate wing of the plantation bloc. This movement was designed to "harness" the social revolution that was the inevitable outcome of Black emancipation and enfranchisement. Upon assuming the presidency in April 1865, the Democratic vice president Andrew Johnson attempted to restore the political and economic power of the leaders of the rebellion. The "Redemption" movement began in mid-May when he reorganized the military departments of the Southwest and stripped Banks of his authority. Then, on May 29, 1865, Johnson declared a general amnesty for rank-and-file Confederate soldiers, issued presidential pardons to most of the rebellion's leadership, and restored their property rights. The former Confederate states were also allowed to organize themselves as they saw fit under a provisional governor. Numerous leaders within the Louisiana Republican Party immediately turned against their African American allies and joined the effort to block African American suffrage. When Governor Hahn became a U.S. senator in 1864, his replacement in office, Republican planter J. Madison Wells, pushed Redemption, campaigned for the ex-Confederate vote, appointed proslavery politician Hugh Kennedy as mayor of New Orleans, allowed the ex-Confederate parishes to reorganize on their own terms, and ordered a new state election with all suspected Black voters purged from the rolls. James Hollandsworth Jr. concludes, "Between them, Wells and Johnson had restored former secessionists to the positions of power they had enjoyed before the war."[15]

Ex-Confederate rule and Black enfranchisement were the focal points of the November 6 election for statewide offices. The Democratic Party convention held in October 1865 resolved that Louisiana was "a government of white people, made and to be perpetuated for the exclusive political benefit of the white race, and. . . . that the people of African descent cannot be considered as citizens of the United States, and that there can in no event nor under any circumstance be any equality between the whites and the other races." The divided, targeted, and desperate Republicans united around a platform promoting African American male suffrage. They then decided to boycott the election, claiming that it was illegitimate due to a lack of congressional authorization. Instead, a plebiscite composed of Black and white Republicans was held to elect a state representative to be sent to Washington, D.C.[16]

The Democratic and Conservative Union Parties supported Wells for governor, and after the election the new legislature was dominated by ex-Confederates whom Hollandsworth described as being "just back from the battlefields." Among the first acts of the new legislature was to declare the Constitution of 1864 null and void. It also passed legislation designed to push African Americans back into bondage. Every adult Black man and woman was given twenty days to establish a stable home and income; those who could not do so would be arrested and "hired out by, by public advertisement, to some citizen, being the highest bidder, for the remainder of the year." Although Wells successfully vetoed the bill, his veto of the results of the 1866 municipal elections in New

Orleans failed. The city of New Orleans was "redeemed" and the Confederate mob leader John T. Monroe was reelected as mayor. After being elected mayor in 1860, Monroe had immediately launched a campaign in which enslaved Blacks living on their own were arrested and free Black leaders were both accused of supporting abolition and constantly harassed by the Metropolitan Police Department. Soon after his reelection in 1862, the Confederate mayor was imprisoned by General Butler. His successor, General Banks, promised to release Monroe if he promised to swear allegiance to the United States. The mayor refused for nine months and was finally released after promising not to return to the city. He reentered the city in 1865 and won the mayoral race in March 1866. Only afterward did he receive a pardon from Johnson, and days later, on May 14, he assumed the office of mayor again.[17]

In 1860 the enslaved Black population in the state numbered 331,726, the number of free persons of color stood at 18,647, and the white population numbered 338,000. By 1863 there were 28,000 Blacks in New Orleans, of whom 10,000 were free. The city was deeply impoverished and more than fourteen thousand persons depended on federal assistance for survival.[18] While many African Americans believed that President Johnson would soon redistribute plantations to those who had endured bondage, they were tragically disappointed. On December 21, 1865, the legislature adopted what Du Bois considered to be "among the worst of the Black Codes" in the South, one that "virtually reenacted slavery." Under the new laws, a worker could not leave his or her place of employment once a contract was signed and the low wages paid were subject to deductions for sickness, idleness, and food. After three days of refusing to work, employees could be forced to work without pay on the levees, roads, and other public works projects. Fines of one dollar per infraction were levied for leaving work without permission, swearing, impudence, and quarreling. An individual could quickly find him- or herself condemned to a lifetime of debt peonage and bondage. The attack on African American children and childhood was, and is, a key plantation bloc institution. Minors (males under age eighteen and females under twenty-one) who were orphans or neglected or whose families were too impoverished to take care of them could be apprenticed by civil authorities to employers until they reached the age of majority. Children were taken from their families and placed in bondage despite the protests of their parents and relatives. Apprenticed minor girls were subject to multiple forms of exploitation, including rape and concubinage. In addition, adults who found themselves destitute and starving could indenture themselves for five years to an employer. All of these arrangements were wrapped with enforced hunger, fraud, coercion, and terror. Du Bois concluded that terrorism directed at Black and white Union loyalists quickly transformed the state: "Thousands were insulted and assaulted. Organized violence was common throughout the state. Negroes were whipped and killed, and no one was punished. Rebel sympathizers were rapidly replacing loyal officials, and the public schools were reconstructed. One hundred and ten of the Northern or loyal teachers were dismissed and their places filled by intolerant Southerners. Union men of business began to give up and move out of the state."[19]

The wave of reaction unleashed by Presidential Reconstruction was supported by a Union army that refused to intervene in the purges and killings occurring throughout Louisiana. Even the Sunday dances at Congo Square were banned. Despite the climate of fear and intimidation, Black newspapers, leagues, and societies united in order to push for universal suffrage and sustainable development and for an end to Confederate rule, terror, and economic exploitation. The National Equal Rights League was formed in Syracuse, New York, at an 1864 meeting of the National Convention of Colored Men. Led by prominent Black abolitionists Henry Highland Garnett, Frederick Douglass, and John Mercer Langston, the organization pushed for universal suffrage, "self-improvement," and the defense of the emancipated. With help from the *New Orleans Tribune*, the New Orleans branch of the organization was established in 1865. Its membership ranged from the recently enslaved who had escaped from rural parishes to the free and wealthy. Although all shared the goal of universal suffrage, when it came to the question of Black working-class leadership, some of the Afro-Creole elite were dedicated to maintaining hierarchies based on class, cultural practices, and phenotype. When speaking before the league's December 27 meeting, Captain James H. Ingraham of the Native Guards argued that the leadership should be drawn from the "colored people of refinement and education." Battle notes that formerly enslaved members of the Black working class were also blocked from assuming political leadership positions by the Afro-Creole elite and their white allies:

> The *Tribune* stated that the two could not afford to separate and strongly supported the guidance which the Creole class was willing to offer the freedmen. . . . By the time the state convention of the Republican party met in New Orleans on September 27, 1865, unity within the Black community for political purposes—had been established. The party was under the direction of a state committee which included White Unionists and five Black men, only one of whom had been a slave. Of the 111 delegates to the convention, all but one of the twenty Black participants were free-born. After nearly two years, the struggle for citizenship rights was still under the careful guidance of the wealthy Creoles of color.[20]

The war and the increasingly unstable political environment provided an impetus for the free-born Creole elite to increasingly identify with the plight of the Black community as a whole. However, this bloc was formed on terms favorable to the elite, who also attempted to naturalize their leadership claims. Elite Creole domination of Black political action became an institution in New Orleans whose manifestations still influenced political decision making within the African American community during the early part of the twenty-first century. However, this institution was repeatedly contested and destabilized by the Blues agenda's emphasis on civil and human rights, economic redistribution, sustainable development, and working-class leadership. For example, several conventions were held and the Freedmen's Aid Association was formed in 1865 to support cooperative forms of agricultural production and land reform. An editorial in the *Tribune* on February 24, 1865, argued that these cooperatives of freed men and women would create a new commons that would bring economic democracy to the state. "These associations of capital, furnished by small shares to freedmen who possess nothing more than their industry, good faith and courage are destined not only to become powerful, but they will also enrich the state. They will inaugurate a new regime, and for the first time give a chance for the field-laborers to obtain their rightful share in the proceeds of the sweat of their brows."[21]

This program for land reform and economic reconstruction was a central pillar of the centuries-old African American development agenda, the Blues agenda. A March 11, 1865, editorial in the *Tribune* argued that economic and democratic progress depended on ending the domination of the plantation bloc:

> The planters are no longer needed in the character of masters. But they intend still to be needed as capitalists, and through the necessity of moneyed help, to retain their hold on the unfortunate people they have so long oppressed. It is that hold that every friend of justice and liberty is bound to break. As capital is needed to work the plantations, let the people themselves make up this capital. Our basis for labor must now be put on a democratic footing. There is no more room, in the organization of our society, for an oligarchy of slaveholders, or property holders.[22]

The civil and human rights crisis in New Orleans and Louisiana reached the boiling point in 1866. The planters in the legislature wanted to restore the antebellum Constitution of 1852, which recognized slavery. Like Lincoln before him, Wells also resisted Black empowerment and sought to harness the social revolution at hand until he realized that it was the only, best, and last hope for democracy. Wells came to the conclusion that if slavery were formally recognized, Congress would return the state to its territorial status. He proposed reconvening the convention of 1864 and recognizing limited Black suffrage. Members of this convention movement also objected to Johnson's rapid re-enfranchisement of secessionists by executive order. They argued that, due to the rebellion, Louisiana was still a territory and that only Congress had the power to organize elections. It was hoped that Congress would eventually approve their amended constitution, reorganize the electoral process, and set specific goals for Louisiana's readmission as a state. Despite challenges to the legality of the convention and threats to attack it, Republican delegates attempted to reconvene the constitutional convention on July 30, 1866. According to Du

Bois, the "prospect of such a consummation was too much for the Louisiana Bourbons and they determined to meet it by reopening civil war."[23]

Planters and ex-Confederates first unleashed a legal and media barrage in order to block Black suffrage and undermine the convention. Second, unbeknownst to Wells, his Democratic lieutenant governor, Albert Voorhies, was engaged in this effort. A member of the Louisiana Supreme Court before the war, Voorhies became the Confederate judge advocate general for the Trans-Mississippi Department. Voorhies sent an emissary with a letter to President Johnson several days before the convention was to convene. He requested and received a promise from Johnson that federal troops would not interfere with the suppression of the convention. A slaveholder, Johnson was considered an ally of the Redemption movement. He denounced Black suffrage as an imposition on whites that should not occur "without preparation, without time for passion and excitement to disappear, and without time for the slightest improvement, whether the one should be turned loose upon the other and be thrown together at the ballot box with this enmity and hate existing between them."[24] Johnson's policy of noninterference in state affairs was celebrated by the former Confederates. Although he was informed in December 1865 by the former director of the Louisiana Freedman's Bureau that antigovernment forces had organized secret societies in New Orleans to undermine federal rule, he viewed the organizations as innocuous benevolent societies designed to support Confederate widows, orphans, and veterans. Voorhies's letter to Johnson declared that the forces aligned with Governor Wells and the convention were planning a coup d'etat in Louisiana that was to be the opening salvo in a national revolution.

> In ordinary times such a proceeding as this, more of a small fraction of a body, which itself did not at any time represent a serious constituency, should be considered a solemn farce. But at the present day, when it is considered that the National government is on the brink of a revolution whose object is to pervert the organic law and when it is apparent, nay even proclaimed, that the revolution to be inaugurated here forms part of a programme of the Radical revolutionists at Washington—it becomes a question of prudence not to treat this matter too lightly, but, taking things at the worst, prepare for all possible emergencies.[25]

On Friday night, July 27, 1866, Black and white Republicans held a rally at the Mechanics' Institute in New Orleans. Inside, political leaders resolved "that, until the doctrine of political equality of all citizens, irrespective of color, is recognized in this State by the establishment of universal suffrage, there will and can be no permanent peace." Outside, speakers addressed a rally of three to five hundred Black and white men with speeches railing against rebel control of city, parish, and state governments. At the conclusion of the speeches at 10:30 p.m., a torchlight procession composed of two to three hundred men, the majority of whom were Black, marched to city hall. Although they were jeered and cheered along the way, when they arrived Dr. A. P. Dostie, a white Republican, reportedly gave the following advice to the marchers: "If you are insulted by any of these bands of men, pay no attention to them. Go home right by them with out saying a word." He then asserted the right to self-defense, "but if they strike you kill them."[26]

Confrontations in the city were common. Many whites objected to the presence of Black troops and the insistence by Blacks of exercising their rights to travel via streetcars and to have access to all retail businesses. Newspapers fueled every encounter on the street as a precursor to a racial conflagration. Yet Union military officials such as General Sheridan, an opponent of Black suffrage, refused to protect the convention when it convened. Consequently, the delegates to the convention and the hundreds of Blacks who gathered outside it were completely vulnerable.[27]

On July 30, 1866, a large crowd assembled outside the Mechanics' Institute, the temporary state capitol and the future site of the French Quarter's Fairmont Hotel. According to Hollandsworth, the "crowd was composed of black men, women, and children dressed in their Sunday best. For them, this was a special occasion, a time to celebrate, and their eager anticipation showed."[28] Harassed along their route, a procession of nearly one hundred Black men, led by members of the Louisiana Native Guard and other Black Union army veterans, moved through the French Quarter to the institute. Despite harassment and attacks, they were intent on securing their freedom, their right to vote, and their right to legally challenge the restored rebel government and to press for Black suffrage and the Blues agenda. More than 137 unarmed leaders and spectators, overwhelmingly African American, were assassinated. One hundred were wounded by police firing squads in the institute and by police and white mobs outside of it. Hollandsworth writes, "Something had to be done about the dead bodies that littered the streets around the Mechanic's Institute. There were fifteen on Dryades between Common and Canal, five at the corner of Dryades and Canal, and another ten or twelve on the neutral ground in Canal. Nine bodies lay at the corner of Baronne and Common, six more at Common and Carondolet. . . . The heat was such that many of the bodies began to swell in the sun. White citizens of New Orleans, men and women, gathered to look and then walked away."[29]

A year later, the U.S. House of Representatives' Select Committee on the New Orleans Riots concluded that Mayor Monroe organized the massacre:

> This riotous attack upon the convention, with its terrible results of massacre and murder, was not an accident. It was the determined purpose of the mayor of the city of New Orleans to break up this convention by armed force. . . . Before the day arrived there was general denunciation of the convention in different circles. . . . A funeral notice, announcing in advance the death of the convention was posted in

the streets on Sunday; declarations were made that the "niggers and half niggers should be wiped out"; . . . Early on Monday the whole police force, numbering between four and five hundred, were massed at their different Stations. . . . Soon after noon an unusual "alarm" was given . . . and then the combined police, headed by officers and firemen, with their companies, rushed with one will from different parts of the city toward the Institute, and the work of butchery commenced. . . . Six months have passed since the convention . . . not one of those men has been punished, arrested or complained of. . . . The gentlemen who composed the convention have not, however, been permitted to escape. Prosecutions in the criminal court under an old law, passed in 1805, were at once commenced.[30]

The congressional committee also concluded that the massacre was preapproved by President Johnson:

The President knew of the condition of affairs in Louisiana in July last. He knew that "rebels" and "thugs" and disloyal men had controlled the election of Mayor Monroe, and that such men composed, chiefly, his police force; he knew that Mayor Monroe, then an unpardoned rebel, had been after his election suspended from discharging the duties of his office by military order; he knew that he himself had subsequently pardoned him. . . . He knew that riot and bloodshed were apprehended. . . . And yet, without the knowledge of the Secretary of War, or of the generals of our armies whose immediate responsibility those military orders had been issued, he gave directions by telegraph which . . . would have compelled our soldiers to aid the rebels against the men in New Orleans who remained loyal during the war. . . . The effect of the action of the President was to encourage the heart, strengthen the hand, and hold up the arms of those men who intended to prevent the convention from assembling.[31]

Once again, New Orleans offered the nation a bloody vision of the South's future. Also revealed was a president who systematically sowed the seeds of the massacre and of many more to come. For his role in the Mechanics' Institute Massacre and for his veto of both the Freedmen's Bureau Act and the Civil Rights Act, a greatly weakened Johnson escaped impeachment by only one vote in May 1868. This often forgotten battle for democracy led by the New Orleans Black community was a turning point in U.S. history that transformed the presidency, the Constitution, and the nation as a whole.

The Radical Reconstruction Plan, 1867–76

National outrage embroiled the country after the Mechanics' Institute Massacre and, as a result, the Republican Party gained numerous seats in Congress. Just as the control of Reconstruction shifted to Congress, Louisiana descended into a state of civil war. The Reconstruction Acts passed in 1867 turned ten southern states into military districts and required that any new constitution adopted by these states enfranchise all of the population except those classes who participated in the rebellion. A state could be restored only after its legislature adopted the Fourteenth Amendment, guaranteeing equal protection before the law. Using his power as the military commander of Louisiana, General Sheridan removed Governor Wells, the state's attorney general, Mayor Monroe of New Orleans, and all of the city's aldermen. When voter registration under the new laws was complete, there were 78,230 Blacks and 41,669 whites allowed to vote in the state.

A new constitutional convention wrote the Constitution of 1868. The document had several strong civil rights clauses: the Black Codes of 1865 were eliminated, employer collusion to fix low wages was outlawed, integrated public schools were created, state-supported African American universities were established, and Confederate leaders were prevented from voting or holding office. Henry Clay Warmoth was nominally elected governor in April 1868 over African American candidate Major F. E. Dumas. Despite being the majority of the electorate, Blacks held only six of the thirty-six seats in the Senate and one-third of the seats in the House.[32]

In response to Radical Reconstruction, a new countermovement arose in Louisiana in 1868. The Knights of the White Camellia, the Ku Klux Klan, and an Italian organization, the Innocents, successfully intimidated Black voters during the 1868 presidential election. Only 276 of 21,000 registered Republicans voted in New Orleans in November of that year. Although General Grant lost the state, he won the presidential election. Afterward the legislature authorized Warmoth to create the Returning Board, a committee that invalidated a large number of elections won through fraud and violence. However, factionalism within the Republican Party set off a new round of conflicts that further undermined Radical Reconstruction. For Du Bois, corruption was so widespread that by the 1872 governor's race, Black voters had no real options. "But what could one choose between men like Warmoth, McEnery, and Carter—a carpetbagger, a planter and a scalawag; a buccaneer, a slavedriver, and a plain thief?"[33]

Led by the African American lieutenant governor Oscar Dunn, Black Republicans initiated a political revolt in 1870. This rapidly growing movement was opposed to Warmoth, who increasingly directed his appeals to planters and Democrats. Upon Dunn's sudden death in November 1871, the Republicans fragmented even further. During the 1872 race for governor both the Republican candidate, William Kellogg, and the Democratic candidate, planter Samuel D. McEnery, declared victory, both established Returning Boards, both took the oath of office, and they established dual legislatures and militias. The First Battle of the Cabildo occurred on March 5, 1873. In what was called the McEnery Coup, armed Democrats attacked the city's integrated militia until

President Grant sent federal troops to quell the violence. Grant declared Kellogg the victor.[34]

For Governor Henry Clay Warmoth, the city in the early 1870s existed in a state of permanent chaos. "New Orleans was a dirty, impoverished, and hopeless city, with a mixed, ignorant, corrupt, and blood thirsty gang in control. It was flooded with lotteries, gambling dens and licensed brothels. Many of the city officials, as well as the police force, were thugs and murderers. Violence was rampant, and hardly a day passed that someone was not shot."[35] He went on to note that, similar to the present period, lobbyists representing "the very best people" descended upon the legislature and used a wave of bribes to deepen state debt, steal parish school funds, provide tax relief for the wealthy, and further impoverish the destitute. Many Democrats refused to pay property taxes. Comprehensive plans for social policies, land reform, and civil rights were destroyed by these crises and by the tragedies of daily violence, political factionalism, and widespread terrorism. In addition, elements within the plantation bloc believed that increased Chinese and European immigration was the solution to continued Black resistance. Policies based on this "starve the beast" plan of plantation state governance would be resurrected during the late twentieth century in order to erase the memory of the Blues agenda that gave birth to the First and Second Reconstructions. This plan was a central pillar of the effort by plantation blocs throughout the South to fully seize the reins of power from the Reconstruction governments through social and fiscal starvation combined with massive public indebtedness. The plan was clearly articulated as a political, class, racial, and regional strategy in the pages of an 1871 edition of the *Floridan*:

> No greater calamity could befall the State of Florida, while under the rule of its present carpetbag, scalawag officials, than to be placed in good financial credit. . . . Our only hope is in the state's utter financial bankruptcy; and Heaven grant that may speedily come! On the other hand, establish for the state financial credit on Wall Street, so that Florida bonds can be sold by Reed & Company, as fast as issued, and you give these foul harpies a life-tenure of these offices. The Temporal salvation of the taxpayers is . . . in having the State's financial credit low so that Reed & Co. can't sell bonds so as to raise money with which to perpetuate their hold on office.[36]

Also attacked were the Black working-class pillars of the regime. The economic panic of 1873 brought five thousand New Orleans families face to face with starvation. In response, by 1875, two thousand African American children, women, and men had been expelled from the city by the military and forced onto plantations.[37] During this crisis efforts were also launched to expel or "bulldoze" Black workers from specific occupations and sectors throughout the city in favor of white workers. In 1874 white longshoremen persuaded federal General Badger to harass Black longshoremen. Although Badger arrested many Black workers, more continued to come. Roger Shugg notes that a new bloc, a

new political and economic alliance, was created between white urban workers
and capitalists united in the effort to intensify Black political and economic
marginalization. This emerging racial division of labor enabled the plantation
bloc to buy the votes and solidarity of white workers without incurring additional costs in terms of wages: "Throughout the city, it was reported in 1874,
employers were hiring Negroes when white men were on the verge of starvation.
Since merchants and planters needed the votes of these laborers to oust the Republican carpetbag government, they were exhorted to 'give preference to white
over black labor.' This policy was adopted by many employers. The steamboat
companies . . . decided to discharge all Negroes and hire whites instead, but 'at
the same wages as are now paid to black for like labor.'"[38]

Despite the growing precariousness of the Reconstruction government, African Americans intensified their organizing efforts. During this period, Blacks
actively participated in Reconstruction clubs, loyal leagues, lodges, and "Companies of the Grand Army," which advocated comprehensive programs for social
justice and development. Campaigns for farm homesteads, public office, and
integrated streetcars and schools were also launched. Also, Black leaders in the
state occupied several major offices: lieutenant governor, state treasurer, secretary of state, and superintendent of public education, as well as serving as congressmen, state senators, and state representatives and holding the governor's
office for forty-three days. Michael Ross notes,

> By the fall of 1870, Republican governor Henry Clay Warmoth and a biracial state
> legislature had ruled Louisiana for over two years, and in New Orleans, evidence of
> radical societal change was everywhere. Black men served on juries, black police of-
> ficers patrolled the streets, and black detectives solved some of the city's most high-
> profile crimes. A well-trained, well-armed black state militia commanded by James
> Longstreet—the former Confederate general who had joined the Republicans—
> drilled on the levee and in public squares. African Americans regularly demanded
> service in the finest saloons, restaurants, and theaters. That fall, the successful in-
> tegration of New Orleans's public schools began.[39]

Yet, according to Du Bois, the emerging Black leadership in Louisiana faced an
enormous array of challenges: "Some looked white, some black, some born free
and rich, the recipients of good education; some were ex-slaves with no formal training. They were faced with an intricate social tangle among the whites.
Economic and social differences were, in Louisiana, more complicated than
any other American state, and this makes the history of Reconstruction more
difficult to follow."[40] Within the tangle of whiteness were the planters who both
served as Confederates officers and returned "embittered and widely impoverished." Also present were northern traders, capitalists, and missionaries and
five to ten thousand Union soldiers whom Democrats called "carpetbaggers."
The local white planters and small farmers who supported the Union were de-

nounced as "scalawags." Then there were the former overseers and slave traders whom Du Bois characterized in the following manner:

> [they] pursued no occupation but preyed on blacks and whites alike, as gamblers, and tenth-rate politicians, drinking and swaggering at the bar, always armed with a knife and revolver, shooting Negroes now and then for excitement. . . . They became demagogic leaders of the Negroes, on the one hand, and murderers and fighters for the planters. . . . Another factor was the numerous poor whites in the northern part of the State. Living close to the subsistence line on the thin soil of the pine hills back of the bottom lands, without schools, with but few churches . . . their ignorance and prejudice bred in them . . . a dread of sinking to the social level of the blacks. The dread, in turn, bred hatred, and it was from this class, instigated very probably by the class above them, that the Colfax and Conshatta murders took their unfortunate rise.[41]

Although Grant sent federal troops into the state three times to restore order after elections, fraud, massacres, and assassinations, the white electorate, North and South, resisted proposals for arming existing and new Black militias. The funeral of General Lee in 1870 marked the beginning of a coordinated cultural mobilization to make the celebration of the Confederacy the civil religion of the South. In New Orleans, the "Lost Cause" bloc was composed of thousands of ex-Confederate soldiers, four Democratic newspapers (the *Daily Picayune*, the *Times*, the *Commercial Bulletin*, and the *Bee*), and the theologian Benjamin M. Palmer. The pastor of the First Presbyterian Church, Palmer was nationally known as "the high priest of the 'Lost Cause'" due to his Bible-based defenses of slavery, segregation, and white supremacy. The funerals of Confederate generals were occasions to assert publicly a united front for the restoration of white rule and the expulsion of Blacks from the electorate. This movement also used social ostracism, economic boycotts, and the press to further undermine Reconstruction in Louisiana.[42]

The parades, festivals, and balls of the Roman Catholic Creoles were suppressed during the Spanish and American periods only to reemerge during the 1820s. Beginning in 1857, the clubs of Protestant American businessmen based in Uptown began to hold parties and balls during Mardi Gras. The founding group, the Mystic Krewe of Comus, came out of the Pickwick Club, which was established in 1857. According to John Kendall, "in 1874 members of the club played a conspicuous part in the attempted overthrow of the radical government." The Knights of Momus is associated with the Louisiana Club, founded in 1872. The King of Carnival was selected from the Rex Society that was associated with the Boston Club, begun in 1841. After the Civil War, early members of the Rex Society included Judah P. Benjamin, the Confederate secretary of state, while the president of the Confederacy, Jefferson Davis, was a "frequent visitor." These clubs, these institutions, which continue to dominate Carnival and the economic life of the city, also used Mardi Gras to justify revolution and massacre.[43] Joseph Roach provides the following description of the 1873 carnival:

> The Comus parade and tableaux for 1873, which appeared 18 months prior to White League's coup d'etat, provide an instance of the "timely" politics of racial hatred bubbling up into the scene of the "timeless" carnival of fantasy and mirth. In a sequence of brilliantly vicious costumes and tableaux, Comus retailed the "The Missing Links to Darwin's Origin of Species," creating a densely inhabited zoological taxonomy of hated public figures from the Reconstruction, such as Ulysses S. Grant as a verminous potato bug or the "Radical" J. R. Pitkin as "The Cunning Fox [carrying a carpetbag] which Joins the Coon." The apostrophe of Darwin, uniting reactionary loathing of modern science with murderous opposition to the Fourteenth and Fifteenth Amendments, culminates in the mock crowning of "The Gorilla," who, holding his banjo in one hand, with the other pushes open the gate of "Darwin's Eden," which the Comus designer depicts as an old Louisiana plantation house. . . . "When the curtain rose on the second tableau the Gorilla had just been crowned, and was seated on his throne under a dais, with Queen Chacona [the Baboon] on his right, and Orang, the Premier, on his left . . ." the tableau offers a symbolic pre-enactment of the coup d'etat in which members of the Mystick Krewe of Comus (among others), attacking "the most absurd inversion of the relations of race" (Platform of the Crescent City White League 1874), violently displaced the reconstructing "monkeys" at the top.[44]

Several new terrorist groups sprang up in Louisiana during this period. Republican voters and officeholders of both races were the objects of destruction. Successors of the Knights of the White Camellia, the White League, spread terror throughout the state. On April 13, 1873, a disputed election for sheriff in Grant Parish led to the massacre of between one hundred and three hundred Black men, including twenty-five prisoners. Known as the Colfax Massacre, this tragedy is considered the bloodiest single event to have occurred during the entire Reconstruction period.[45] By 1874 the White League was terrorizing the countryside with posses numbering several hundred men. In August 1874 in Red River Parish, five white Republican officials were lynched in what is known as the Coushatta Massacre.[46]

Finally, on September 14, 1874, more than eighty-four thousand members of the Crescent City White League attacked and defeated the six hundred members of the integrated Metropolitan Police and three thousand members of the Black militia. Known as the Battle of Liberty Place, the conflict was fought along Canal Street and involved the use of Gatling guns and artillery. Order was restored only after federal troops intervened. The subsequent political negotiations allowed Kellogg to stay in office but gave the Democrats control over the state House of Representatives. A controversial monument honoring White League members who fell in battle still stands near the site.[47] The prolonged political, social, economic, cultural, psychological, and guerilla warfare against the Reconstruction government reached its peak during the presidential election of 1876. In *Black Reconstruction*, Du Bois describes the Louisiana counterrevolution in the following manner: "Organized clubs of masked, armed men, formed as recommended by the central Democratic committee, rode through the country at night, marking their course by the whipping, shooting, wounding, maiming, mutilation, and murder of women, children, and defenseless men, whose houses were forcibly entered while they slept, and, as their inmates fled, the pistol, the rifle, the knife and the rope were employed to do their horrid work. Crimes like these, testified to by scores of witnesses, were the means employed in Louisiana to elect a President of the United States."[48]

The governor's race of the same year again resulted in two governors, two legislatures, two sets of presidential electors, and two armed camps. Du Bois suggests that Blacks were "pawns" in a larger struggle:

> Evidently, the Negro voter, and even the office-holder, could not be held to blame for the anarchy and turmoil, which are the history of Reconstruction in Louisiana. Practically, so-called Reconstruction in Louisiana was a continuation of the Civil War, with the Negro as pawn between the two forces of Northern and Southern capitalists. The Northerners were determined to use the state for their own interest, but willing to admit universal suffrage under property control; while planters, united in secret organizations with poor whites, were determined to reduce the labor vote by disenfranchising the Negro. Between these two forces, the Negro was the victim and peon. His intelligent and sacrificing leadership was beaten back, deceived, and ham-strung, and finally discredited by charging it with plans to "Africanize" Louisiana. The shrewd and venal and dishonest Negro elements were characterized as typical and used as an excuse for cheating and lawlessness by elements in the white population just as dishonest and much more influential. Back of this smoke screen lay the real charge, which was the attempt to subject this state so rich in raw materials, and so strategic for trade, to a dictatorship of labor, rather than an oligarchy of capitalists.[49]

The agenda of working-class Afro-Louisianans cannot simply be reduced to a struggle between North and South, capital and labor. Codified over the course of a century and a half and manifest during the Civil War and Reconstruction, the Blues agenda was viewed by the plantation bloc as a mortal threat to its regionally distinctively authoritarian movements, alliances, institutions, daily practices, and representations. The principles of social justice and sustainability at the core of the Blues agenda were used to create a representational grid in order to critique the social order, create parallel institutions, and construct a symbolic moral economy. This approach ensured that working-class African Americans in Louisiana and the South became a self-assertive national and global force as opposed to mere "pawns" and "peons." As the "Lost Cause" became the civil religion of much of the white South, the Blues became the civil religion for much of the Black South.

The Blues and plantation-bloc dialectic that defined the Lower Mississippi Valley became the epicenter of southern and national political schisms. The Mechanics' Institute Massacre represented the first attempt in the South to overthrow Presidential Reconstruction. After a series of other massacres, the Battle of Liberty Place represented the first attempt by a southern plantation bloc to overthrow Radical Reconstruction. The elections and coup of 1876 and 1877 would mark the formal demise of the 250-year African American First Reconstruction movement in the South. During the following nine decades New Orleans and Louisiana remained centers of reaction. Yet the repeated revitalization of the Blues agenda by Afro-Louisianans during this long tragedy remains one of the most remarkable accomplishments in U.S. history.

The Bourbon Plan and the Second New Orleans Renaissance, 1876–96

They have learned nothing and they have forgotten nothing.

Charles-Maurice de Talleyrand

The movement for the overthrow of Reconstruction accelerated as the gubernatorial election of 1876 approached. Before the election white posses roamed the countryside terrorizing the Black and Republican electorate. After the balloting was complete the Republican candidate, former marshal Stephen Packard, and the Democratic candidate, former Confederate general Francis T. Nicholls, both declared victory and took the oath of office in separate ceremonies on January 9, 1877. On the following day Nicholls sent three thousand members of the White League to attack and occupy the Cabildo, the New Orleans home of the Louisiana Supreme Court and the Metropolitan Police Department. Federal troops and the metropolitan police force were quickly overwhelmed, and Nichols completed the coup by replacing the entire supreme court.[50]

The Louisiana movement coincided with the national movement to overthrow Reconstruction. The national presidential election of 1876 was also disputed. Whether Democrat Samuel J. Tilden or Republican Rutherford B. Hayes would declare victory hinged on the resolution of disputed elections in Louisiana, Florida, and South Carolina. As part of the agreement to award Hayes the presidency, the federal troops that defended Reconstruction governments, communities, and partisans were withdrawn from these states, all of which were still under military control. The movement was institutionalized by the new Louisiana constitution approved by voters and Congress in 1879. Written by the Democratic majority, it officially returned "home rule" to the state. According to Joel Gray Taylor, the same class that controlled Louisiana before the war, "planters in the country and the merchants, bankers, and brokers of New Orleans," would remain in control of the state for another half century.[51]

Designed to reproduce the hegemony of the dominant plantation bloc, several other institutional power centers dominated the state during this period, according to Mark Carleton and William Ivy Hair. First, the New Orleans Ring was a political machine closely allied with the highly profitable Louisiana Lottery. Second, a massive prison-industrial complex emerged that has undermined civil and labor rights from the 1870s to the present. Samuel James, along with several legislators and government bureaucrats, made up the James Gang. An engineer, an associate of P. G. T. Beauregard, a major in the Confederate army, and a future president of the Pickwick Club, James bought the eighteen-thousand-acre Angola cotton plantation in West Feliciana Parish in the late 1860s. In 1870 James and his associates were awarded a twenty-one-year contract to manage the state's convict lease system in exchange for a small annual fee. The gang's members became millionaires by leasing men to planters, lumber companies, levee districts, and railroads. By 1884 the brutality of the system led the *Daily Picayune* to conclude that anyone sentenced to more than six years should be given the death penalty as a humanitarian gesture. In this convict lease system that overwhelmingly relied on Black labor, more than 20 percent of the men died in 1892 alone.[52]

The third center of institutional power was the plantation bloc known as the Bourbons. The term *Bourbonism* has been used to describe the restored plantation blocs in several Southern states in general and the Louisiana cotton and sugar blocs in particular. The House of Bourbon was a French and Spanish family dynasty that ruled France from 1594 to 1848. Although Louis XVI and the House of Bourbon were overthrown in 1792 by the French Revolution, after the defeat of Napoleon in 1815, the Bourbons were restored to power. They were then overthrown again and restored in 1830 before being overthrown for the last time in 1848. The absolutism and ultraconservatism of this aristocracy were ridiculed by the French bishop and diplomat Talleyrand when he concluded that, after multiple revolutions seeking democracy and justice, the Bourbons "have learned nothing, and they have forgotten nothing." Another quote often used to depict the Bourbon philosophy toward poverty is "let them eat cake." The term *Bourbon* was increasingly used during the 1880s to describe the militarized, authoritarian, planter-dominated regimes in each southern state that led the violent movement to overthrow Reconstruction, disenfranchise Blacks and impoverished whites, and create the institutions of debt peonage and prison slavery. Yet, according to William Holmes, the principles that guided the House of Bourbon were more fully restored in Louisiana than in any other state: "Louisiana Bourbons were ultraconservatives who considered any 'whisper of moderation' as 'rampant pseudo liberalism.' Without pretense of subscribing to a *noblesse oblige* attitude, they identified closely with the propertied interests and espoused rabid racism that elsewhere was identified with the poor whites. Nowhere else did public services sink so low, as was illustrated by the fact that in the 1880's Louisiana was the only state, North or South, to show an absolute rise in the per cent of white illiterates."[53]

The Bourbon Constitution of 1879 reduced state taxes on properties that were already significantly undervalued by tax administrators, who historically allowed planters and commercial interests to escape payment altogether. This tax cut strategy was inserted in the state constitution along with a reduction in the interest paid on bonds and restrictions on the legislature that prevented it from issuing bonds or contracting any debt "except for the purpose of repelling invasions or for the suppression of insurrection."[54] Appropriations could be made only through constitutional amendments requiring two-thirds approval of both legislative houses and a majority of voters. The legacy of Bourbon rule was the creation of state fiscal and tax institutions that reduced expenditures for public works, education, social services, and governmental institutions to below antebellum levels. The Louisiana landscape became littered with destroyed schools and rutted roads, while the state debt and tax burdens were increasingly placed on the backs of workers and small farmers. By 1890 the state had the highest rate of Black illiteracy in the nation, 72 percent. Mark Carleton, Perry Howard, and Joseph Parker argued that public education was still reeling from Bourbonism a century after the overthrow of Reconstruction.[55] During the 1980s many fiscal and racial elements of Bourbonism were restored and used to create a new national movement developed under the banner of Reaganism, a philosophy of limited governance developed under the banner of "starve the beast," as well as international social and economic policy institutions developed under the banner of neoliberalism.

What has been called "Classical Bourbonism" flowered during the terms of Governor Samuel D. McEnery (1881–88), a cotton planter from Ouachita Parish. Francis Nicholls, the leader of the 1877 coup, returned to serve as governor from 1888 to 1892. He was succeeded in office by St. Mary Parish sugar planter Murphy Foster Sr., who served from 1892 to 1900. In his summary of the period, Carleton notes that "for almost a generation following the end of Reconstruction, therefore, Louisiana experienced the absolute and uninterrupted rule of a small group of fiscal archconservatives who utilized race, electoral fraud, physical violence, and eventually disenfranchisement to sustain themselves in office."[56]

The Bourbon system of cultural representation was partially organized around attacking the extension of democracy and social spending that occurred during Reconstruction. It was also geared toward defining Bourbon-bloc interests as being identical to the interests of its white working-class allies who were being impoverished by its policies. Despite the fact that New Orleans was home to several major corporations and thirty-five millionaires by 1892, this bloc was able to build new fortunes by keeping the promise to block the Blues agenda and to eliminate Black competitors from farms, jobs, communities, and the electoral process. "The Bourbons' 'plea of poverty,' consequently, 'was purposely exaggerated' so that the 'privileged few' could 'use the poverty of the majority as the specious excuse for avoiding taxation upon themselves.' Professing sympathy with taxpayers, the Louisiana Bourbon Democrats actually desired 'a government of should-be taxpayers who paid little or nothing.'"[57] A key component of the bloc's cultural representation grid was fanning the flames of racial hatred in order to legitimize the theft of labor, land, and state wealth. For example, Roach notes that during Mardi Gras, Comus "celebrated the final collapse of Reconstruction in 1877 with a triumphant float parade entitled 'The Aryan Race.'"[58] Additionally, corruption, theft, debt bondage, imprisonment, torture, and assassinations committed in the name of white supremacy were not considered crimes. Considered the voice of Bourbonism, the editor of the *New Orleans Daily States*, Henry J. Hearsey, denounced the emancipation of the enslaved as "a crime" and insisted that when white mobs burned Blacks accused of rape, they were obeying a "divine impulse."[59] For William Ivy Hair, Louisiana had become the epicenter of Southern fascism:

> But, it is unlikely that Negroes in any other state suffered more than those in Louisiana. . . . Available evidence also points to the conclusion that Pelican state blacks were subjected to a greater degree of violence than Negroes in other parts of the south during the late nineteenth century. Why was this so? The answer lies partially hidden in the labyrinthine social history of the antebellum and colonial Louisiana. Somehow, the commingling of the English-speaking and Creole-Cajun cultures had resulted in a milieu of political instability and unusual insensitivity to human rights. Long before the Civil War, the state had been notorious for its lawlessness and its maltreatment of slaves.[60]

Although Blacks remained a majority of registered voters as late as 1888, white supremacist Democrats were able to solidify their hold on state offices through "shotgun sovereignty": violent intimidation at the polls, ethnic cleansing or "bull dozing," the falsification of ballots, and forcibly "voting" the living and the dead under the principle that "a dead darky always makes a good Democrat and never ceases to vote." The parishes with the greatest Black majorities also had the greatest number of votes cast for the Bourbons, who used these "forced votes" to politically dominate the state.[61]

Finally, during this period New Orleans developed as a massive port, rail, and storage complex organized around the shipment of southern cotton and sugar, along with midwestern grain and coal. It was also the main port of entry for the coffee and banana trade from Central America and the Caribbean. Immigrants, merchants, and political leaders from these countries increasingly called the city home. Even though cotton production doubled from five million bales in 1859 to ten million by the late 1890s, cotton and grain were increasingly shipped eastward via the new rail hubs of Memphis, Vicksburg, Cincinnati, St. Louis, and Louisville. In addition, the city's manufacturing base stagnated by 1880; it employed only 1 percent of the population. Furthermore, a recession in the cotton sector during the late 1880s deepened the regional economic crisis.[62]

To address the economic decline of the city, the New Orleans World's Industrial and Cotton Exposition of 1885 was organized to market the city to northern manufacturers and financiers. The campaign emphasized regional reconciliation, patriotism, economic development, Latin American and Caribbean trade opportunities, and the presence of a compliant, yet skilled, Black workforce. Organized by the National Cotton Planter's Association and financed by the U.S. Congress, the exposition was led by individuals including Edmund "King Cotton" Richardson of Tensas Parish, the second-largest plantation owner in the world, and E. A. Burke, owner of the *New Orleans Times-Democrat* and a renowned white supremacist. Burke viewed the exposition's Colored Department exhibit as a tool to manage inherent inferiors, an effort "to reach out our hand to our brother in black; to shed upon that unfortunate race the sunlight of science and invention, and implant in him the desire to come out of the slough of ignorance and make a manly effort to occupy with us the improved farm, the workshop, and the factory." For Robert Rydell, the leaders of the New South increasingly redefined progress as a southern variant of fascism: a herrenvolk movement comically referred to as "Jim Crow" and "a classless society of Anglo-Saxons, ready to lead the rest of the nation in the imperial duties of subjugation and uplift."[63]

The Bourbon movement had a horrific impact on African Americans' social conditions, community life, and human rights—with consequences that would last for generations. By 1880 the population of New Orleans had grown to more than 200,000 persons: 57,617 Blacks and 158,859 whites. Many of the Black residents had fled to the city from the surrounding plantations, where they had worked as "field hands, engineers, drivers, overseers, bricklayers, coopers, carpenters, wagon makers, blacksmiths, harness makers, nurses, tanners, woodworkers, and sugarmakers." As described by Duplain W. Rhodes, many rural families had been bulldozed off their lands: "If you owned land, you had to get out, and the easiest thing to do is to kill you. Just hung him if you could catch him. They got rid of a schoolteacher, left the body on the street with sign on it as a warning to all blacks in that location. My daddy had to make himself not to be found. He went into the woods. My mother started selling what we had. My daddy came at night and took my mother in a wagon and a horse. They left there and went here (New Orleans) from Thibodaux."[64]

The year 1881 was considered a landmark in depravity. Among the sixteen African Americans lynched in Louisiana was Jane Campbell, a Claiborne Parish woman who was burned at the stake. In the northeast Louisiana delta's More-house Parish, a man was "trussed up inside the carcass of a cow, leaving only his head sticking out, so that buzzards and crows would pick his eyes out."[65] The *Chicago Tribune* and the Tuskegee Institute put the number of African Americans lynched in the state between 1882 and 1903 at 232, the third-highest state total in the nation. Hair suggests these figures are misleading, given that as a percentage of the total population, Louisiana had the second-highest rate of lynching. In addition, the figure of 232 excluded the Thibodaux Massacre of 1887, the dozens of vigilante killings reported in the local press, and the dozens of other slayings not reported in the local press. The upper classes and the local press actively participated in lynching and bulldozing campaigns—the ethnic cleansing of Blacks from their homes, farms, or jobs. For example, the Shreveport Plan of 1889 proposed in the city's *Daily Caucasian* would have required that Blacks be restricted to only a few occupations: "bootblacks, waiters, porters, cooks, clerks, and teachers." In 1890 the legislature attempted to remove Blacks from specific public spaces. The railroad segregation law passed in that year provided for "separate but equal accommodations for whites and coloreds." After African Americans challenged this law in the case of *Plessy v. Ferguson* in 1896 the U.S. Supreme Court sided with the legislature and, consequently, legitimized militarized racial segregation throughout the United States for the next six decades. After playing a central role in designing and implementing the overthrow of Reconstruction and the institution of apartheid in the South, the Bourbon bloc found its model for African American destitution and persecution adopted nationwide following the *Plessy* verdict.[66]

Although rural families fled to New Orleans in search of refuge, in the city they found a desperate Black community being bulldozed from long-held occupations and trades. Then as now, extremely high rates of Black unemployment were represented as the "natural" products of laziness, ignorance, and immorality.[67] Approximately 80 percent of the households in New Orleans rented, and renters, according to Shugg, "paid more for poorer quarters . . . than in any other old American city." Pauperism became both an institution and a central feature of life as both Black and white homeless boys roamed the streets, subsisting off coffee and fish caught from the Mississippi River. A large segment of the growing ranks of the Black dispossessed found themselves in the city's workhouse and chain gangs. Many lived in shacks in or near malarial swamps, while many others lived in overcrowded hovels with unpaved streets filled with garbage in the front and contaminated privies in the back. Even after the yellow fever epidemic devastated the city in 1878, high rates of smallpox perpetually plagued Black communities.[68]

A central feature of the Bourbon death economy was extremely high rates of morbidity and mortality between 1860 and 1880: the annual death rate for Blacks was thirty-two to eighty per thousand, while it was only five to thirty-one per thousand for whites. According to Blassingame, so "many Negroes were crowded into dilapidated huts and tenements that they were easy prey for pulmonary consumption, small pox, and pneumonia. Living in overcrowded and frequently badly ventilated, uninhabitable tenements, surrounded by filth, drinking unsanitary water, subsisting on insufficient diets, Negroes were naturally the major victims of such communicable diseases as small pox and cholera." This social disaster was compounded by the elimination of the Freedman's Bureau's medical services programs in 1882. Many residents relied upon "Indian or voodoo doctors" as their primary care physicians. In addition to amazingly high rates of infant mortality, 450 per 1,000, the rate of adult mortality due to disease, poverty, overwork, and violence left many children orphaned. Yet, according to a German visitor writing in 1876, in New Orleans "the Negro is kind hearted toward people of his own color and would not lightly abandon one in need of help."[69]

African Americans responded to these multiple crises by expanding the breadth and depth of their social, cultural, and political organizations. Blassingame notes that the institutionalization of benevolent societies and the social and pleasure clubs played a key role in sustaining community life by creating a community-based planning network that provided basic social services during the prolonged crisis that was Bourbonism. Migration to the city also led to a flourishing of associational life and to the Second New Orleans Renaissance:

> The Negro societies and benevolent associations were the most important agencies involved in organized efforts to solve community social problems. Negro societies in the days before the rise of Negro insurance companies provided the major form of social security against sickness, death, and poverty. They aided orphan asylums, Negro veterans, and the indigent; gave religious education to children; and fought against segregation and for racial uplift. For individual Negroes the societies provided status, a sense of belonging, some form of organized social life, a guarantee of aid to the sick and to the children and widows of deceased members. They also assured members an impressive and proper burial by paying for the bands to lead funeral processions, taking care of burial expenses, holding special rites over the body, marching in special regalia in the funeral procession, and wearing mourning badges for the deceased.... Usually the societies held wakes over the bodies of deceased members and fined those members who did not attend the wake and funeral.[70]

Spirituals, rural secular music, and urban brass bands began a historic interaction during this period. Spirituals such as "Before I'd Be a Slave, I'd Be Buried in My Grave" were still popular, and some were revised by New Orleans University singers. Musical skills brought to the city included expertise in the banjo and the fiddle/violin and in drumming. The brass bands in New Orleans were at the center of parties, parades, conventions, and funerals. As Blassingame also points out, they helped maintain the balance between death and life, which was echoed in the constant funeral processions of the period as well as the celebrations represented by second lines.[71]

Major mass meetings, parades, and festivals were organized around the anniversary of the Emancipation Proclamation, the abolition of slavery in Haiti, the death of Lincoln, and the life of John Brown. Also, masked balls were held during a season that began in January with Mardi Gras and ended on St. Joseph's Eve, March 18. In addition to a year-round schedule of major dances, there were also numerous readings, orations, and lectures on history and current events. Variety theaters, the opera, classical music performances, and drama companies contributed to Black cultural life in the city. Hundreds of social clubs formed the pillar of African American associational life and political economy. They also served to circulate wealth used to support speakers, entertainers, seamstresses, craftsmen, builders, and musicians as well as businesses and social and political movements. The 226 societies listed on the books of the Freedman's Bank included "benevolent associations; militia companies; rowing clubs; masonic, Odd Fellow, Eastern Star and Knights Templar Lodges; religious societies; social and literary clubs; orphan-aid associations; racial improvement societies; and baseball clubs."[72]

One of the defining features of Black autonomy in New Orleans was the resistance to cultural imposition. Consequently, the Bourbon mobilization targeted cultural practices in "the Land of a Thousand Dances." Dude Bottley recalled that "Negroes were prohibited from congregating in any public park under penalty of fine and imprisonment. So that was the end of Congo Square and the Sunday evening festivities moved to an open-air area uptown." Julio Finn argues that the forms of accommodation, censorship, and cultural assimilation emanating from the Black economic and religious elites contributed to the decline of African dances such as the Black Annie, the Pas Mala, the Strut, the Walkin' the Dog, and the Ballin' the Jack during this period. "The Black Christian Church, ever ashamed of black culture, laid down strictures about dancing, and the faithful followed them—waltzin', polkain', and mazurkain' with a panache which did full credit to the spiritual advisors." With Reconstruction's collapse in 1877, city police once again resumed their attacks on Vodou practitioners, which disproportionately impacted women, as they led this institution. In 1897 the city council actually outlawed trance artists from operating in the city.[73] Increasingly, many African American middle-class organizations adopted the imperial discourse of uplift and Black working-class immaturity. In doing so, they advocated a two-stage theory.

The second stage, ending racial subjugation, would occur only after a prolonged period of moral tutelage organized by Black middle-class reformers. This uplift model was at odds with the lived experience of the Reconstruction generation, which witnessed a powerful class of leaders emerging from among

the freedmen and freedwomen. Consequently, J. J. Spellman, the Colored Department's African American superintendent at the New Orleans World's Industrial and Cotton Exposition, selected sixteen thousand exhibits that celebrated the freedom generation, the abolitionist movement, higher education,
Black scientific and mechanical achievements, and the Haitian revolutionary
Toussaint L'Ouverture. Spellman believed the exposition marked a new era
of racial unity "where the greatest part of us are identified with the development and progress" of the South and "demonstrate a capacity for all branches
of industry." His views reflected the perspective of the Radical Reconstruction
political leadership, which still held sway in the Black community. The Blues
agenda present in the organization of the exhibits was diametrically opposed
to the representations adopted by new Black economic leaders who organized
the Colored Department at the Atlanta Exposition a decade later, in 1895. The
latter used the occasion to obliterate from Black memory and public discourse
the Blues development tradition, the Reconstruction era's working-class leadership, and their advocacy of internationalism, human rights, and sustainable
development. In Atlanta, Booker T. Washington announced, "Agitation of questions of social equality is the extremist folly." The local Black press in Atlanta
urged Blacks to boycott the exposition because it had become a circus of denigration where their leaders, like Washington, had become part of the show.
In its support of the boycott, Atlanta's *People's Advocate* suggested that "if they
want to see on all sides: 'for Whites Only,' or 'No Niggers or dogs allowed,' if
they want to be humiliated and have their man and womanhood crushed out,
then come!"[74]

Also during this period, the size of Catholic, African Methodist Episcopal,
Congregational, and Baptist congregations expanded rapidly. Many churches assisted with family unification and created survival programs for the hungry and
homeless. According to Blassingame, the Protestant movement in the city exhibited deep class, theological, and ontological divisions between the upper-class
Protestant churches, which increasingly selected college-educated ministers,
and the Blues churches:

> Lower-class churches, composed primarily of former slaves and illiterate immi-
> grants from the parishes, had an entirely different form of religion. These people
> had a strong belief in the presence and power of God in everyday life; they empha-
> sized revelations, visions, dreams, and inward expression of the Divine presence.
> Their services, a mixture of grief and sadness about their weary life on earth, pro-
> vided an emotional release for them. The sermons and songs about their bondage,
> and their passionate prayers for Divine aid, gave to their services a reality, vividness,
> and emotionalism, which created a sense of shared suffering, and hope, which
> caused the congregation to shout, cry, and raise a joyful noise to the Lord. In spite
> of the emotion, there was a deep practical strain running through sermons, which

usually compared the Negro's lot with that of the Jews and which urged him to protect and enlarge his freedom.[75]

The Mardi Gras Indian Movement

I'm a Indian ruler from the 13th Ward
Blood shiffa hoona I won't be brought,
I walk through fire an' I swim through mud
Snatched the feathers from a eagle,
drank panther blood

Got a itty-bitty spy got a heart of steel
Shank won't get you his hatchet will
Gedde may hocko m'yoo na no
He shoot the gun in the jailhouse door

I'll bring my gang all over town,
drink fire water till the sun go down.
We get back home, we gonna kneel and pray . . .
we had some fun on the holiday?
Meet de boys on the battle front (3x)
The Wild Tchoupitoulas gonna stomp some rump!

    The Wild Tchoupitoulas (with the New Orleans band the Meters),
    "Meet de Boys on the Battlefront," *Wild Tchoupitoulas*, **1976**

As part of the resistance to Bourbonism, movements informed by the Blues development tradition repeatedly emerged during this period. One of the new Black working-class institutions created was the Mardi Gras Indians. According to several accounts, Chief Becate Batiste's Creole Wild West nation was founded in 1883. George Lipsitz has shown how this practice draws from African culture but cannot be categorized as an African ritual. Chiefs, queens, nations, warriors, ancestor worship, the celebration of nature, and the other institutions established by the Mardi Gras Indians worked to defend a community and a culture under relentless attack. This movement also fought to occupy and control public spaces for their processions at a time when Blacks were being "bulldozed" from farms, jobs, communities, rail car seats, and a variety of other public spaces.[76]

At the height of the Bourbon reaction, the Mardi Gras Indian movement was gaining momentum. In this context, the Bourbon elite decided to add a Black krewe to the procession of Rex, the king of Mardi Gras. The entry of the African American Zulu Social and Pleasure Club into the Mardi Gras beginning in 1909 was viewed by some as a carnival-day release organized around the mocking of white authority. However, the costumes of Zulu ensured that the krewe was also fully engaged in the officially promoted derision of Black American and African culture. Despite being led by their own king, the Zulus performed in a historic space of denigration situated between the Bourbon elite and white crowds. Roach notes that "tossing coconuts, as the riders in Rex and other krewe floats toss plastic beads and other trinkets, Zulu royalty, garbed in grass skirts and black-face, have always walked a thin line between ridiculing and reinforcing the imagery of abject racial hatred with which Mardi Gras in New Orleans is historically replete."[77]

The Black urban working-class labor movement was another institutional site for consciousness raising, cultural development, and working-class leadership that solidified around resolute resistance to Bourbonism, terror, and workplace exploitation. What is referred to as "biracial unionism" emerged in Louisiana beginning in 1880 when skilled and unskilled, Black and white laborers in thirteen unions formed an association. In 1881 ten thousand dockworkers in New Orleans, 30 percent of whom were Black, united to launch a strike for higher wages.[78] A decade later, twenty-five thousand Black and white workers in forty-two unions launched the New Orleans general strike of 1892 on November 3. Workers seeking better conditions, wages, and hours, along with the firing of nonunion employees, brought the city to a standstill. Newly elected governor Murphy Foster, a planter and grandfather of future governor Murphy "Mike" Foster, called out the state militia on November 11 and the strike was broken three days later. Throughout this period, the Bourbons responded to the mobilization of Black labor, the growing labor movement, and "biracial" organizing and alliances with increased violence.[79]

The Black rural labor movement was another important institutional site where Bourbon rule was contested. In 1880 Black wage workers in the cane fields of the southern sugar parishes launched several strikes. After the March 17 strike in St. Charles Parish, thirty miles west of New Orleans, was violently repressed by the state militia, a new strike was launched in St. John the Baptist Parish on March 29. The strike's governing council demanded that the seventy-five-cents-a-day wage rate be increased and summarized their demands with banners that read, "PEACE—ONE DOLLAR A DAY" and "A DOLLAR A DAY OR KANSAS." The latter slogan referred to the Exoduster movement that organized Blacks to leave the South for small farms and independent Black towns in Kansas and Oklahoma. After the state militia broke this strike in April, new labor actions were launched in Ascension, St. James, St. Bernard, Jefferson, and Plaquemines Parishes.[80]

In *Bourbonism and Agrarian Protest*, William Hair examines in detail the statewide authoritarian effort to suppress the rural Black labor movement in the Sugar Bowl, south and east of New Orleans, and how this led to a militarization of rural life. The Knights of Labor union entered the state in 1883; it quickly organized urban and rural workers across racial lines, and its members won political offices. Black and white organizers from the union led an 1887 strike by six thousand to ten thousand Black sugar workers in five parishes against the members of the Louisiana Sugar Planters' Association. They demanded higher pay and payment in cash rather than notes redeemable only at plantation commissaries. Governor McEnery sent ten companies and two batteries of the state militia, one unit with a Gatling gun, to evict the strikers and their families from their homes in November. Armed skirmishes occurred throughout the region, and this led hundreds of evicted families to flee to Thibodaux in Lafourche Parish for refuge. By November 21 the militia had been replaced by "armed bands of white vigilantes, composed of local 'organized citizens' plus a number of grim-visaged strangers to the community. These newly arrived men were alleged to be 'Shreveport guerillas well versed in killing niggers.'" On the following day, this group of terrorists employed by the planters attacked and killed thirty Blacks, wounding hundreds more. Additional bodies were found scattered throughout the swamps. Two African American leaders of the strike, Henry and George Cox, were imprisoned and later taken from jail, never to be seen again. By December, Black workers had been forced back onto the sugar plantations. A more permanent militarization of rural life occurred after the emergence of the Regulating Movement, which "aimed at discouraging economic or political assertiveness on the part of Negroes."[81]

An attempt to combat the further militarization of urban and regional life under the banner of Jim Crow was also launched by the Afro-Creole leadership of New Orleans. The Comite des Citoyens (Citizens Committee) was organized to fight discrimination in 1890. One of its members, Homer Plessy, intentionally sat in the "whites only" section of a train bound from New Orleans to Covington, Louisiana. After his arrest, the Comite des Citoyens collected funds to finance a suit and several appeals, claiming that the recently enacted law requiring racially separate accommodations violated the Equal Protection Clause of the Fourteenth Amendment. As noted earlier, in the 1896 decision in *Plessy v. Ferguson* the U.S. Supreme Court both spread the Bourbon racial militarization nationally and simultaneously fueled the creation of new African American civil rights and cultural movements both locally and nationally.[82]

Finally, small farmers and urban and rural workers throughout the state joined together to create the populist movement and institution. This campaign to eliminate the Bourbon death and destitution political economy resulted in a regional crisis that continues to reverberate throughout the state to this day. According to several accounts, the populist movement in the state began with the formation of the Louisiana Farmers' Union by white small farmers from Lincoln and five other northern parishes in 1881. By 1890 this organization had joined the three-million-member Farmers' Alliance. The latter began in Texas during 1877 as the National Farmers' Alliance and Industrial Union before spreading throughout the South and to the Great Plains. This populist movement was allied with the one million members of the Colored Farmers' Alliance, which also spread from Texas to encompass the South. The latter had fifty thousand Black farmers as members in Louisiana, primarily in the Red River cotton parishes. The goal of the alliance was to improve rural life, incomes, education, and democracy by forming cooperative storage facilities, mills, gins, stores, and credit. In addition to supporting a massive school construction program, the movement sought to sell crops directly to buyers in New England and Europe in order to avoid the exorbitant fees taken by Bourbon middlemen bankers, insurers, merchants, and speculators, particularly those headquartered in New Orleans. John A. Tetts of the Louisiana Alliance believed that the organization "forced the 'half Ku Klux and half desperado' white cotton farmer of the South out of his provincial shell, and into an awareness of class interest which transcended racial and/or regional boundaries." However, Blacks were justifiably suspicious of the alliance due to the presence of white regulators who were responsible for numerous acts of terror and the pattern of back-door negotiations with Democrats and Bourbon planters.[83]

Despite endless factionalism, a multiracial, multiethnic, multireligious, multiclass, and multiregional alliance composed of disillusioned Democrats, Cajuns, Blacks, Republicans, and several sugar planters arose to challenge Bourbon rule. This movement also linked with the national Populist Party or People's Party movement that, beginning in 1889, emerged in the Southwest, the Great Plains, and then in the South in alliance with the Knights of Labor. An extension of the Farmers' Alliance, the Populist Party's Omaha Platform of 1892 favored the direct election of U.S. senators, soldiers' pensions, immigration restrictions, a graduated income tax, abolition of armed workplace guards, popular referendums, presidential term limits, low-cost agricultural loans, and agricultural price supports.[84]

A partial precursor to the New Deal, this program was denounced by the Bourbons as "hayseed socialism." Yet many African Americans began to join. In the midst of this growing crisis, the gubernatorial election pitted Governor McEnery, who had the support of the Bourbon Democrats and the New Orleans lottery, against planter Murphy J. Foster's Reform Democrats, who ran on a platform that emphasized their opposition to both the lottery and the corruption of McEnery. The federal government forced the lottery out of business just before the April 1892 open primary. Foster defeated McEnery, two Republicans, and the Populist candidate, Tannehill. Out of forty thousand votes cast in New Orleans, the Populists received only seventy-one, due in part to fraud.[85] One of Foster's first major acts in office was the breaking of the New Orleans general strike of 1892. Hair notes that the gubernatorial election held four years later was defined by the Great Depression of 1893, a collapsing agricultural economy, a populist mobilization, and shifting alliances. The European financial crisis resulted in decreased prices for cotton and sugar. This in turn led to desperation and fears of a revolution. The 1896 election centered on tensions between Democrats and

Republicans, who in turn were in alliance with the People's Party and the "Lily Whites."[86]

The Lily Whites dominated the Populist Party convention of 1895 and their gubernatorial candidate, St. Mary Parish sugar planter John N. Pharr. One of the wealthiest persons in the state, Pharr favored Black voting rights, although he evicted numerous Black families during the Sugar Bowl strike of 1887. Throughout the state, the Democrats were under siege. Charles Janvier, John M. Parker, and other New Orleans business leaders broke with the Democrats and formed the Citizens League to run a separate slate of candidates for the municipal and legislative elections. According to Hair, even "in the most 'bulldozed' cotton parishes Democratic landlords seemed to be having an unusual amount of difficulty in discouraging Negro participation in the approaching election."[87]

Hair concludes that nowhere "in the South did Populism encounter so many obstacles or as much brutality." On election day, April 21, 1896, the fusionists were able to secure victories in the north-central parishes. However, there was massive voter intimidation and fraud in the majority Black northern Louisiana cotton parishes along the Mississippi and Red Rivers. Blacks "voted" for St. Francisville planter Murphy J. Foster Sr. He carried seven majority white parishes and twenty-three majority Black parishes and barely won New Orleans. On the other hand, Pharr carried twenty-five predominantly white parishes and four predominantly Black parishes in south Louisiana.

Before the legislature convened on May 14, Democrats' refusal to count Black populist votes in Natchitoches Parish resulted in hundreds of armed white populists assembling for an attack on the courthouse before they were dispersed by the state militia. Black populists seized stuffed ballot boxes in St. John the Baptist Parish and prepared to engage the militia before they too were dispersed. The *New Orleans Daily Picayune* predicted "war and rapine, and blood from the Arkansas line to the Gulf of Mexico if the populists did not submit" to the stolen election. On May 8 the Populist Party chairman called upon "white men of the state to meet in Baton Rouge." Reports circulated that nine thousand whites from the northern hills were preparing to march on the capitol, where they would be joined by supportive sugar-parish militias with artillery and troops capable of taking the capitol. In anticipation, paramilitary units were organized among Democrats in Baton Rouge and the Florida parishes (East Baton Rouge, East Feliciana, Livingston, St. Helena, St. Tammany, Tangipahoa, Washington, and West Feliciana). On May 6 the Democratic State Central Committee issued a proclamation indicative of the "Let them eat cake / Starve the beast" ethic of Bourbonism. It revealed the "beast" as the Black working-class empowerment movement defined as the Blues development tradition. It was also clear that the "beast" was the alliance between the Black working class, white organized labor, and white small farmers united under the banner of populism. The Central Committee denounced the "monster, horrid, formless and crowned with darkness" that was attempting to overthrow democracy and uplift that "great horde of ignorant blacks who yearn for social equality." It warned that "this land shall not be a Hayti or San Domingo." Hearsey, the publisher of the *Daily States*, concluded that "dictatorship" was "the most suitable form of government for Louisiana," and dictatorship is what the Bourbons delivered.[88]

The Bourbon Disenfranchisement Plan and the Jazz Renaissance, 1896–1915

It is the religious duty of Democrats to rob Populists and Republicans of their votes whenever and wherever the opportunity presents itself and any failure to do so will be a violation of true Louisiana Democratic teaching. The Populists and the Republicans are our legitimate political prey. Rob them! You bet! What are we here for?

Shreveport Evening Judge, December 15, 1895[89]

Resistance to the crisis generated by the Bourbon movement led to unprecedented alliances between the African American, labor, and populist movements. In turn, this alliance spawned a statewide crisis during the gubernatorial campaign in 1896. During the 1896 general election the Bourbon bloc launched a mobilization to defeat the historic Blues and populist agenda proposed by the People's Party. This mobilization was followed by the creation of several new institutions designed to reproduce Bourbon power. First deployed was the Bourbon press, with continual attacks on Blacks, white populists, and the threat of "social equality." After having "aroused the desired baser emotions," Bourbon journalists gave way to Bourbon thugs who employed violence throughout the state to intimidate Blacks and whites away from fusionism. Louisiana's recorded total of twenty-one lynchings in 1896 "exceeded the combined total for every other state" and represented one-fifth of all lynching in the United States. In one instance the state militia was called in to halt the violent efforts to suppress Black voter registration in St. Landry Parish, thirty miles west of Baton Rouge. One militia member recalled witnessing a Black woman Populist-Republican activist being "unmercifully whipped" with barbed wire by her Democratic attackers.[90]

The abandonment of the Populist-Republican alliance by the New Orleans Citizens League during the election enabled the full restoration of Bourbon rule. After the reelection of Foster as governor, several new institutions were created to reproduce Bourbon hegemony. Registration and election laws were soon passed that dramatically reduced the Black and white working-class and small farmer vote. Louisiana soon became a southern-wide laboratory for policies designed to intensify racial and class oppression. The constitution approved in 1898 contained several voter disenfranchisement provisions: a property requirement of $300, a poll tax requirement, and a literacy requirement. The first use of the grandfather clause in the United States also occurred in Louisiana during this period. It excluded all Blacks whose grandfathers had been enslaved, while most whites whose grandfathers had voted during slavery were allowed to register. Similar to slavery, a system of apportionment based on population rather than voter registration expanded the power of the planters who ruled in the predominantly Black regions now subjected to mass disenfranchisement. Between 1896 and 1904 the number of whites registered to vote in Louisiana declined by 35 percent due to the new laws, from 164,088 to 106,360. However, 96 percent of registered Black voters were erased from the rolls. The number of Black voters fell from 130,344 to 5,320 during the same period, and by 1940 only 866 Blacks were registered to vote in the state.[91]

Louisiana essentially became a one-party dictatorship. The new primary system established in 1906 resulted in the Democratic "white primary" being equivalent to the general election. Simultaneously, segregation mania gripped New Orleans, the state, and the nation. An antimiscegenation law banning marriages between Blacks and whites was enacted in 1894 and a law banning marriages between Blacks and Native Americans was enacted in 1920. In between these initiatives, concubinage was made a felony in 1908 and the purity of blood law, "the one-drop rule," defining Blackness was enacted in 1910. This last provision collapsed the legal foundations of the mixed-race caste system and undermined the Afro-Creole elites' claims for legally recognized privileges. This occurred in spite of the widely held belief, enunciated by future governor Huey Long, that the pure whites in Louisiana could all be fed with "a nickel's worth of red beans and a dime's worth of rice." Other aspects of life were also increasingly segregated by state laws and city ordinances: streetcars and prostitution in 1902; bars in 1908; shows and circus ticket offices in 1914; and jails in 1918. The Catholic Church contributed to this movement by establishing African American parishes in 1895 and 1916.[92]

The Bourbon bloc represented the new regime as a triumph over the inherent evil and immorality embedded in the working class. For example, new monies for public education were blocked under the principle that "the education of a bad citizen will increase his power for evil and make him a worse citizen." Also, Bourbons refused aid to the drought- and starvation-stricken northern parishes because food assistance "demoralized labor."[93] One journalist concluded that the end of the era of racial and class conflict in Louisiana had arrived and the defeat was one with profound political, economic, and psychological dimensions. "The people are thoroughly cowed. . . . They are under complete subjection. They will bow the knee, receive the yoke and pass on, hewers of wood, drawers of water, beasts of burden; without spirit, without complaint, without resentment." Reflecting on the Bourbon restoration in 1899, the white Populist leader Hardy Brian regretted that we "refused to take up the gun [and] so we lost. The fight will be won some day, but by [unchristian] methods."[94]

By 1890 New Orleans was the twelfth-largest city in the United States, with a population of 242,000 persons. The city's population grew by over 40 percent after the turn of the century: from 287,000 in 1900 to 339,000 by 1910.[95] The Bourbon system of racial and class apartheid made the city an extremely deadly place to live. Mark Carleton and William Hair highlight several aspects of Bourbon planning that turned the city into the Western world's burial ground: "Although the well-to-do drank imported spring water, everyone else consumed cistern water brimming with mosquito larvae or untreated water from the Mississippi, which also served as the municipal garbage dump and sewer. New Orleans . . . was reportedly the only major community in the Western world without a sewage system. Federal census figures also listed New Orleans as having one of the highest death rates among American cities."[96] Despite such conditions within the city, the worsening of rural conditions for Blacks spurred migration to New Orleans. More than 90 percent of Louisiana's population lived in rural areas at the beginning of this period. The sharecropping regime on cotton plantations and farms and the wage regime on sugar plantations were defined by enforced dependency, destitution, hunger, and violence. The export orientation of these sectors ensured that wealth generated by the state's land and resources was directed away from meeting local needs. The intensification of economic bondage and widespread terrorism led forty thousand Blacks to flee from rural Louisiana, Mississippi, and Arkansas to New Orleans between 1890 and 1910. They brought to the city the scars of prolonged social warfare, highly developed social networks, a collective social vision, and the remarkable determination and resiliency that was deeply embedded in the Blues intellectual tradition.

Thomas Brothers argues that many of the founders of Jazz in New Orleans were part of this exodus seeking refuge from rural terror, sharecropping, and debt peonage:

[Louis Armstrong's] mother came from Boutte, fifty miles to the west of New Orleans, and Mahalia Jackson's family came from a cotton plantation on the Atchafalaya River, about a hundred miles to the north. Joe Oliver's family came from Abend, near Donaldsonville, some sixty miles upriver, and bassist George "Pops" Foster from McCall Plantation nearby. Henry Allen, whose son Henry "Red" Allen, Jr. was a successful rival to Armstrong during the swing era moved from Lockport in 1890 to work on the docks. Charles Hamilton's father brought his family from Ama around 1910 so that his children would have a chance to go to school. Johnny and Baby Dodds's father Warren came from Alabama, where he had learned to play "quills," an African American instrument made out of bamboo pipes. Cornetist Punch Miller grew up in Raceland, where he sang blues to himself while he worked the sugar cane fields. Trombonists Harrison Barnes and Sunny Henry moved to the city from the Magnolia Plantation, where they learned the ring shout and congregational heterophony. Cornetist Chris Kelly and trombonist Jim Robinson came from the Deer Range plantation, also downriver. Louis Jones from Mississippi arrived after working in labor camps in Arkansas, Missouri, Illinois, and Tennessee.[97]

Brothers also notes that some of the migrants were fleeing the suppression of their culture. Also significant is that not only were the members of this first Jazz generation from rural areas, they were deeply steeped in the Blues tradition. Another factor typically left out of Jazz historiography is that these future cultural pioneers moved to Uptown neighborhoods, according to Brothers. He argues that this is where the Jazz movement was launched, not in the downtown neighborhood of Tremé or the Storyville red light district:

> Clarinetist Louis James was from Thibodeaux, where African-American bands were suppressed in the wake of the bloody massacre of some fifty blacks in 1887, and where James worked in the fields for twenty-five cents a day. Cornetist Willie Hightower came from Nashville. Kid Ory and clarinetist Lawrence Duhe came from the Woodland Plantation near LaPlace, where they learned how to rag tunes. Cornetist Oscar Celestin came from Napoleonville, cornetist Hypolite Charles from Parks, drummer Zutty Singleton from Bunkie, cornetist Jimmy Clayton from Jaspar County, Mississippi, and Professor James Humphrey from Sellers, upriver in St. Charles Parish. Trombonists Buddy and Yank Johnson came from McDonaldsville, cornetist Edward Clem and trombonist Kid Thomas Valentine from Reserve. Virtually all of these migrating musicians and their families relocated to one of the subsections of uptown New Orleans, to the Irish Channel, River Bend, Carrollton, Back of Town, the Battlefield.[98]

They arrived in a city that was exceedingly dangerous. Before Red Summer and the Elaine Massacre in 1919, before the Atlanta riot of 1906, terror stalked the streets of New Orleans. Although born in 1901, Louis Armstrong's recollections of his youth are applicable to understanding the nature of mob violence in 1900 and how it could break out at any time in the city: "It seemed that the only thing they *cared* about was their Shot Guns. . . . So they get full of their *Mint Julep* or that *bad* whiskey, the poor white Trash were Guzzling down, like water then when they get so Damn Drunk until they'd go out of their minds—then it's Nigger Hunting time. . . . Then they would Torture the poor Darkie as innocent as he may be."[99]

The Robert Charles Affair

Didn't he ramble, ramble,
Rambled all around, in and out of town,
Didn't he ramble, ramble,
Rambled 'till the butchers cut him down
"Didn't He Ramble," standard Jazz funeral march[100]

At 10:00 p.m. on Monday, July 24, 1900, on Dryades Street between Washington Avenue and Sixth Street, Mississippi Delta native Robert Charles was sitting on a doorstep talking to sixteen-year-old Leonard Pierce. A few minutes later the police issued orders to shoot him on sight. From within the Blues epistemology, the African American leader and theorist Ida B. Wells-Barnett examined this event in her classic pamphlet published two months later, *Mob Rule in New Orleans: Robert Charles and His Fight to Death, the Story of His Life, Burning Human Beings Alive, Other Lynching Statistics*. Although the pamphlet was written at the beginning of the twentieth century, it exemplifies how many of the principles, the bioethics, associated with the disposability of Black life were revealed repeatedly during the early twenty-first-century disasters that preceded Hurricane Katrina. As Wells-Barnett notes,

> This instruction was given before anybody had been killed, and the only evidence that Charles was a desperate man lay in the fact that he had refused to be beaten over the head by Officer Mora for sitting on a step quietly conversing with a friend. Charles resisted an absolutely unlawful attack, and a gunfight followed. Both Mora and Charles were shot, but because Mora was white and Charles was black, Charles was at once declared to be a desperado, made an outlaw, and subsequently a price put upon his head and the mob authorized to shoot him like a dog, on sight. . . . This authority, given by the sergeant to kill Charles on sight, would have been no news to Charles, nor to any colored man in New Orleans, who, for any purpose whatever, even to save his life, raised his hand against a white man. It is now, even as it was in the days of slavery, an unpardonable sin for a Negro to resist a white man, no matter how unjust or unprovoked the white man's attack may be. Charles knew this, and knowing to be captured meant to be killed, he resolved to sell his life as dearly as possible.[101]

At 2:00 a.m. Charles's home was surrounded by a police detail. A captain and a patrolman were killed when they attempted to seize him, and the other officers fled. When they returned several hours later with reinforcements, they discovered that Charles was gone. A general alarm was sounded in the city and "citizens" were called to join the "man hunt." Officers flooded the streets and arrested numerous Black men deemed "impertinent" or "game niggers." A July 25 account in the *Times-Democrat* partially captures the rebellious attitude that existed within the African American community: "The police made some arrests in the neighborhood of the killing of the two officers. Mobs of young darkies gathered everywhere. These Negroes talked and joked about the affair, and many of them were for starting a race war on the spot. It was not until several of these little gangs amalgamated and started demonstrations that the police commenced to act. Nearly a dozen arrests were made within an hour, and everybody in the vicinity was in a tremor of excitement."[102] Wells-Barnett writes that the mass arrests of Blacks were soon followed by the organization of a white mob numbering over three thousand. "Unable to vent its vindictiveness and blood-thirsty vengeance upon Charles, the mob turned its attention to other colored men who happened to get in the path of its fury. Even colored women, as has happened many times before, were assaulted and beaten and killed by the brutal hoodlums who thronged the streets."[103] When the mob was prevented from lynching a young man at the police station, a Black man near the crowd was shot and a Black newsboy was stabbed. Then the mob split up and proceeded to abuse every Black person encountered: a downtown streetcar passenger was shot and beaten repeatedly before he died; seventy-five-year-old Baptiste Philo was shot and killed on his way to work at the French Market; sixty-year-old Hannah Mabry was fatally shot in her home and her son, daughter-in-law, and infant grandchild disappeared; a man walking on the levee near the French Market was shot multiple times by white longshoremen; and then "a number of Italians, who had joined the howling mob, reached down and stabbed him in the back and buttock with big knives." In the Storyville red light district, white women sex workers urged the mob forward. Here the mob found a man on a streetcar, shot him, and then dumped his lifeless body in the gutter. Barnett-Wells notes that although Charity Hospital rapidly filled with wounded children, the elderly, and women, the Bourbons slumbered peacefully: "The killing of a few Negroes more or less by irresponsible mobs does not cut much figure in Louisiana. But when the reign of mob law exerts a depressing influence upon the stock market and city securities begin to show unsteady standing in money centers, then the strong arm of the good white people of the South asserts itself and order is quickly brought out of chaos."[104] The New Orleans wing of the Bourbon bloc quickly assembled a posse of one thousand to assist the police. Yet the rioting continued. The search for Charles was thwarted by Black community members who hid him until he was discovered on Friday in a small building at 1210 Saratoga Street:

> Still defying his pursuers, [he] fought a mob of twenty thousand people, single-handed and alone, killing three more men, mortally wounding two more and seriously wounding nine others. Unable to get to him in his stronghold, the besiegers set fire to his house of refuge. While the building was burning, Charles was shooting, and every crack of his death-dealing rifle added another victim to the price, which he had placed upon his own life. Finally, when fire and smoke became too much for flesh and blood to stand, the long sought for fugitive appeared in the door, rifle in hand, to charge the countless guns that were drawn upon him.[105]

No criminal charges were filed against members of the mob. Conversely, many Blacks were jailed or fined. One of those sentenced was Matilda Gamble, who received a sentence of twenty-five dollars or thirty days for commenting on the slaying of the officers, "It was a pity more were not shot." Wells-Barnett concludes her appeal by arguing for a reordering of the iconography of New Orleans, the South, and the United States:

By only those whose anger and vindictiveness warp their judgment is Robert Charles a desperado. . . .On the contrary, his work for many years had been with Christian people, circulating emigration pamphlets and active as [an] agent for a mission publication. Men who knew him say that he was a law-abiding, quiet, industrious, peaceable man. . . . So he lived and so he would have died had not he raised his hand to resent unprovoked assault and unlawful arrest that fateful Monday night. That made him an outlaw, and being a man of courage he decided to die with his face to the foe. The white people of this country may charge that he was a desperado, but to the people of his own race Robert Charles will always be regarded as the hero of New Orleans.[106]

According to pianist Jelly Roll Morton, there was a song written for Charles but it was wise to forget it "in order to get along." Clarinetist Louis "Big Eye" Nelson's father was murdered by the mob near the French Market on July 27. After his father's death, he recalled that he began "playing harder than ever."[107]

King Bolden's Cultural Revolution

After the Civil War, the militarization of race relations and its institutionalization became a key pillar of social and spatial planning in the Lower Mississippi Valley and in the South as a whole. According to Derrick Ward, the first wave of urban race riots that followed the end of the Civil War revolved around undermining Black freedom and southern Reconstruction: New Orleans, Louisiana (1866, 1868, 1874); Memphis, Tennessee (1866); Meridian, Mississippi (1870); Vicksburg, Mississippi (1874); and Yazoo City, Mississippi (1875). As I discuss in *Development Arrested*, during this period the Blues emerged as a working-class music, as the codification of memory and resistance, a philosophy, and a sustainable development agenda. This tradition had become a southern institution before the beginning of the second wave of urban race riots. New Orleans was once again the epicenter of schism during this new error of terror. *Plessy v. Ferguson* and the Robert Charles Affair signaled the beginnings of a national campaign to legalize segregation and disenfranchisement. Officially sanctioned mob violence and massacres greeted Blacks migrating from rural areas to the urban centers of the South, including New Orleans in 1900 and Atlanta in 1906. This new era of repression spawned another African American cultural revolution.[108]

Jelly Roll Morton recalled that back "in 1901 and 1902, we had a lot of great blues players that didn't know nothing but the Blues. . . . There's always been Blues in New Orleans."[109] By 1900 New Orleans pianists were known for their Ragtime "stomps" and their Blues or "slow drags." Among the most famous Blues pianists were Tony Jackson and Morton. The latter's next-door neighbor was Mamie Desdoumes, a popular Blues singer whose "Mamie Blues" spoke of women asserting their independence within relationships: "I got a husband and I got a kid man too / My husband can't do what my kid man can do." Another important Blues pianist was Game Kid, a "howler," whose most famous lyric spoke to the breadth of the Blues: "I could sit here and think a thousand miles away / I got the blues so bad I cannot remember the day."[110]

The piano Blues movement was eventually overshadowed by a cultural revolution led by Charles "Buddy" Bolden, who built a Blues institution, a house within the Blues, that eventually came to define New Orleans. Brothers notes that at "the same moment the Robert Charles riots made clear how desperate the situation was, Bolden's star was rising. Political power was in decline, musical power in the ascent. They heard Bolden's brassy defiance as both a proclamation of vernacular values from the plantations and a new, urbanized professionalism." Later labeled Jazz, the right of individual and community self-defense, the ethic of social justice, the critique of plantation relations, the desire to create sustainable communities, and the sound of rebellion against fascism were deeply embedded in the Blues movement led by "King Bolden." William Barlow suggests that the Blues were central to Bolden's project of revolutionizing dance music. In addition to his band playing and singing the Blues, "Bolden's most significant musical innovation was to rearrange the New Orleans dance band to better accommodate the blues. . . . Bolden positioned the rural folk blues at the center of his musical experiments and thus paved the way for other musicians to develop original and experimental styles."[111]

Well known as a player of popular waltzes, quadrilles, and rags, Bolden resided in the same Central City district that was home to Robert Charles, famed trombonist Edward "Kid" Ory, and Morton. Born in 1901, Louis Armstrong grew up several blocks to the east.[112] Bolden and his peers sparked a deep cultural revolution when they rebelled against these genres, professional musicians, and the New Orleans Bourbon bloc. During a time of intense class differentiation in the Black community, Jazz marked a working-class Blues insurrection. Bolden and others proceeded to jazz up, rag, Bluesify, Africanize, and re-Africanize rhythms, songs, genres, schools of musicians, and popular dance. According to Danny Barker, many of the Afro-Creole rhythms and folk songs, still sung in French creole, also became pillars of the Jazz movement. Although he played all over the city, the Uptown audiences at Lincoln Park lionized him and his music between 1900 and 1906. Former sugar plantations, Central City, and other Uptown neighborhoods increasingly became the home of Black rural refugees. They brought their Blues with them. The music emerged from, and was placed at the service of, a growing New Orleans Black working class attempting to impose its social vision upon a region organized around its brutal exploitation. In this music were found their aspirations, stories, hollers, moans, work songs, children's rhymes, humor, voices, dialogues, sexuality, fantasies, rowdiness, parodies, tears, bondage, trials, tribulations, triumphs, African rhythms, and the rhythms of their daily lives. Bolden's interpretation of Blues music, community, consciousness, protest, and spirituality made him a social hero. His ability to bring into the house of the Blues the city's numerous African and European musical traditions made him a global icon.

It has been said that Bolden could play the trumpet so loud that he could be heard in towns ten miles away. According to trombone player Bill Matthews, "That boy could make the women jump out the window. On those old, slow, low down blues, he had a moan in his cornet that went all through you, just like you were in church or something." Another observer reported what occurred when Bolden's band played "Home Sweet Home" for Black troops departing for Cuba during the Spanish American War. Some "of the men on board were so overcome by nostalgia they jumped off and swam to shore." According to Warren "Baby" Dodds, Bolden was thought to have composed the epic to Blues life "Didn't He Ramble," a standard still played by brass bands returning from burials.[113]

The Jazz Blues that emerged in New Orleans during this period preserved the fearless criticism of the dominant plantation-bloc social order, including the endless ridicule of its official morality. For example, the song most closely associated with Bolden's movement was alternatively known as "The Funky Butt Blues," "Buddy Bolden's Blues," and "I Thought I Heard Buddy Bolden Say." Donald Marquis suggests that the "song was sung up and down the Mississippi and had probably been carried to New Orleans by upriver boatmen." As played by Bolden and his band, the song had numerous verses, some of which were scatological, sexually explicit, satirical, and insurrectionary in Bourbon New Orleans. Banjo player Lorenzo Staulz would "sing about the Civil War; about how General Grant made Jeff Davis kiss his behind and how General Sherman burnt up Georgia riding on Robert E. Lee's back. The crowd would scream and holler." According to Jazz pioneer and Eagle Band member Sidney Bechet, the police brutally attacked audiences when the song was sung: "When we started off playing Buddy's theme song, 'I Thought I Heard Buddy Bolden Say,' the police would put you in jail if they heard you singing that song. I was just starting out on clarinet, six or seven years old; Bolden had a tailgate contest with the Imperial Band. Bolden started his theme song, people started singing, and policemen began whipping heads. The Eagle Band was good for the blues. . . . They played Bolden's theme song, but they did not sing any words to it."[114]

Kidd Jordan suggests Bolden was a rebel and an opponent of the Bourbon restoration. Many believe that this "crime" and not insanity led to his 1907 commitment, at age twenty-nine, to the state insane asylum in Jackson, where he would remain until his death twenty-five years later. *Plessy*, the Charles Affair, Ragtime, brass bands, the Blues, and Jazz were the bonds that increasingly united Afro-Creoles and African Americans in southeastern Louisiana. This historic confluence marked the birth of a new working-class consciousness, spirituality, and social vision. It came to symbolize freedom and democracy for a people often forced into perpetual states of bondage and fugitivism. Their music was quickly demonized as the music of primitives performed in brothels as part of a strategy of demonizing the culture and the communities that gave birth to it and sustained it. Even in its appropriation before and after Hurricane Katrina and the failure of the levees, the culture and its people are still denigrated as part of ongoing attempts to mask the regional, national, and global significance of the working-class, multiethnic alliance created on the streets of New Orleans.

CHAPTER 3

Hemispheric UNIA and the Great Flood, 1915–1928

In the early part of the twentieth century New Orleans was considered one of the most conservative cities in the South due to the small number of interlocking boards of directors that rigidly controlled the city's political, economic, and cultural institutions. For example, in 1905 Charles Janvier simultaneously served as president of the Canal Bank, as a member of the Board of Liquidation of City Debt, as chairman of the state Democratic Party's Central Committee, and as president of the Boston Club. He was also a member of the White League in 1874 and president of the Citizens' League in 1896. Closely linked to the Chase Bank in New York, Canal Bank was considered both the largest bank in the South and one of the largest in the world.

Other centers of Bourbon and Anglo power included the Union, Boston, Pickwick, and Louisiana Clubs. Beginning in the 1850s, many of the founders of the clubs dominated the banking, planting, and shipping sectors in Louisiana and adjoining states. Several members held key positions in the Confederacy during the Civil War, in the White League after the war, and in the krewes that dominated Mardi Gras. In 1857 several of these clubs created an anglicized version of the Creole Mardi Gras Carnival. Parading under the krewe names of Rex, Momus, Comus, Proteus, Atlantis, and Mystic, the clubs and their members have dominated Mardi Gras and the city's power structure from the nineteenth century to the present.[1]

The New Orleans wing of the Bourbon bloc was composed mainly of representatives of the leading banks (Canal Bank, Hibernia Bank, Whitney Bank, and the Marine Bank and Trust Company), major law firms, cotton merchants and financiers, major planters, and shippers, all of whom had strong ties to national and international financial centers. This bloc controlled the city's finances after Reconstruction via the Board of Liquidation of City Debt. Established in 1880, the board controlled the government of New Orleans based on its control of the city's revenue, bonds, and budget. This fiscal absolutism combined the economic power of the board's members to give the Bourbon bloc fee simple ownership over the regional state. John Barry suggests that the body operated as a dictatorship. The nine lifetime members of the board were selected from among the four major private clubs while the mayor and two councilpersons held extremely marginalized ex officio positions: "Though the mayor, the governor, and the voters had no say over who became a syndicate member, the syndicate members dictated decisions about nearly all large public expenditures. Elected officials controlled only current operating budgets. The syndicate members answered to no one but themselves—and their colleagues in the club. Between 1908 and 1971 only twenty-seven men served as syndicate members; virtually all were either bankers or bank directors."[2]

The century-long history of the board's domination of New Orleans provides a particularly relevant lesson on the disastrous intergenerational consequences of privatization and other forms of plantation political economy, which serve as pillars of the current global economic paradigm referred to as neoliberalism. Barry argues that New Orleans's shadow government was "unique in the United States, and probably the world." For over a century, until a city charter revision in 1995, the Board of Liquidation of City Debt was able to use city bonds and bond indebtedness to support the projects of fellow club members. Although city revenues were deposited in their banks, the city received no interest payments during a 115-year period. In addition to robbing the populace and starving the city's operating budget, the board defeated proposed social expenditures while manipulating property tax, insurance, water, sewer, and utility rates: "First, every day the city deposited *all* the money it collected in the board's bank accounts. . . . The board paid off whatever notes and interest were due, then gave any money left over to the city government. In the 1920s, payments on bonds absorbed between 39 and 45 percent of all city taxes, leaving little for the city to spend on anything else. Second, the city could issue no bonds—not for schools, not for roads, not for lighting—without the board's consent."[3]

Another key component of New Orleans's Bourbon regime was the Democratic Party machine run by the Choctaw Club, also known as the "Old Regulars." Although the machine controlled the votes of a large percentage of the Anglo, Creole, Italian, and Irish working class, white supremacy and corruption cemented its alliance with the Bourbons. The organization was created by longtime mayor Martin Behrman (1904–20), who once proclaimed, "You can make corruption illegal in Louisiana but you can't make it unpopular." The Choctaw Club Democrats often determined local and state elections by buying and selling votes, stuffing ballot boxes, and using police intimidation and violence.[4]

In the former strongholds of the Populist Party in the northern parishes, the revolt against Bourbonism disintegrated into the rebirth of the Ku Klux Klan after 1920. The party's membership in New Orleans peaked at only three thousand primarily because its nativist program of "one hundred percent Americanism" was strongly opposed by local Catholics.[5] Statewide efforts to suppress the organization emerged only after party members physically attacked members of the planter class. In the northeastern Louisiana Delta parish of Morehouse, two planters' sons were murdered in 1922 after they reportedly ridiculed the Klan and flaunted its interracial dating proscriptions. In response to this challenge by the Klan to the Bourbon class hierarchy, Governor John M. Parker (1920–24) vowed to defeat the organization.

A Democrat, Parker owned numerous plantations in Mississippi and Louisiana as well as a mansion in the Garden District of New Orleans and had impeccable Bourbon credentials. He served as president of both the New Orleans Cotton Exchange and the New Orleans Board of Trade. In addition to being a board member of the Illinois Central Railroad, he was a personal friend of both Mississippi Delta planter Leroy Percy and President Theodore Roosevelt. In 1891 a young Parker had helped organize a mob that stormed a New Orleans jail in order to lynch eleven Italians thought to be involved in the murder of the city's police chief. By the early 1920s Parker and several other major cotton producers and commission merchants were handling more than one million bales a year.

In response to Parker's threat, the Klan "erected wooden headstones on the lawn of the governor's mansion." Soon afterward the bodies of the two missing men were found in Lake Lafourche. According to investigators, each "man had broken arm and leg bones; their hands and feet had been cut off or mashed off; each had his penis and testicles cut off." Not only were there no convictions for these crimes, but in 1923 the emboldened leaders of the Morehouse Klan began organizing branches in the Mississippi Delta. Yet, once the Klan had made its contribution to the militarization of national urban and rural race relations after World War I, its appeal to the upper classes waned. By 1924 internal conflicts and state regulations led to a dramatic decline in national membership. In Louisiana a watershed moment came when the former warden of the notorious Angola Prison was elected governor in 1926. Governor Henry L. Fuqua and the state legislature approved a law designed to suppress the Klan: membership lists were to be filed with the state, the lists were to be open for public inspection, and masked disguises were banned except during Mardi Gras. While the law proved to be a major setback for the Klan, the organization's social theories and methods remained influential in Louisiana for decades to come.[6]

The U.S. policy of Caribbean, Central American, and Pacific colonization adopted during the 1890s served as the foundation for the renewed national alliance between the southern planter blocs and northern regional blocs dominated by finance and manufacturing capitalists. This national Bourbon movement also united regional forms of working-class whiteness under the national banner of new political, economic, racial, and imperial projects. While maintaining its unique and historic position as the hemispheric center of plantation ideology, white supremacy, militarism, and corruption, New Orleans Bourbonism underwent a new round of globalization during this period. For example, after

Haitian dictator Jean Vilburn Guillaume Sam massacred nearly two hundred political prisoners, a successful popular uprising was launched. Fearing the new movement would challenge the Haitian American Sugar Company and other U.S. interests, on July 28, 1915, the night after Sam was overthrown, U.S. naval and marine forces anchored in Port-au-Prince harbor and seized the capitol. The Haitian constitution was torn up in favor of a new one written by the secretary of the navy, Franklin D. Roosevelt, in 1917. The document allowed foreign ownership for the first time. U.S. firms rapidly seized the most fertile lands, on which they established sugar, rubber, and sisal plantations supported by the brutal exploitation of labor. Under this privatization scheme, members of the U.S. plantation bloc and its allies, including Roosevelt, hoped to enrich themselves through massive property theft and speculation. However, intense resistance to colonization by the Haitian people continued until U.S. troops left the island in 1934.

In his 1920 investigation of the U.S. occupation, National Association for the Advanced of Colored People (NAACP) leader James Weldon Johnson sought to understand "why the United States landed and has for five years maintained military forces in that country, why some three thousand Haitian men, women, and children have been shot down by American rifles and machine guns." Johnson discovered that the Bourbons "have found in Haiti the veritable promised land of jobs for deserving democrats and naturally do not wish to see the present status discontinued." Beneficiaries of this colonial affirmative action project included the head of the Haitian customs service (a former Louisiana parish clerk), the superintendent of public instruction (a Louisiana schoolteacher), and a Louisiana state politician, John Avery McIlhenny, who was appointed national financial advisor by the occupation authority. McIlhenny was born to an Avery Island planter family that eventually made a fortune selling hot sauce. As a financial advisor to the government of Haiti, his primary accomplishment, according to Johnson, was organizing "the complete transfer of the Banque Nationale d' Haiti to the National City Bank of New York."[7]

New Orleans was also an important center for the importation of bananas, coffee, sugar, and raw materials. Between 1900 and 1932 the United States militarily intervened more than twenty-five times in the Caribbean and Central America to protect this trade. The derogatory term *Banana Republic* was used to denote the Bourbonization of these nations based on a package of military dictatorship, white supremacy, massive corruption, massacres, and extreme labor exploitation. In 1911 a *New York Times* headline proclaimed, "New Orleans Junta Plots: City Full of Central American Revolutionaries Planning Upheaval." Bourbon foreign policy was distinguished from that of the United States and its other regional blocs. The city hosted annual meetings of Central American and Caribbean revolutionaries who came regularly to secure arms, ships, and financing or entire mercenary armies. "As the hotbed of revolution and the Mecca of

filibusterers," the article explained, "New Orleans is preparing for another annual upheaval in Central America, and unless the United States steps in, almost
the entire strip of land, from the southern border of Mexico to Panama within
the next six months may be in upheaval."[8]

The little-studied phenomenon of conflicting regional imperialisms within
the United States was epitomized by the activities of Samuel "Sam the Banana
Man" Zemurray (1887–1961), a central figure in the story of imperial Bourbonism. His New Orleans–based Cuyamel Fruit Company controlled plantations in Honduras, a small shipping line, and a southeastern U.S. distribution
network allied with the Boston-based United Fruit Company. After U.S. officials
operating at the behest of the Morgan Bank of New York threatened his operation, he overthrew the government of Honduras in 1910 with the assistance
of former president Manuel Bonilla and the infamous Louisiana mercenaries
Guy "Machine Gun" Molony and Lee Christmas. In 1930 Zemurray sold his
firm to United Fruit Company (now Chiquita), which at the time controlled
70 percent of the banana market. New Orleans–based Standard Fruit (now
Dole) controlled most of the remainder of the market. After United Fruit suffered substantial losses, Zemurray seized control of the board of directors and
essentially ran the corporation from 1932 to 1951. Known as El Pulpo (the Octopus), the company continued its long tradition of promoting authoritarian
dictatorships in the banana-, sugar-, cacao-, and coffee-producing nations of
Central America, South America, the Caribbean, and Africa. Zemurray crafted
planter-friendly industrial codes during the New Deal for his ally President
Franklin Roosevelt. He also used his huge fortune to financially support the
anti–Huey Long forces in Louisiana during the 1930s, and, in 1954, organized
the overthrow of the Arbenz government in Guatemala. In its efforts to preserve
plantation-dominated regimes, the firm wrought physical, social, and psychic
violence throughout the hemisphere and beyond. Chilean poet Pablo Neruda
captured the Bourbon disposability of human life ethic in his epic 1950 poem
"La United Fruit Co.":

> The Fruit Company, Inc.
> reserved for itself the most succulent,
> the central coast of my own land,
> the delicate waist of America.
> It rechristened its territories
> as the "Banana Republics"
> and over the sleeping dead,
> over the restless heroes
> who brought about the greatness,
> the liberty and the flags,
> it established the comic opera

....
the dictatorship of the flies,
....
drunken flies who zoom
over the ordinary graves,
circus flies, wise flies
well trained in tyranny.

Among the bloodthirsty flies
the Fruit Company lands its ships,
taking off the coffee and the fruit;
the treasure of our submerged
territories flows as though
on plates into the ships.

Meanwhile Indians are falling
into the sugared chasms
of the harbors, wrapped
for burial in the mist of the dawn:
a body rolls, a thing
that has no name, a fallen cipher,
a cluster of dead fruit
thrown down on the dump.[9]

Enclosures in New Orleans

In addition to producing horrific human, civil, and economic conditions abroad, the Bourbon bloc used many of the same theories and methods to devastate the lives and communities of Louisianans, particularly the African American cotton and sugar workers. Although profiting from the transport of corn and wheat, the New Orleans regional economy was still dependent upon the processing and distribution of sugar and cotton. The largest sugar refinery in the world operated just outside the city limits in the St. Bernard Parish town of Arabi.

During this period, Louisiana was also undergoing major demographic and sectoral transformations throughout the state. Although 90 percent of Louisiana was rural, by 1920 the population of New Orleans reached 387,000 persons. The cities of Baton Rouge, Monroe, Shreveport, and Lake Charles also grew significantly during this period.[10] The cotton sector boomed during World War I as prices rose to record levels. During the 1920s the petrochemical industry took off based on the exploitation of oil, gas, and sulfur reserves in the region. In turn, this industry fueled a boom in construction, oil infrastructure, railroads, retail, services, utilities, and shipping. By 1920 approximately 57 percent of the employed males in the state were working in nonagricultural jobs and a new managerial class populated by a significant number of white northerners was firmly established in New Orleans.[11]

New Orleans also underwent a shift in settlement patterns. A new drainage technology, the screw pump, enabled both the settlement of former swampland and the movement of residential developments northward toward Lake Pontchartrain. Several campaigns were launched to ensure that Blacks would not have access to these new communities. In 1924 the city council passed an ordinance mandating residential segregation that, according to Packard, "required anyone moving into an area to receive written consent of the people already living in the area, the city characterizing its bald racism as representing a zoning ordinance within the power of the city's policing authority." Although the ordinance was struck down by the U.S. Supreme Court, almost simultaneously efforts were launched by residents in the new all-white subdivisions, such as Gentilly, to end African American access to Seabrook Beach and other neighboring recreational areas.[12]

The national campaign for spatially organized and militarized racial segregation, that is, ghettoization, began soon after the Plessy v. Ferguson decision of 1896. This movement resulted in the expulsion of Black residents and communities from majority white zones and their concentration in designated Black zones. One of the defining features of the new urban segregation movement was the organized removal of "white vice" from white districts and its imposition in Black neighborhoods. An international seaport and the most open city in the fundamentalist South, New Orleans used an 1897 ordinance to push adult prostitution, child prostitution, gambling, drug trafficking, drug abuse, and other "white vices" out of the central business district and into the Storyville District adjacent to the historic African American neighborhood of Tremé, just north of the French Quarter. For Buzzy Jackson, "the creation of Storyville as a distinct business zone was just another example of this drive toward segregation—in this case, a desire to isolate vice from virtue." Gerald Neuman observes that the ordinance also created an officially sanctioned "Black vice" zone in the more heavily African American neighborhoods of Uptown: "The city also enforced racial segregation within Storyville, requiring white and black women to occupy separate brothels, and prohibiting black men from patronizing either white women or the more luxurious of the black brothels. The 1897 ordinance provided for a separate district several blocks to the north, but the city did not officially activate it until February 1917, when the city limited prostitutes 'of the colored or black race' to the uptown district and reserved Storyville for prostitutes 'of the Caucasian or white race.' Meanwhile, the uptown district operated as a locus of unlawful prostitution."[13]

The Storyville red light district was planned as a segregated and militarized sexual-social playground that fostered social unity among white men from all classes, regions, and nations around several common themes: plantation bloc hegemony; the white supremacist ideal, gender domination, sexualized violence, and the exploitation of Black and white women; the exploitation of children; the destabilization of Black communities and family life; the naturalization of Black communities as vice zones; and the celebration of moral duplicity in the Southern Bible Belt. Although African Americans were employed in Storyville, they were restricted to just a few occupations: domestics, service workers, sex workers, and musicians. In this socially toxic and racially charged environment, the Blues and Jazz simultaneously became the soundtrack both for the celebration of Bourbon exploitation and for racial and gender suffering, resistance, wage earning, and affirmation. Jackson provides a description of how these contradictory traditions encountered each other on the street:

> The original "Sin City," Storyville was a creative experiment in urban planning: from 1898 to 1917, the nearly forty-square block neighborhood of stately Victorian buildings (former residences), with their balconies and ballrooms, was set aside as an adult playground. While prostitution was never legalized in Storyville, it was officially prohibited only outside its boundaries, a form of tacit decriminalization. It was well known to all—residents, tourists, sailors on leave—that Storyville was the place to go for a good time, and early blues and jazz provided the soundtrack. "Hundreds of men were passing through the streets day and night," said Jelly Roll Morton. "The chippies in their little-girl dresses were standing in the crib door singing the blues."[14]

Neuman suggests that these "anomalous zones," bubbles in the social fabric, usually emerged due to a confluence of unique events. However, it should also be noted that once established, these racially segregated zones or enclosures took on a life and logic of their own.

An infrastructure of distinct sectors, institutions, organizations, laws, practices, discourses, and regimes of profit making emerged to defend and reproduce these enclosures in New Orleans. Bankers, lawyers, landlords, real estate speculators, and law enforcement were particularly adept at squeezing wealth from these red light districts. The Storyville District began declining before the outbreak of World War I. Laurence Bergreen argues that the war brought the arrival of "a new breed of customer . . . sailors who wanted to have sex as quickly and as cheaply as possible, and music be damned. They became targets for predatory pimps, gamblers, and thugs." The death of several sailors and a panic surrounding venereal disease were used to justify increases in police raids and in the imprisonment of many white and Black women sex workers. Influenza also led to the closure of the cabarets, honky-tonks, and dance halls that nightly employed numerous pianists and more than two dozen bands. In August 1917 a representative of the Department of War warned Mayor Martin Berhman that either he could shut down the district or the navy would. The city complied in October.[15]

The closure of Storyville was closely followed by an attack on Jazz itself. In a famous 1918 editorial entitled "Jass and Jassism," the editors of the *New Orleans Times-Picayune* expressed the sense of panic that the popularity of Jazz aroused among the dominant economic and cultural bloc. It also expressed the bloc's commitment to destroying this new cultural movement. First, the editors placed supposed Black "primitivism" on par with the perceived dangers of communism and Bolshevism:

> Why is the jass music, and therefore, the jass band? As well ask why is the dime novel or the grease-dripping doughnut? All are manifestations of a low streak in man's tastes that has not yet come out in civilization's wash. Indeed, one might go farther, and say that jass music is the indecent story syncopated and counter-pointed. Like the improper anecdote, also in its youth, it was listened to blushingly, behind closed doors and drawn curtains, but, like all vice, it grew bolder until it dared decent surroundings, and there, was tolerated because of its oddity.[16]

The editors then argued that the sensibilities of those who appreciated Jazz were similar to those of wild beasts:

> Prominently, in the basement hall of rhythm, is found rag-time, and of those most devoted to the cult of the displaced accent there has developed a brotherhood of those who, devoid of harmonic and even of melodic instinct, love to fairly wallow in noise. On certain natures sound loud and meaningless has an exciting, almost an intoxicating effect, like crude colors and strong perfumes, the sight of flesh or the sadic pleasure in blood. To such as these the jass music is a delight, and a dance to the unstable bray of the sackbut gives a sensual delight, more intense and quite different from the languor of a Viennese waltz or the refined sentiment and respectful emotion of an eighteenth century minuet.[17]

Finally, the leadership of the newspaper pledged that New Orleans's elite would suppress the new cultural revolution's threat to civilization: "In the matter of jass, New Orleans is particularly interested, since it has been widely suggested that this particular form of musical vice had its birth in this city—that it came, in fact, from doubtful surroundings in our slums. We do not recognize the honor of parenthood, but with such a story in circulation, it behooves us to be last to accept the atrocity in polite society, and where it has crept in we should make it a point of civic honor to suppress it. Its musical value is nil, and its possibilities of harm are great."[18]

The cultural war against Jazz occurred at the same time the Bourbon elite was continuing its war against Black voting rights and leadership. Civil rights were further diminished with the approval of a new state constitution in 1921. Its "understanding clause" allowed the use of arbitrary tests to block Black voters from registering.[19] Disenfranchisement, widespread violence, and the growth of racial segregation led to a fracturing of the Black political community, the preservation of intracommunity schisms, and the strengthening of white-dominated patronage networks. A. P. Tureaud, the leader of the New Orleans branch of the NAACP, concluded that, prior to World War I, historic ethnic and geographic divisions within the Black community were rigidly maintained. There was little mingling between "Creole Negroes" of the Seventh Ward and "what we called the American blacks above Canal Street." Adam Fairclough suggests that although linguistic differences were fading as the use of the Creole language declined, Catholicism became more of a defining feature of Afro-Creole identity. This process was partially reinforced when the church widened its patronage system by opening a number of primary and secondary schools for Black children.[20]

Another growing Bourbon patronage network linked elite whites with the Black middle-class leaders who emerged from social organizations, religious bodies, the professions, small businesses, educational institutions, and the greatly diminished political organizations. According to Fairclough, in New Orleans a few approved leaders were allowed to plead with judges and politicians for some slight mercies. The leader of the "Black and Tan" wing of the Republican Party, Walter Cohen, occupied this position for decades.[21]

The Bourbons and northern capitalists who directly benefited from the sharecropping, indebtedness, despotism, and racial wage system of the South crafted a complimentary system of patronage. Without access to local and state resources, Black communities and a section of the Black leadership became heavily dependent upon northern philanthropy. This relationship was allowed to blossom because a semblance of legitimacy and social peace was important to northern capitalists who were flooding the South with investments in land, labor, and manufacturing. Second, the Bourbon leadership gained new investments, public relations benefits, compliance from existing Black leaders, and the production of a new generation of compliant Black leaders. Third, the projects supported in the South didn't fundamentally alter existing racial relations.

For example, the Atlanta-based Commission of Interracial Cooperation was a central conduit for grants from the Chicago-based Julius Rosenwald Fund. This aid built 372 rural schools in Louisiana between 1914 and 1922; a third of all Black children in the state were educated in these schools.[22] However, the majority of the commission's projects in the state were confined to New Orleans. On its board of directors sat white businessmen, planters, bankers, and cotton and sugar merchants who ensured that the small health, recreation, and education projects funded wouldn't violate the system of rigid segregation or disrupt notions of Black inferiority. One leading board member concluded that poverty plagued Blacks because they weren't "fully aware of opportunities in Louisiana." He further argued that Blacks lacked civic pride and had a tendency to "spend their idle time in shooting craps [and that they stayed] awake half of the night . . . in emotional [religious] orgies." Consequently, the efforts of Black middle-class leaders allied with northern capitalists often produced both minor successes and prolonged exercises in circularity. This history is extremely instructive for students of the activities of the contemporary nonprofit industrial complex and its activities in New Orleans after Hurricane Katrina.[23]

Human Rights and Blues Sustainability Ethic

To understand New Orleans's role as an African American sacred place, as a city of refuge, it is necessary to remember that throughout this period the human rights crisis faced by African Americans in the urban and rural areas continued to intensify. Rural Black workers were trapped three ways based on their exploitation as workers and through forced economic competition with both impoverished whites in the state and impoverished workers in the various dictatorships of the global plantation system. The whipsaw of this racialized global racial division of labor ensured that multiple forms of bondage, impoverishment, and terror would haunt rural and urban African American communities for decades to come. For example, as Barry notes, in Amite, fifty miles north of New Orleans, "several farmers were indicted on charges of kidnapping a family of Negroes at gunpoint, taking them into Mississippi, and selling the whole lot for a twenty-dollar bill; the Negroes were forced to work without pay for weeks under armed guards." The stories of the many individuals and families who were trapped on plantations and in prisons and labor camps still remain untold.[24]

The Blues sustainability ethic took many manifestations in the New Orleans region. First, it was defined by interlocking relationships between nature, family, community, and ontology. The world's greatest gospel singer, Mahalia Jackson, was born in New Orleans in 1911. Her family lived in the Sixteenth Ward section known as Front of the Town because it sat behind the levee and in front of railroad tracks and the Garden District:

> It was a mixed-up neighborhood, with Negroes, French, Creoles and Italians all trying to scratch out a living. The Negro men in the neighborhood worked around the river, on the docks and the steamboats and the banana boats. My father moved cotton on the river docks in the daytime, barbered people at night and preached on Sundays. He made enough to get along, but we never had much money. We lived in a little old "shotgun" shack. It rained about as much inside our house as it did outside, and we were always putting out pots and pans to catch the water and sweeping it out with brooms, but those floors were always scrubbed clean.[25]

Reflecting on her childhood in the city, Jackson recalled how the activities of catching seafood and game and growing, harvesting, purchasing, bartering, cooking, and eating food undergirded resistance, affirmation, ritual, art, and dignity:

In New Orleans good things to eat are an important part of your life. . . . What with the river and tropical fruits and Louisiana farm country outside the city, all kinds of real good food have always been cheap. . . . In my time you could always go out on the river and catch buckets of fish and crabs and shrimp. In our little gardens we grew okra, green beans, red beans, tomatoes, pumpkins, peas, corn and mustard greens. We kept chickens and goats. We had the markets where you could buy any piece of the pig from his head to his tail and fish from the ocean as well as the river. From the swamps we got soup turtles and baby alligators and from the woods we got raccoon, rabbit and possum. From the trees we picked peaches, figs, bananas, pecan nuts and oranges. I was brought up to believe that good food was important for the strength it gave you and it was a matter of pride to prepare it properly.[26]

A second linchpin of this Blues complex was the intense dedication of parents to passing local knowledge, traditions, and social surveillance to their children. Musician Danny Barker recalled the education of a childhood friend, Mr. God Lord the Lifter, who grew up in a family of women who worked for the Bourbon elite as cooks and housekeepers: "As Lifter sat around the dinner table at night, he heard all sorts of stories, tragic and funny, that his grandmother, mother and aunts related to one another. Lifter was allowed to hear these stories because it is the belief in New Orleans, 'Let them children know so they won't be no damned fool.'"[27]

A third part of the Blues sustainable development complex was the dozens of neighborhood social aid and pleasure clubs that provided health care, pension, and funeral benefits, along with support for Black businesses. The neighborhood and ward complex of large extended families, social and pleasure clubs, churches, healers, businesses, schools, other organizations and clubs, brass bands, musicians, artisans, workers, labor leaders, Mardi Gras Indians, and second lines provided an endless supply of community-centered leadership, development initiatives, and institutionalized planning. Distinctive neighborhood rituals, cooperation, and competition also served to foster a unique sense of identity, unity, and innovation.[28] Charles Siler argues that the second line is an African ritual that functions to unite neighborhoods and preserve Black access to public space:

[Processionals] are an integral part of African culture and, in New Orleans, the second line is the archetypal expression of celebration. The second line is usually associated, outside of the area, with the jazz funeral tradition, which is only one place where it occurs. There are a variety of first lines—marching clubs, Mardi Gras Indian gangs, funerals, brass bands, and a variety of other, some newly created, celebrations. The name, Second Line, describes the followers of the first line. These are the drummers, dancers and others who follow the primary activity and give it support. The second line and its reflection of Louisiana's Senegambian connection links us to a processional dance called the Saba.[29]

The communal complex of the New Orleans region also supported the Blues ontology. This philosophy fostered complementary realist, utopian, and prophetic traditions whose statements on oppression, social justice, love, life, and destiny circulated widely outside the official physical and doctrinal boundaries of the Black church and the Black elite. One of the architects of the Gospel Blues, Mahalia Jackson, recounted how her cousins performed with Ma Rainey and how she felt personally moved by Bessie Smith. Jackson believed that the Blues worldview played a central role in sustaining African American life and community:

> I played Fred's records all day long. . . . Bessie Smith was my favorite. . . . She dug right down and kept it in you. Her music haunted you even when she stopped singing. . . . I don't sing the blues myself—not since those days when I was a child. . . . But you've got to know what the blues meant to us then to understand properly about them. The Negroes all over the South kept those blues playing to give us relief from our burdens and to give us courage to go on and maybe get away.[30]

Interaction with and appreciation of nature manifested in many forms.

Blues and Jazz culture also operated to lessen neighborhood and interethnic conflicts within the African American community. Afro-Creole and African American musicians and audiences increasingly encountered each other in workplaces, citywide organizations, and the entertainment districts. Danny Barker remembered that the closure of Storyville did not close the two-square-mile Black red light district stretching "from Old Basin to New Basin, from South Rampart Street to North Claiborne Avenue." It was, "according to many noted authorities on the subject, just about the largest and most organized Red Light District in the Western Hemisphere. . . . The tallest and largest buildings in the section were the Parish Prison and Charity Hospital. Most the jazz joints were scattered about here—that is cabarets, honky tanks, dives, sporting houses, gambling dens. The main drag for the Negro underworld was South Rampart Street."[31]

Although the closure of Storyville and the migration of many Jazz and Blues artists away from the city are often portrayed as leading to the decline of Jazz in the region, often overlooked is the deepening of the Blues tradition in the city. Mahalia Jackson remembered that during her childhood, Ragtime, Jazz and Blues were to be found everywhere, particularly after phonographs and records became widely available: "The famous white singers like Caruso—you might hear them when you went by a white folks' house but in a colored house you hear the blues. You couldn't help but hear the blues—all through the thin partitions of the houses—through the open windows—up and down the street in the colored neighborhoods—everybody played it real loud."[32]

Another key component of the expanding New Orleans Blues university system was the piano professor. During the 1920s, music in the city was transformed by never-recorded barrelhouse boogie-woogie piano greats such as "Sullivan Rock," Frank Duston, "Rocker," Willie "Drive 'Em Down" Hall, "Kid Stormy Weather," "Boogus," and Robert Bertrand. In addition to playing at specific venues, these scholars would meet regularly to engage in legendary "bucking" competitions. Isidore "Tuts" Washington was among the numerous musicians to graduate from this school. Born in 1907, he received his initial music education from the brass bands that were constantly parading through the streets, in part due to the city's extremely high mortality rate: "There was always bands out in the street, 'cause nearly everybody got waked by a band then. On weekends, sometimes there'd be two or three bands on the corner tryin' to 'buck' each other to see which one was the best. All us kids would run behind the bands, they call it second linin' today. I'd like to hear the 'Tin Roof Blues.' [sings] 'Don't you get too funky 'cause your water's on.' That was kicks."[33] Washington was playing the piano by the age of ten. "I started out playin' the blues 'cause that was what the people liked to hear. I'd sneak around the joints and listen to 'em play the blues and boogie woogie. They had a gang of blues players then; see, every joint had a piano in it 'cause this was before they even had radios and jukeboxes." The Black red light district behind Rampart and Perdido Streets had become a central place for Blues piano experimentation. "We used to have a joint in the back of the precinct that we called the 'Fuck Around.' I run up on on a gang of blues players there in the Twenties. 'Black' Merineaux, Fats Pichon, Little Brother Montgomery, Burnell Santiago, Kid Stormy Weather, Hezekiah—they was all blues players. Some nights there'd be three or four of us in there and we'd 'buck' each other to see which one was the best." The piano professors of the city continued their tradition of reinterpreting and preserving Louisiana's rich musical traditions while simultaneously incorporating ideas from throughout the United States and the world.[34]

Once the New Orleans Blues/Jazz Renaissance began to migrate, it rapidly transformed the nation. Lonnie Johnson left New Orleans and settled in St. Louis with his brother James "Steady Roll" Johnson in 1920. Soon afterward, most of his family in New Orleans died during an influenza epidemic. Johnson initially played with the Jazz-O-Maniacs and soon married Blues singer Mary Williams. Singing and playing the guitar, mandolin, banjo, and piano, he was the most recorded Blues performer in the nation between 1925 and 1932. In addition to recording with Victoria Spivey, Texas Alexander, Louis Armstrong, and Duke Ellington, he influenced generations of guitarists. William Barlow notes that "the one-string vibrato he mastered with his picking technique created a high-pitched wailing sound easily used to approximate the human voice." Johnson indicted the social order in several songs, including "There Is No Justice." "Boys it's a pity, but I sure can't understand / They say the judge is for justice / But he still framed an innocent man."[35]

Just prior to the closure of Storyville, bands composed of African American and Afro-Creole musicians began to carry the New Orleans Renaissance onto the riverboats plying their trade up and down the Mississippi River Valley, while others boarded trains for Los Angeles and Chicago. Freddie Keppard's Original Creole Orchestra arrived in Los Angeles as early as 1911 and was followed by Kid Ory in 1919.

In Chicago, Ory, the New Orleans Creole Jazz Band, Jelly Roll Morton, Joe "King" Oliver, and many others attracted a massive following.[36] Migrants from Mississippi and Louisiana were transforming the city as the African American population of 45,000 in 1910 grew to 235,000 by 1930. The Blues and Jazz pulsing from the hundreds of bars, restaurants, casinos, and dance halls became the soundtrack of rapid urbanization and industrialization throughout the nation. Louis Armstrong became a key figure in this cultural revolution, the first Chicago Renaissance, known as the Jazz Age. According to Mutt Carey, he was one the most important Blues innovators to emerge in New Orleans: "Armstrong came out to Lincoln Park in New Orleans to listen to the Kid Ory Band. . . . I let Louis sit in my chair. Now at time I was the 'Blues King' in New Orleans, and when Louis played that day he played more blues than I ever heard in my life. It never did strike my mind that blues could be interpreted so many different ways."[37]

Oliver brought the twenty-one-year-old Armstrong up from New Orleans in 1922. He soon helped to construct a new sound based on several interventions: a mastery of the Blues; a mastery of the styles of Oliver and Bunk Johnson; a loud and "hot" sound; reaching unheard-of of high notes; and the ability to make the trumpet talk. Signature songs he developed with pianist Lil Hardin, his future wife, such as "Dipperrnouth Blues" and "Gut Bucket Blues," extended the Blues tradition in new directions. Playing with the Fletcher Henderson Orchestra, Armstrong took New York by storm in 1924.[38]

Some cultural critics responded to the music by variously defining it as apolitical dance music, a white aesthetic innovation, an indicator of social crisis, a symbol of African American degeneracy, or the "jungle" soundtrack of a new era of colonialism. What is missed is that the nationalization of the New Orleans Blues/Jazz Renaissance during the early 1920s gave the world a new language of social experimentation, social realism, and cultural freedom. As it traveled along the road to becoming a global culture, it immediately transformed the literature, theater, dance, art, and architecture of the age. The specific antiracist, democratic, internationalist, African American, and working-class pillars of the sustainable Blues development tradition and the Blues epistemology gave Jazz its aesthetic, freedom ethic, flexibility, and social vision, as well as its political agenda. This allowed the tradition to become central to the efforts of working-class Blacks, Asian Americans, Latinos, whites, and colonized communities to organize new imagined and real alliances. Simultaneously, the Bourbons' Storyville crucible prepared New Orleans Renaissance intellectuals for the task of creating new communities in the midst of elite-organized vice playgrounds dedicated to racial, class, and gender denigration.

The Movements against Bourbonism: Garveyism and Ghettoization

The reorganization of national and international racial relations, along with World War I (1914–18), were also signal events in the nationalization and the globalization of the Blues epistemology. Wartime labor shortages spurred Black urbanization in the South and urbanization in and migration to the North. Although some viewed the flight of several hundred thousand Blacks out of the South as an exodus to the Promised Land, many of the migrants were met with profound segregation and violence, during and after the war. Consequently, the Blues development tradition's emphasis on sustainable working-class communities, human rights, economic redistribution, cultural autonomy, and dignity found fertile ground in the cities of the South, North, and West. It provided a foundation for a new age of African American and African diaspora social movements.

In the half century prior to the 1920s, pogroms, invasions, and colonialism transformed the African diaspora and led to a shift in consciousness. To address this crisis, African Americans launched multiple movements, many of which addressed human rights in the United States, Africa, and the Caribbean. The Niagara Movement's human rights campaign was launched in 1905. Several leaders of this movement were founders of the NAACP in 1909. The New Orleans branch of the NAACP was founded in 1915. Outside of New Orleans, Baton Rouge, Alexandria, and Shreveport, efforts to establish new branches in rural areas of Louisiana were typically crushed. The New Orleans branch and its newsletter, the *Vindicator*, focused on and played central roles in the 1927 U.S. Supreme Court ruling striking down the residential segregation ordinance of 1924.[39]

The vortex created by the conflict between the Blues and Bourbon development traditions also played a central role in the rise and demise of the Universal Negro Improvement Association (UNIA). The organization's emphasis on cultural dignity, cooperative economic development, working-class leadership, democratic participation, self-defense, anticolonialism, and African repatriation resonated throughout the South, the rest of the African diaspora, and in Africa itself.

Yet Marcus Garvey and the leadership of UNIA were faced with the intensification of repression by the U.S. federal government and European colonial powers. The movement also faced the intensification of political repression, ghettoization, poverty, and of organizational and class conflicts within African American communities. Finally, the intensification of the historic Blues movement and its agenda for civil rights, land reform, and human rights in the South created internal contradictions within UNIA that could not be reconciled.

Throughout the United States, Blues universities penetrated UNIA. Although dedicated to many of the same goals as the Garvey movement, these institutions were also concerned with the immediate defense of children, women, and men from the predatory plantation regimes of the South. They were also concerned with defending the emerging communities of Black migrants in the Northeast, Midwest, and West. Blues working-class universities are scattered throughout African American history. They have often been rendered invisible by class, regional, and cultural biases within African American historiography. Another conceptual dilemma derives from their being subterraneanly embedded within organizations, institutions, and movements with contradictory goals and agendas. Yet this phenomenon seems less contradictory when we remember that the Blues emerged from maroonage, fugitivism, masking, and other resistance practices perfected during slavery. The goal of acquiring skills, resources, and information necessary to preserve and expand the Blues sustainable development agenda within hostile environments often came at great individual, family, and community costs. But new insights were gained, new experiments were undertaken, new specializations and flexibilities were developed, and the agenda was carried forward.

The working-class Blues universities are rendered invisible by the several elite uplift models deployed among and by African Americans. Much of the discourse on African American uplift, improvement, and development takes a civilizationist approach, which assumes that members of the Black working class will revert back to their essential primitive nature without constant and stern tutelage by their racial and class superiors. This post-Reconstruction tradition comes by the rhetoric of colonialism honestly. Born in 1839 to missionaries in Hawaii, General Samuel C. Armstrong founded Hampton Normal and Agricultural Institute in Hampton, Virginia, in 1868. Critics charged that the educational model adopted by the school was the same used in Hawaii, on Native Americans, and in other colonial contexts. It was designed to create an assimilated and apolitical elite who believed themselves to be morally, culturally, and intellectually superior to the vast majority of their fellow African Americans. In 1874 Armstrong described his project to a former Williams College classmate: "I have a remarkable machine for the elevation of our colored brethren. . . . Put in a raw plantation darkey and he comes out a gentleman of the nineteenth century." The prized product of this machine, Booker T. Washington, went on to serve as the first principal of Alabama's Tuskegee Institute from 1881 to 1915. By the 1920s the Armstrong/Washington/Tuskegee model of industrial education and elite formation was internationalized and applied in Africa by British, German, and South African colonial authorities.[40]

In 1914 Marcus Garvey and Amy Ashwood founded the Universal Negro Improvement Association (UNIA) and African Communities League in the British colony of Jamaica. Their goal was to create an industrial school modeled on

Booker T. Washington's Tuskegee Institute.[41] After Washington's death in 1915, Garvey cancelled plans to visit Tuskegee and traveled to Harlem in New York City to raise funds for the project. The New York branch of UNIA was formed in May 1917 by thirteen members.

The United States officially entered World War I on April 6, 1917, and expanded production in the United States rapidly increased the demand for labor. Between 1916 and 1917 some ten thousand to twelve thousand Blacks migrated to East St. Louis, Illinois, to work in that city's rapidly expanding industrial plants. Many of the migrants were from Louisiana. On July 2 and 3, 1917, white mobs attacked the Black community, which was viewed as economic competition. Estimates of the number of Blacks killed during the East St. Louis Riot range from thirty-nine to two hundred, while at least six thousand were displaced.[42]

For many observers, the riot and massacre signaled either a new era of oppression for African Americans or the nadir following the triumphs of abolition and Reconstruction. In the immediate midst of this crisis, Garvey delivered a famous speech on July 8, 1917, "The Conspiracy of the East St. Louis Riots." The speech and a subsequent pamphlet in which it was reprinted laid the massacre at the feet of the New Orleans Bourbon bloc:

> The East St. Louis Riot, or rather massacre, of Monday [July] 2nd, will go down in history as one of the bloodiest outrages against mankind for which any class of people could be held guilty. (Hear! Hear!) This is no time for fine words, but a time to lift one's voice against the savagery of a people who claim to be the dispensers of democracy. (cheers) . . . For three hundred years the Negroes of America have given their life blood to make the Republic the first among the nations of the world, and all along this time there has never been even one year of justice but on the contrary a continuous round of oppression. At one time it was slavery, at another time lynching and burning, and up to date it is wholesale butchering. This is a crime against the laws of humanity; it is a crime against the laws of the nation, it is a crime against Nature, and a crime against the God of all mankind. (cheers)[43]

After arguing that the massacre was both a state crime and a sin, Garvey referred to a debate in New Orleans between the mayor of East St. Louis and the Bourbon leadership:

> Mayor Mollman of East St. Louis . . . fostered a well arranged conspiracy to prevent black men migrating from the South. . . . Two months ago I was in New Orleans completing a lecture tour of the United States, and on the 26th of April Mayor Fred W. Mollman arrived in the city on a trip from St. Louis. In New Orleans he was met by Mayor Behrman and the New Orleans Board of Trade. For months the farmers of Louisiana were frightened out of their wits over the everyday migration of Negroes from great farming centers of the State. They wrote to the papers, they appealed to the Governor, the Mayor and the Legislature and the Board of Trade to

stop the Negroes going away, but up to the 26th of April nothing was done to stop the people.... In an interview [Mollman] said that some of the largest industries in the country were established in East St. Louis and there were strikes for the last few months. He believed the labor conditions in East St. Louis were responsible for the number of Negro laborers going to that city.... His interview did not make pleasant reading for the farmers and others interested in labor in New Orleans and Louisiana so that the very next day he appeared at the Board of Trade where he met the farmers and others and in discussing the labor exodus with them, he promised that he would do all he could to discourage Negroes from Louisiana going into East St. Louis as the city did not want them.[44]

Rural oppression and destitution fueled the migration from Louisiana, Arkansas, and Mississippi. White workers had launched a series of campaigns to organize the plants in East St. Louis, but the union policy of white supremacy excluded Black workers, thereby enabling employers to rapidly replace striking white workers with Blacks. A toxic environment was created as manufacturers' need for labor, white workers' need for employment, the state's need for legitimacy, the Bourbon bloc's need for cheap Black labor, and Blacks' need for work intersected. According to Garvey, this stalemate was broken by the Bourbon leadership:

His [Mollman's] remarks to the people whom he met were published under big headlines in the newspapers, so that the Negroes could read that they were not wanted in East St. Louis, but that did not deter the blackmen of Louisiana who were looking for better opportunities than the South offered with lynching and Jim Crowism. On the 5th of May the New Orleans Board of Trade elected Mr. M. J. Sanders its president, and Mr. W. P. Ross as delegates to attend a transportation conference at St. Louis to be held on May 8–9.... It isn't for me to suggest that Mayor Mollman met these gentlemen again. One thing I do now know; the first riot started on May 28 after a conference of labor leaders with Mayor Mollman. On that day, May 28, crowds of white men after leaving the City Council stopped street cars and dragged Negroes off and beat them. Then the night following three Negroes and two white men were shot.... On the 29th of May, a day after the first disturbance, and when three Negro men had been killed, Mayor Mollman sent a dispatch to Governor Pleasant of Louisiana advising the Negroes of Louisiana to remain away from East St. Louis.[45]

Garvey theorized that the tragedy was not just a confluence of events, it was a plan, one that would be repeated over and over again during the next few years as racial pogroms, labor repression, and the rise of the Ku Klux Klan came to define the postwar period for African Americans:

Because nothing was done to crush the originators and leaders of the first riot the Negro haters of East St. Louis took fresh courage and made their final attack on our defenseless men, women and children on Monday, July 2nd and which resulted in the wholesale massacre of our people. When we read in the white press a report like what I will read to you, we can conjure to our own minds the horror of the whole affair. . . . "East St. Louis, July 2nd. Negroes are being shot down like rabbits and strung up to telegraph poles." . . . The whole thing my friends is a bloody farce, and that the police and soldiers did nothing to stem the murder thirst of the mob is a conclusive proof of conspiracy on the part of the civil authorities to condone the acts of the white mob against Negroes. (Hear! Hear!) In this report we further read that as the flames of fire would drive a Negro man, wom[a]n or child from a dwelling, their clothes burning, the mob would set up a great shout and rifles and pistols would be fired. So far no Negro was known to escape as the whites had a merciless net about the Negroes, and the cry was "kill 'em all."[46]

For Garvey, the East St. Louis Riot was a battle over human rights, particularly the right to migrate and to earn livable wages. White supremacy combined with Black disunity enabled the Bourbon bloc and other leadership groups to generate oppression throughout the African diaspora:

The mob and entire white populace [of] East St. Louis had a Roman holiday. They feasted on the blood of the Negro, encouraged as they were by the German American Mayor who two months ago went to New Orleans and promised to keep the Negroes out of East St. Louis. . . . I can hardly see why black men should be debarred from going where they choose in the land of their birth. I can not see wherefrom Mayor Mollman got the authority to discourage black men going into East St. Louis, when there was work for them, except he got that authority from mob sentiment and mob law. It was because he knew that he could gain a following and support on the issue of race [is] why he was bold enough to promise the white people of Louisiana that he would keep Negroes out of East St. Louis. He has succeeded in driving fully 10,000 in one day out of the city, and the South has gone wild over the splendid performance. . . . Can you wonder at the conspiracy of the whole affair? White people are taking advantage of black men to-day because black men all over the world are disunited. (Loud and prolonged cheers).[47]

The East St. Louis Riot, massacre, and enclosure fundamentally transformed Black America. The NAACP conducted its famed silent march of eight thousand Blacks down Fifth Avenue in New York City on July 28, 1917, to denounce the event, while Garvey's speech and pamphlet made him a national figure. Garvey scholar Robert Hill suggests that the event was also personally transforming, a Blues moment. "It is that speech that marks the turning point of Garvey away from Jamaica, away from a preoccupation with matters related to the West Indies and now he's not looking for support for what he is hoping to accomplish in the West Indies, but, rather, he is now sucked into the vortex of American race relations."[48]

Garvey's analysis was also popular among African Americans because it appeared as if he were ready to take on the bedrock of economic, racial, political, and cultural oppression in the United States, Louisiana, and the rest of the Lower Mississippi Valley. Yet he was equally passionate in denouncing the persecution of Black soldiers and community members in Houston during 1917 and he condemned the twenty-six riots and massacres that occurred during Red Summer 1919. The establishment of several key institutions by the UNIA—the *Negro World* newspaper (1918), the Black Star Line (1919), and the African Orthodox Church (1921)—also captured the imagination of African Americans, Caribbean peoples, and Africans.[49] The movement also built cooperative economic, social service, and cultural institutions throughout the United States. By 1920 the UNIA claimed more than a million members in one thousand divisions located in forty countries. Both pan-African and anti-imperialist, the UNIA promised to transform the African diaspora into a massive transatlantic development zone. In Africa the movement and its allied organizations in the Congo, Ghana, Senegal, Sierra Leone, Nigeria, South Africa, Namibia, Kenya, and Angola threw Belgian, British, French, Italian, Portuguese, and South African colonial regimes into a panic between 1921 and 1922. In the United States the movement was increasingly surveilled by the federal government. In New Orleans the movement was viewed as a vehicle for social and economic transformation.

Activist working-class women, men, and families were at the center of the founding of the New Orleans Division (NOD) of the UNIA. Noted activist Alaida Robertson organized the NOD in her home in October 1920. Her husband, Sylvester, a bank porter, served as the president before becoming a state commissioner. The treasurer was Mamie Reason, a forty-year-old domestic and seamstress who later became a leader in the Spiritual Church movement.[50] Garvey sent Adrian Johnson from New York to aid the organizing effort in February 1921. The NOD grew by uniting with existing organizations, which were allowed to join the movement without losing their distinctive identity. The number of dues-paying members increased from seventy to twenty-five hundred in five months and then increased to four thousand by the fall of 1921. Key engines in the growth of the organization were the West Indian Seamen's Association and the Black Longshoremen's Association.[51] Along the Atlantic and Gulf Coasts, Black longshoremen, shipbuilders, navy yard workers, and railroad workers were among the most intense supporters of the movement. For example, T. A. Robinson was both an officer in the Longshoremen's Association and the vice president of the NOD in 1921 before becoming its president in 1922.[52]

Early in 1921 Garvey traveled to the Caribbean, South America, and Central America to form new branches. He arrived in New Orleans on July 13, 1921, despite the efforts of the U.S. Department of Justice and Immigration Office to block his return.[53] According to Queen Mother Audley Moore, the new militancy of the African diaspora and the attempt to suppress it were both in evidence when Garvey lectured in New Orleans:

> They didn't want Garvey to speak in New Orleans. We had a delegation to go to the mayor, and the next night, they allowed him to come. And we all were armed. Everybody had bags of ammunition, too. So when Garvey came in, we applauded, and the police were lined man to man along the line of each bench. So Mr. Garvey said, "My friends, I want to apologize for not speaking to you last night. But the reason I didn't was because the mayor of the city of New Orleans committed himself to act as a stooge for the police department to prevent me from speaking." And the police jumped up and said, "I'll run you in." When he did this, everybody jumped up on the benches and pulled out their guns and just held the guns up in the air and said, "Speak, Garvey, speak." And Garvey said, "As I was saying," and he went on and repeated what he had said before, and the police filed out [of] the hall like little puppy dogs with their tails behind them. So that was radical enough. I had two guns with me, one in my bosom and one in my pocketbook, little 38 specials.[54]

According to Claudrena Harold, Garvey was widely celebrated by the city's Black citizens. "Enormously popular among blacks living in the uptown section of New Orleans, Garvey addressed an enthusiastic crowd of fifteen hundred supporters. . . . The electrifying orator emphasized the need for race pride, improved relations between diasporan and continental Africans, and the development of black-owned industries." He argued that the "time has come . . . for the strongest race of people on earth, barring the Chinese, to break the bonds of oppression. . . . The world is without sympathy. You must form your own future. . . . I am not preaching radicalism. We are not organizing to fight the whites, but to protect what is ours, if it takes our lives." Garvey remained in the city for three days under the watchful eyes of the recently created Federal Bureau of Investigation.[55]

Mary Rolinson notes that within a few months of UNIA's founding, New Orleans had three divisions downtown "plus additional locals in the uptown Carrollton district and the outlying communities of Algiers, Westwego, Kenner, and Gretna." S. V. Robertson went on to become a state commissioner and organized twenty divisions in the sugar parishes between New Orleans and Baton Rouge. After becoming high commissioner for Alabama, Louisiana, and Mississippi in 1923 he "traveled further and further to the north in Louisiana and Mississippi. . . . At the 1924 convention [he was] the record holder for 'having brought more members into the ranks of the UNIA than any other commissioner.'" A second-generation longshoremen, state commissioner Thomas W. Anderson was also instrumental in establishing new divisions.[56] Based on Rolinson's calculations, between 1921 and 1926, eighty divisions of the UNIA were founded in Louisiana, the largest number in the South, and the state ranked second only to Florida in terms of membership. She suggests that in addition to powerful organizers, several other factors contributed to the rapid growth of the movement in the state: "This large unit's membership was quite diverse, unlike other Deep South divisions. In addition Garvey visited the Crescent City several times, and his presence had an enormous impact. Louisiana hosted large numbers of West Indian–born black slaves in 1850, more than any other state slave or free. . . . Another unique feature in Louisiana's organization was the Black Star Line, which was more of an inspiration to those working directly along the lower Mississippi River, one of the world's busiest maritime commercial centers."[57]

Rolinson also argues that the Garvey movement flourished in Mississippi and Louisiana when the NAACP could not because the former posed less of a challenge to the regional political economy:

> Because . . . the uncompromising segregationist white political structure of Mississippi under leaders like James K. Vardaman and Theodore Bilbo effectively prevented the incursion of any organization advocating social equality, only avowedly nonpolitical or separatist organizations like the National Negro Business League and the UNIA could exist in the state. . . . Louisiana's Black Belt showed a very similar pattern, with only five weak urban branches of the NAACP at Shreveport, Alexandria, New Orleans, Baton Rouge, and Monroe, and two rural ones at St. Rose and Clarence. In contrast, the UNIA had eighty divisions in Louisiana in the 1920s.[58]

Harold argues that the UNIA was offering challenges to the intersection of the ideologies of white supremacy and class supremacy that were not a central focus of the NAACP:

> Education, occupation, and social background were not determining factors in an individual's eligibility for office in the New Orleans UNIA. Washerwomen, carpenters, cooks, longshoremen, porters and common laborers held positions of authority within the division and its various auxiliaries. . . . Occupying leadership positions within the movement was a source of pride for many laboring people in New Orleans and elsewhere. No one recognized this more than the noted sociologist E. Franklin Frazier. "A Negro might be a porter by day, taking his orders from white men . . . but he was an officer in the black army when it assembled at night in Liberty Hall." Quenching the black workers' thirst for "self-magnification . . . made the Negro an important person in his immediate environment."[59]

Harold also concludes that Garveyism was more popular in Uptown neighborhoods than it was in the Creole districts of downtown. "Garvey's promotion of race pride resonated deeply in the hearts and minds of many who struggled to navigate the city's complex color line. His exaltation of blackness and celebration of those physical characteristics . . . [that] were often portrayed as aesthetically unattractive in white popular culture—appealed to many blacks who wanted to counter pejorative images of blackness, develop a more positive self-concept, and publicly articulate their own standards of beauty." In an article published in the *Negro World* on March 24, 1923, several NOD women leaders expressed their frustration with the Black economic and political leadership and its class and color elitism: "We are not members of the Negro 400 of New Orleans, composed of the class spending their time imitating the rich white, with card parties, eating parties, and studying Spanish so as to be able to pass for anything but a Negro. We are not ashamed of the race to which we belong and we feel sure that God made black skin and kinky hair because He desired to express Himself in that type as well as in any other."[60]

Indigenous forms of sustainable cultural and economic development critical to the working-class Blues epistemology were able to flourish within the UNIA. For example, according to Harold, the NOD became a site for the celebration of expression, imagination, solidarity, and daily life:

> Garvey himself was impressed by the numerous cultural activities offered by the local division. "We had a time in New Orleans," Garvey boasted after returning from the city in 1921. "I spoke for two nights in the National Park in New Orleans, where we had thousands of people. They had a large plaza and they had midnight dances and other amusements." An important cultural center, the New Orleans UNIA provided an institutional space where men and women could listen and dance to the syncopated sounds of the division's jazz band, showcase their various talents, debate the meaning of human existence, laugh and cry over life's joy and pains, and criticize the ways of white folks and the black elite without fear of reprisal. Within the confines of the division's Liberty Hall, women and men communed with individuals who shared their political viewpoints, cultural tastes, and working-class status. UNIA functions offered members of the community temporary respite from the drudgery of work, household duties, parental responsibilities, and the general demands of everyday life.[61]

The UNIA was also viewed as a mechanism for addressing the rising rates of Black unemployment. According to Harold, "Substantial decline in the volume of foreign trade, production cutbacks, and business closures had resulted in decreased employment opportunities and severe wage reductions for black and white laborers in New Orleans' leading industries. The election of John M. Parker to the Louisiana governorship and Andrew McShane as mayor of New Orleans provided additional ammunition to the city's commercial elite in their ongoing war with labor over wage increases, the work process, and the use of non-union employees." The UNIA's proposal to develop the Black Star Line, an Atlantic trade network, new businesses and cooperatives in the United States, and industries, farms, and colleges in Africa promised economic salvation to thousands of Louisiana's Black workers.[62]

Democratic participation, the valorization of Black working-class culture, cooperative economic development, comprehensive and autonomous planning, and globalization were key elements of the UNIA that were parallel to key pillars of the Blues development agenda. The demands of the Blues political and economic agenda continued to push the UNIA movement to specifically address the fascist practices occurring in the southern states in general and in the vortex of the Lower Mississippi Valley in particular. The anger in the region was expressed repeatedly in the pages of the *Negro World*, particularly by columnist John Edward Bruce, "Bruce Grit," who called for the lynching of white men who raped black women. In the face of this growing southern militancy, Garvey wavered. Although initially a proponent of the federal antilynching bill in 1921, Garvey later withdrew his support. He expressed a suspicion of Republican leaders, politicians in general, voting, and state reforms. The growing human rights, civil rights, and community self-defense demands and projects of Black southerners threatened Garvey's diplomatic negotiations and his attempt to build an economic base not subject to full-scale government repression.[63]

Many of the contradictions present in the UNIA reached a crossroads during the August 1922 convention: women were pushing for a greater leadership role, federal authorities indicted Garvey for using the mail to fraudulently raise funds for the Black Star Line ship, and he was widely condemned for his secret June 1922 meeting in Atlanta with the imperial wizard of the Knights of Ku Klux Klan, Edward Young Clarke. For Hill, Garvey and the UNIA were fundamentally transformed during that historic year:

> Following the dissolution of the Black Star Line Corporation in April 1922, Garvey modified the UNIA's previous militant stand by seeking external sources of support to buttress the organization's faltering resources, thereby diluting its appeal as the symbol of racial autonomy. By early 1922, the question of Africa began to be subordinated to Garvey's search for white allies. The first intimation of this political shift came on 13 February 1922—two days before Garvey's indictment in New York—when Garvey publicly praised Mississippi state senator T. S. McCallum's resolution urging the U.S. Congress to acquire land in Africa for "the founding of a national home for the American Negro" as the solution to America's race problem. . . . Garvey's African redemption program was thus realigned to coincide with the philosophy of the white American Colonization Society; this ideological shift was underscored by Garvey's 25 June meeting with Ku Klux Klan leader Edward Young Clarke in Atlanta, Georgia, a gesture reminiscent of the "Southernizing" strategy that conservative black politicians advocated after the collapse of Reconstruction in the late 1870s. The same shift away from militant self-reliance and toward racial accommodation, with the consequent reduction of the rhetoric of racial oppression, was manifest in Garvey's outreach to European governments with colonies in Africa.[64]

The revelation of negotiations between Garvey and the leader of the Klan tore the movement asunder. The head of the American section of the UNIA, Reverend James Eason, spent three months in New Orleans before the 1922 convention. His criticism of Garvey's leadership style, his management of various enterprises, and the overture to the Klan led to countercharges that he was undermining the organization. During the August convention he was charged with disloyalty, financial improprieties, and inappropriate sexual behavior. He was impeached along with two other members of the executive council. When questioned about the events by a reporter with the African American–owned *New York Age*, T. A. Robinson, president of the NOD responded, "To follow Garvey any longer one would have to be a rank fool. . . . The New Orleans Branch of the U.N.I.A. will either quit following Garvey and the outrageous methods he employs in handling the affairs of the association and line up behind some other fairer man who will organize a similar movement in opposition to it, or split up in factions aiming at the same end for the good of the Negro people of the United States." In a private meeting with Garvey after the convention, NOD treasurer Mamie Reason charged him with "ruining the colored race" and promised that she would tell the people of New Orleans "exactly what he stood for." Garvey called her a "traitor to the cause" and expelled her from the UNIA.[65]

UNIA soon found itself swirling in the New Orleans vortex. Eason formed the Universal Negro Alliance and received immediate support from Robinson and Reason. By the time he arrived in the city in October to build a branch, Eason was placing more emphasis on fighting for human and civil rights in the United States than on African repatriation. In November the UNIA sent the leader of the Universal African Legion, Esau Ramus, to New Orleans to disrupt Eason's organizing efforts. After delivering a speech on January 1, 1923, to an audience at St. Johns Baptist Church, Eason was shot outside the building. He died two days later, but not before identifying two UNIA members as his assailants. Ramus disappeared from the city, while the Black Baptist Ministerial Alliance and the leader of the NAACP, George Lucas, pledged to help law enforcement find the perpetrators.[66]

Two weeks after the murder several nationally prominent African American leaders such as *Chicago Defender* publisher Robert S. Abbott and NAACP field secretary William Pickens signed an anti-Garvey letter dated January 15, 1923, and had it delivered to the U.S. attorney general. The signatories declared "this tocsin [*sic*] only because they foresee the gathering storm of race prejudice and sense the imminent menace of this insidious movement, which cancerlike, is gnawing at the very vitals of peace and safety—of civic harmony and interracial concord." They requested the U.S. attorney general to "use his full influence completely to disband and extirpate this vicious movement, and that he vigorously and speedily push the government's case against Marcus Garvey for using the mail to defraud. This should be done in the interest of justice; even as a matter of practical expediency." Among the many charges they leveled at the UNIA, five of the twenty-nine points had to do with the Eason killing:

On January 1, this year, just after having made an address in New Orleans, the Rev. J. W. Eason, former "American Leader" of the Garvey movement, who had fallen out with Garvey and was to be the chief witness against him in the Federal Government's case, was waylaid and assassinated, it is reported in the press, by the Garveyites. Rev. Eason identified two of the men as Frederick Dyer, 42, a longshoreman, and William Shakespeare, 29, a painter. Both of them are prominent members of the U. N. I. A. in New Orleans, one wearing a badge as chief of police and the other as chief of the Fire Department of the "African Republic."[67]

Three weeks after the Eason murder, the U.S. Justice Department launched a campaign of repression against the NOD in order to accumulate evidence to prosecute Garvey and the UNIA. In late January federal officials raided a meeting, seizing membership lists and arresting nine leaders. Three weeks later twenty New Orleans Police Department (NOPD) officers raided a meeting held at the Negro Longshoremen Hall. Documents were seized and ten leaders, including two women, were arrested and charged with unlawful assembly and inciting a riot. Two of the arrested, Effie Hathaway and Florence Watterhouse, joined with a third woman to write a letter to Mayor McShane condemning the harassment campaign. In it they explained the multidimensional character of the UNIA and the strengths that had carried the organization through this moment of crisis. "The Universal Negro Improvement Association is our church, our clubhouse, our theater, our fraternal order and our school, and we will never forsake it while we live; neither will our men forsake it." The NOD was further disrupted by the national governing body's attempt to replace the division's working-class leadership with a teacher and a college professor, both of whom had little organizing experience. Several members claimed that this was an undemocratic attempt to replace proven working-class leaders with "respectable" college-educated men beholden to the national leadership group.[68]

Dyer and Shakespeare were convicted of Eason's murder in 1923. The convictions were overturned in 1924, after the Louisiana Supreme Court ruled that evidence linking Ramus to the crime was wrongfully excluded. Harold argues that the organization was able to survive and rebuild after the conflicts of 1922 because it was both a broad coalition and a dynamic institution. Rolinson suggests that the local organizations continued to thrive by retaining an emphasis upon freedom from white supremacist forms of economic and cultural domination. In addition to rejecting theories of black inferiority, it supported Black workers in their campaigns against exploitative employers while simultaneously promoting Black business development and the creation of cooperative economic institutions.[69] The national organization also continued to promise to employ millions of desperate workers in Africa and the Americas. The hopes of the emigrationists and supporters of the pan-African development zone were renewed when the UNIA formed the Black Cross Navigation and Trading Company in

1924 and purchased a ship that was renamed the *Booker T. Washington*. Yet, according to Harold, funds were not found for a comprehensive rural development program proposed by NOD president Isaac Chambers at the 1924 convention. Sharecropper cooperatives were to be created in order that "cotton and other produce of the Negro could be bought, thereby preventing white capitalists from obtaining this produce at a ridiculously low figure, as was the case at present to the undoing of the farmer." The national organization continued to ignore the Blues development agenda and its emphasis on the realization of full human and cultural rights and on the fundamental economic transformation of the South, the United States, the African diaspora, Africa, and the plantation world.[70]

By February 1925 Garvey had been convicted of mail fraud and was confined to a cell in the federal prison at Atlanta. His first message from behind bars was a combination of condemnation and prophecy:

> Continue to pray for me and I shall ever be true to my trust. I want you, the black peoples of the world, to know that W.E.B. Du Bois and that vicious Negro-hating organization known as the Association for the Advancement of "Colored" People are the greatest enemies the black people have in the world. . . . After my enemies are satisfied, in life or death I shall come back to you to serve even as I have served before. . . . When I am dead wrap the mantle of the Red, Black and Green around me, for in the new life I shall rise with God's grace and blessing to lead the millions up the heights of triumph with the colors that you well know. Look for me in the whirlwind or the storm, look for me all around you, for, with God's grace, I shall come and bring with me countless millions of black slaves who have died in America and the West Indies and the millions in Africa to aid you in the fight for Liberty, Freedom and Life.[71]

The desires and activities of the New Orleans locals suggests that one of the key undercurrents to be found in the history of the UNIA is the effort of African Americans to revitalize the historic Blues development agenda. Although the Blues agenda's principle of mass democracy was fractured by numerous leadership schisms, the focus on emigration, and Garvey's pragmatism, the organization simultaneously served as a Blues university. The UNIA experiment demonstrated to several generations that the African American working class was an inexhaustible fountain of leadership. It also revealed that the Blues agenda had global resonance and that the African American working class could successfully form alliances with, and provide leadership to, national and global communities. This was the invisible meaning of UNIA. Yet, on the other hand, New Orleans and southeastern Louisiana was a global community two centuries before the arrival of Garvey. The centuries-long campaign for human rights was magnified by the historic campaign to preserve and expand African American, Afro-Creole, and regional cultural autonomy. The Blues communities of Louisiana and Mississippi experienced levels of racial, social, and economic violence

at the hands of the Delta and Bourbon plantation blocs unknown in the rest of
the United States. Garvey initially benefited from exposing this dilemma and
then faltered when he attempted to ignore its centrality.

The Great Flood of 1927

On the eve of the Great Depression, the Great Flood of 1927 transformed the
region and the nation. The modern Mississippi River had become a man-made
engineering disaster. When the region's levees began to collapse, the Bourbon
and the Delta blocs once again exhibited to the world their capacity for transforming a major disaster into a biblical-scale tragedy. In New Orleans, the mid-
1920s were increasingly defined by an economic depression that gripped most
of the South. Cotton prices declined dramatically after World War I. The boll
weevil infestation, exhausted soils, and competition from Indian and Egyptian
cotton producers combined to produce a collapse of the agricultural economy.
Early in 1927 the heaviest rainfall recorded in five decades pushed the rivers that
flowed into the Mississippi River to flood stage. By April levees began to collapse
in Missouri, Arkansas, and the Mississippi Delta.[72]

Rather than evacuate the city, the Bourbon bloc favored a plan designed to
relieve pressure on the New Orleans levees by dynamiting levees in St. Bernard
and Plaquemines Parishes. The decision was ultimately made by the three members of the Board of Liquidation: James Butler, president of the Canal Bank;
Rudolph Hecht, president of the Hibernia Bank; and lawyer J. Blanc Monroe,
leader of the Whitney Bank's board of directors and a future president of the
American Bankers Association. Their recommendations for demolition were
agreed to on April 19 by the mayor, the presidents of all the major banks in New
Orleans, and leaders of the city's Cotton Exchange, Board of Trade, Stock Exchange, Dock Board, Association of Commerce, and Levee Board. On April 23
an incident occurred that would resonate eighty-eight years later in the debate
over the collapse of the levee in the Lower Ninth Ward after Hurricane Katrina.
An oceangoing molasses tanker mysteriously slammed into a St. Bernard Parish
levee three miles below the city and opened a break. The attack was anticipated
by St. Bernard levee guards and the breach was quickly repaired.[73]

Despite widespread resistance, on April 25, fifty-seven Bourbon-bloc economic and political leaders, including the governor, signed an agreement
outlining how they would proceed if the demolition was approved: compensation efforts would be supported, a reparations commission would be established, and the evacuees would be provided for. According to Barry, six of the
fifty-seven signatories were government officials and thirty-five were members
of the Boston Club. Of "the sixteen who were not, most—like Edgar Stern,
president of the New Orleans Cotton Exchange and son-in-law of Julius Ros-

enwald, who built Sears into one of the world's largest businesses—were Jews, who could not belong." Of the five attorneys who wrote the legal opinion in favor of the governor's power to deliberately destroy a region, all were from New Orleans, three "reigned over Carnival as Comus, the fourth as Rex and the fifth, Monte Lemann, was Jewish and could not participate in Carnival." The Board of Liquidation overcame the intense opposition of the mayor, the head of the Army Corps of Engineers, the governor, and the president of the United States on the road to liquidating entire communities in the two parishes. On April 29 the dynamiting of the levees commenced and continued for the next nine days.[74]

City officials placed approximately half of the ten thousand displaced persons in a New Orleans warehouse. After exhausting its existing resources, the Red Cross soon refused to provide additional assistance. The subcommittee formed to provide food, housing, employment, education, and transportation aid balked at Bourbon suggestions to create "concentration camps" because it would create bitterness among the Blacks, whites, Native Americans, and others in, and outside, the camps. It also informed the board that expenses for food were running $20,000 a week above what was budgeted. True to Bourbon form, the "starve the beast" planning principle was unleashed on the displaced. Butler, Hecht, and Monroe decided to deduct food money from final damage settlements. Monroe dominated the Reparations Commission and denied most claims, the right to legal counsel, and the awarding of partial payments, that is, no money would be distributed until all appeals were extinguished. Barry notes that most "refugees needed money desperately. By refusing partial payments, Monroe was starving them into submission." He then disallowed $23 million of the $35 million in claims submitted and agreed to settle on only $3.9 million of the remaining $12.5 million worth of claims outstanding. From this latter amount he deducted $1 million for food and shelter expenses. The city agreed to pay $2.9 million, of which $2.1 million went to two firms. The remaining $800,000 was split among 2,809 claimants, and another 1,024 people received nothing. Little help was forthcoming from the federal government or President Herbert Hoover's flood relief director for the state, former governor John M. Parker.[75]

In the midst of general destruction, African Americans in need were uniquely abused. In mid-June, an elderly African American woman whose home was underwater settled for just twenty-seven dollars in order to feed herself. Momentarily, the board agreed to continue to feed those whose settlements were less than $100. However, several weeks later a "group of black refugees pleaded for an extension of food payments, explaining that the marshes from which they had earned income—they had gathered moss and sold it as mattress filling—were waist deep in mud. But for these people, aid had ended. They were informed, 'As long as we continue to feed you, you are not going to work.'" NAACP branches from around the country, along with other organizations, sent clothes and funds to the New Orleans branch to aid flood victims and to assist Blacks in the rural areas who were held at gunpoint to prevent them from leaving the flooded plantation districts of Louisiana and Mississippi.[76]

The New Orleans Bourbon bloc was roundly condemned by then-governor Oramel Simpson and by his campaign opponent, Huey Long, who repeatedly denounced them as "plutocrats" and as "the self-appointed rulers of the state." The return to classical Bourbonism during moments of crisis defines the New Orleans plantation bloc, then and now. In a prophetic rebuke, the *Memphis Commercial Appeal*, the conservative voice of the Delta plantation bloc, condemned the Bourbons in an editorial headlined "New Orleans Babbitry": "If New Orleans is ever flooded the world will not know unless there is some outside newspaper man there. The newspapers of New Orleans have not told their own people the actual situation. It's business depression that's feared. Many of the leaders of the town had much rather take a chance at loss of life and destruction of property than face the possibility of the grain market slumping a couple of notches, the price of cotton falling 50 to 100 points, or New Orleans stocks going under the least of a strain."[77]

Similar to Katrina, there were five disasters associated with the flood of 1927. There was the manmade disaster of Bourbon-bloc race, class, and gender relations that existed prior to the storms. Second, there was the manmade disaster created by engineers who designed and built a flood-protection system with inherent technological flaws. Third, suffering was exponentially increased by the demolition of the levees and by other decisions made during the initial crisis. Fourth, there was the manmade relief disaster. Finally, intergenerational economic and psychological damage was wrought on the population of southeastern Louisiana. The consequences of Bourbon logic sparked new resistance movements among white populists and within working-class Black communities.

An outpouring of Blues songs were written to document the Great Flood of 1927. In "Helena Blues," Lonnie Johnson depicted the situation faced by many Black men. His character asserts the Blues ethic of "always running," "hell hound on my trail," to describe being a fugitive by resisting forced labor on the collapsing levees. This ethic would inform and guide the regional and national movements spawned from this tragedy:

> I want to go back to Helena, but the high water got me barred
> . . . .
> They want me to work on the levee
> . . . .
> I was so scared the levee would break, lord, and I might drown
> . . . .

The police run me from Cairo all through Arkansas (2x)
they put me in jail behind those cold iron bars

The police say, "Work or go to jail," I say, "I ain't totin' no sack!
I ain't drillin' no levee! . . . and I ain't driving no nails!"[78]

The Blues tradition encourages us to focus on the visions promoted by the dispossessed. It offers a conception of the struggle against Bourbonism that would come to define the region for the rest of the century.

CHAPTER 4

The Share the Wealth Plan

Longism, 1928–1940

Well, your riddle please, a tell it to me
Of how an eater came forth meat?
Well, your riddle please, ah tell it to me
Of how the strong of it came forth sweet?
Well, if I had my way
Well, if I had—a wicked world
If I had my way, oh Lord, I'd tear this building down
    "Blind" Willie Johnson, 1927[1]

In December 1929 the wandering Blues theologian and singer "Blind" Willie Johnson sang "If I Had My Way I'd Tear This Building Down" in front of the New Orleans Customs House. The building was the site of the 1874 Battle for Liberty Place, one of the first of many massacres that culminated in the violent overthrow of Reconstruction in Louisiana and the South. According to varying accounts, Johnson was arrested by the police and charged with attempting to incite a riot. His arrest was an expression of the mounting fears of the Bourbon bloc. Throughout the state and the nation, the condemnation of the Bourbon regime had taken on the dimensions of a religious crusade.[2]

The reaction to the Mississippi Flood of 1927 fueled multiple social movements. In Louisiana the tragedy fueled Huey Long's victory over Governor Simpson in 1928. Long relentlessly attacked the New Orleans Bourbon bloc, its bankers, its "lying newspapers," the New Orleans Ring political machine, and Standard Oil, the world's largest oil corporation. According to political scientist V. O. Key, on the eve of the Great Depression the Bourbon bloc, along with its regional and sectoral allies, was unrivaled in the South. Dismal education rates and the lack of public services were an index of "the efficacy of financial oligarchy. . . . Louisiana was a case of arrested political development. Its Populism was repressed with a violence unparalleled in the south, and its neo-Populism was smothered by a potent ruling oligarchy." Many scholars assume that the plantation bloc's political economy and its epistemology were doomed by industrialization, urbanization, and modernization. This is a particularly dangerous assumption as it applies to those trapped in the confines of these regimes. The intersection of distinct racial, class, gender, sectoral, and regional alliances, along with specific social-spatial fixes, ensured that these regimes would be able to reproduce their hegemony into the twentieth and twenty-first centuries.

I will quote several critics of Bourbonism at length in an effort to capture the gravity of the Great Depression in Louisiana and the challenges faced by working-class Blacks in the state. Key's analysis of the interlocking sectors of Louisiana's "oligarchy" is instructive:

> The tears of the people of Louisiana had in reality lasted for generations. While no measuring rod is handy for the precise calibration of the tightness of oligarchies . . . the combinations of ruling powers of Louisiana had maintained a tighter grip on the state since Reconstruction than had like groups in other states. . . . The New Orleans machine bulked large in state politics and had established itself early. In every respect it was an old-fashioned machine effective in its control of the vote and, in turn, itself beholden to the business and financial interests. Add to the mercantile, financial, and shipping interests of New Orleans, the power wielded by the sugar growers, an interest peculiar to Louisiana, then add the cotton planters of the Red River and the Mississippi. The lumber industry constituted perhaps a more powerful bloc than in any other southern state and also enacted a spectacular drama in exploitation apparent even to the most unlettered. Later came oil. Like other industries it hoped to minimize taxation, but in Louisiana state ownership of oil-bearing lands gave petroleum a special interest in politics. Add to all these, the railroads and gas and electrical utilities, and you have elements susceptible of combination into a powerful political bloc.[3]

While in 1949 Key described Bourbonism as an oligopolistic dictatorship comparable to fascist regimes, in 1935 Huey Long's ally Reverend Gerald L. K. Smith compared the state's political economy to feudalism:

> Nine years ago, Louisiana was a feudal state. Until that time it was ruled by the feudal lords in New Orleans and on the big plantations: the cotton kings, lumber kings, rice kings, oil kings, sugar kings, molasses kings, banana kings, etc. . . . The common people in New Orleans were ruled, domineered over and bulldozed by a political organization known as the Old Regulars. The great mass of people in the city and the country worked like slaves or else lived in an isolation that excluded opportunity. Labor unions were very weak and the assembly of workers was prohibited in most industrial centers. It was not uncommon for labor organizers to be beaten or assassinated.[4]

According to Smith, organized corruption pervaded every aspect of daily life in the Bourbon-dominated society:

The great corporations ruled the state and pushed the tax burden onto the poor. The Chambers of Commerce spent money in the North urging industry to come South for cheap labor. Illiteracy was as common as peonage. The commissary plan was in force in mills and on plantations; it kept the workers from receiving cash and left them always in debt to the employer. The highway system was a series of muddy lanes with antique ferries and narrow bridges with high toll charges. Great forests sold for a dollar an acre, to be "slaughtered" and removed with nothing left to enrich the lives of stranded cut-over populations. Families north of New Orleans were forced to pay an $8 toll to cross Lake Pontchartrain into New Orleans and return.[5]

Finally, Smith claimed that the Bourbon regime's public festivals were actually celebrations of cultural domination, organized destitution, and multiple forms of social violence:

> Of course, we had our grand and glorious aristocracy, plantation mansions, the annual Mardi Gras festival, horse races, and those staunch defenders of the old South, the newspapers. Of course, the old Louisiana aristocracy, with its lords, dukes and duchesses, had to be preserved, regardless of what happened to the people. State institutions constituted a disgrace. The insane were strapped, put into stocks and beaten. The penitentiary was an abyss of misery, hunger and graft. . . . Ten thousand aristocrats ruled the state while 2,000,000 common people wallowed in slavery with no representation in the affairs of the state. Half of the children were not in school. Great sections of the adult population could not read or write. Little consideration was given to Negro education. Professional training was available only to the sons of the privileged.[6]

The rebellion led by Long included impoverished white workers and small farmers from the state's northern and southern parishes. Although African Americans had launched repeated movements against Bourbonism over the course of nearly two centuries, by 1928 there were only two thousand Black registered voters, 0.5 percent of the 750,000 Black adults in the state. John Barry notes that voters in flood-ravaged Plaquemines and St. Bernard Parishes chose to ally with Long "and helped him wrest control even of city affairs from the city."[7]

Once in office, the former railroad commissioner from Winfield initiated several programs designed to break the legacy of Bourbon-bloc development planning by providing a new regime of public assets: free school textbooks, free school lunches, adult night schools, public health clinics, increases in oil company payments, and a massive state employment program organized to construct new highways, schools, and hospitals. According to Fairclough, these initiatives were financed through the taxation of oil and gas production:

> Oil derricks pockmarked the countryside, making Louisiana the nation's third biggest producer of crude petroleum and second biggest supplier of natural gas. . . . Indeed, oil helped to make Louisiana the most urbanized of the southern states: it

boosted the growth of Shreveport, Monroe, and Lafayette, fostered Baton Rouge and Lake Charles as ports and industrial centers, and gave the stretch of the Mississippi River between Baton Rouge and New Orleans one of the world's biggest concentrations of refineries and petrochemical plants. Oil became Louisiana's second largest industrial employer, and oil revenues helped the Long dynasty to finance a welfare system that provided services and benefits unmatched in the rest of the South.[8]

Long's biographer T. Harry Williams suggests that he was one of the first white Southern politicians of the twentieth century who did not run on a platform that celebrated the Confederacy while simultaneously demonizing Blacks and the North. When Hiram Evans, the imperial wizard of the national Ku Klux Klan, attacked Long in 1934 for having an "un-American attitude" toward authority, he issued the following rebuke: "Quote me as saying that that Imperial bastard will never set foot in Louisiana, and that when I call him a sonofabitch, I am not using profanity, but am referring to the circumstances of his birth."[9] Barry notes that the "bankers, the lawyers . . . despised him. . . . In the evenings they literally sat around their drawing rooms discussing ways to murder him. He laughed and stripped them of power and forced New Orleans to its knees."[10] The Bourbon bloc and its New Orleans political machine were clear about the threat posed by the reemergence of populism. During one of the several impeachment proceedings conducted against him, Long accused Bourbon-allied Standard Oil of passing out enough proimpeachment bribe money in Baton Rouge to "bum a wet mule." Although equally committed to purchasing allies, Long believed that he was fortunate to have had Bourbon opponents.[11]

Garvey theorized that the Bourbon movement was central to the East St. Louis massacre and that it threatened to transform the national social order. Similarly, Long theorized that the philosophy of Bourbonism manifest during the Great Flood of 1927 threatened both Louisiana and the nation. He argued that President Franklin Roosevelt's administration had adopted the theory and practice of Bourbonism. He was also able to mobilize millions. The populist forces assembled around Long viewed their movement as a national one. His election to the U.S. Senate in 1932 provided a national platform from which to attack the New Deal's support for large banks, its support for an industry-controlled wage and price system, and its failure to directly assist the millions of newly impoverished Americans. In 1934 Senator Long launched the "Share Our Wealth Campaign," whose agenda was designed to address the ravages of the Depression while simultaneously launching his bid for the presidency. Share Our Wealth Clubs spread throughout the South, with twenty-seven thousand distinct clubs with 7.7 million members established by 1935.[12] During a May 1935 congressional hearing, Long articulated the rationale for the movement, indicting the national social order for what he viewed as its celebration of greed and starvation:

We looked upon the year 1929 as the year when too much was produced for the people to consume. We were told, and we believed, that the farmers raised too much cotton and wool for the people to wear and too much food for the people to eat. . . . In fact, these statistics show that in some instances we had from one-third to one-half less than the people needed. . . . Because the people could not buy the things they wanted to eat, and needed to eat. That showed the need for and duty of the Government then and there, to have forced a sharing of our wealth, and a redistribution, and Roosevelt was elected on the pledge to do that very thing. But what was done? Cotton was plowed under the ground. Hogs and cattle were burned by the millions. The same was done to wheat and corn, and farmers were paid starvation money not to raise and not to plant. . . . Less and less was produced, when already there was less produced than the people needed. . . . God forgive those rulers who burned hogs, threw milk in the river, and plowed under cotton while little children cried for meat and milk and something to put on their naked backs![13]

Using both a theory of labor value and the tenets of the Social Gospel movement, Long argued that God is the author of the theory that wealth is collectively produced and therefore must be collectively shared. To do otherwise was both a crime and a sin:

It took the genius of labor and the lives of all Americans to produce the wealth of this land. If any man, or 100 men, wind up with all that has been produced by 120,000,000 people, that does not mean that those 100 men produced the wealth of the country; it means that those 100 men stole, directly or indirectly, what 125,000,000 people produced. . . . Their fortunes came from manipulated finance, control of government, rigging of markets, the spider webs that have grabbed all businesses; they grab the fruits of the land, the conveniences and the luxuries that are intended for 125,000,000 people, and run their healers to our meetings to set up the cry, "We earned it honestly." The Lord says they did no such thing. The voices of our forefathers say they did no such thing. In this land of abundance, they have no right to impose starvation, misery, and pestilence for the purpose of vaunting their own pride and greed.[14]

During a radio address in January 1935, Long specifically indicted the Roosevelt administration for its alliance with the leading capitalists of the age:

President Roosevelt was elected on November 8, 1932. . . . This is January 1935. We are in our third year of the Roosevelt depression, with the conditions growing worse. . . . We must now become awakened! We must know the truth and speak the truth. There is no use to wait three more years. It is not Roosevelt or ruin; it is Roosevelt's ruin. . . . When I saw him spending all his time of ease and recreation with the business partners of Mr. John D. Rockefeller, Jr., with such men as the Astors, etc., maybe I ought to have had better sense than to have believed he would ever break down their big fortunes to give enough to the masses to end poverty—

maybe some will think me weak for ever believing it all, but millions of other people were fooled the same as myself. I was like a drowning man grabbing at a straw, I guess. The face and eyes, the hungry forms of mothers and children, the aching hearts of students denied education were before our eyes, and when Roosevelt promised, we jumped for that ray of hope.[15]

In the same broadcast he outlined the seven points of his "Share Our Wealth" plan for addressing the economic crisis. His sustainable development program focused on redistributing wealth, providing basic necessities, and guaranteeing universal employment, education, old-age pensions, and debt relief:

(1) The fortunes of the multimillionaires and billionaires shall be reduced so that no one person shall own more than a few million dollars to the person. . . . (2) We propose to limit the amount any one man can earn in one year or inherit to $1 million to the person; (3) Now, by limiting the size of the fortunes and incomes of the big men, we will throw into the government Treasury the money and property from which we will care for the millions of people who have nothing; and with this money we will provide a home and the comforts of home, with such common conveniences as radio and automobile, for every family in America, free of debt; (4) We guarantee food and clothing and employment for everyone who should work by shortening the hours of labor to thirty hours per week, maybe less, and to eleven months per year, maybe less; (5) We would provide education at the expense of the states and the United States for every child, not only through grammar school and high school but through to a college and vocational education. . . . We would give every child the right to education and a living at birth; (6) We would give a pension to all persons above sixty years of age in an amount sufficient to support them in comfortable circumstances . . . ; [and] (7) Until we could straighten things out and we can straighten things out in two months under our program—we would grant a moratorium on all debts which people owe that they cannot pay.[16]

According to Williams, the program's principles of sharing the wealth were not new. He suggests that while many analysts have traced its origins to Long's encounters with socialism and populism growing up, Long himself would often claim he learned these principles from the Bible. Yet the evidence suggests that the program was inspired by his study of the Radical Reconstruction era and the Freedman's Bureau in particular.[17]

Although the Long movement tapped deeply into the Blues sustainable development tradition that emerged during Reconstruction, like populists in the past, he also built a statewide political machine that incorporated elements of the Bourbon bloc. As new alliances and schisms emerged, the state entered into another period of instability. His alliance with the Old Regulars (the Choctaw Club) and their leader, New Orleans mayor T. Semmes Walmsley, began in 1932. The machine was promised various infrastructure projects in exchange for delivering votes for Long's candidates and programs. After three failed grand juries and threats of martial law, Long's opponents forced the examination of New Orleans ballot boxes after the 1932 election. Approximately 512 Choctaw Club and Long officials were indicted for miscounting eighteen thousand votes. Prosecutions were halted only after the Long legislature passed a bill changing the standard for determining guilt of voter fraud to willful intent.[18]

Long's attempt to raise taxes and his criticism of Roosevelt led some whites within the crowds that attended his speeches throughout the state to vehemently express their hostility. These conflicts coincided with the setting of two suspicious fires at his New Orleans home. His attacks on Roosevelt were detrimental to both the plantation bloc that benefited from the Agricultural Adjustment Administration's enclosure movement and to the New Orleans Democratic machine, which hoped to benefit from a variety of New Deal programs. In this tense environment, the election of 1932 and two disputed congressional elections led to confrontations between the state's troopers and militia, on the one hand, and local police, local militias, and armed crowds, on the other. Williams details how Long's 1935 threat to increase the taxes levied on the oil industry nearly resulted in an armed coup: "The news struck Baton Rouge right after New Year's Day in 1935: the Standard Oil Company had laid off a thousand employees and had intimated that it would probably have to move its huge refinery to another state. 'Now the blow has fallen,' lamented the *State-Times*, which went on to inform its readers of the reason for the company's decision. It was the five cents a barrel tax on refined oil enacted by the legislature in December, at the demand of 'a mad ruler drunk with power,' whose only purpose was to 'wreak private vengeance' on the company."[19]

White-collar oil workers immediately held a mass meeting in Baton Rouge that included calls to hang the legislature and the governor. The Square Deal movement that emerged soon established chapters throughout the state. The several hundred members of the Baton Rouge chapter garbed themselves in blue shirts and began military training. Members of the state movement included Mayor Walmsley of New Orleans and former governor Parker. After the organization seized a Baton Rouge courthouse in January 1935, Governor Allen, a Long ally, imposed martial law in the capital and in East Baton Rouge Parish. Long charged that Standard Oil had organized an assassination attempt and a coup. Six months after the tax was repealed, Senator Long revealed another assassination plot during a speech before the U.S. Senate. While he was gearing up for a campaign to defeat Roosevelt in the 1936 presidential primaries, national, state, and Bourbon leaders were reportedly planning his political and physical demise. He was shot in the state capitol building on September 8, 1935, by Dr. Carl Weiss, the son-in law of a longtime opponent, and he died two days later.[20]

For several observers of the period, deepening poverty and the Share the Wealth movement pushed Roosevelt to adopt elements of the African American Reconstruction agenda and the Blues agenda that were part of the goals of the Share the Wealth movement. During what is called the "Second New Deal," unemployment, subsistence, labor rights, and housing shortages were directly addressed. However, the mass expulsion of African Americans from the South had already been set in motion and thousands of communities were being starved into nonexistence by the New Deal. Unlike the situation with the First Reconstruction, the Roosevelt administration did not comprehensively address African American voting, civil, and human rights in the South. After Long's demise, his Share the Wealth allies (Gerald K. Smith, Father Charles Coughlin, and pension advocate Francis Townsend) challenged Roosevelt by launching the National Union for Social Justice and running a candidate in the 1936 presidential election. After a poor showing, Smith and Coughlin veered off into forms of dissent more profitable and acceptable to the dominant regional and sectoral blocs: white supremacy, anti-Semitism, anticommunism, and racially restrictive local industrial development campaigns.[21]

Long's legacy continues to be intensely debated. Key argues that the "virtual dictatorship" of Huey Long was an example of the principle that "the longer the period of unrestrained exploitation, the more violent will be the reaction when it comes."[22] The African American reaction to Longism varied according to class, region, and the memory of previous regional alliances. Several Black Share the Wealth clubs were formed in Louisiana and in several northern states. Part of the attraction was the stated position that racism was one of the most powerful tools used to defeat the proposed economic reforms. In response to critics who denounced the encouragement of Black political activity, Long argued that the organization was for all poor people and that you "can't help poor white people without helping Negroes. It has to be that way."[23]

Despite this formally expressed position, racial discrimination was still present in the movement. Although celebrated in the Black press, Long opposed the federal antilynching bill. Fairclough disputes claims that Longism benefited African American communities by citing racially disparate cuts in school construction funding, per pupil spending, and teacher salaries along with his acceptance of the widespread theft by parish school boards of monies designated for dilapidated Black schools in order to build "decent white schools": "Longism built upon Louisiana's well established traditions of political thuggery, electoral chicanery, flagrant disregard for civil liberties, and racial oppression. . . . Huey Long and his supporters . . . did little for black Louisianans. Long himself did not question white supremacy. Equally important, he did not challenge the structure of local political power that kept African Americans in subjugation."[24] The many contradictions embedded in the Long movement posed a threat to working-class Blacks repeatedly caught between the populism and Klan pogroms of schizophrenic white Democrats. Dependent on long-term alliances with southern and northern capitalists, African American middle-class leadership organizations were equally perplexed. For example, when interviewed by the NAACP's future executive director, Roy Wilkins, in 1934, Long stated that his "Every Man a King" program meant "everyman, niggers along with the rest."[25] Thirty years after Long's death, African American civil rights leader Reverend John Henry Scott of Lake Providence, Louisiana, reflected on the contradictions of the movement and its impact on African American political consciousness:

> Personally, I held Huey Long in high esteem because at the time, I didn't have knowledge to understand that the occasional bone he threw to the Negro was just a decoy to keep us from seeing what was really happening . . . so when Huey Long was gunned down in 1935, I couldn't help but shed a few tears. He had seemed a little Christian-like to me when he was encouraging people to "Share the Wealth." I admired his ambition. I admired his climbing high. I admired his nerve in the things that he would say and get away with. . . . And most of all I admired how he took on the upper crust whites and won. He made a lot of Negroes believe that if a change could come for poor whites, a change could come for us too.[26]

In addition to restoring value to the Bourbon bloc's agricultural empire, the New Deal greatly benefited its interests within New Orleans. From the 1700s onward, new levee and drainage projects had been intimately tied to preserving and intensifying class and racial hierarchies. As the city moved northward during the 1920s, the Orleans Levee Board began preparing plans to construct a massive levee that would create two thousand acres of public land adjacent to Lake Pontchartrain. Completed by the federal Works Progress Administration (WPA), the project resulted in land for the construction of a new municipal airport in 1934 and the construction of the New Orleans campus of Louisiana State University (now the University of New Orleans) after World War I. Pierce Lewis notes that the Bourbon bloc also used the WPA project to enrich itself. Half the acreage was "summarily and casually" turned over to private developers to pay the levee district's debts. The subsequent Lake Vista project was a series of planned residential communities, the Lakeshore/Lake Vista and the Lake Terrace/Lake Oaks neighborhoods. Ironically, Mayor Maestri described it as a "poor man's project" designed to create affordable housing. Yet, according to Lewis, corruption was so deeply embedded in the workings of the city that "nobody was really surprised when Lakefront became the wealthiest area in the New Orleans metropolitan area—amid public outcries that the law had been persistently violated during the auctioning of land."[27]

Despite the multiple crises of the age, the Bourbon bloc's grid of cultural representation continued its work of naturalizing hierarchy and oppression. For example, in 1935 one white writer, Perry Young, reviewed Mardi Gras and attempted to imagine the happiness and pride Blacks took in the opportunity to dance with heavy lit torches during Carnival parades:

> In the white parades no element is more essential, or more sincerely part and parcel, than the thousand or fifteen hundred black torchbearers and muleherds, white-shrouded, cowled, that dance before the cars, between them, alongside, toiling, but dancing. They think that they belong, and they earn the affiliation. A dollar apiece they get, or a dollar and a half, the way is long, the asphalt hard, the blazing torches hot and heavy—but they dance. Not for the dollar and a half they do it for being part of the parade—a part that can't be done without—a part that cook and chambermaid, scrubwoman and black mammy, admire as much as madame on the Avenue admires the masks that might be son and heir, lord and master, or fine and chosen true-love.[28]

According to Young, African Americans saw the ritual of Mardi Gras as part of their identity despite the fact that they were trapped in lifelong menial positions within Carnival and within the local economy. This racial representation of the happy servant or slave has deep roots in the region's history.

There is no doubt that the hegemonic Bourbon bloc's very existence was dependent upon economic, political, social, cultural, and psychological alliances with Black individuals and collectives. Family, religious, community, and other bonds also provided numerous links across racial and class boundaries. Yet the happy slave tradition is predicated on a denial of the presence of the Blues intellectual tradition. This mask would have us forget that during this period the Great Flood of 1927, the Great Depression, Bourbonism, racial violence, discrimination, disenfranchisement, and "starve the beast" policies propelled the region's African American community to deepen and expand the Blues sustainable development tradition. The new sites created to preserve body, mind, and soul produced numerous movements that continue to shape the present.

When the Saints Come Marching In

The New Orleans anthem "When the Saints Go Marching In" was originally a spiritual developed during the era of enslavement. Drawn from the biblical Book of Revelations, it honors those "saints" and prophets who dedicated their lives to the realization of justice. It also expresses a profound rejection of the permanence of the oppressive regimes, "the world of trouble," under which African Americans endured. It inextricably links the principles of sustainable development, environmental justice, social justice, and working-class leadership and a recognition of the individual and collective suffering so eloquently expressed in the Spirituals and Blues development traditions. Finally, the song also expresses an anticipation of the fall of repressive regimes and their leaders. This prayer was first played by brass bands as a dirge on the way to the cemetery and was then made "hot" and celebratory for the second line returning from burial. Louis Armstrong's recording of "The Saints" during the 1930s established the song as one of the most popular titles in U.S. history. Although it has remained a popular dance tune for generations, the social theory embedded in the powerful lyrics was typically excluded from Armstrong's repertoire. Many were shocked when the song with the complete Armstrong lyrics was played as a dirge by Bruce Springsteen and his band during the 2006 Jazz and Heritage Festival in New Orleans:

> We are trav'ling in the footsteps
> Of those who've gone before
> But we'll all be reunited (but if we stand reunited)
> On a new and sunlit shore (then a new world is in store)
> O' when the saints go marching in
> When the saints go marching in
> O Lord I want to be in that number
> When the saints go marching in
> And when the sun refuse (begins) to shine (2x and refrain)
> When the moon turns red with blood (2x and refrain)
> On that hallelujah day (2x and refrain)
> O when the trumpet sounds the call (2x and refrain)
> Some say this world of trouble
> Is the only one we need
> But I'm waiting for that morning
> When the new world is revealed
> When the revelation (revolution) comes (2x and refrain)
> When the rich go out and work (2x and refrain)
> When the air is pure and clean
> When our leaders learn to cry
> O Lord I want to be in that number
> When the saints go marching in

**Louis Armstrong, "When the Saints Go Marching In," traditional
spiritual and New Orleans funeral hymn and second line song**

The revival and resurrection of the saints is a key component of the New Orleans-region Blues epistemology. The belief in reassembling and strengthening communities, past and present, has undergirded each New Orleans renaissance. During the Great Depression the national and Bourbon political economies divested numerous communities, families, and individuals in the region. This major transformation of urban and rural African American life in Louisiana was once again accompanied by new Blues cultural movements that provided sustenance, social justice, and social vision.

The total population of New Orleans increased from 458,000 to 494,000 between 1930 and 1940. The African American population increased from approximately 130,000 to 149,000 during the same period. In 1940 the white population of 327,729 included 19,681 foreign born and 65,766 native whites with foreign or mixed parentage. Among those with mixed parentage, Italians were the most numerous, followed by German, Irish, English, Scotch and Scotch-Irish, and Jewish people. As late as the 1930s, no single district in New Orleans was home to one exclusive ethnic or racialized group—contrary to the increased segregation of Blacks throughout urban America.[29]

During the 1930s unemployment intensified in the city and many Black firms and organizations succumbed to the economic pressures of the Great Depression. In the rural areas, the Agricultural Adjustment Act enclosed communities and led to the elimination and expulsion of ten thousand of the seventy-eight thousand African American farm families in the cotton and sugar regions during the 1930s. Fairclough notes that the Bourbon bloc discouraged a mass exodus into the city by erecting a series of blockades that included the use of hunger as a weapon:

> At least half of the South's urban black population depended on state and federal relief. In New Orleans, blacks made up about a third of the population but half of the unemployed and two-thirds of the families on relief. . . . The city set lower relief payments for blacks, and during the recession of 1937–38 the city's Department of Public Welfare began turning black families away, insisting that blacks compose no more than half of relief rolls. In the opinion of Katherine Radke, director of Xavier's school of social work, these restrictions threatened "the slow starvation of a large section of the population."[30]

Although African Americans were steadily engaged in building a wide variety of programs and institutions to address issues of sustainability and survival, according to Claude Jacobs and Andrew Kaslow, economic crisis and state policies exacted a deadly toll:

> By the mid-1930s one estimate is that New Orleans had approximately six hundred black churches. In addition, the neighborhoods were home to other groups: benevolent societies, which provided health care, insurance benefits, and burial for members; social and pleasure clubs; Mardi Gras associations; and secret fraternal orders such as the Masons, Eastern Star, and the Knights of Pythias. The city's black population had one of the highest death rates in the country, with tuberculosis and pneumonia taking a great many lives. Despite this high mortality, between 1920 and 1930 the black population increased twice as fast as the white. Following the closing of the Flint Medical School, growth in the number of black physicians in the city slowed, and cures for many illness continued to depend on the region's wealth of home remedies, *tisanes*, local curers, and neighborhood drugstores that sold a variety of patent medicines as well as "conjure" items.[31]

In terms of political power, during the 1930s, 50 percent of the state's population was African American, yet they accounted for only 1 percent of the registered voters. The "Black and Tan" faction of the moribund Republican Party was increasingly marginalized and its access to federal patronage was completely eliminated by the "Lily White" faction after 1936. Several actions were taken to counter the increasing political marginalization of Black voters. After the white Orleans Parish registrar told a Black audience they did not possess the intelligence to vote, activists formed the Seventh Ward Civic League and the Eighth Ward Civic League in 1927 to train potential voters. This movement expanded to become the citywide Federation of Civic Leagues. However, the excuses used to block the registration of trained voters seemed limitless. NAACP leader A. P. Tureaud noted that a "third grade student holding the position of deputy registrar will insist that a college graduate can not give him a reasonable interpretation of the Constitution."[32]

Although Long and the legislature abolished the poll tax in 1934, registrars continued to tear up Black voter applications at the Orleans Parish office. The registrar claimed that the poll tax didn't "change the status of the nigger one bit. . . . Some of these niggers don't even know when they were born. It's comical as hell, we get a regular picnic out of it. Oh sure, their coming down here all right but we're turning 'em down by the hundreds because they don't qualify." By 1940 the number of registered African American voters in the state declined to less than one thousand persons, of whom four hundred lived in New Orleans.[33]

The Bourbon battle to deny African Americans access to public education also intensified. The city had only one public high school, which served 130,000 Black students. The school board rejected the Rosenwald Fund's effort to create a Black trade school dedicated to the "Negro trades" because it might attract Black students from other parts of the state.[34] This conflict was also manifest in debates over higher education. Dillard University was established in June 1930 through the merger of New Orleans University and Straight College. The Flint-Goodridge Hospital and nursing school were also part of the Dillard complex. Established in the neighborhood of Gentilly, Dillard, its white board of trustees, and its white president represented a tenuous marriage between the Black middle class and northern and Bourbon capital and philanthropy. The model of interracialism and racial uplift advocated by this tripartite alliance remained hostile to much of the Blues development agenda.[35]

Yet it was leadership against human rights abuses that was most needed during this period. In the rural areas of Louisiana brutal attacks occurred. On Christmas Day 1928, in the town of Eros, near Monroe, two white men arrived at the home of a Black man in order to deliver a dog to his landlord. The NAACP's annual report of 1929 concluded that the man was not home but his wife, four daughters, and grandchildren were. "The white men ordered the black women to line up and be killed. The women, thinking the men were jesting, made no effort to escape. They were fired upon. A girl 15 and another [aged] 20 with a baby in her arms were killed. The mother and another of the daughters were wounded." After an extended campaign by the NAACP, a rare event occurred. The two white men were convicted and given sentences of life in prison.[36]

In Washington Parish, north of New Orleans, Jerome Wilson was tried and convicted for defending his family's farm. In 1935, after the Louisiana Supreme Court granted him a new trial, he was seized by eight men from the Washington Parish jail and hammered to death.[37] A year later, in 1936, what has been called "the last mob lynching" in Louisiana occurred in Lincoln Parish. W. C. Williams was hung from a tree and then shot at for ten minutes. Thousands of whites came afterward "hunting for shells, drops of dried blood on leaves, pieces of bark from the oak tree and other souvenirs."[38]

In the New Orleans region a bloody record of unofficial, semiofficial, and official human rights abuses also defamed this decade. Surprisingly, a white New Orleans police officer was convicted of murder. In 1930, while working in a New Orleans restaurant, fourteen-year-old Hattie McCrary was sexually assaulted by a white police officer, Charles Geurand. When she resisted, he shot her. In the African American community, McCrary was viewed as a martyr who "gave her life to save her honor." The NAACP viewed the successful campaign to convict Geurand as part of an overall effort to ensure that "our women are no longer shot down by white brutes for fun." Reflecting the rebirth of collective militancy, a NAACP meeting held at the First Mount Calvary Baptist Church asked participants, "What [will] . . . The Colored Men give to Safeguard the Honor of the Future Mothers?"[39] At roughly the same time, Henry Freeman and Dave Hart were shot and murdered by sheriffs while in their cell at the Gretna jail, just south of New Orleans in Jefferson Parish. Although the decline in semiofficial mob violence was celebrated by some observers as a sign of progress, others suggested that it was replaced by a new era of official violence. In a 1940 editorial, the *Louisiana Weekly* cautioned readers against being too quick to celebrate the decline of the public-spectacle lynching, because a new form had taken root. "The illegal police murders . . . and various mysterious homicides and lynchings have not ceased."[40]

The Mardi Gras Indian and Spiritual Church Renaissance

A central part of the African American response to Bourbonism, the Great Flood of 1927, and the Great Depression was yet another Blues renaissance. Masked in feathers and crowns, hidden by a language unintelligible to the uninitiated, and guarded over by spies, wildmen, warriors, chiefs, queens, axes, and pistols, this renaissance remained invisible outside the region for decades. Similarly, the Spiritual Church movement was protected by a syncretic congregation of African,

Native American, and neighborhood saints. Comprehending the breadth and depth of these two related Blues movements is made exceedingly difficult by intellectual traditions that view African American working-class communities as either irrational, immature, insignificant, or tragically, homogenous. Conversely, the Blues methodology reveals hundreds of practices used by thousands of social architects creating from within working-class communal traditions. When these practices and practitioners are viewed collectively, we are able to discern a Blues cultural revolution occurring during the 1930s from the movements and communal universities created by the Mardi Gras Indians and the Spiritualist churches.

As early as the 1850s, Mardi Gras evolved into an expression of Bourbon hegemony and southern nationalism. A historian of Carnival, Joseph Roach argues that the emerging Bourbon bloc, like the leaders of other plantation blocs, imagined themselves as monarchs. They replaced the randomness of the Creole Mardi Gras with "the regulated entry of Anglo 'royalty.' Rather than opening the streets for willy-nilly mischief, krewe parades occupy them in a style evoking the civic entries of Renaissance princes."[41] This annual celebration and coronation was fundamentally challenged by organic intellectuals from within the African American community. The late nineteenth-century resistance movements of Native American nations inspired the birth of the Mardi Gras Indians among Blacks in New Orleans. Similarly, as Roach notes, during the 1930s the Mardi Gras Indian movement represented a challenge to Bourbon control by asserting autonomy over African American culture, territories, streets, and bodies, if even for a day: "The spectacular appearance of the gangs on the fringes of 'official' carnival enacts a scene of defiant counter-entitlement, and the wide, arm-length gestures of Big Chiefs, Spy Boys (scouts), Flag Boys, and Wildmen claim the space through which they move as if to abrogate the 'law' of manifest destiny on the very borders of a contested and 'lawless' frontier."[42]

The discussion that follows examines the origins of the Mardi Gras Indian tradition and its role as a working-class university, a Blues university that continues to impact social change and cosmology in the region. We begin with the origins of the Mardi Gras Indians, which have been the subject of numerous debates. George Lipsitz argues that one of the ways the Mardi Gras Indians "subvert" the spectacle of Mardi Gras is by "declaring a powerful lineage of their own, one which challenges the legitimacy of Anglo-European domination." To understand the lineage of naming chiefs and queens in New Orleans, Native American traditions must be acknowledged, particularly the history, practices, and intellectual traditions preserved within the Blues system of organic scholarship. African traditions were similarly preserved within the broad Blues folkloric grid.[43]

Due to the prevalence of the Eurocentric thesis that Africans were a people without culture, it took American academic scholarship several centuries to begin the process of acknowledging and systematically investigating African retentions in the United States. The growth of the comparative study of Africa and the

African diaspora revealed that many aspects of official and unofficial carnivals and festivals in the Western Hemisphere could be understood simultaneously as the masked extension of African practices and as the masked celebration of newly indigenous African American, Caribbean, and Latin American communities, their spirituality, and their resistance. These studies also revealed that the practice of designating kings and queens in Africa had been retained throughout the Western Hemisphere. Shane White's essay on festivals in colonial New England is instructive.[44] Recent scholarship has increasingly focused on tracking the preemancipation and postemancipation dispersion of cultural practices and ideologies in the African diaspora. As Michael Smith suggests, this has enabled a reconceptualization of the port of New Orleans and the contributions made by the seamen, travelers, musicians, music, and ideas that have flowed through it:

> There was considerable cross-fertilization and reinforcement of African heritages in Latin American and Caribbean port cities. Before the Cuban Revolution, a strong shipping trade linked the major ports of Cuba-Santiago, Matanzas, and Havana with New Orleans. Members of *Rumberos* groups with whom I spoke in Matanzas and Santiago said they had visited New Orleans and drummed at Mardi Gras Indian practices. And parades I followed in Santiago strikingly resembled those of New Orleans. Some New Orleans Indians were seamen as well and told me they participated in similar cultural practices elsewhere in the West Indies and South America. Furthermore, a gang in Trinidad shared the same name, "Red, White, and Blues," with an early twentieth-century gang in New Orleans, reinforcing the evidence of international cross-cultural fusions.[45]

Another emerging field of scholarship is revisiting the multiple interactions between Blacks and Native Americans. Soon after their arrival in the Louisiana colony, Africans were relating to Native Americans as trading partners, comrades in arms, opponents, spouses, and family members. The French spent decades trying to break alliances between the two groups. By 1781 the Spanish governor banned "masking, the wearing of feathers, gathering at local taverns, and public dancing by negroes" during Carnival. Yet such practices continued and were reinforced by the thousands of Haitians who entered the colony and state, bringing with them a similar tradition. These multiple eighteenth-century influences led Kalamu ya Salaam to conclude,

> Clearly, the historical background suggests that the idea of 'masking Indian' is more than two hundred years old. Rather than an anomaly, the Mardi Gras Indians are in fact simply a manifestation of a much broader and older cultural trend than is often supposed. Rather than unique to New Orleans, Mardi Gras Indians are better understood as representative of the historic merging of African and Native peoples—a merger which happened throughout the so-called "new world" both because of as well as in spite of African enslavement and Native genocide.[46]

Salaam goes on to argue that African American and American cultural identities were uniquely shaped by the original indigenous nations:

> Paradoxically, the high visibility of Native peoples in the USA may be because the armed resistance of Native Americans, especially in the "wild west," had a longer, stronger, and more successful history in the United States than anywhere else in the Americas. Active, armed Native resistance to colonialism continued through the turn of the twentieth century. Additionally, there was a higher incidence of African and Native amalgamation in the United States unlike in the Caribbean where the native populations were generally physically eliminated altogether and thus did not provide the opportunity for amalgamation on the order of Seminoles and Blacks in Florida or Blacks and Natchez in the Louisiana territory. In any case, there is a strong historical basis for Native-American images in the general American cultural consciousness as well as a more pronounced and subversive meaning of these images for African-Americans.[47]

The academic study of African American working-class ontology, epistemology, culture, and social movements—that is, the Blues epistemology—is still in its infancy. Although questions related to the impact of Native American resistance on African American consciousness are still emerging, there are several insights that are critical for future studies. During the 1990s, Big Chief Robert Lee put forth the theory that the Mardi Gras Indians were an extension of the antebellum fugitivism ethic. "It all started when young men ran away from their masters and lived with the Indians as Indians. After slavery, they began to spread out, but they never forgot the tribes they lived with. At first, the Native Americans thought we were making fun of them. But they found out better." Thus the centuries-long Native American movement to retain their communities and their culture became firmly rooted in African American ontologies and epistemologies. According to Roach, by the nineteenth century masking had become an embedded institution: "Some of the earliest accounts of 'masking Indian' at Mardi Gras date from the time of the Seminole Wars which followed the Haitian revolutions of the 1790s and the Louisiana rising of 1811. 'Masking Indian' thus draws upon a violent genealogy of performance that illuminates the continued preoccupation of the Black Codes with slave assembly and recreation."[48]

The theory Lee and Roach put forward contradicts the often accepted narrative that the Mardi Gras Indian tradition was birthed as a result of a performance of Buffalo Bill Cody's Wild West show in December 1884 at the World's Industrial and Cotton Centennial Exposition. Members of the show, including Plains Indian warriors and chiefs, were observed by Black residents on Mardi Gras day and at the numerous performances held during the next several months. These performances were credited with inspiring Becate Batiste to mask in the early 1880s and to create the Creole Wild West tribe. Another "Wild West" show in the city was credited with motivating "Brother" Robert Sam Tillman to mask as a Native American chief and lead the Creole Wild West after 1897, when it moved uptown. It has been argued that Becate's and Tillman's decisions to mask as Plains Indians was an act of imitation unrelated to the historical memory of the centuries-old alliance between African Americans and the indigenous nations of the region, who dressed in a very different manner.[49]

Another way of examining the origins debate is to recognize the movement of the 1880s as a revival of the longer tradition established by Lee and Roach. The decisions by Becate and Tillman to revitalize and expand the masking tradition and to mask as Plains chiefs occurred during the height of the "Indian Wars" and the nadir of the Black Reconstruction movement. After Cody's show left New Orleans, the famous Sioux chief Sitting Bull (Tatanka Iyotanka) joined the forty-city tour. A year before the Colfax Massacre in Louisiana, the chief had captured the imagination of the country. In 1872, "during a battle with U.S. soldiers protecting railroad workers on the Yellowstone River, Sitting Bull led four other warriors out between the lines, sat calmly sharing a pipe with them as bullets buzzed around, carefully reamed the pipe out when they were finished, and then casually walked away." Native American intellectual and physical resistance to social domination during the 1880s contributed to the revitalization of the Blues traditions of honoring Native Americans, resistance, and cultural affirmation. It provided an important "counternarrative" for New Orleans organic intellectuals during a time defined by despair and massacres. Although subject to multiple interpretations and permutations, the Black–Native American alliance against oppression was both a fundamental pillar of the Blues human rights traditions and an expression of Blues internationalism.[50]

The Mardi Gras Indian renaissance can also be viewed as the construction of a new university system that continues into the present period. During the 1920s and 1930s, several Mardi Gras Indian tribes were active: the Creole Wild West, the Yellow Pocahontas, the Wild Squatoolas, the Red, White and Blues, and the Golden Blades. Their working-class membership was also united by occupational, family, organizational, racial, and neighborhood ties: construction workers, longshoremen, truckers, plasterers, dock workers, seamen, former members of the Garvey movement, domestics, Native Americans, religious leaders, musicians, singers, dancers, hustlers, fugitives, and rebels. Participants were also fathers, mothers, wives, brothers, sisters, sons, and daughters. The social network that defined Indian life often included membership in one of the social and pleasure clubs and a series of practice sessions over the course of the year that incorporated second lines, brass bands, neighborhood bars, and the streets. It was also not unusual for a participant to move between tribes and for a tribe to become inactive. This tightly knit Blues grid of overlapping memberships solidified collective social bonds while the year-long preparation of the suits involved sustained individual sacrifices and artistic challenges.[51]

Biographies of the members and their successors reveal a strong network organized around families, apprenticeship, neighborhoods, music, art, religion, and the intergenerational transmission of knowledge. Salaam's interview with one of the legends of the tradition is instructive. Allison Marcel "Tootie" Montana was born on December 16, 1922. He was a member of a Seventh Ward Afro-Creole family that played an instrumental role in the creation and preservation of the tradition. Montana recalled that his family had "Indian blood mixed in." His great-uncle was Becate Batiste, the previously mentioned founder of the Creole Wild West in the 1880s. After the Creole Wild West moved uptown, west of Canal Street, at the turn of the century, the Yellow Pocahontas tribe was formed in the Seventh Ward and was led by Henri Marigny. Montana's father, Alfred Montana Sr., was the Big Chief of the Yellow Pocahontas during the 1930s and 1940s. Although he began his participation in his father's tribe at age seven, as a teenager Montana masked as a skeleton.[52]

The uptown Creole Wild West was originally led by "Brother Tillman" (Robert Sam Tillman) and then, according to several accounts, by his son, "Big Chief Brother Tillman" (Cornelius Tillman), who led the organization during the 1920s and 1930s. A member of the latter's tribe in the 1930s, Paul Longpre, described the younger Tillman as the ultimate practitioner of fugitivism, "a desperado. He was a legend in his time. Never worked for nobody. When it came around Carnival time, he'd go into hiding. If the police knowed where he was, they would go after him, put him in jail 'till after Carnival. Because at Carnival, he was clean treacherous." His death was announced just before Mardi Gras in 1927. The many mourners who attended the funeral were joined by members of the NOPD who wanted to personally confirm his demise. "They put him in the hearse, bringed him to Holt Cemetery. He got out of the casket inside the hearse. . . . On Carnival morning he had on an Indian suit—returned from the dead!"[53]

Another important chief was Daniel Lambert, Big Chief Copperwire. Born on March 30, 1900, he was one of fifteen boys and five girls who grew up in "a house near Melpomene and Rocheblave by the old Melpomene Canal." Although his father was skilled in carpentry and plumbing, desperate conditions forced Lambert to quit school after two years and seek work. He enlisted in the army during World War I and boxed briefly before working for many years as a truck driver. Lambert was a close friend of Big Chief Brother Tillman. A great singer of Indian songs, Lambert founded and led the Wild Squatoolas, whose territory covered much of Uptown and a part of downtown. According to scholar Maurice Martinez, the Wild Squatoolas were "one of the largest Black Indian groups in New Orleans, numbering more than 100 members in costume." Lambert's sister Johanna was known as "Shake Babe" because of her ability to out dance all rivals. A Blues woman, she is also considered to be one of the first Mardi Gras Indian queens. However, in an interview with Martinez, she claimed, "I was more than a queen. I was the first woman chief."[54]

A 2001 *New York Times* obituary chronicled the life of another central figure to emerge during this period. Born in 1915, Big Chief Robbe (longshoreman and Blues man Robert Nathaniel Lee) began sewing costumes for Brother Tillman at the age of eleven. His family's apartment lacked electricity, so he sewed by candlelight, making magnificent suits from feathers and rhinestones. As a young boy he traveled to Indian practice sessions at Lambert's house, where he was taught songs, dances, chants, and ethics. In 1929 he became a Spy Boy for Creole Wild West. Lee also befriended Jazz legend Louis Armstrong and for many years sang the Blues at fish fries and clubs while accompanying himself on the piano. His legendary peacemaking skills helped move the Mardi Gras Indians away from the violent confrontations of the 1930s. Big Chief Robbe eventually became the chief of the Golden Blades, the White Eagles, the Ninth Ward Hunters, and the Golden Arrows and the first Chief of Chiefs of the New Orleans Mardi Gras Indian Council in 1985. Later he was invited to speak at Yale University. After receiving an award from the mayor in the 1990s, Lee recalled that in years past, Indians were not allowed to pass in front of city hall. He refused to migrate in order to record his Blues because "in Ohio or Chicago they didn't have anybody masking as Indian. So why would I want to go?" A similar lifelong commitment was expressed by Joseph "Big Chief Monk" Boudreaux of the Golden Eagles in a 2007 interview. He was a teenager when he started masking with his father, Raymond, who was a member of both the Creole Wild West and the Wild Squa-toolas. "I wouldn't know what to do on Mardi Gras Day if I didn't run with the Indians," Boudreaux explained.[55]

According to Salaam, one of the key elements of the Mardi Gras Indian tradition was the ritualized creation of a new, real and imagined, social Blues order. "The formation of societies with secret codes, a specific hierarchy, plus regulations and obligations to be met serve as a major focus of socialization by organizing and teaching young men how to be responsible members of their community."[56] Thus one of the goals of this tradition is to create, preserve, and structure a community and its imagination through year-long practice sessions involving the performance of specialized music, dance, song, linguistic, history, design, and congregational traditions. According to longtime participant Isaac "Ike" Edwards, masking began on Mardi Gras Day and continued every Satur-day night until St. Joseph's Night.[57] Another important aspect of this movement is the creation of an ongoing discourse on what constitutes culture, beauty, and power. The Mardi Gras Indian complex, institution, and explanatory grid has opened wide avenues for indigenous Black New Orleans to make astounding local, regional, and global connections. Salaam notes that the "desire to pro-duce beauty in dress, beauty in song, and beauty in dance pushes each Indian to and beyond their creative limit. The chiefs in particular tend to be men who take extreme pride in their personal appearance. . . . The multiple levels of masking are sometimes so complex that even the participants are not self-consciously aware of all the possible meanings." For example, Montana recalled a trip to a New York museum during the 1980s that "was shocking" because he saw three-thousand-year-old Aztec and African designs and beadwork that resembled his own. The Mardi Gras Indian university within the Blues tradition enabled many African Americans in the city to repeatedly bring forth new conceptualizations of, and linkages between, Black, Native American, Caribbean, African, and American culture.[58]

In addition to supporting a wide-ranging discourse on Black, U.S., and world aesthetics and history, Mardi Gras Indian rhythms, drumming, songs, chants, and hollers served as a foundation for the intergenerational transmission of knowledge through local music. Charles Siler concludes that they preserved the Bamboula rhythm and dance. "For nearly one hundred and twenty years the Bamboula, associated with Louisiana Congo Square legacy, was kept intact within that tradition." The tradition also informed and manifested itself in the music and lives of numerous New Orleans musicians: Jelly Roll Morton, Louis Armstrong, Danny Barker, Smiley Lewis, Sugarboy Crawford, Guitar Slim, Champion Jack Dupree, Professor Longhair, the Dixie Cups, James Booker, Ernie K-Doe, Mac Rebennack (Dr. John), Fats Domino, the Meters, and the Neville Brothers. It also played a critical role in the development of several genres: brass bands, Blues, Jazz, Rhythm and Blues, Funk, and Hip Hop.[59]

The Mardi Gras Indian language represented a combination of African languages, Native American languages, and several Creoles—French, Spanish, English—and a vocabulary unique to the tradition itself. There are traditional chants sung as refrains, like "Two-Way Pocky Way," and there are chants delivered as boasts without end by the chiefs. Thematically, many of the chants are similar to Yoruba epic poetry, the bad man Blues, gangsta rap, and Old Testament prophecies. They establish a universe where injustices are reconciled by supernatural powers wielded mercilessly. According to Salaam, the "loose translations of some of the chants refer to 'refusing to bow down' and 'kiss my ass.' The militant assertion is more than simply macho-inspired behavior, especially when presented in the guise of Indians, the people who waged armed struggle against colonialism." This assertiveness was present in the 1930s battle chants of the Red, White, and Blues:

> Get out the dishes,
> Tu-way-pa-ka-way!
> Get out the pan,
> Tu-way-pa-ka-way!
> Here comes the Indian man,
> Tu-way-pa-ka-way!
> Oh the Red, White, and Blues!
> Tu-way-pa-ka-way!

> Bravest Indians in all the land,
> Tu-way-pa-ka-way!
> They are on the march today,
> Tu-way-pa-ka-way!
> If you should get in their way,
> Tu-way-pa-ka-way!
> Be prepared to die,
> Tu-way-pa-ka-way![60]

The tradition can also be examined as the progenitor of specific social changes in New Orleans, including a peace movement within the African American community. This insight is part of a larger debate regarding the relationship between cultural movements and social change. For example, during the 1930s Richard Wright asserted that the Blues combined investigation and social vision. In 1937 Wright argued that the hard edge of the Blues actually produces the reverse of the social isolation, nihilism, and narrow social visions that underclass theorists have assigned to impoverished Black communities over the last quarter century. It serves as the foundation for new, transformative social movements: "Lacking the handicaps of false ambition and property, they have access to a wide social vision and a deep social consciousness. They display a greater freedom of initiative in pushing their claims upon civilization than even the petty bourgeoisie. Their organizations show greater strength, adaptability and efficiency than any other group or class in society."[61]

Though the Mardi Gras Indian tradition, festivals, and carnivals could be examined as pure entertainment inconsequential to the larger social and political agenda of African Americans, such a conclusion denies the significance of the educational opportunities provided by the music and the processionals. Musicologist John Miller Chernoff, for example, argues that music and dance in Africa and the African diaspora are often at the center of a wide array of critical social institutions:

> In African societies, music fulfills functions which other societies delegate to different types of institutions. In Africa, musical events provide a focus for personal character and encourage the socialization of indigenous philosophical and moral ideals: respect, patience, flexibility and adaptability, collectedness of mind, composure in the exercise of power and in the toleration of powerlessness, a sense of pluralism, and a sense of balance in the perception of personal character and generational filiation. Music serves a crucial integrative function within many types of institutionalised activities, and musicians perform a complex social role in community occasions. Music and dance sometimes provide the generative dynamics of large and small scale social movements.[62]

Although it is impossible to completely categorize all of Africa in one broad stroke, Chernoff's observations appear to be particularly applicable to African

Americans in the United States. Deeply embedded in the Spiritual and Blues traditions, in all of their many variations, are organic philosophies and philosophers. The boundaries among secular and sacred, entertainment and social activism are so consciously, unconsciously, and consistently blurred as to be irrelevant. Such blurring of boundaries is the foundation of many African American, national, and global institutions. In addition, the Blues tradition has evolved to where it provides fundamental cultural, class, gender, and racial critiques of all American disciplines and institutions. Essentially, it is the hidden foundation of the socially just society that many have fruitlessly searched for since the overthrow of slavery.

Chernoff also asks for a reconsideration of the daily and seasonal practices from which social activism is born. In this vein, carnivals or festivals can be reconsidered as an opportunity for political education and for garnering support for social movements. Roach cites Congolese cosmologist Fu-Kiau Bunseki on the ways in which festivals can become social movements: "Festivals are a way of bringing about change. People are allowed to say not only what they voice in ordinary life but what is going on within their minds, their inner grief, their inner resentments. . . . They carry peace. They carry violence. The masks and the songs can teach or curse. . . . Parades alter truth. Parades see true meaning."[63] During Mardi Gras season, highly organized processionals are deployed when the martial, protonational royal court strategically moves across hostile territories according to a highly developed system of rank. Big Chief Allison "Tootie" Montana provides the following description of how the Mardi Gras Indians move through contested spaces: "You've got first chief, which is Big Chief; First Queen; you've got Second Chief and Second Queen; Third Chief and Third Queen. First, Second, and Third chiefs are supposed to have a queen with them. . . . Your fourth chief is not called fourth chief, he's the Trail Chief. From there on it's just Indians, no title. You also have your Spy Boy, your Flag Boy and your Wild Man. Your Spy Boy is way out front, three blocks in front of the chief. The Flag Boy is one block in front so he can see the Spy Boy up ahead and he can wave his flag to let the chief know what is going on. . . . The Wild Man wearing the horns is there to keep the crowd open and to keep it clear. He's between the Flag Boy and the Chief."[64]

This processional also has a second line composed of neighbors and friends who dance and provide musical accompaniment and both moral and physical support. In later years, Flag Girls, Spy Girls, Lil' Chiefs, and Lil' Queens have become key components of this ritual. Also, the organizational structure, ritualized encounters, language, dances, and signs have migrated to other cities. For example, in Los Angeles the sign for peace, the opening of arms into a raised "V," is still used as a greeting. The interconnectedness of neighborhoods, families, co-workers, friends, art, music, dance, processionals, education, and drilling were pillars of these conscious community-building strategies.

If the Mardi Gras Indian tradition is a movement, what is its agenda besides unifying communities around aesthetic principles? How does the movement assist the community as a whole, which is faced with atomizing attacks launched to preserve Bourbon racial and class hegemony? During the Depression, the use of public space by Blacks was intensely resisted. Additionally, within the Black community, horns, axes, spears, rifles, pistols, battle rhymes, and warriors were all deployed to clear the way on Mardi Gras Day. Smith argues that the ensuing battles between nations were an extension of the Maroon tradition, a subset of the antienclosure principle of fugitivism, which still defines the present-day city: "Traditional social and pleasure clubs . . . abide by all city regulations. . . . The largely underclass black Indian gangs remain outlaws. They remain tribal and anonymous, perform their own music, and march through the city on the back streets, where they come and go as they please. Being the carriers of the Maroon tradition, the black Indians refuse to subject themselves to the humiliation of being monitored and controlled by hostile authorities. To do so would betray the function and historical meaning of their independent spirit."[65]

Berry notes that the territorial conflicts of the 1930s had deep roots in the city's history of racial oppression. The Mardi Gras Indians were key instruments in the centuries-long campaign to open the streets of the city:

> Violence at the hands of whites provoked in some Indians a militant strain, suppressed through normal life, yet freed in Carnival. In the 1850s Irish Channel whites openly terrorized blacks entering the area. By the 1920s, in the same neighborhood, whites dressed as cavemen fought the Indians with spike-studded cypress clubs. Most of the Indians, especially, the uptown tribes, came from impoverished households. Even in the Seventh Ward, with the "self-help" tradition of Creoles, Tootie [sic] Montana recalled "men who'd walk the streets here, real dangerous people. I'm talking about men who'd kill you with their fists. Stone killers. Today people run to the Indians. During them days, people would run away from the Indians."[66]

He goes on to suggest that the Indians were, and are, the key instruments in the unlocking of barriers between the downtown Afro-Creoles and the uptown African Americans: "The emergence of Indian celebrations in the early decades of this century was marked by a dichotomy similar to that between the first jazzmen. A cultural gulf divided the downtown Creole wards and the uptown black neighborhoods. . . . [The] . . . uptown-downtown competition was hardly peaceful."[67]

These battles over the reordering of social-spatial relations culminated in a ritualized face-off at the battlefield, the Claiborne and Poydras Streets battlefield. Montana recalled his father's role in these conflicts:

> They had a Magnolia Bridge, not too far from where the Superdome is now. It was a little pontoon bridge. Any tribe that crossed over that bridge meant they were going

to humbug—they used the word "humbug" to mean fight. But my daddy crossed it every year. My daddy was a son-of-a-gun. And he had people with him like Spy Boy Dolphy and Lil Yam Springham. They used to mask with capes over their shoulders. They didn't wear those big heavy crowns like I wear because they had to run. When they would get ready to meet another tribe they would close that cape, fold their arms, and have their hand right on that gun in their waistband. When they'd meet the enemy they would tell them humba. Humba is a Creole word that means get down, set down, or put down.[68]

According to Martin, Lambert also refused to be denied. "Danny Lambert was a leader of men . . . and a guardian of Black culture. . . . He could have been a military general." According to Berry, the violent clashes between the Indians subsided during the early 1930s. Peace was achieved due to several transformations: an increased police presence, interneighborhood migrations, a decline in inter-Black conflicts, and the demonstration that "the Indians were unafraid-of white police or of each other."[69]

The tradition of Indian celebration and battle is still practiced, in part due to the ethical statement it repeatedly makes to each succeeding generation. A few weeks before he died, Big Chief Robbe reiterated the ethic of caring that is central to the tradition: "I want them to think of me like I think about Brother Tillman. . . . I'm just a good friend who knew the game and didn't mind telling anyone how it goes."[70] For Herreast J. Harrison, wife of Chief Donald Harrison, the Mardi Gras Indian tradition became part of the backbone of modern New Orleans culture because it both celebrated the ancestors and led to the adoption of the ethic of the refusal to "bow down" in a region where Black subservience was part of the official state religion: "I see it as a reconnecting force for me and anyone watching Mardi Gras Indians and knowing anything about what has happened to us as a people will realize that this is the unifying force that reconnects us to the motherland. It's a beautiful thing. The men are very strong. . . . If they are of a belief, there is no force, no institution, or anything that will sway them from what it is they believe."[71]

Finally, in addition to being a Blues university and a Blues cultural and social movement, the Mardi Gras Indian tradition was also a Blues spiritual movement. Lipsitz notes that "dancing in African cultures is a form of public worship, a visual demonstration of belief just as the dance itself is a visual expression of the music. Like their African counterparts (and forebears), Mardi Gras Indians in New Orleans manifest their values about art and life through performance of a 'danced faith.'"[72] Salaam argues that during "dancing, singing, and parading on Mardi Gras day (or at Indian practices), the Mardi Gras Indians often enter the spirit world of possession akin to catching the spirit in Black church services or being ridden by loa in a voodoo service." Montana expressed this danced moment of faith as "spirit, with a feeling. If there are five or six chiefs in my practice, I'll out dance all of them until they are short-winded and they have to run outside looking for air. I'll still be on the dance floor soaking wet. Look like I can't stop. My duty was to out dance every one of them. I'm just dancing with a spirit. I'm not just dancing to be dancing."[73] Practice and parades were always begun with the song "Indian Red."

> Mighty cooty fiyo
> We are Indians, Indians
> Indians of the nation,
> the wild wild creation
> We won't bow down, we won't bow down
> Not on the ground, not on the ground
> Oh, how I love to hear them call my Indian Red.[74]

Several participants recalled that this song and "Take That Flag Down" were mapped out during this period by Eugene Honore, Second Chief of the Yellow Pocahontas and a seven-foot-two-inch-tall Choctaw. According to Montana, "I sing Indian Red like my daddy sang it. It's a hymn, like a spiritual." For Big Chief Donald Harrison of the Guardians of the Flames, "Indian Red was a hymn with a double meaning, sung at the beginning of Mardi Gras day and sung over the body of men lost in battle. . . . Being an Indian is a religious experience, believe me. You have to see the spirit that these cats [have] on Mardi Gras day[—]it's completely spiritual. The earliest Mardi Gras Indian that I know of came from the Sanctified Church and the Sanctified Church is the closest to Africa."[75]

The Spiritual Church Renaissance

Several goals are central to the Blues development tradition: participatory democracy, economic justice, cultural autonomy, building sustainable working-class communities, and recognizing important works regardless of a person's gender, age, ability, religion, ethnicity, race, and nationality. As discussed previously, support for this agenda could emerge in a limitless number of organizational forms. The Spirit Houses and Spiritual Churches of New Orleans were built on the syncretic blending of African, Native American, Catholic, Baptist, Pentecostal, and Spiritualist traditions. They express many components of the Blues tradition. Siler notes that understanding religious syncretism in Louisiana is a complex undertaking:

> Throughout the state there are "Spirit Houses" that represent the diversity of West African survivals that are considered a part of so-called mainstream traditions. We also find the mixing of religious practices such as Yoruba and Haitian VooDoo with Catholicism. The mixing of African religions with those imposed by slave masters

grew out of the need of the enslaved for survival. This blending of religions (which included selecting "saints" to represent African gods) provided a disguise for the continuation of the African's own belief systems. Information regarding this practice is supported by research in Africa, as noted by Dr. John Mbiti, who indicated that Africans tended to convert the missionary and conquering religions on that continent by blending them with traditional beliefs.[76]

Jacobs and Kaslow suggest that there are several contending schools of thought on the origins of the Spiritual Church in New Orleans. One genealogy emphasizes an African lineage, Voodoo Marie Laveau, and the blending of African, Protestant, and Catholic religions in Louisiana and the Western Hemisphere. Another school of thought privileges the European tradition of Spiritualists and the "prophets, healers, mediums, advisors and circles" associated with it. A third narrative focuses on a still evolving understanding of the works of Reverend Mother Leafy Anderson. There are several versions of the story of Anderson's arrival in New Orleans. Jacobs and Kaslow claim that she resided in Chicago and, beginning in 1913, founded several Spiritualist churches and missions. By 1920 institutions organized under her Eternal Life Christian Spiritualist Association could be found in Little Rock, Memphis, Pensacola, Biloxi, Houston, and New Orleans. Another history was assembled by African American sociologists St. Clair Drake, Horace Clayton, and E. Franklin Frazier, who conclude that Anderson brought this tradition from New Orleans to Chicago. In 1931 anthropologist Zora Neale Hurston wrote an article, "Hoodoo in America," that placed the date of the founding of the New Orleans congregation at 1918. Jacobs and Kaslow place Anderson's arrival in the city in 1920. It is also claimed that Mother Anderson's work centered on the downtown Black Creole neighborhoods and that her success led to the construction of two major churches, the Holy Aid and Comfort Church and the Helping Hand Church, before her ministry moved uptown. Conversely, it is also suggested that she owned a house and had several churches in Uptown before moving to New Orleans and that this was her initial base of operation.[77]

What is known is that Anderson's ministry developed rapidly in Uptown among Blacks and some whites, particularly Italians. Her organization received a state charter in 1920, but only after she was harassed, surveilled, and jailed by authorities who suspected her of "practicing hoodoo, witchcraft, or fortunetelling." Several hundred Blacks and whites attended her Amelia Street Church and thousands more attended the Eternal Life Christian Spiritualist Association's 1926 convention in New Orleans. She concluded the gathering by introducing several "spirit guides" into the religious movement: Father Jones (Father John), White Hawk, the Virgin Mary, and Black Hawk.[78]

Although Anderson died in December 1927, other African American women took up the leadership of the movement. Mother Catherine Seals was born in

Kentucky in 1887. At the age of sixteen, while working as a domestic in New Orleans, she was paralyzed by a stroke. "After a white healer refused to pray for her because she was black, she received a vision" and her health improved. In the Lower Ninth Ward she built the Holy Manger beginning in 1922, which was then supplanted by the larger Temple of the Innocent Blood in 1929. This "village" became the center of the Spiritual movement in the city. Her funeral in 1930 was attended by several thousand mourners.[79]

Mother C. J. Hyde soon led the rapidly growing movement with her protégée Mother Estelle Keller-Morris (aka Mother Crosier). By the 1930s approximately one hundred of the six hundred African American churches in the city were part of the Spiritual Church movement. According to Archbishop E. J. Johnson, at the height of the Great Depression they were drawing many members from other denominations:

> They was migrating out of them [other] churches like mad. You see, the Spiritual church in 1927, '30, '35, '37, if you didn't get there let's say ahead of time, you weren't going to get in. No kind of way! They didn't have too many big churches [buildings]. But the folk used to have meetings in halls, any kind of hall, big places. They would have tables and boxes, and make altars. People saw something in the Spiritual church and used to have some mighty good readers at that time. Prophets! And a lot of good healing. Folk saw Christ in these people, more than they did in those other churches.[80]

Several foundations of the Blues were present in the Spiritual Church and other major religious movements during the Depression, such as Father Divine's International Peace Mission movement and Charles "Daddy" Grace's United House of Prayer for All People. There was an intense ethic of caring and empathy for the Black working class, along with other oppressed and impoverished people, who were treated by the larger society as if they were disposable. This sustainable development ethic helped many of those abandoned by the state and capital by promoting multiple forms of class unity and action. The motto of Mother Anderson's congregation was "Helping One Another." Services held by Anderson and Mother Crosier were organized around praying for the sick and troubled, delivering messages of prophecy and hope for individuals, and healing the afflicted. Mother Seals was known as a "miracle worker." A complex soon developed composed of hundreds of ministers, reverend mothers, prophets, healers, advisors, and ritual workers engaged in daily intercessions. The troubled traveled from throughout the United States and other countries to seek out New Orleans healers. Some advisors were thought to have the ability to change the outcome of legal cases along with the minds of prosecutors and judges. They were engaged in trying to realign the human world and divine intervention.[81]

Community building and the visioning of a democratic community life were also among the Blues ethics present in the Spiritual churches. During ser-

vices congregants could contribute prayers, songs, testimonies, and dance. All
the members were equally capable of being "hit" by various spirits during the
service. During the several evening services held each week, members shared
messages, news, songs, and meals with each other and with visitors. Jacobs and
Kaslow argue that people attended "not because Spiritual people have 'turned
away from world' or are averse to secular activities as are members of Holiness
dominations. Rather, large numbers of older female members, limited economic resources, and the spirit of fellowship in the congregation help build
attendance."[82]

Another Blues ethic present was the democratic participation of and leadership by working-class Black women. By 1936 Reverend Thomas Watson and
other leaders moved to organize the blossoming movement by establishing the
Divine Spiritualist Churches of the Southwest (the Southwest Association). "No
longer was Jesus unnamed, as in Leafy Anderson's ELCSA or was Christianity
only implicit, as in Mother Crosier. . . . Boldly, Reverend Watson had undertaken both the task of organizing independent church leaders, as well as the first
known step to try to legitimate the churches in the eyes of the New Orleans religious establishment. . . . For the first time in New Orleans, there is reported use
of the term 'bishop' for officers who were elected to head the new organization."[83]

The Southwest Association adopted mainstream Christian organizational
forms, discourse, and the priestly tradition, in part to limit growing efforts
in several states to prosecute church leaders and members for the "crimes" of
fortunetelling and Vodou. Within the newly organized Spiritualist tradition
attempts were made to confine women to several roles: psychics, mediums,
healers, fortunetellers, and so on. This effort caused several types of internal
conflicts. Board member Mamie Reason, the first treasurer of the New Orleans
Division of the UNIA, opted to retain autonomous control over her church.
When Reverend Watson attempted to complete the legitimation process by de-
nying the right of women to become bishops, Bishop Bessie Johnson broke with
the organization. She and Reason formed a new association. As other women
leaders joined, the number of women bishops grew rapidly.[84]

Although women often held powerful positions and sacred roles in many
religions, they were increasingly marginalized by the spread of monotheistic
religions, capitalism, and colonialism. Numerous African religions recognized
women leaders based on their gender, their lineage, or their special individual
gifts. While aspects of these practices were preserved in the bush arbors and
ring shouts during slavery, the nineteenth and twentieth centuries witnessed
organized campaigns by white and Black denominations to severely limit the
religious leadership of Black women. At least three factors contributed to the
survival of the tradition of Black women's leadership. First, there were African
retentions such as matrilineal descent, religious leadership as a family vocation,
and the exalted status given to those who could heal, deliver prophecy, have

visions, and speak to the spirits and ancestors regardless of gender. Second, strong bonds of class and racial solidarity had emerged from several centuries of community campaigns that often were organized by women. Third, historically strong bonds between women emerged from their efforts to create or maintain spaces of cultural, economic, and social autonomy. There was a confluence of all three factors in New Orleans's Spiritual churches.

The theological foundations of the Spiritual Church continued the tradition of conferring sainthood upon distinguished working-class Blacks. As discussed in an earlier chapter, St. Malo received such a designation in the early eighteenth century. In an interview conducted during the 1980s, Archbishop E. J. Johnson provided the following explanation of this democratic tradition:

> When you ask for help you don't know who it's going to be. Could be your grand-mama, grandpa, your parents, anybody. Sometimes those people come and help you too. Somebody that has gone that has cared for you, loved you in life. They help you when they pass. . . . Moses would be considered a saint, although he wasn't canonized by the Catholic church. But anybody that's serving God in any way, they're known as saints. . . . We honor the saints. As they say, so a man lives, so he dies. Well what saints was accustomed to doing in life, that's what people expect them to do after they pass.[85]

Several key saints, each with his or her own altars and feasts, are often relied upon to guide people through the world: Father John or Father Jones heals, Queen Esther provides support for courageous women, Uncle Bucket provides financial blessings, and St. Patrick defeats enemies. Another important guide, Black Hawk, was introduced by Mother Anderson in 1926. A leader and warrior, Chief Black Hawk (1767–1837) engaged in a fifty-year battle against colonialism in Illinois, Iowa, Wisconsin, and Canada. His peoples lost fifteen million acres and suffered a massacre of hundreds during the Black Hawk War of 1832. In the Spiritual churches, songs, prayers, and ceremonies are dedicated to Black Hawk to seek his guidance and protection for oppressed people. In other Afro-Catholic syncretic religions in the Western Hemisphere, St. Michael has been given the role of the defender against oppression and wickedness. According to Stephen Wehmeyer, some Spiritual churches added another Native American saint named Yellow Jacket who would guide and protect those who stole from the rich in order to give to the poor. Though not universally present in all Spiritual churches, the Black Hawk saint was widespread. Jacobs and Kaslow describe a 1980s-era altar:

> On an Indian altar in one of the major churches in the city, there is another clue to the meaning of Black Hawk. Here, in addition to the representation of the Indian spirit and the statue of St. Michael, there is also a picture of the late Dr. Martin Luther King. Together, these three figures communicate a message of militancy.

Although church members are not black nationalists, some have been active over the years in voluntary civil rights organizations, including the NAACP and the local voters' league. In addition, some churches express racial pride by using black crucifixes and statues of black saints. Here, in St. Michael, the guardian of Israel, Black Hawk, the defender of the Indian nation, and Dr. Martin Luther King, are . . . the figures of three champions of oppressed races, symbols of strength and victory.[86]

The Spiritual Church movement also contributed to the evolution of Black political activism. In 1931, during the Depression, Mother Kate Francis led a barefoot march calling for jobs. Mother Estelle Keller-Morris became a noted civic leader, a board member of the NAACP, and a participant in the interdenominational support for the People's Defense League in the 1940s.[87] The scholarship on the Spiritual churches is still evolving. The wide cultural contribution of this movement, its relation to other religious institutions, and its impact on other social movements is yet to be fully comprehended. What is clear is that democracy and social justice are both imagined and planned within this institution. The critical importance of Depression-era African American movements such as the Mardi Gras Indians and the Spiritual Church has yet to be fully incorporated into the body of African American Studies, much less U.S. academic research. The Blues epistemology offers the only method capable of understanding the intersection of Black working-class consciousness, regional identity, social vision, social movements, development thought, and planning.

Another aspect of the expansion of the Blues epistemology during this period was the Zydeco renaissance. In southwestern Louisiana, Afro-Creole musician Amédé Ardoin used his accordion to inject the Blues into Creole and Cajun music. According to Michael Tisserand, "He brought the blues into Cajun like nobody else before him. His impassioned vocals and syncopated accordion work defined the Creole style and pointed the way to zydeco." Known for Blues waltzes and Blues sung in Creole, Ardoin was also familiar with African religious and dance music. At Cajun venues it was not unusual to find Cajun women openly crying when he played or for him to be threatened and chased because of this. He stopped playing for years after being chased and beaten. Like another musical genius, Buddy Bolden, he died in a Louisiana state asylum. One of his most powerful songs, "Les blues de la prison," concerned Bourbon and Cajun justice:

> O parti à la prison un condamné
> La balance de mes jours
> Ma pauvre maman s'ennuie autant
> et elle peut pas me rejoinder
> O jusqu' à, yaïe, O
> la porte de la prison fermée sur moi
> Ils ont oublié la clef.

Je crois ils l'ont jetée,
Ils vont jamais la retrouver encore

Oh, I'm going to prison condemned
For the rest of my days,
Oh, for the rest of my days
My poor mother misses me so
and she can't come to me.
Oh, right up to, oh
the prison door that closed me in
They've forgotten the key,
I think they must have thrown it away
And they'll never find it again.[88]

Finally, during this period older organizations were transformed and new so-cial movements emerged. The influence of philanthropic alliances and African American middle-class leadership began to dissipate as the Depression deep-ened. The NAACP's membership declined dramatically and numerous branches expired. Membership in the New Orleans branch fell from 505 in 1928 to 74 in 1930 before rising to 750 members by 1934. Lee Sartain suggests that the core membership of the organization belonged to occupational, class, and social net-works that enabled a degree of economic independence: teachers, physicians, nurses, morticians, insurance and realty executives, professional beauticians, preachers, classical musicians, and so on. The middle-class-dominated New Orleans branch was also defined by family ties and by multiple memberships in a select number of religious, fraternal, economic, civic, and political organi-zations or firms: the Colored Knights of Pythias and the Star of Calanthe, the Knights of Peter Claver and its Ladies Auxiliary, the Prince Hall Masons and the Eastern Star, the Young Men's Christian Association and the Young Women's Christian Association, the Louisiana Industrial Insurance Company, the Stan-dard Industrial Life Insurance Company, the Unity Industrial Life Insurance Company, the *Louisiana Weekly*, Flint-Goodridge Hospital, the Urban League, the Federation of Civic Leagues, and the Republican Party.[89] Reportedly, by 1933, during the height of the Depression, the New Orleans branch of the NAACP had become so passive that the national office assumed it had expired. Despite their frailty as a group, the elite fought to maintain their leadership of the African American community while simultaneously maintaining its social and physi-cal distance from the Black working class. Political scientist Ralph Bunche and other researchers associated with Gunnar Myrdal's *American Dilemma* project described the branch as a "closed corporation" that solely represented the Black upper classes. One of the members of the executive committee interviewed during the Myrdal project argued that the "downtown group has a traditional culture which the 'uptown' group cannot understand." Another member noted that when "leadership comes from uptown it is bizarre as only it can be from an uncultured group." Still another leader argued that "the 'downtown' people came in close contact with the European old-world culture; the quadroon mistresses mingled with the best European whites. Poor whites are just as crude as the poorest, darkest and most-kinky-headed Negroes 'uptown.'"[90]

The growth of the New Orleans branch in the mid-1930s was predicated on the skills of the national NAACP field secretary Daisy Lampkins. Although many elites feared the effects of admitting new members, women in Louisiana and across the nation flowed into the organization. The legal system rarely protected Black working-class and middle-class women from many instances of sexual assaults, rape, sexual exploitation, and police beatings or from the major and minor insults that they experienced daily. The commonality of segregation enabled cross-class alliances. However, according to Sartain, the agenda set by the NAACP and other elite organizations avoided many of the issues related to working-class starvation while claiming special rights for their families. Using a classic uplift argument, they claimed that white attacks were undermining the stability and authority of middle-class Black patriarchal families, the greatest ally of white elites, and therefore only served to foster working-class Black immorality and violence:

> Women who were members of the NAACP directed their energies and resources into a battle against segregation that would reinforce middle-class values and prevailing gender perceptions, such as the patriarch-led family. Local NAACP campaigns in Louisiana tended to reinforce this point. . . . White segregationists tended to defend lynching by arguing that it was a means to protect white feminine purity from the savagery of black men. The antilynching campaign at the local level . . . deliberately reversed this notion. The idea that black men were lynched simply for sexual transgression was a falsehood debunked early on by the national office, and local cases in Louisiana turned the antilynching issue into one of protecting black men, their wives, and the family unit from white aggression and persecution.[91]

The organization also participated in legal battles. Human rights abuses were portrayed as attacks on the Black family, Black women, and Black manhood. Hattie McCrary was depicted as a teenaged martyr who "gave her life to save her honor." The NAACP viewed the successful campaign to convict McCrary's attacker Geurand as part of an overall effort to ensure "our women are no longer shot down by white brutes for fun."[92]

In the northeast Delta and in the sugar parishes, hundreds of African Americans and some whites joined the communist-allied Sharecroppers Union (SCU). After a cotton-pickers' strike in Lowndes County, Alabama, was violently suppressed in 1935, the union established locals in Louisiana and moved its headquarters to New Orleans in 1936. Greta de Jong suggests that African Americans "used the union to attack inequalities and injustices that were the foundations of the white supremacist social order" and "embraced the union as an ally in their ongoing fight to gain fair compensation for their labor, adequate education for their children, a chance to participate politically, and protection from violence." In other words, the organization was evaluated based on its support for the Blues epistemology and social agenda, which predated the union's arrival.[93]

In order to secure protection for open organizing, the predominantly white staff of the majority-Black SCU merged the organization with the all-white National Farmers Union (NFU) in 1937. The NFU granted a charter to the renamed SCU, the Louisiana Farmers' Union (LFU). The tenants, sharecroppers, and wage laborers in the organization sought the transformation of African American rural life by attempting to achieve reforms that are still being actively resisted in the region. To improve the plight of women the organization demanded "equal pay for equal work, higher wages for domestic workers, free medical attention for pregnant women, and a maternity insurance system." Other goals included fair crop settlements, legal assistance, increased school funding, longer school terms, free school transportation, loans to support the purchase of farms, access to federal farm programs, agricultural extension assistance, credit, quality housing, medical care, equal enforcement of the law, and guarantees of the right to organize. By the late 1930s some of the membership and staff began to advocate the armed self-defense of their persons, families, and communities. Planters and state officials increasingly feared both the increased militancy of the union and the arrival of federal investigators. The LFU grew to three thousand members by 1940 despite numerous encounters with planter-organized violence, evictions, and imprisonment, along with the withholding of aid and the seizure of equipment by the federal officials working within the Resettlement Administration.[94]

Others in the region consulted the spiritual world to address human rights abuses. A front-page article in the January 20, 1940, edition of the *Louisiana Weekly* reported that a St. Bernard Parish sheriff who had killed several Black men had suddenly been hospitalized in New Orleans:

> Information from Hotel Dieu says that [Sheriff] Stander is resting nicely, but cannot have any visitors. Rumors have it that there is little hope for him. "In secret places, Deep in St. Bernard Parish, the Voodoo queens are holding seances on Stander; they have delivered Oscar Smith [the latest victim] out of the spiritual world upon him. He is going to haunt Stander all of his entire life," a person close to the "Voodoo gods" emphatically stated, refusing to give her name. Rumors say that several dead, black cats with red lemons in their mouths were found under Stander's house, however, this could not be verified.[95]

On the eve of World War II, the New Orleans Bourbon bloc was faced with multiple challenges. In addition to the growth of African American working-class movements, Longism was the official ideology of many working-class whites and small farmers. Additionally, labor unions viewed the Roosevelt regime as a defender of workplace rights, organizing, and fair wages. Many African Americans saw the New Deal government as an advance in the fight for civil rights, economic security, and political power and subsidies for the family budgets of the dispossessed. Yet the federal government was simultaneously subsidizing all the racial, class, and gender hierarchies associated with Bourbon institutions, the cotton enclosure, the state of Louisiana, and the city of New Orleans. Although federal intervention would intensify during World War II, the Bourbon bloc viewed the Roosevelt administration as an ally that would, in the final analysis, defend and valorize its regime and those of the other plantation blocs of the South.

CHAPTER 5

The Double V Generation and the Blues Agenda, 1940–1965

At the height of the war against tyranny overseas and the mobilization of what has been referred to as the "greatest generation," wartime labor shortages exposed domestic social fissures in terms of race, class, and gender that continue to haunt New Orleans, Louisiana, and the United States.[1] During World War II the Bourbon bloc sought to profit from the war mobilization while simultaneously preserving its racial regime. This work was greatly assisted by the elimination of large sections of Black, rural, working-class communities through President Franklin Roosevelt's Agricultural Adjustment Act (1935). Those African Americans who found their way to New Orleans or to the centers of war production were typically denied both employment and relief. Similar to the present, tens of thousands of African Americans were effectively expelled from the state through discriminatory employment practices, an educational-spending blockade, the manipulation of racially segregated housing markets, governmental budget cuts, hunger, and officially sanctioned violence and terror. Yet those who stayed launched new mobilizations that fundamentally transformed the city, region, state, and nation.

Wartime employment discrimination and violence were used to preserve the servile economy and racial hierarchy by committing massive thefts of employment opportunities, income, family stability, community stability, land, and other resources. This can be seen first through the terror that continued to reign in rural areas. Rural expulsion, migration to the West and North, and wartime labor demands rapidly depleted the ranks of agricultural labor and created a severe labor shortage. In the cotton and sugar parishes, force was used to prevent tenants from leaving. The *Louisiana Weekly* reported that Blacks were "picked off the Streets" and forced into the fields, while the state Department of Agriculture forbade farmworkers from leaving their home parishes. Second, despite the labor shortage, occupational segregation was maintained. Blacks were denied employment in several of the rapidly expanding war industries in Louisiana: weapons production, oil drilling and refining, shipyards, supply depots, and so on. Third, local governments and employers conspired to undermine African American education, training, hiring, and occupational advancement. The state refused to train Blacks as welders, and the Delta Shipyards in New Orleans refused to follow federal directives to hire skilled Blacks.[2] The mere request for a school to train Black welders in New Iberia resulted in local deputies beating NAACP leaders and dumping them on the road outside of town in May 1944. FBI agents sent to investigate these kidnappings and expulsions were told by the local sheriff that Blacks had become too demanding and that it "seems about time that several Negroes resist arrest. . . . Then they will quiet down for a while." The sheriff was referring to the historic practice of killing innocent and unarmed Blacks in order to pacify the larger community. For successfully violating African American civil and human rights, the sheriff was elected vice president of the Louisiana Sheriff's Association and his deputies were cleared by the federal grand jury impaneled in New Orleans.[3]

In order to maintain the racial division of labor during this transformational period, violence was used to silence both advocates of Black employment and Black workers themselves. In February 1944 several Black longshoremen were beaten on the docks of New Orleans by their white coworkers as state troopers watched without intervening. As a result, two thousand Black shipyard workers walked off the job. When they were hired, Blacks were typically confined to menial jobs or to the most dangerous and deadly jobs available. Black occupational advancement was so anathema to the Bourbon bloc and its allies throughout the state that the leaders of Shreveport refused the offer of $67,000 in federal funds for a health center for whites because it would require them to accept a hiring quota of twelve Blacks per hundred workers. Then as now, affirmative action for Blacks in segregated occupations was often viewed as antiwhite violence. Along with many white workers and business owners, the mayor of Shreveport refused to let the federal government "cram the Negro down our throats."[4]

The Bourbon impoverishment institutions also adapted to social changes wrought by the Depression and the war. Victims of employment discrimination and other forms of bias were forced onto relief in New Orleans. African Americans made up a third of the city's total population but only half of the eleven thousand families on relief. They also represented the overwhelming majority of the six thousand families denied relief following massive cuts in the city's budget in 1942.[5]

Simultaneously, throughout the rural South, regional plantation blocs and their northern financial and industrial allies organized to undermine the most progressive rural components of the New Deal. Farm Security Administration programs designed to support higher agricultural wages and to provide home, equipment, and farm loans to tenants and sharecroppers were targeted in particular. After several rounds of budget cuts and program mergers, the Farm Security Administration was replaced by the Farmers Home Administration in

1946 and the Bourbon restoration was signaled once again by mass starvation. Greta de Jong notes that the "displacement of plantation workers continued with little to cushion the effect, relegating many people to the status of seasonal wage laborers forced to work for low pay during the harvest seasons and dependent on public welfare services at other times of the year." The increasing impoverishment of Louisiana farmworkers coincided with a decline in contributions from liberals to the Farm Workers Union, the flight of its members to urban centers, and the rapid growth of the anticommunist movement. In response to this campaign, many union members sought war works employment in Texas and California. Political repression, a financial crisis, and declining membership led to the union's charter being revoked in December 1941.[6]

Finally, war mobilization brought tens of thousands of troops into Louisiana from all over the South and the United States. Thousands of African American soldiers came to the state's training camps. Many of those who arrived were already aware of the goals of the national "Double V" movement launched within the African American community: victory against fascism abroad and at home. What these soldiers experienced was the latter, as segregation and racial violence intensified. A conflict in Alexandria on January 10, 1942, resulted in the shooting of thirteen African Americans: a civilian woman and twelve soldiers. Later, when Raymond Carr, a Black military police officer, was killed by a state trooper in Alexandria for no reason, a state jury refused to indict the trooper and the U.S. Department of Justice refused to pursue the case. After Black soldiers charged with raping a white waitress in Grant Parish were sentenced to death, President Roosevelt intervened and commuted their sentences to life imprisonment. In the midst of these and other conflicts, U.S. senator John Overton attempted to allay white fears of the rising tide of resistance: "We do all that we can to avoid any racial antagonism. In order to do this we let the negroes understand—and they do understand—that here in Louisiana we have a white man's government, run by white men. Here in Louisiana we permit neither social or political equality."[7] Conditions within New Orleans were defined by rapid population growth, continued destitution, urban redevelopment, and new forms of segregation. Between 1940 and 1950, the population of the city grew from 494,000 to 570,000. The African American population was roughly 182,000 by the end of the decade, or 31 percent of the total population. While the city's white population grew by 47,311 (14 percent), the Black population grew by 33,597 (23 percent). Wartime production and widespread unemployment, combined with agricultural displacement, fueled the increase in the African American population.[8]

The Blues ethic of caring and sharing was central to African American survival during the Depression and the war. This ethical tradition can also be conceived of as the "gumbo ethic" or philosophy. Individuals and families survived by contributing what they could to the collective pot. Born in 1924, noted drum-

mer Earl Palmer described the workings of this philosophy that pervaded much
of the Black community in general and his neighborhood of Tremé in particular:

> It's not that my mother didn't make no money—she sent money home. But you
> see, we were such that a whole unit within our family might not be working. If my
> Uncle Freddy was out of work, his family moved in and we all bunked together. One
> time there must have been five different branches of the family staying together:
> my aunts and uncles and their children and my grandparents and my mama and
> me. My mama raised three children that wasn't even related to us! We always took
> people in, man, it didn't matter, it was so cheap to live. You got used to living cheap
> like that, where you always wanted something. It was part of life.
>
> That's pretty poor when you're getting half rice, half bread, and half beans, but
> I was never hungry. In New Orleans your mama could always go to a family down
> the street and say, "Listen, we ain't got nothing now, take care of my baby, feed my
> baby." You'd go over there and eat and didn't feel anything wrong with it. Their child
> might do the same next week. They themselves might do the same next week![9]

During this period the Bourbon bloc continued to blockade educational opportunities for African American youth. By 1940, despite increases in school
funding, 60 percent of the Black children in the state attended schools built
with the assistance of northern philanthropists. Communities responded by
pushing for improved facilities and for an increased number of high schools and
teachers. Lee Sartain notes that increasing the number of Black high schools was
a priority, in part because there were so few in the state:

> School buildings were old and made of wood, such as the dilapidated two-room
> structure in St. Charles Parish. In East Carroll Parish there were no libraries in the
> black's schools and no buses for students to get to classes. Furthermore, students
> did not have access to many of the essentials for proper teaching, such as black-
> boards, tables, and schoolbooks, which if available were often second-hand from
> white schools. Progression on to higher school grades was often only possible in
> the cities and larger towns. Indeed in twelve Louisiana parishes, even as late as 1956,
> there were no high schools for black students at all. In addition rural areas had their
> school terms limited by the harvest season and, for similar reason, [students] were
> primarily taught an industrial syllabus. However, Louisiana's cities suffered from
> comparable problems. In Shreveport some schools had no electricity and could not
> accommodate all their students, so church buildings were used to house them.[10]

Considered the oldest Black urban neighborhood in the United States, Tremé
during the 1930s and 1940s differed from some of the nearby Seventh Ward
communities. According to Tony Scherman, the "Seventh Ward was the stronghold of the descendants of the old *gens de couleur libre*, antebellum New Orleans' French-Speaking, Catholic Creoles of color. The Seventh was staid and
genteel, its residents fighting a rearguard battle for their ebbing prestige. 'In

the Seventh Ward,' says restaurateur Leah Chase, who grew up there, 'everyone thought they were the Pope.'" Palmer remembered that in Tremé there was more demographic heterogeneity:

And there was people like the Spadonis—the family was white.... but they were raised right there on St. Ann between Galvez and Johnson and they were part of our neighborhood. They was a little mixed but they were mostly white. Everybody knew it, nobody cared. Because they didn't act white, they didn't want to be white, they were uncomfortable in the white culture. Johnny Spadoni would work a white job to take care of his family, but he'd never go to Bourbon Street and drink. He drank at the bar across the street. The Spadonis didn't even go to a white school; they put down on paper they were black and went to black schools.... In those days in New Orleans, if you were white and decided to be black, they let you.... Of course they had a lot of light-complected blacks that didn't want to be around blacker blacks; call you nigger fast as any white man. There was a little animosity there all the time. You didn't find it so much in my neighborhood, because we had a mixture of the passé a blancs, the real light-complected blacks you saw in the Seventh Ward, and the darker ones you saw uptown. The Treme was a mixture.[11]

Tremé and many of the city's neighborhoods would soon undergo a fundamental transformation due to shifts in federal and city housing policies. The pillars of the second wave of national Black ghettoization, the "federal ghetto," were put in place during this period. The Bourbons tried to lead the nation in restricting the movement and location of Blacks, requiring separate public accommodations in 1890 (the origins of *Plessy v. Ferguson*), adopting restrictive housing covenants in 1915, and attempting to implement racial zoning in 1924 before it was declared unconstitutional. New Orleans escaped the full impact of the main movements embedded within the first national racial ghettoization, the racial militarization of urban space, which occurred as African Americans left the South for northern cities during the Great Migration: the mob violence of the Red Summer of 1919, the national Ku Klux Klan movement after World War I, an ongoing campaign of private intimidation and terrorism by neighborhood associations, the nationalization of restrictive covenants developed by the real estate industry, and intensified urban racial policing.[12]

Large-scale ghettoization proceeded in New Orleans only after new technologies emerged that opened urban swampland for residential development. Yet as new lands were drained, the unavailability of financing during the Depression blocked the construction of new housing. Established in 1933 to provide financing for homeowners facing foreclosure, the federal Home Owners Loan Corporation developed a racial rating system to rank which neighborhoods qualified for mortgage loans. Defined as redlining because of the red lines drawn around undesirable neighborhoods, this practice quickly became one of the most powerful tools for the national spatial organization of racial exploitation.[13]

The Federal Housing Administration (FHA) was created by the National Housing Act of 1934. Racial composition was used to determine the creditworthiness of loans, mortgage interest rates, the cost of insurance, and the likely future appreciation or decline in value of every home and neighborhood in the nation. Integrated neighborhoods were deemed inherently threatening to property values. "Lenders were explicitly told to add restrictive covenants to contracts and deeds" or face the withdrawal of subsidized mortgages and insurance. This particular federal ethnic cleansing policy mandated lily-white neighborhoods and suburbs on the one hand and impoverished all-Black communities on the other. Charles Abrams suggests that the policies of Roosevelt's FHA could have been "culled from the Nuremberg laws." Similarly, Martha Mahoney concludes that "the FHA advocated zoning and deed restriction to bar undesirable people. The agency categorized occupancy by racial minorities with other nuisances to be guarded against for their impact on an area, such as the presence of 'stables' or 'pig pens.'" The FHA and the postwar Veterans Administration (VA) systematically denied loans to African Americans and neighborhoods with a significant African American presence. Consequently, these policies led to a massive disinvestment in the relatively integrated neighborhoods of New Orleans while simultaneously reinforcing long-term segregation and impoverishment.[14]

Used to build public housing in the city, the Housing Act of 1937 also intensified segregation. The Housing Authority of New Orleans (HANO) was created in the same year and, according to Daphne Spain, "was the first such agency in the United States to receive federal funds for slum clearance and publicly subsidized housing." Arnold Hirsch notes that the use of the program in the South provided new tools to create racially segregated neighborhoods:

> If the North now needed the supplementary power of the state to separate whites and blacks, the South (which had long used the state to enforce racial policy) quickly resorted to geographic concentration and distance to structure race relations in the postwar era. Whether viewed as regional convergence or the nationalization of the race issue, northern and southern cities were becoming more alike. . . . Historically, smaller, nonindustrial southern cities with their older black populations were less segregated residentially than their northern counterparts. The alacrity with which southern municipalities seized the federal tools when they became widely available in the 1930s served as a clear indication that local governments had their own agendas and lacked only the means to carry them out. Local control of federal resources and implementation of national policy would have even greater implications for race relations later on, with the coming of the civil rights era. . . . If southern cities found New Deal racial and housing policies congenial, they also quickly learned to use other government programs to similar effect.[15]

As in the post-Katrina era, the segregationist housing policies of the Roosevelt administration provided a federal mask behind which the Bourbon bloc could effectively operate without engaging in overt local racial battles. By the end of 1941 HANO had built two white projects with 1,826 units and three Black projects with 2,309 units, and another Black development was under construction. Mahoney notes,

> By 1940, six public housing projects opened for tenants: four for blacks (Magnolia, Calliope, Lafitte, and St. Bernard) and two for whites (St. Thomas and Iberville). St. Thomas and Magnolia, the uptown projects, replaced severely decayed housing. St. Thomas was racially mixed. Iberville and Lafitte were located relatively close to the center of the city, replacing the old "Storyville" area. Lafitte occupied a historically mixed neighborhood of whites, Blacks, and Creoles. Calliope was located on vacant land near an industrial site. . . . St. Bernard lay in an isolated area, on sparsely developed land far from downtown. Streets in the area were still poorly developed.[16]

Mahoney further notes that, as originally conceived, public housing in the city dramatically limited access for the most destitute residents on relief: "Twenty percent of the tenants were drawn from each of five categories to occupy the housing. No more than 20 percent of the spaces in any project could be assigned to families on relief, including New Deal work-relief programs. The other categories were domestic workers, 'shipping industry' (probably longshoremen), 'automobile industry' (including taxi drivers), and 'miscellaneous.' Black tenants demanded and received a staff of black social workers to process their applications."[17] Despite the current idyllic discourse on building mixed-income housing developments, problems in the rest of the region limited the success of such public housing during the 1940s. First, an intense housing shortage existed. This was compounded by federal, state, and local policies, along with private practices, that severely limited where African Americans could move, live, and visit for recreational purposes. For example, laws still prevented Black access to Audubon and City Parks. Additionally, the residents of the newly created all-white Gentilly subdivision fought successfully to end Black access to Seabrook Beach on Lake Pontchartrain. Whites also had access to private- and government-sector jobs not available to Blacks. The latter faced higher rates of unemployment, higher rents, and widespread overcrowding in the face of a declining number of affordable units. Additionally, landlords and realtors were intensely opposed to new construction. Although public housing was a stepping-stone for many whites, it was a life raft for the tens of thousands of African Americans on the waiting list. Mixed-income developments in this instance meant that those on the waiting list were sacrificed upon the altar of the Bourbon real estate market. Then and now, super-profits were generated by the refusal to provide subsidized and affordable housing to low-income African Americans.[18]

Finally, during this period, those who found themselves ensnared by the Bourbon justice system encountered unrelenting abuse. According to Adam Fairclough, the wartime "files of the NAACP and the black press also bulged with allegations of police brutality against civilians, ranging from wrongful arrest and

the use of arbitrary dragnets to the most sadistic forms of torture and death."
Among these accounts were more than a few incidents where New Orleans police officers murdered African Americans while they were handcuffed.[19]

The Junker Blues and the Double V Movement

Postwar, the sounds of the Double V generation evolved into the high energy of Jump Blues, the hollers and piercing sounds of the Blues honkers and
shouters, the Blues theory of relativity embodied in Be Bop and its breaking of
the space-time continuum, and the mellow and cool West Coast Blues and Jazz
produced by displaced Texan and Louisianan communities.

An important figure during this period was William "Champion Jack"
Dupree, born in 1910 in New Orleans. In several interviews, Dupree stated that
he lost both parents in a fire set by the Ku Klux Klan. While living at the Colored
Waifs' Home for Boys he met Louis Armstrong and learned the piano. When he
left the home at age fourteen, he survived by boxing and by learning to play the
Blues and boogie-woogie from greats such as Willie "Drive 'Em Down" Hall, Tuts
Washington, and a very young Roy "Professor Longhair" Byrd. By 1938 Dupree
was living in Indianapolis. During a famous Chicago recording session in 1941,
he recorded Hall's "Junkers Blues." Told from the perspective of an Angola prison
inmate, the multiple versions of this iconic song express the intersection of alienation, addiction, and the desire to find happiness during the crisis of the "zoot"
generation. Still gripped by the chaos of the Great Depression, this generation
was being asked to sacrifice their lives in battle for a society that refused to recognize its own humanity. While the Double V elements of this generation looked
forward to transforming the United States, the zoot segment was profoundly
alienated and rebelled against the dominant aesthetics and ethics. Although the
zoot movement was considered new in the 1940s, the sense of alienation from
many aspects of the Black, Creole, and white social orders had deep roots in New
Orleans. "Junkers Blues" expresses the desire to escape within an unjust world:

> Some people call me a junker
> Cause I'm loaded all the time
> I'm just being happy and I feel good all the time
> Some people say I use a needle and some say I sniff cocaine
> but that's the best old feeling, in the world that I've ever seen
> Say goodbye to whiskey and so long to gin
> I just want my reefer
> I just want to feel high again.[20]

This song's open defiance of prohibitions on certain forms of drug use and its
rhythm would eventually serve as the foundation for songs central to the two

New Orleans Rhythm and Blues renaissances: Professor Longhair's "Tipitina," Antoine "Fats" Domino's "The Fat Man," and Lloyd Price's "Lawdy Miss Clawdy." After spending several decades in Europe, Dupree's sense of alienation was still present in a 1977 interview. There he expressed the belief that the "Blues was built on ill treatment, everyday hardships and politics. Today it's the same as it was back in slavery times and as long as black people live, it will always be the same."[21]

Dupree saw two pillars of American society, the plantation development tradition and the Blues development tradition, as inextricably intertwined phenomena possessing the forces of necessity and inevitability. The "Junkers Blues" then force us to ask an unavoidable question: What is the reality the addict is trying to manage and how destructive is it? The Blues have often been condemned as pathological for their refusal to engage in contrived optimism. Yet there are many intellectual traditions that profess a perpetual sense of hope and progress. The Blues add a serious counterweight by demanding a realism supported by empirical proof, rather than a selective reading of history or an imagined golden future. Consequently the hard, and hard-living, women and men who crafted the Blues tradition are seen as relics of the racial past by some and as prophets by others.

Despite the hard realism of the Blues, it does not teach resignation. In a 1960 essay, Richard Wright notes that "their burden of woe and melancholy is dialectically redeemed through sheer force of sensuality, into an almost exultant affirmation of life, of love, of sex, of movement, of hope." Larry Neal expresses a similar position when he writes, "The blues are basically defiant in their attitude toward life. They are about survival on the meanest, most gut level of human existence. They are, therefore, lyric responses to the facts of life. The essential motive behind the best blues song is the acquisition of insight, wisdom." Finally, in 1937 Wright argued that the hard edge of the Blues actually produces the reverse of the social isolation, nihilism, and narrow social visions that underclass theorists have assigned to impoverished Black communities over the last quarter century. It serves as the foundation for new, transformative social movements.[22]

The Blues intellectual Paul Robeson reached a similar conclusion in a 1952 speech entitled "The Negro Artist Looks Ahead." He argued that an understanding and appreciation of Blues culture were prerequisites for political and social progress in the United States. Robeson served in the leadership of campaigns designed to defeat fascism, African colonialism, racism, and the waves of terror that defined the South before, during, and after World War II. A student of world music and a historian of African American song, particularly Spirituals and the Blues, Robeson argued that attempts by progressives to subsume the Blues epistemology, ethics, and development tradition were self-defeating exercises:

Negroes have carried on an important struggle in the United States throughout the history of this country, even before there was any significant progressive movement in the U.S.: this is a lesson progressives must learn—and accept it as a duty and a privilege to join in the struggle. The progressive movement must understand with crystal clarity that the Negro people have never retreated or compromised in their aspirations, and progressives must follow a dynamic path with them. For if they do otherwise, they will find themselves conscious or unconscious allies of reactionaries and pseudo-liberals. Progressives must re-orient themselves to the qualitative change that has come about in the unalienable and rightful demand of the United States Negro. The Negro men and women of the United States want equality for everybody, in everything, everywhere, now.[23]

The Blues agenda and working-class leadership in New Orleans and Louisiana reemerged through informal and formal mass movements advocating fundamental social transformation. Numerous daily encounters in the state signaled that the generation that had witnessed the Great Flood, evictions, brutality, and war had experienced a dramatic shift in consciousness. The daily conflicts occurring in the military camps scattered throughout the state were a key omen. Scherman argues that while Black correspondents attempted to romanticize the role of Black soldiers in the segregated military, most were confined to inferior barracks, served the worst food, and required to endlessly perform the most degrading labor. In one letter several Black soldiers noted that their commander, Major Sheridan, was "a rough dried, leather neck Negro hating cracker from Louisiana. . . . Calls our women everything but women. Misuses soldiers, treat us as if we were in a forced labor camp or chain gang." Another soldier based at Camp Claiborne in Alexandria described the dangers that lurked outside the gates: "Now right now at this moment the woods surrounding the camp are swarming with Louisiana hoogies armed with rifles and shot guns even the little kids have 22 cal. rifles and B & B guns filled with anxiety to shoot a Negro soldier."[24]

In the summer of 1943, Black soldiers stationed at a camp near Lake Charles rebelled; one year later, Black soldiers attacked abusive white officers and military police at Camp Claiborne. According to one report, a conflict with a Black soldier on Rampart Street in New Orleans nearly evolved into a major racial confrontation. In the city, overcrowded public spaces were the sites of numerous disputes. NAACP leader A. P. Tureaud recalled a 1943 incident in which an African American woman threw a white "conductorette out of the street car when the conductorette attempted to strike her with the controls."[25]

Additionally, white employers suddenly found the fourteen thousand Black women in domestic service to be too "'independent,' 'impudent and impertinent,' 'rude and undependable,' 'sassy,' and 'unappreciative.'" Sixty-eight percent of employed Black women in 1940 were domestics. On average, full-time domestics worked six and one-half days a week for approximately eighteen cents an hour.

Rumors of Black women organizing into Eleanor Clubs, Disappointment Clubs, Aggravating Clubs, and a union caused a panic among white households. One white housewife expressed her longing for the "good old days" before the growing militancy of working-class Black women:

> To tell you the truth, I think they're making too much money. You see them buying things at grocery stores that they've never been used to. Their husbands probably all have defense jobs, and they're horribly independent. There don't seem to be many faithful "darkies" around. So many agitators have come down here and stirred them up. I don't think they really want to work; you know how they are—give them an inch and they want a mile. I've always thought our southern Negroes were pretty good, and I hope I'll live to see the day when they'll be glad to work for you again.[26]

Although the NAACP provided legal representation for some of those involved in disputes with military and police officials, new organizations, strategies, and tactics were emerging. The new interracial union movement gained a foothold in the city, as did the Southern Negro Youth Congress, which was associated with the radical National Negro Congress. This movement signaled the rise of union-based working-class leadership at the expense of the old-line Black commercial and professional elite. In 1939 social worker Ernest Wright was hired to lead the *Louisiana Weekly's* Community Responsibility Program. He organized a popular series of community forums to address voting rights, police brutality, racial discrimination, and labor organizing. In 1940 Wright became involved with insurance agents seeking better pay from the four largest Black insurance companies. The agents organized as a local of the United Office and Professional Workers Union within the interracial Congress of Industrial Organizations (CIO) and quickly launched a strike. The companies brought in their agents from other parts of the state, armed them, and sent them out to collect payments. The college-educated agents on strike accepted help from members of the National Maritime Union, such as former prizefighter "Battling Siki" and the longshoreman "Poydras Street Black." They led a successful direct action against the strikebreakers and the companies settled. Although Wright and Zachary Ramsey, the first president of Local 101 of the Insurance Guild, were given sixty days in the parish prison for various assault charges, upon their release a contingent of five thousand community members met them and paraded along Canal Street to a welcome-home rally at Shakespeare Park, Uptown. This watershed interclass conflict was similar to events occurring within Black communities throughout the country. Combined community, political, and labor mobilizations fostered the reassertion of the Blues agenda.[27]

Known as the "People's Champion," Wright became part of the regional staff of the CIO in 1941. He immediately brought three thousand laundry workers,

who earned only nine cents an hour, into the ranks of the Amalgamated Cloth-
ing Workers Union. After escaping a lynching in 1942 while attempting to organize sharecroppers in the city of Natchitoches, he became general secretary
of the New Orleans Industrial Union Council and its twenty-eight unions and
thirty-five thousand workers in 1945. Wright and chairperson Elizabeth Sanders
also led the People's Defense League campaigns against the denial of the ballot
and police brutality. The league held a "Memory Day" for Felton Robinson. A
"mental patient with no history of violence, Robinson was killed in his home by
a Twelfth Precinct policeman who fired two shots as the man lay helpless and
bleeding on the floor while his wife begged the officer not to kill her husband."
After another, similar incident, the mayor refused to meet with the league until
Wright brought some "thuggish looking Negroes" to his office.[28]

Tensions mounted in New Orleans after rumors circulated that Blacks were
planning an armed uprising on May 1, 1943. Archbishop Joseph F. Rummel and
other white members of the Urban League responded by criticizing the Black
press for forcibly demanding civil and human rights. To ease these tensions, the
new African American president of Dillard University, Albert Dent, cofounded
the Citizens Committee on Race Relations. Yet the committee's demands for
lakefront beach access, police accountability, and a hostel for Black seamen were
all denied.[29]

Despite the wide array of wartime tensions and setbacks, NAACP victories in
the federal courts gave many a glimmer of hope that the restoration of voting
rights was eminent. In April 1944 the U.S. Supreme Court struck down the
whites-only primary in *Smith v. Allwright*. Voter registration drives were immediately launched by the NAACP, the People's Defense League, the CIO's Political
Action Committee, the Prince Hall Masons, the Knights of Peter Claver, the
Louisiana Progressive Voters League, the International Longshoreman's Association, and the Interdenominational Ministerial Alliance. However, some parish
registrars continued to block registration through the use of arbitrary tests and
intimidation. In the 1946 case of *Hall v. Nagel*, Thurgood Marshall of the NAACP
Legal Defense Fund and A. P. Tureaud of the New Orleans Branch of the NAACP
used the denial of registration in St. John Parish to successfully argue that those
denied access to the ballot should be allowed to appeal directly to the federal
courts for relief.[30]

Recounting the setbacks of the period, a *Louisiana Weekly* editorial concluded that the Bourbon regime had arrived at a crossroads and that democracy "will never survive the present crisis as a frozen or half-caste concept. The
struggle to preserve it must on all fronts be linked with the struggle to extend it.
The victory must be complete if it is to be at all. We must overthrow Hitlerism
within as well as Hitlerism without." Due to economic enclosures and constant
brutality, by the mid-1940s many of the historic rural Black communities of
Louisiana and their Blues agenda lay in shambles while recent migrants to the

city were intensely pushing the agenda forward at every turn. The Bourbon bloc then began to turn the force of its repressive machinery toward silencing urban liberals, progressives, and radicals. Yet according to Ernest Wright, the Double V generation in Louisiana was "in a belligerent mood, having to risk their lives for democracy and still be subject to lynch mobs at home."[31]

As in the past, the consciousness of this Blues generation provided the foundation for numerous individual and collective actions that were both a mystery and a direct challenge to elite Black leadership organizations. This is not to say that these organizations didn't understand change was at hand. For example, in 1945 Donald E. Byrd, president of the NAACP Louisiana state conference, wrote that "tolerance and patience . . . [being] at an end . . . [we] must not wait another 80 years for the white man to give us justice." Yet as the conflicts on the ground multiplied, the ability of the middle class to symbolically claim leadership was rapidly diminishing. Fairclough notes that soldiers "clashed with military authorities; civilians argued with bus drivers and policemen; and shipyard workers walked off the job. Blacks were speaking and acting in a way not seen since Reconstruction." The Bourbon effort to suppress this militancy would define southeastern Louisiana for the next two decades.[32]

The Things I Used to Do, I Don't Do Them Anymore, 1945–1954

I am in blood
Stepped in so far that, should I wade no more,
Returning were as tedious as go o'er.
William Shakespeare, *Macbeth*[33]

When confronted by the growing alliance between African Americans, national unions, and progressive movements, the Bourbons pushed for the expulsion of these groups from rural areas and then from the economic and political life of the urban areas. The rural movement was led in part by the Louisiana Delta Council, which controlled twelve northeast cotton parishes, and by the American Sugar Cane League, which dominated key sections of the twenty-five southern parishes, the "Sugar Bowl." Both relied on the federal Agricultural Adjustment Act's enclosure policies and the subsequent mechanization movement to finance rural expulsions. The rural population in Louisiana declined by 286,000 persons during the 1940s and by another 334,000 persons during the 1950s. The farm population accounted for 36 percent of the total state population in 1940, 21 percent in 1950, and only 7.2 percent by the 1960s. Cotton production declined from 2 million acres in the 1930s to 352,000 acres by 1966. During the same period, the number of farms in the state declined by half, the number of Black farmers declined by two-thirds, and the number of tenants and sharecroppers declined by ninety-five thousand persons, or 89 percent. According to Fairclough, by 1960 "machines harvested 96 percent of the cane, 60 percent of the cotton and all of the rice." Numerous African American rural communities collapsed during this period, while starvation and flight to the cities became a central narrative of rural Black Louisiana life.[34]

Enclosure and expulsion also defined changes within the urban racial division of labor, as well as life in the areas of employment, housing, human rights, and politics. Blacks were bulldozed from already segregated urban occupations. At the end of the war, layoffs in manufacturing, shipbuilding, petroleum, and other industries were occurring just as returning veterans, Blacks and white, were demanding work. Mahoney notes that as "GI's returned looking for work, employers preferred whites. Therefore, black unemployment rose sharply in the late 1940s." Both employers and unions expelled Black workers, who were further impoverished by their exclusion from the occupations and industries that benefited from the long oil boom stretching from the late 1940s to early 1960s. Industrial unions played a key role in exacerbating poverty and racism by excluding African Americans from membership. Similarly, craft unions such as those for plumbers, electricians, and machinists barred the hiring of Black apprentices, the only route to enter those occupations.[35]

The veteran benefit programs served as a great reservoir of wealth creation for the next several decades. White southern veterans received a disproportionate share; 20 percent of veterans lived in the South, yet the region received 35 percent of all veterans' benefits. While Black veterans made up one-third of the South's total, they received few benefits. They were often denied veterans' unemployment benefits. Of those who did secure jobs through the U.S. Employment Service, more than 92 percent were forced into unskilled positions, while 86 percent of their white counterparts were placed in professional positions. The majority of Black veterans were also denied access to on-the-job training programs and to college benefits. Segregation ensured that those who did secure college benefits typically earned less than white high school dropouts.[36]

Mahoney notes that the "longshore industry was the most important exception to the rule of exclusion, employing blacks in significant numbers. Jobs along the waterfront were generally stable, well-paid, and ranked among the best jobs Blacks could obtain." Although jobs on the docks and with the railroads were somewhat stable, six of every ten employed Black people held highly unstable positions as private domestic household workers, laborers, or service workers. The largest increase in Black employment was for unskilled common laborers, while private household work, "a primary source of employment for Black women, declined by nearly one third in the 1940s." Manufacturing employment in New Orleans increased from 34,950 to 46,500 jobs during the 1940s but declined by 3,000 jobs during the 1950s. In the New Orleans racial division of labor, industries and firms reserved menial jobs for Black workers, while positions as clerks, stenographers, bank tellers, sales assistants, bus drivers, firefighters, and police officers were reserved for whites. Additionally, Blacks could not be hired for government jobs involving public contact.[37]

Although they made up one-third of New Orleans's population in 1950, African Americans were almost totally excluded from utility, municipal, and downtown white-collar employment: they accounted for 0.08 percent of the New Orleans Public Service, Inc., utility workforce, 0.015 percent of the phone company workforce, and 0.054 percent of the city government workforce. The state government of Louisiana had one of the lowest rates of Black employment in the South and the nation, with even janitorial and landscaping jobs being reserved for whites.[38]

Federal, state, and local government officials promoted, financed, and co-ordinated the multiple racial blockades and expulsions launched within New Orleans sectors and communities during the late 1940s. Blacks were also de-nied access to the growing number of suburban jobs and communities. Housing segregation reinforced suburban employment discrimination in at least four different ways, according to Mahoney: through the time and money required for commuting, the lack of information about firms that were hiring, the fears of employers about revolts from white workers if Blacks were hired, and the inability of Blacks to pressure suburban employers.[39] While the number of white workers in the state increased by eighty-three thousand due to an influx from Mississippi, the number of Black workers in the state declined by forty-six thousand. During the late 1940s and early 1950s, the pillars of urban and rural planning rested on industrial, occupational, and residential redlining policies. The toll on devastated African American communities resulted in a net total of ninety-two thousand Black Louisianans being forced out of the state by its racial starvation polices, while a net total of forty-two thousand whites were welcomed to the state with open arms and opportunities.[40]

By the 1960s over half of the Black residents of New Orleans lived in poverty.[41] "One of every three black families earned less than $1,000 a year, a poverty rate more than double white families in New Orleans."[42] This massive social disaster did not prevent some white leaders, such as former state senator Fritz Eagan, from naturalizing Black worker exploitation as simply "the southern way of life":

> We always had servants, and even the poor people in the community would have people of the black race that would do services for them, whether cleaning up their houses or their yards or whatnot. The black community at that time were domes-tics, they were repairmen, cleanup type of people. We always had black maids in our house. You couldn't call them nannies, I don't guess, but they were black people that took care of the children as they went up. . . . There's a relationship between people of those different races that's very close. They were the servants, but if they had any problems, you hear any Southern person say this, usually they were solved

by the white family. . . . There wasn't any turnover in help. If you had a maid in your house, even today if you go to some of the Garden District homes, they have maids that have been with them for 50 (years), their entire life was shared in that house.[43]

The threat to de jure racism posed by a mobilized Black community and an increasingly activist federal bench led various hegemonic blocs around the country to race to perfect those institutions that could ensure de facto racism. As Spain notes, the romance associated with New Orleans's backyard pattern of housing development and its integrated neighborhoods masked a tale of two cities:

> But by 1950 there were numerous segregated blocks emerging in the city. Fifty-seven percent of all blocks had less than one percent black housing units, while eight percent had less than one percent white. This could be interpreted to mean that thirty-five percent of all blocks were integrated. A housing profile for New Orleans blacks in 1950 shows that such integration did not insure equality, however. Fewer than twenty-five percent of blacks were home owners compared to forty-four percent of whites; median rent for blacks was $13 less per month than for whites; and black owner-occupied homes were valued at $3,800 as compared with $10,000 for whites. Four-fifths of all black dwellings were dilapidated or lacked plumbing, and forty percent were overcrowded. . . . "Nonsegregation for Negroes in New Orleans seemed to mean the right to crowd into old and poor dwellings as whites left them for new housing."[44]

Beginning in 1939 the Roosevelt administration, major banks, and the real estate industry organized the federal ghetto. After World War II, these same forces simultaneously subsidized racially organized suburbanization and Black ghettoization. The FHA and the VA financed more than half of the homes built immediately after World War II. By 1950, 5 percent of Black veterans used VA loans to purchase homes, compared to 13 percent of white veterans. Those Blacks who did receive a FHA or VA loan were forced to use it to purchase a house in a segregated neighborhood or in a rapidly segregating neighborhood that was being devalued according to the FHA's racially coded appraisal system. Other federal decisions regarding the placement of veterans hospitals and other facilities enhanced and reproduced segregation. According to Michael Brown and his colleagues, segregation was a wealth-generating engine for numerous white suburban communities: "These federal policies underwrote a new pattern of white accumulation and Black disaccumulation throughout the country. . . . White families prospered as suburban developments were constructed, while black families were left holding a losing hand. After World War II, federal housing and urban renewal policies facilitated rigidly segregated neighborhoods and disinvestment in black communities."[45]

The federal "second ghetto" in New Orleans reproduced the plantation-bloc development tradition of Black working-class social, economic, and political incapacitation while enabling extraordinary rents to be exacted from a captive population.[46] Begun in the 1920s, the large-scale drainage of New Orleans's swamps opened up new land for residential development, particularly after World War II. The operation of a unified front composed of banks, developers, landlords, and homeowners ensured that these developments were all white. Mahoney argues that the VA's and FHA's subsidies were the pillars of urban and suburban residential segregation for the next several decades:

> Given federal and private restrictions on lending, and the fact that discrimination against blacks was still open and legal, these were actually decisions to create *white* neighborhoods. . . . Years later, a municipal assessor recalled that "10,000 GI's returned to New Orleans ready to settle down. And they could not get a mortgage in central city, the Irish Channel, or the Lower Garden District [the older sections of the city with historically racially mixed population patterns]. . . . Moderate-income white families found apartments in attractive new developments, often built with federal mortgages. No such options existed for blacks. . . . Severe housing pressures for blacks resulted in relatively high rents and scarce vacancies in black neighborhoods. In the spring of 1949, the Housing Authority had 46,000 pending applications for public, low-rent housing. The fact that federally subsidized "private" housing was closed to blacks was one of the factors increasing black ghettoization during this period. Black families "doubled up" and black neighborhoods remained geographically compact.[47]

In the midst of this housing blockade, Mayor Morrison launched a campaign of neighborhood demolition and public housing construction during the early 1950s. The demands of realtors and white homeowners to maintain segregation resulted in five thousand new units of public housing being attached to existing Black public housing developments such as Desire, Magnolia, and Calliope. Substandard materials were used to build the new units and vibrant existing neighborhoods were demolished. Mahoney notes that the "Magnolia extension displaced the spacious homes of black doctors and ministers near Flint-Goodridge Hospital as well as the remnants of the old slum area nearby." In the planned chaos of urban renewal, public housing became a poverty-generating institution. Families whose income began to rise were rapidly evicted and replaced by the more impoverished on the waiting list. Thrust onto a housing market defined by exorbitant rents, the evicted were quickly reimpoverished. Any major or minor family disaster would requalify the evicted for public housing. Yet by then they would be last on the list of nearly fifty thousand families.[48]

The city did not protect African Americans from terrorism within their households or in the community as a whole. As in other southern states, empowered Black veterans were brutalized after the war. On August 8, 1946, John C. Jones, a twenty-eight-year-old veteran, was lynched in Minden. Although he was engaged in investigating the theft of an oil lease from his grandfather by

Premier Oil, the official transcript stated that his crime was looking at a naked white woman through a window as he walked across her yard. The five deputies accused of his murder were acquitted.[49]

The Louisiana Civil Rights Congress (LCRC) was organized in 1948 by Dr. Oakley Johnson, a white professor of English at Dillard University and a communist. One of the death penalty cases the organization worked on involved Milton Wilson, who was charged with rape and the murder of a white couple in St. Charles Parish, a few miles from New Orleans. Arrested on another matter, Wilson "confessed" to the crime after being severely tortured in the state's execution chamber. The first trial was delayed because he was urinating blood clots. His conviction after a second trial in 1947 was overturned after the formation of an active Milton Wilson Defense Committee, widespread outrage over torture, and judicial recognition of the inadmissability of a forced confession. On appeal, the Louisiana Supreme Court and the U.S. Supreme Court upheld his conviction and Wilson was executed in 1951.[50]

The LCRC also handled several cases just outside of New Orleans in bordering Jefferson Parish. Accused of raping a white woman in her Metairie home, Paul Washington and Ocie Jugger refused to confess for two months. The LCRC noted that their confession came only after they "were dragged on a tour of police stations. . . . Their mouths were sealed with adhesive tape and they were handcuffed. Police and deputies beat them with blackjacks, choked them with garottes, slugged them with rubber hoses and chains, kicked, starved, denied them water, threatened them with shooting, gave them no sleep or medical attention—all during a period of weeks in which no one but officers were allowed near them." Both were electrocuted in 1952. In another case, Gretna sheriff Beauregard Miller killed Elliot Brooks for resisting arrest in 1946. Brooks was the eighth Black man killed by Miller under similar circumstances. Also in Jefferson Parish, in February 1948, after getting on the wrong bus, a Black woman asked for her nickel back. When she was denied, passenger Roy Cyrus Brooks got into an argument with the bus driver about returning the fare. A deputy was called and as Brooks was being walked to the parish courthouse, the deputy shot and killed the forty-four-year-old. After seven minutes of deliberation, the jury acquitted the officer. Finally, Black prisoners in Orleans and Jefferson Parishes were routinely beaten to death while in custody. This did not prevent Bourbon leaders from promoting the routinization of physical and psychological torture. New Orleans mayor Chep Morrison defended torture by arguing that the extraction of a confession often required "a certain amount of coercion above and beyond normalcy."[51]

Another pillar of the civil rights institution, the political party system, was also reformed to preserve racial hegemony. Key elements of the southern plantation bloc realized that the U.S. Supreme Court's *Smith v. Allwright* decision in 1944 would end the white primary in the South and with it the system of one-party dictatorship. A debate broke out within the plantation bloc over whether it was easier to maintain racial and class hegemony by operating within an increasingly integrated, labor-influenced Democratic Party that would eventually end Black disenfranchisement or by creating an autonomous structure. After President Truman decided to integrate the military in July 1948, southern delegates at the National Democratic Party Convention walked out. This Dixiecrat revolt was followed by the formation of the State's Rights Party (the Dixiecrats) and the nomination of Strom Thurmond of South Carolina as the party's presidential candidate. Louisiana's U.S. senator Allen Auslander supported Truman while U.S. senator Russell Long ran on both slates. However, the strong support of the Plaquemines Parish leader Leander Perez helped Thurmond carry four states: South Carolina, Alabama, Mississippi, and Louisiana. The election marked the birth pangs of a movement that would transform the Republican Party and national politics from 1954 to the present.

During this period of institutional restructuring, the plantation bloc of the region deployed a two-pronged cultural strategy. First, it deployed the rhetoric of racial panic to counter what some viewed as impending doom. In 1950 the Louisiana legislature passed a law to bolster the existing prohibition on interracial relationships. It banned the "marriage or habitual cohabitation" of "a person of the Caucasian or white race and a person of the colored or Negro race." According to Earl Palmer, the law was increasingly being ignored despite severe consequences:

> By the fifties it was pretty flagrant. . . . Sugar Boy Crawford was always flirting [*sic*] with white women. He got beat up about that, the police beat him up. One Sunday morning the police found Lee Allen and a white girl named Patty Driscoll drunk and half-dressed in a parked car with the door wide open. Right on Canal Street, people streaming past going to church. The cops like to have killed Lee, beat him every time a new shift came on until they finally let him go. You didn't want to go to jail in New Orleans, you might never come out. You don't know how those days were. They could kill you if they wanted and say you'd committed suicide. Who was going to argue? Who was going to investigate?[52]

In the second strategy, which was similar to that of the Mississippi Delta, several representatives of the dominant plantation bloc moved away from the public discourse on inherent racial inferiority and began to use the sociological categories of poverty, crime, and deviancy to define, defend, and mask their exploitative regional, racial, class, and gender projects. Born in Terrebonne Parish, Allen Ellender entered the U.S. Senate in 1937 and served for thirty-six years. Not only did he believe that African Americans were "inferior to the white man," he thought that the character of Blacks was defined by "inherent dishonesty, laziness, slothfulness." Black professionals and businesspersons were "sub-mediocre," and as soldiers Blacks were "inferior." He also believed that any

"'Negro' of notable ability owes success to white blood." For the senator, not only were Blacks incapable of governing, they were the blood enemies of civilization: "Negro blood has degraded and ultimately destroyed every white civilization they were allowed to mongrelize."

Fairclough concluded that the Louisiana Bourbons and their allies, in keeping with their Mississippi Delta counterparts, understood perfectly that the new institution of American social science, with its theories of poverty, crime, disease, and deviancy, was a glove that fit perfectly the racialist theories of the post-Nazi, anticolonial, and Cold War global intellectual environment of the 1950s. This was evident in Ellender's new interest in demography: "'I do not particularly like to quote venereal disease statistics about any group, or to cite crime rates' . . . the Senator informed a black correspondent. 'But these are things we must recognize. . . . Your race is not perfect, that is something you must understand.'" Indeed, Ellender often called up statistics on crime and disease that he had collected for three decades.[53]

According to Coleman Warner, despite the halfhearted effort to mask the continuation of racial, class, and regional domination, many African Americans recognized the shift from de jure racial institutions to de facto institutions for what it was: "If more white people had read the *Louisiana Weekly*, they would have found an NAACP official's description of segregation as 'a modernized, streamlined slavery that replaces ankle irons with "For White Only" signs; that replaces slave quarters with the slum ghetto; that replaces three meals a day with the starvation wage of maids and porters; that replaces the master's bullwhip with the torch of the mob and the policeman's club.'"[54]

The New Orleans Rhythm and Blues Renaissance I

Music so high you can't get over it
So low you can't get under it
    The Temptations, "Psychedelic Shack" (1970)[55]

Having participated in the defeat of fascism abroad, the Double V generation returned home with the intent to defeat it domestically. Instead, they witnessed the dismantling of their movements, the diminution of their rights, the dismantling of their rural communities, and the intensification of urban segregation. They began to produce a powerful, irrepressible music, which undergirded a new era of social inquiry. The music was dedicated to social justice, human rights, sustainable development, and the celebration of the sanctity of local Black cultural traditions and its heroes. In addition to revitalizing the local Blues pantheon, the New Orleans Renaissance once again crafted the thoughts and sounds of a new world.

The infrastructure of the New Orleans Rhythm and Blues Renaissance rested on eight pillars. First was the community itself, the audience. The second pillar was the insistence on carrying through the Double V movement. The third pillar was the new places of congregation and experimentation that emerged within the African American community. Many new show places, nightclubs, and restaurants were opened after the war, including the famed Dew Drop Inn, the Caldonia, the Club Rocket, and the Tijuana. These venues consistently hosted national Rhythm and Blues acts. Many of the bars and clubs of Tremé were sites of intellectual exchange, affirmation, and experimentation: the Crystal Club, the Keno, the Struggle Inn, and the Gypsy Tea Room. Other historic clubs included the Joy Tavern in Gert Town, the Hideaway in the Ninth Ward, Al's Starlite Inn in the Seventh Ward, and the Shadowland in Uptown.[56] According to Palmer, the "Dew Drop Inn was the best place in town. It was our hangout, *the* club for blacks. We called it the Drop. . . . Most local musicians came in every night after work, and it was where out-of-town musicians came when they wanted to hear some music, some black music."[57]

Fourth, New Orleans audiences and performers were closely connected to larger regional music currents through booking networks that linked bars, clubs, auditoriums, and dance halls: the southern Louisiana Silver Circuit, the Texas Sugarcane Circuit, and the Gulf States Circuit.[58]

Fifth, the rise of Black radio and disc jockeys greatly expanded the local audience for New Orleans–produced music. Legendary disk jockeys such as Ernie the Whip, Okey Dokey, Dr. Daddy-O, Poppa Stoppa, and Jack the Cat focused on introducing local talent. Due to segregation, Blacks were not allowed to be on air, but Dillard professor Vernon Winslow wrote scripts and selected songs for the program *Jam, Jive and Gumbo* with a series of white disk jockeys named Poppa Stoppa beginning in 1948. When Winslow read the script one day, he was fired and then hired by another station. Under the name Dr. Daddy-O, his *Jivin' with Jax* show became a hit on WMRY and was heard as far away as East Texas.[59]

Sixth, before World War II, Victor, Okeh, Decca, and other labels would make rare visits to the city to record Jazz and Blues. De Luxe Records came to the city in 1947 to record Roy Brown, Paul Gayten, and Annie Laurie in a high school gym with equipment the label owners brought with them from New Jersey.[60] Around the same time, former bricklayer Cosimo Matassa created a recording studio in his record shop. Eventually this studio and another one he built later became the focal point of his recording business. He was both owner and engineer at J&M Studios, which recorded almost all of the Rhythm and Blues records produced in the city for a twenty-year period.[61]

The seventh pillar of the renaissance centered on J&M itself. J&M Studio Band became nationally known for its sound, skills, and professionalism. It was led by producer, arranger, trumpet player, and longtime band leader Dave Bartholomew. The son of a well-known New Orleans tuba player, Bartholomew was born in 1920 in Edgard, Louisiana, thirty miles west of New Orleans. While in his teens, he cut sugarcane by day and played trumpet at night. During the late 1930s, Bartholomew played in the leading New Orleans band, led by pianist Walter "Fats" Pichon, and on the S.S. *Capitol*, a steamboat that carried passengers between New Orleans and St. Paul, Minnesota. After three years in the army during World War II and a few engagements with Duke Ellington, he started his own band in 1946 with Bartholomew on trumpet, Earl Palmer on drums, Clarence Hall and Joe Harris on alto saxophone, Meyer Kennedy on saxophone, Red Tyler on baritone saxophone, Frank Fields on bass, Edward Franks or Salvador Doucette on piano, Ernest McLean on guitar, and Theard Johnson on vocals. The group primarily performed ballads and big band arrangements during the late 1940s. Although the band played a number of places and styles, many of the musicians were adherents of Be Bop and they would assemble regularly at the Dew Drop Inn to play this revolutionary music with future legends Ed Blackwell, Alvin Batiste, Harold Battiste, and Ellis Marsalis.[62]

When record companies came to the city to record, they often chose the Studio Band to back individual performers such as Roy Brown, Blues artist Jewel King, and balladeer Tommy Ridgley. Bartholomew also sang on several records under his own name, including the 1949 hits "Country Boy" and "Mr. Fool."[63] With the addition of Lee Allen on tenor saxophone, the Bartholomew group formed the heart and soul of the J&M Studio Band, which became the engine behind the classic Rhythm and Blues songs of Fats Domino, Shirley and Lee, Smiley Lewis, Joe Turner, Ray Charles, and Little Richard.[64] Other important musicians of the period came to New Orleans to immerse themselves in the renaissance, including Ray Charles, Ornette Coleman, Big Joe Turner, Charles Brown, Pee Wee Crayton, Lowell Fulson, Amos Milburn, and Roosevelt Sykes. Tours led by Nat King Cole, Elmore James, Charlie Parker, Sonny Stitt, and Sonny Boy Williamson were also backed by the Bartholomew band. Although the musicians of the renaissance were heavily recruited by major touring bands, their love of family and community led most of them to remain in the city.[65]

The final pillar of the renaissance was that, after several artists made the national charts with locally produced records, thousands of new songs were developed in the city by hundreds of singers and musicians, young and old. Not since the age of Bolden had the city witnessed a cultural renaissance on such a massive scale. According to Jeff Hannusch, between "the years 1950 and 1970, New Orleans had a commanding position as one of the largest sellers of single records in the United States. In the neighborhood of two hundred and fifty New Orleans' singles graced the national R&B and pop charts during these two decades."[66]

Many of the artists of the renaissance experienced the same brutal working conditions, constant displacements, exploitation, censorship, and terror that were experienced by their audiences. This reality was reflected in their Blues. One of the inaugurating events of this cultural movement occurred when Roy Brown scored a major national hit in 1948. Brown was born in New Orleans in

1925 and raised in the heavily Cajun town, where he sang in the church choir and cut sugarcane. He moved to Los Angeles in the early 1940s, not long after Zydeco legend Amédé Ardoin was run over, reportedly by a car driven by angry white patrons outside of Eunice.[67] Brown developed an appreciation for the Blues while working as a vocalist in the clubs of Shreveport and Galveston, and he soon joined the ranks of the Blues shouters, singers who shouted their songs over source "roaring riffs and honking saxes." He also sang crying and pleading gospel-tinged Blues, fast boogies, and slow Blues.

Brown and his band, the Mighty Men, entered J&M Studios in 1947 to record "Good Rockin' Tonight." Alvin "Red" Tyler, recalled, "Prior to this there were no big rock 'n' roll artists in the stature of Roy Brown at the time. You had artists who were pretty good but Roy Brown really took the country on fire with 'Good Rockin' Tonight.' Although the song was exceedingly popular, its distribution was hampered. One record label manager recalled that 'it was considered filth. They had a definition in those days of the word "rock" meaning the sex act.'"

Brown had fifteen hits between 1948 and 1951; however, this Jump Blues, Rock and Roll, Rhythm and Blues, and Soul pioneer was marginalized after 1951.[68] Yet his shouts and his band's name, the Mighty Men, signaled the determination of the Double V generation to be heard over the roar of the segregationists. The goal was also to transform a southern society committed to daily denigration. The psychological impact of the regime and its repetitive enclosures of Black life were captured by Brown in his haunting 1950 hit "Hard Luck Blues":

> Well, Rocks in my pillow!
> The cold ground is my bed,
> The highway is my home
> So I might as well be dead.
>
> . . . .
>
> I'm travelin' and travelin'
> Seems the road has got no end.
> And I ain't got nobody
> In this mean old world to call my friend.
>
> I got so much trouble
> Sometimes I could cry,
> I'm gonna find my mother's grave
> Fall on the tombstone and die.[69]

Another aspect of the New Orleans Rhythm and Blues Renaissance was the ability of the current generation to recall traditions and practices reaching back to the colonial period and to Africa. When this historical memory was combined with the innovations of the present generation, the historic Blues aesthetic, epistemology, and agenda were all revitalized.[70]

Numerous instances of recalling and combining occurred during the renaissance. For example, Professor Longhair (Henry Byrd) preserved and embodied many historic traditions while creating new soundscapes. Born in Bogalusa in 1918, Byrd was brought to New Orleans at age two months by his mother, Ella Mae. She taught him how to play piano and several other instruments. He was introduced to music outside the home at Delpee's Club at Calliope and Franklin. The Byrd home was razed during the 1950s to build the new city hall and federal building. As a youth, he received musical instruction from Blues pianists Sullivan Rock, Kid Stormy Weather, and Tuts Washington. He continued his piano studies in between street dancing, performing in medicine shows, boxing, and gambling. By the mid-1930s he was accompanying singers and collaborating with pianist "Champion Jack" Dupree and guitarist Sonny Boy Williamson (Rice Miller). During the Depression Byrd found work in the federal Civilian Conservation Corps building levees. Mistreatment in the army led to a medical discharge in the mid-1940s. Afterward he worked as a cook and partner in a soul food restaurant.[71]

Around 1948, during the intermission of a Bartholomew-led show at the Caldonia Inn, Byrd mounted the stage. The crowd demanded more and Bartholomew's band was fired. According to disk jockey Dr. Daddy-O, Byrd "was the kind of performer that gave me a gut reaction the first time I saw him. They made him wear these long-toed shoes, because he would kick the piano so hard he would break the front of it." Professor Longhair became known for his hair, speaking his own language, a pounding two-hand attack, kicking the piano, and walking on the keyboards, as well as his mastery of Ragtime, Jazz, Blues, Zydeco, Calypso, and Rhumba beats. In 1949 he recorded "She Ain't Got No Hair" and "Mardi Gras in New Orleans." The latter classic was a Blues organized around the Congolese rhumba rhythm popular in Cuba. He explained later that this Mardi Gras anthem was written at the request of community members who wanted to mark the importance of the celebration: "Well, the people was askin' for carnival numbers. At that time they wanted a good carnival number. They had numbers about Christmas, they had New Year's, most of all the holidays":

> Going down to New Orleans, I got my ticket in my hand (2x)
> When I get to New Orleans I want to see the Zulu King.[72]

In "Professor Long Hair's Blues," Byrd announces that he is also conversant with the rootwork tradition that preserved African culture, religion, and philosophy in the region:

> Well y'all know I'm not a doctor but you didn't know I was not a doctor's
>   son (2x)
> I intend to do my father's work until the day he comes.[73]

Recording variously as Professor Longhair and His Shuffling Hungarians, Roy Byrd and his Blues Jumpers, Roy "Bald Head" Byrd, and Professor Longhair and

His Blues Scholars, Byrd had several hits. In 1953 he entered J&M Studios and recorded the classic second line anthem "Tipitina," a remake of the "Junker Blues."[74]

Smiley Lewis was also key in the renaissance. Born Overton Lemmons in DeQuincy, Calcasieu Parish, in 1913, Lewis arrived in New Orleans at the age of ten. By the mid-1930s he was supporting himself by playing the Blues guitar, driving trucks, and shoeing horses. After his home on Thalia Street was razed to construct public housing in 1943, his wife and children moved into the Laffite housing development. He formed a Blues trio with Tuts Washington and scored two hits in 1950 with the backing of Bartholomew's Studio Band. In 1952 he had success with "The Bells Are Ringing" and his 1955 classic, "I Hear You Knocking (But You Can't Come In)," which was covered by white artists Elvis Presley and Gale Storm. In the same year Lewis had limited success with "Gumbo Blues." The song implicitly addresses the trauma brought on by migration and lost love, offering return as a form of physical and psychological healing:

> Yeah, When you left New Orleans Baby
> You were feeling kind of low
> Yeah grab you a fast train baby
> and come on back to the old Gumbo.[75]

Although several white artists made fortunes covering the songs of Smiley Lewis, he remained impoverished. His body of work also includes "Dirty People" and "Tee-Nah-Nah." Both songs capture the historic human rights tragedies visited upon Black residents of Louisiana. In "Dirty People," Lewis protests the criminalization of an entire community and the numerous instances of police brutality occurring throughout the city.

> Public enemy! Public enemy number one!
> Don't go outside that man got a big machine gun
> Dirty, dirty people done the poor boy wrong
> Those dirty, dirty people done the poor boy wrong.[76]

Protesting the oppressive conditions of the Louisiana prison-industrial complex using the lens of Blues realism, "Tee-Nah-Nah" was sung to the "Junker Blues" rhythm of Champion Jack Dupree and earlier generations. According to Tuts Washington, it "was one of those prison songs they used to sing up in Angola (prison plantation). 'Tee-Nah-Nah' went everywhere; every time I turned around I heard it on the box. We traveled all over on that record. Florida, Mississippi, Oklahoma":

> Six months ain't no sentence
> No, and one year ain't no time.
> They got boys in Angola yeah doin' one to 99
> Tee-Nah-Nah Nah Nah Nah.[77]

Other songs of the period supported the resolve of the community in various ways. For example, in 1947 Mahalia Jackson recorded the Blues-based "Move on Up a Little Higher." Simultaneously an invocation to move higher and an exploration of the earthly sacrifice, struggle, and crucifixion of the oppressed, this inspirational song became the bestselling gospel record up to that time. It also garnered Jackson a record contract with CBS, a weekly radio show, and a large national and international audience:

> One a-these mornings
> soon one morning
> I'm gonna lay down my cross, get me a crown. . . .
> Soon as my feet strike Zion
> Lay down my heavy burdens
> Put on my robe in glory
> Going home one day and tell my story. . . .
> Gonna fly, Lord, and never faulter
> I'm gonna move up a little higher.[78]

The younger generation also played a key role in the renaissance through their rediscovery of older rhythms and movements. In 1952 Art Rupe of the Los Angeles–based Specialty Records went on a scouting trip to New Orleans. There he recorded seventeen-year-old Lloyd Price, who brought "Lawdy Ms. Clawdy" to J&M Studios. Based on a combination of the "Junker Blues" and a local saying, in the record Price provided the wailing vocals, Fats Domino played piano, and the Studio Band provided the accompaniment. This Blues reached number one on all the Billboard sales charts. Its success demonstrated conclusively that the Orleans sound was national and that Black radio was reaching into southern, northern, and western white homes. Price followed this song with the hits "Restless Heart" and "Ain't That a Shame" before being drafted in 1953.[79]

Born in Uptown in 1934, James "Sugar Boy" Crawford learned to play piano from a neighbor and learned the trombone at Booker T. Washington High School. His band of high school students was introduced to the city in 1952 on Doctor Daddy-O's Saturday morning radio show. The group didn't have a name until Daddy-O dubbed them "The Chapaka Shawee" (roughly translated from the Creole as "we aren't raccoons"), which was also the title of an instrumental the group played. This appearance led to regular work at the Shadowland and the Pentagon clubs, as well as an Aladdin Records contract. Under the name "Sugar Boy and His Cane Cutters," their first release was "I Don't Know What I'll Do" on the Chess label. In 1953 the band recorded "Jock-A-Mo." A combination of two traditional Mardi Gras Indian chants, the record became a local and national classic.[80] In a 2002 interview, Crawford discussed the origins of the song:

[I] lived at 1309 La Salle Street. We called the neighborhood "The Bucket of Blood," because there were a lot of barrooms around there. It seemed like every Saturday night there was a cutting or shooting there. It was also a neighborhood where there were a lot of Indian tribes. . . . It came from two Indian chants that I put music to. "Iko Iko" was like a victory chant that the Indians would shout. "Jock-A-Mo" was a chant that was called when the Indians went into battle. I just put them together. . . . It wasn't my idea to call the song "Jock-A-Mo"—Leonard Chess did that. If you listen to the song, I'm singing C-H-O-C-K as in Chockamo. Not J-O-C-K, as in Jock-A-Mo. When Leonard listened to the session in Chicago, he thought I said "Jock-A-Mo." When I saw the record for the first time I said, "That's not the title, it's 'chock-a-mo.'"[81]

The song captured the warrior chants heard on the Mardi Gras Indian battle-field, an area bordered by Claiborne, Galvez, Tulane, and Perdido Streets. The song also expressed the militant spirit embedded in the Mardi Gras Indian tradition and in the New Orleans Black community as a whole. It became a classic that has been repeatedly covered by numerous artists:

> My grandma and your grandma were
> Sittin' by the fire,
> My grandma told your grandma:
> "I'm gonna set your flag on fire."
> [Chorus] Talkin' 'bout, Hey Now! Hey now! Iko, Iko unday
> Chock-a-mo fee-no ai nane. Jock-a-mo fee na-ne.
> Look at my king all dressed in red.
> Iko, Iko unday.
> I bet cha five dollars he'll kill you dead
> Chock-a-mo fee na-ne.[82]

Given the multiplicity of styles present in the city during this period, there is an ongoing debate as to whether there was a distinctive New Orleans sound. Several participants in the renaissance provide telling insights. Ray Charles spent a great deal of time in the city developing his new soul sound, collaborating with other artists, and developing his own band. During a 1953 session he played on and helped arrange Guitar Slim's record "The Things That I Used to Do." Charles described the new soundscape in the following manner:

This was also a period in my life when I spent some time in New Orleans—several months at a time. I lived in the Foster Hotel, which was only a couple of blocks away from the Dew Drop Inn—Frank Painia's place, the heart of all musical activities. . . . There were good sounds in New Orleans back then—this was 1953—and I sat in with as many of the cats as I could. The blues were brewing down there, and the stew was plenty nasty. . . . I made a record with Guitar Slim, and that turned out to be a big smash. . . . He was a country boy, and I liked him very much.[83]

Eddie Jones, "Guitar Slim," was born in Greenwood, Mississippi, in 1926. By 1950 the Blues vocalist and guitarist was working at the Dew Drop Inn, and he began recording a year later. In 1954 he released "The Things I Used to Do," one of the largest hits to emerge from New Orleans. The song sold more than a million copies. According to songwriter Al Reed, the sartorial splendor, music, performances, and attitudes of Guitar Slim revitalized the Blues aesthetic in the city:

> [He] had cords on his guitar that was something like 200 feet long. This guy would play on stage with his band, he would get off the stage, walk out of the door at the club, go out into the middle of the street . . . and never drop a beat. . . . Big passing automobiles would stop and just listen to this guy play and watch him walk. And he wore these loud clothes, like red suits, cherry red, snow white, and the loudest greens. . . . I think he had a greater impact on the electric sound than any other guitarist. . . . And Chuck Berry was not using that sound at the time. I hear them speak of Jimi Hendrix. Jimi Hendrix was a late comer. . . . He [Guitar Slim] was a backwoods country boy, he came to New Orleans with just what he had on his back, didn't even have an instrument to play. . . . He would lift you above and beyond the clouds when he played; he would create sensations within your body that really played tricks with your mind. He was the first man to do this.[84]

Several writers suggest that there were multiple rhythms circulating in New Orleans and J&M Studios. Hannusch claims that "New Orleans rhythm and blues did not acquire its distinctive identity over night. . . . A number of rhythms styles have been popular: 6/8 rock and roll piano triplets; Latin and rhumba tempos; 4/4 swinging second line drumming; and riffing stop-time horn patterns."[85] In addition, Bartholomew and the J&M Studio Band were engaged in crafting a fundamentally deeper and stronger sound.[86] Although Matassa did not take credit for the New Orleans Sound, some began to call it the Cosimo Sound. However, pianist Mac "Dr. John" Rebennack also credits the origins of the signature rhythm, their exponential deepening of the bass line, to the J&M Studio Band: "That was the start of what eventually became known as the New Orleans Sound with the guitar doubling the bass line, the baritone and tenor doubling the bass line, making it a real strong sound and playing around it. It got to be known as 'Cosimo's Sound' but it was the musicians' sound because they were playing the music. But it was his little mix job that got the credit."[87]

The creation of modern bass culture was defined by the ritualistic search for the bottom, the deepest depths of sound and human experience. This philosophical lyrical and sonic search and the movement of bass into musical prominence went on to revitalize the Blues epistemology while simultaneously building the foundations of Rhythm and Blues, Soul, Reggae, Funk, and Hip Hop. One of the best descriptions of the meaning of this innovation was rendered by Black British dub poet Linton Kwesi Johnson in his song "Bass Culture." Johnson concludes that the new bass sound was "di beat of the heart, this pulsing of blood . . . pushing against the walls that bar Black blood / . . . when the beat just lash / when the walls mus' smash . . . when oppression scatah."[88]

On the eve of the landmark *Brown v. Board of Education* decision, the New Orleans Rhythm and Blues renaissance was reassembling historic patterns of community building in the face of new forms of repression. The release of Guitar Slim's slow Blues "The Things I Used To Do, Not Gonna Do No More" in January 1954 metaphorically spoke to the end of an era of patience and compliance and the beginning of a period where the walls of segregation were pushed down. As crafted in New Orleans, the architecture of bass culture promised a transformative search for meaning and freedom.

The Crossroads

Court challenges, voting, boycotts, and mass protests increasingly defined the southern landscape. The Double V generation was pushing the Blues agenda forward in new and historic ways despite facing a wave of repression. Twenty thousand Black voters were registered in Louisiana by 1948, 2.4 percent of the total population of Blacks in the state. Orleans and Jefferson Parishes accounted for half of this number, while thirty-one parishes had no registered Black voters. Registration rates were generally higher in the twenty-five southern Louisiana parishes due to regional conflicts in the state and the growing opposition to segregation within the Catholic Church. Yet when Alvin H. Jones of the Louisiana Progressive Voters League attempted to register six persons in the predominantly Cajun St. Landry Parish in 1950, he was attacked at the registrar's office: "I was slugged with the butt of a gun and was pounded with a pair of brass knuckles. They left a hole in my head. I didn't stagger and they didn't knock me down."[89] As Black registration rose, politicians increasingly campaigned to secure African American support. Earl Long received the endorsement of the league during his 1948 campaign for governor.[90] In the same year, Long's plan to increase educational expenditures and equalize teacher salaries was approved by the legislature. Spending on Black children increased from $16 to $116 per pupil between 1940 and 1955. In addition, Grambling University received increased funding and a law school was established at Southern University in Baton Rouge to forestall efforts to integrate LSU's law school.[91]

In New Orleans, parks, beaches, restaurants, water fountains, lunch counters, buses, streetcars, churches, hospitals, public housing, public and private schools, and public libraries continued to be rigidly segregated. In 1947 the NAACP organized a boycott of Canal Street stores that refused to allow Black women to try on hats. This campaign was suppressed by police harassment and a court injunction.[92] To appease his African American supporters, whom he privately referred to as "darkies," Mayor Chep Morrison improved several parks, recreation centers, playgrounds, and pools that had been neglected for decades. Admittance to City Park was achieved in 1952, and the public libraries were integrated in 1954. For the Black middle class, a new subdivision with a park and municipal golf course was built in 1956, Pontchartrain Park. New Orleans became the last major southern city to integrate its police force. The two Black policemen hired during this period were the first on the force since 1915.[93] Yet Palmer recalled that segregation on public transportation continued to be strictly enforced: "I saw a white guy get thrown off a city bus once for sitting in the Black section. 'Can't sit there, it's the Black section.' 'I can sit anywhere I want.' 'Not with niggers you can't.' Threw him off the bus. One time Mike Serpas, a white trumpet player we called Cheese painted himself green. Got on the bus and said, 'Where do you want me to sit, I'm green!' Threw him off, too."[94]

Segregation allowed many institutions to extract rents from African American consumers by, among other things, eliminating Black businesses and charging monopoly fees and prices. Just thirty miles from New Orleans, resistance to these practices in the capital city of Baton Rouge reverberated throughout the South. In 1950 the city declared all of the independent bus companies illegal, and Black ridership soon reached 80 percent of the total on city-owned buses. In January 1953 bus patrons were confronted with a 50 percent increase in fares, from ten cents to fifteen. Reverend T. J. Jemison of Mount Zion First Baptist Church remembered looking out the church's window one day and seeing buses full of exhausted Black women domestics standing in the aisles over empty seats reserved for whites. "I thought that was just out of order, that was just cruel," he recalled.[95] Willis Reed, publisher of the *Baton Rouge Post*, formed a group that met at homes and schools to plan a bus boycott that would send an economic message to the city. In February 1953 Reverend Jemison appealed to the city council, and two weeks later the body passed an ordinance enabling open seating so long as Blacks entered from the back and whites entered from the front.

White bus drivers successfully resisted the ordinance for three months until an exhausted domestic worker, Martha White, sat in a "whites only" designated seat in June. When she refused to move the police were called. When she was threatened with arrest, all the Black riders rose to her defense and insisted on being arrested with her. Although Jemison convinced the police not to make arrests, the bus drivers' union launched a strike on June 15 in order to have the open seating ordinance repealed. They returned to work four days later after the attorney general declared the law unconstitutional. Simultaneously, the United Defense League organized a mass meeting among African Americans in order to plan a bus boycott and a free car pool effort. The boycott began on June 20 and soon crosses were burned at Jemison's church and home. From that point forward, an armed member of his church served as his bodyguard.

Support for the Baton Rouge bus boycott grew so quickly that the June 22 meeting had to be held at Memorial Stadium. On June 24 the city council approved Ordinance 251, which required open seating except for two white seats in the front and two Black seats in the back. Jemison's decision to accept the compromise disappointed many who believed that it ended a mass movement capable of challenging segregation in Baton Rouge, Louisiana, and throughout the South. The Baton Rouge movement was closely studied by other activists and was successfully deployed by the leaders of the more well-known Montgomery, Alabama, bus boycott of 1955. Lasting a year, the Montgomery movement transformed Rosa Parks into an international icon and propelled a young Reverend Martin Luther King Jr. into the ranks of national civil rights leadership. The erasure from memory of the Baton Rogue episode is just another example of how the deep roots of African American working-class innovation, leadership, and resistance present in the Louisiana Blues agenda continue to be masked.[96]

During this period the NAACP pursued a legal strategy of securing equalization under the "separate but equal" principle of *Plessy v. Ferguson* while at the same time exposing its contradictions. The NAACP Legal Defense Fund and the Louisiana Colored Teachers Association launched a campaign to equalize teachers' salaries in 1942, and after several dismissals, the state courts ordered equalization in 1943.[97] By the early 1950s the organization dedicated itself to pursuing legal decisions supporting full integration. The initial targets were long established higher education institutions that could not be easily duplicated under the *Plessy* rubric. Marshall and Tureaud successfully sued to integrate Louisiana State University's undergraduate degree program and its law school in 1950. The supporting opinion was written by federal judge J. Skelly Wright, a thirty-eight-year-old member of New Orleans's Bourbon elite. However, these eases did not directly affect K-12 education. Fairclough notes, "Overcrowding was especially acute in New Orleans, where Black enrollment increased 28.9 percent in 1947 and a further 10.8 percent in 1948. . . . While fifteen white elementary schools were half-empty, 23 of the Negro schools operated the 'platoon' system of double shifts. Even so, the *Louisiana Weekly* estimated that perhaps a quarter of the city's black children were not in school."[98]

Despite this growing social disaster, the school board approved only a fraction of the school superintendent's $40 million plan to improve Black schools and open underutilized white schools for Black use. This action led the NAACP to file *Bush v. New Orleans Parish School Board* in 1948 in order to improve the availability of educational facilities and opportunities. The case would work its way through the courts for another twenty years before being resolved.[99] The silence in which many rural and urban Louisiana communities suffered had much to do with elements of the national Black leadership defining progress in terms of activism within a Democratic Party still dedicated to segregation, North and South. At the conclusion of World War II, radicals, socialists, communists, progressives, liberals, Blacks, and Blues advocates of direct action were increasingly expelled from public life. For example, in 1947 the Southern Conference for Human Welfare moved its headquarters from Nashville to New Orleans. Among its six hundred members in Louisiana were Black leaders, white liberals, socialists, and union leaders. Hoping to establish a broad alliance for interracial social reform, the organization appealed to members of the Bourbon bloc: Edgar Stern, president of the New Orleans Cotton Exchange, Catholic Archbishop Rummel, Samuel Zemurray of United Fruit, and the newly elected mayor, Chep Morrison. However, due to its refusal to purge communists and socialists from its ranks, the group was ostracized by the Bourbon elite, the NAACP, and the Catholic Church. The Southern Conference for Human Welfare soon found itself the subject of an attack led by the plantation-bloc leaders who dominated the U.S. House of Representatives' Un-American Activities Committee (HUAC).[100]

Gerald Horne contends that the multiple purposes of McCarthyism have often been overlooked. This movement to expel a wide range of activists from public life was led by a new alliance formed between previous combatants who joined together to resist the transformation of the racial order: the southern plantation bloc, elite Catholics, and white supremacists in the North, South, and West. For Horne, the anticommunism of McCarthyism was defined very broadly: "[The] phenomenon often subsumed under the rubric 'McCarthyism' had a particularly sharp racist edge. Robert Griffith has noted Senator Joseph McCarthy's close ties to the Dixiecrats—especially Senator James Eastland; indeed, the repressors of Blacks and Reds tended to march in lockstep. And of course being a Black Red was the commission of more than a chromatic sin. Donald Crosby sees the motive force behind McCarthyism emerging from elites among Catholics in the South and elsewhere."[101]

HUAC attempted to eliminate much of the Double V era leadership before the *Brown* decision. Paul Robeson's passport was cancelled in 1950, and W. E. B. Du Bois was arrested in 1951. Numerous cultural leaders, labor activists, civil rights activists, communists, and socialists were called before HUAC and the U.S. Senate's Internal Security Committee and questioned about their activities over the previous two decades. In the South, a wide range of progressive thinkers and activists were increasingly targeted.

During the same period in New Orleans, members of the Progressive Party were subjected to police harassment and eleven radical unions in the city were expelled from the CIO. Professor Johnson at Dillard was fired for refusing to answer questions about his alleged affiliation with the Communist Party, and in 1951 the LCRC and the Louisiana Committee on Human Rights were disbanded. In an attempt to protect itself from McCarthyism, the NAACP purged Civil Rights Congress members and socialists from its local and national branches beginning in 1950. Additionally, the Afro-Creole elite's domination of the NAACP headquarters continued to foster conflict within the New Orleans branch and between it and other state branches. Thoroughly isolated from many of its former allies and riven with internal conflicts, the state NAACP became increasingly susceptible to Bourbon attacks.[102] Other Black leadership organizations also fractured around the question of electoral endorsements. The new Black political organizations attempted to deliver a small but growing number of votes to competing white politicians, some of whom were open supporters of white supremacist policies.[103]

In the face of rising union mobilizations that the church supported, the sugar planters, many of whom were Catholic, also mobilized. They relied on planters who were also representatives in the state legislature to introduce a right-to-work bill designed to severely limit labor's ability to organize in the state by outlawing the union shop. Although the legislation was opposed by the Catholic Church's leadership, the bill passed in July 1954. Despite these setbacks, things had changed. Although the strike ended within a week and many of the demands were not met, the workers, families, organizers, and priests involved considered the strike itself a minor victory. One Black member stated, "We won the strike the day we went out. Men for the first time. The white folks became aware that we are Negroes."[104]

For many years an annual parade of schoolchildren was held at Lafayette Square in New Orleans to honor John McDonogh, a Baltimore-born shipping executive, slave trader, and New Orleans slaveholder who willed a large donation to New Orleans schools for the education of whites and freed Blacks. Black children were traditionally required to march in the rear. They were absent on May 8, 1954. The boycott of this ceremony by African American organizations, parents, teachers, and principals marked the beginning of a new era in the city. The era of mass movements had returned to the South and it moved to the insistent rhythms of New Orleans music.[105]

CHAPTER 6

The Second Reconstruction, 1965–1977

The Neo-Bourbon War on Poverty and
Massive Resistance in Concrete

The passage of the Civil Rights Act of 1964, the Economic Opportunity Act of 1964 (the War on Poverty), the Voting Rights Act of 1965, and the Fair Housing Act of 1968 did not signal the demise of the plantation bloc in the South or the creation of a color-blind society. Yet African Americans' mobilizations, along with major federal economic and legal interventions, did alter the practices and composition of these regimes. I offer the term *neoplantation* to describe a period, set of practices, and ideology defined by the multiple institutional reforms that accompanied African American re-enfranchisement. Similarly, I use the term *neo-Bourbon* to capture the new power structure that emerged in the New Orleans region.

From 1965 to 1977 an intense battle was waged to eliminate segregationist institutions in the nation as a whole. The growing Blues-based Black political, social, and cultural movements pushed for the systematic elimination of plantation-bloc hegemony in the South. Yet the massive resistance institutions created prior to this period continued to defend these regimes while systematically and simultaneously undermining African American movements and federal interventions. The Bourbon bloc used urban renewal, the War on Poverty, new suburban political allies, new policing practices, and other policies to defeat the intensifying movements for sustainable development and social justice that reemerged from the Blues tradition. In keeping with previous periods, a part of this campaign was dedicated to incorporating significant elements of the Black political, economic, and cultural insurgency into a new governing alliance, what I call the neo-Bourbon bloc.

Although this bloc was highly unstable, some still remember its birth as marking the golden age of ethnic, racial, gender, and class reforms in the region. However, during this same period, the African American community in New Orleans was enclosed by a series of social, spatial, physical, political, educational, and fiscal barricades. Second, a set of policies were deployed that channeled limited regional and national resources, both public and private, to support declining

Bourbon economic sectors and institutions. Other resources were appropriated and confiscated in order to create neo-Bourbon profit centers and institutions. The new neo-Bourbon state was able to simultaneously preserve Bourbon command over the economy and major institutions while incorporating elements of the Blues agenda pushed by African American social movements.

When members of the working class, African American students, and numerous organizations pushed for a more fundamental realization of the Blues agenda, their voices were forcibly silenced. These movements were also silenced by a new period of resource starvation that followed the massive withdrawal of federal War on Poverty funds during the late 1960s and early 1970s. Many aspects of the sustainable Blues development agenda, the movements that revitalized it, and the War on Poverty were demonized over the next four decades by academics, journalists, politicians, prosecutors, police, and those members of the African American community allied with the neo-Bourbon regime.[1] Yet, as in previous generations, the Blues agenda was preserved by working-class organic intellectuals operating within communities, cultural traditions, families, churches, schools, homes, workplaces, and other organizations, as well as in the prisons used to cage this alternative development path.

While the Second Reconstruction marked the elimination of de jure segregation, it also marked an increased reliance on the built environment to ensure de facto racial segregation. As in many ghettoized communities around the country, infrastructure policies produced and reproduced numerous social and racial disasters. Hurricane Katrina uncovered the corruption and racism that had created a network of inferior levees bordering many of New Orleans's African American communities. Yet forty years earlier, in 1965, Hurricane Betsy had revealed the presence of two historic disaster-generating Bourbon engineering failures of epic proportions. The devastation of the wetlands wrought by oil- and gas-industry dredging brought hurricanes closer to the city while the construction of the Mississippi River–Gulf Outlet (MR-GO) created a highway for rapid entry of hurricanes and storm surges into the heart of the city, the Lower Ninth Ward.

Billion-Dollar Betsy

Now, cryin' won't help you,
prayin won't do you no good,
When the levee breaks, mama,
you got to move!

Memphis Minnie, "When the Levee Breaks" (1929)

The dawn of the Second Reconstruction in 1965 was accompanied by a powerful hurricane. After crossing over Florida, Hurricane Betsy's wind speed reached

150 miles an hour just before it struck the Gulf Coast below New Orleans with twelve-foot waves. The city was battered by 105-mile-an-hour winds late on the night of Thursday, September 9, 1965. After a levee failed, from twelve to fourteen feet of water covered the Lower Ninth Ward and four feet of water covered Claiborne Avenue in Tremé. Lois Tilley was at her Lower Ninth Ward home during a break from Southern University. Approximately fourteen feet of water surrounded her house before she left aboard a pirogue navigated by a friend. Before she left, she looked out her second-floor window at a sight that stayed with her for the rest of her life: "In that water, there were babies floating, along with the snakes. . . . I saw that. I know that." The water was so high that rescue teams often tied bodies to trees and rooftops so they could be found later.[2]

The storm took a total of eighty-one lives, mostly in the Lower Ninth Ward, and it left 80 percent of this community under water. Following the storm, people seeking shelter walked through water above their waists carrying children in their arms. Others had to be rescued from rooftops. Many current residents believe this disaster was the beginning of the economic decline of the Lower Ninth Ward. They and other observers argue that the residents did not receive sufficient financial assistance in the form of grants, loans, and other support to revitalize the area. Consequently, the lack of aid led many longtime residents, commercial firms, and manufacturers to abandon the community.[3]

Approximately 250,000 residents fled the city before Hurricane Betsy arrived. More than 185,000 of the remaining residents were forced into shelters opened at schools, churches, the city auditorium, and other government buildings. Conditions in the city worsened due to the loss of electricity in ten thousand homes and the presence of at least one hundred alligators that crawled out of Bayou St. John. Several days after the hurricane struck a large number of residents remained in shelters: fifty thousand persons in New Orleans, twelve thousand at the naval air station in Algiers, and thirty thousand in St. Bernard and Plaquemines Parishes. In those parishes water levels also reached fourteen feet.[4]

Time magazine noted that property "damage in the delta would total at least $1 billion, and shipping losses, including 700 vessels sunk or grounded, would amount to another billion." "Billion-Dollar Betsy" placed a spotlight on MR-GO, which had been completed earlier in the year. This channel funneled the storm surge into the Lower Ninth Ward.

Writing in 2006, Todd Shallat described the concerns raised about MR-GO prior to its completion:

> In 1964, for example, the New Orleans District [of the Army Corps of Engineers] advocated building a phalanx of steel gates that would have lain across the path followed by Katrina. The next year Hurricane Betsy drove a monstrous swell into the city's Ninth Ward. Six thousand houses sustained serious damage. Twenty thousand people barely escaped with their lives. Betsy, said an insurance spokesman, was

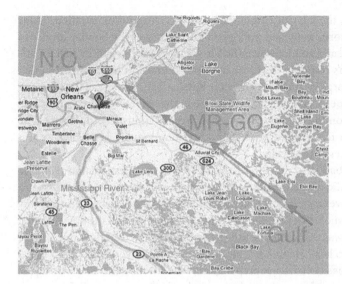

FIGURE 5.
Mississippi River–Gulf
Outlet (MR-GO). Map
by Greg Palast in
"Bush'd Again? New
Orleans, Mr. O and Mr.
Go," *Huffington Post*,
August 27, 2010.

"the worst natural disaster in the history of America—greater even than the San Francisco Earthquake and the Chicago Fire combined." Damage estimates ran as high as $2.4 billion—more costly than any storm on record, the inflation-adjusted equivalent of $13 billion today.[5]

Hurricane Betsy occurred during the height of the Vietnam War and the civil rights movement. Yet the response of the state and federal governments differed dramatically from the response to Hurricane Katrina. President Lyndon Johnson visited New Orleans on September 10, one day after the storm. A visit to a shelter established at George Washington High School was part of his itinerary: "Johnson had pressed his way through hundreds of refugees huddled in the darkened school corridors. The electricity was out, and they were eating cold beans and raw carrots from paper plates on the floor. Many begged the President for water, which was also cut off."[6] The National Guard soon entered the city. Governor McKeithen used the functioning radio stations to appeal to the residents of the state to do their "brotherly" duty: "Open your hearts and homes. . . . Sorrow and sympathy are not enough. . . . The disaster and misery that all of us saw in New Orleans and southern Louisiana yesterday must make us answer the question Cain asked of Able, 'Am I my brother's keeper?' And the answer must be 'Yes,' and the time is now."[7]

President Johnson returned on September 12 and remained in constant contact with several federal leaders and agencies in order to coordinate the relief effort: Secretary of Defense McNamara, the Army Corps of Engineers, the Federal Housing Agency, the General Services Administration, the Small Business

Administration, the Job Corps, and the Food and Drug Administration. Three days after the storm army and navy personnel were serving Sunday dinner to the twelve thousand residents who fled to the naval air station in Algiers. Although Johnson's response to Hurricane Betsy differed dramatically from that of President George W. Bush to Hurricane Katrina, the response of the Bourbon bloc was the same in 1965, in 1927, and in 2005. After the storm, disaster capitalism descended on the city. Merchants soon were charging five to six times the regular price for ice, gas, groceries, and other commodities. Hotel owners also raised their prices dramatically.[8]

In 1965 a debate also raged over the city's lack of an evacuation plan and the failure to build adequate levees. In town for a speech, nuclear physicist and atomic bomb inventor Edward Teller was amazed by the Bourbon disposability ethic. "It is incredible that people only had 20 minutes between the time they first knew the water was rising and the time it reached a height over their heads to get out. Then it's too late." He was quickly denounced by Mayor Schiro, who stated that New Orleans's civil defense preparations were "the best there is." During the 1965 mayoral race, Schiro was attacked again by challenger James E. Fitzmorris, who argued that the mayor failed to heed a 1964 report by the Army Corps of Engineers recommending the construction of hurricane flood-control levees. In November Schiro avoided a runoff election by a mere five hundred votes.[9]

Finally, the Bourbon bloc was not the only group of plantation elites implicated in the disaster. Shallat argues that Johnson's celebrated quick response had less to do with empathy than it had to do with opportunity. His family was part of the movement of southern plantation-bloc capital into large-scale urban and suburban development:

> Six hours into the flooding, President Lyndon Johnson was stepping from *Air Force One* onto the tarmac at New Orleans's Moisant Field. "I am here," he said, "because I want to see with my own eyes what the unhappy alliance of wind and water have done to this land and its people." Wind and water and man, he might better have said, because the storm had landed hard where Texas investors, the president's wife Lady Bird Johnson among them, planned to levee off 32,000 acres for 250,000 people in a new suburb and industrial park. New Orleans East, as it was called, would need flood protection; so would the north-shore suburbs, Jefferson Parish, the Port of New Orleans, the Port of Venice, Morgan City, and a dozen or more other storm-battered sites. . . . Johnson pressured Congress to approve $250 million for Gulf Coast hurricane projects, including a $56-million down payment on New Orleans levees.[10]

The actions of the Bourbon bloc during the Great Flood of 1927 and Hurricane Betsy continued to resonate throughout the southeastern Louisiana region in 2005. After Hurricane Katrina, accusations were made that the neo-Bourbon bloc destroyed levees in predominantly African American neighborhoods of the Lower Ninth Ward and west of the Industrial Canal. In 2005 Dr. Robert Bullard, professor of sociology at Clark Atlanta University and director of the Environmental Justice Resource Center, observed how the intellectual legacy of 1927 informed theories of attacks on Lower Ninth Ward levees during Hurricane Betsy and Hurricane Katrina:

> Hurricane Betsy was a hurricane that hit New Orleans. . . . This is 1965, what happened in New Orleans . . . in terms of the levee breaching and the Lower Ninth Ward being flooded . . . [was] that there are still people in the Lower Ninth Ward who believe that the levee was breached on purpose by the mayor and his officials to save the white areas. . . . In some cases, it is an urban myth. In other cases, people believe it, and therefore, it becomes real. And probably the reason why there were fewer deaths in the Lower Ninth Ward is because people, older people who remember Betsy and remember being trapped in their attics with no way to get through . . . [many people had] hatchets and axes in their attics and were able to chop through. . . . So we have the story of the breaching of the Ninth Ward—of the levee and flooding of the Ninth Ward on purpose.[11]

In the same year, a similar question was posed to Charmaine Marchand, representative for the Lower Ninth Ward, in the Louisiana House of Representatives. Her response was crafted from a multigenerational encounter with the Bourbon politics of submersion and disaster: "They blew the locks in the levees to save Uptown, to save the French Quarter, the richer upriver areas, in Betsy, at the expense of us. . . . Katrina brings back those old fears. Was this intentional? Did they do this to us again? We're still the dumping grounds for the city of New Orleans. That's what's going through people's minds in the community right now."[12]

Both comments address the deep fear embedded in the minds of many Black residents about their own position within the neo-Bourbon worldview and regime. In both disasters, questions have been raised as to whether these fears are products of racial paranoia detached from reality. Certain crucial evidence is often left out of this debate. For thousands of years levees have been broken to save areas controlled by the powerful. The politics surrounding death by submersion in New Orleans stretch back at least three centuries, and during most of this history Black residents were forced to live in the city's swamps and other flood-prone areas. Throughout the history of the region, race, wealth, and power determined where levees were built, how they were built, and how they were maintained. This history, when combined with the multidimensional nature of flood control and the reality of "massive resistance," should give us pause before we randomly dismiss claims of intentional malice. Only in light of the burden of Bourbon history can we understand the Blues narratives that reflect simultaneously on the proven, the hidden, the possible, and the seemingly impossible. For example, the Ninth Ward was more than a metaphorical dumping ground. As Bullard notes, after Hurricane Betsy the city government created a toxic landfill in the predominantly Black Upper Ninth Ward:

> Hurricane Betsy created not only devastation, but it also created a landfill that created a Superfund site in a black neighborhood, the Agriculture Street Landfill. Most of the debris from Hurricane Betsy in 1965 was put in a landfill in a black neighborhood in New Orleans, and so the people in the Agriculture Street community, Press Park area, have been fighting for decades to get their community relocated from this Superfund site. And it's ironic that they may get their neighborhood cleaned up from this Superfund site because of Katrina. Just before December 2004, there was a major lawsuit—the lawsuit actually went to trial, and the case was declared a class action, and it's still pending in court right now, even though . . . the contamination is much wider than the site itself.[13]

Although it would seem impossible that city officials would respond to the devastation of one Black community by devastating another, this is the tragic trajectory of Bourbon logic. Discussions of the Lower Ninth Ward's devastation by Hurricanes Betsy and Katrina have often hidden the role played by MR-GO. In addition to contributing to the massive destruction of the city's cypress swamp wetland buffer, during both hurricanes the channel acted as a funnel for a storm surge aimed directly at the Lower Ninth Ward, as a hurricane highway. This vulnerability was recognized in 1964 and was proven during Hurricane Betsy in 1965. Still, MR-GO was not only kept open, it was constantly dredged and widened. The few powerful shipping companies that benefited from this multibillion-dollar boondoggle over the years fought against its closure even after Katrina definitively proved that the channel was little more than a dagger aimed at the city. MR-GO was not part of a conspiracy concocted in the minds of paranoid Blacks; it was a planned, billion-dollar reality. It was one of many infrastructure projects designed to preserve the hegemony of a neo-Bourbon regime whose trademark is the daily reproduction of social, economic, cultural, and environmental disasters.

A vast network of oil and gas pipelines, along with shipping channels, carved up the wetlands of the region and made southeastern Louisiana more vulnerable to hurricanes. According to Todd Shallat, the system of gates proposed in 1964 to block the storm surge into the Lower Ninth Ward was partially funded by Congress after Hurricane Betsy. However, environmentalists resisted the completion of the system and the allocated funds were diverted. The Army Corps of Engineers eliminated "the gated barriers from the hurricane-protection design by 1984. During two decades of delays, the cost of the gates ballooned from $85 million to $924 million. . . . Reluctantly the Corp[s] returned to a simpler, but less-effective system of earthen and concrete levees, though it was common knowledge that lakeside earthen embankments were not enough to withstand another Betsy."[14]

The possibility and probability of the 2005 Katrina disaster was known for over four decades. The belief in the disposability of the Lower Ninth Ward in particular, and African American neighborhoods in general, was not the product of Black paranoia but rather a key pillar of Bourbon philosophical thought and urban planning for over a century and a half. MR-GO, oil and gas pipeline construction in the wetlands, corruption, and the inferior, and deadly, levees constructed by the Levee Board and the corps laid waste to the Lower Ninth Ward, New Orleans, and the parishes of St. Bernard and Plaquemines. Neither a once-in-a-century natural catastrophe nor the most elaborate conspiracy theory can compete with the consequences of the daily workings of the Bourbon regime.

The Second Reconstruction Blues in New Orleans

The first seven months of 1965 fundamentally transformed African American consciousness: the assassination of Malcolm X, Selma, Bogalusa, the passage of the Voting Rights Act, the Watts Rebellion, and Hurricane Betsy. In the wake of these events, a Black electorate staged multiple confrontations with the Bourbon regime that had worked hard to repress it for nearly three centuries. In contrast to the First Reconstruction, Blacks were now a part of a political party that contained both the leading supporters and the leading opponents of the Second Reconstruction.

During this period of intense political conflict, the historic redistributive agenda embedded in the Blues development tradition informed numerous organizations. This movement had to simultaneously face new forms of "massive resistance," including the appearance of policies and programs that were intentionally designed to misdirect and thwart fundamental social change. The Black middle class was engaged in a struggle, often against its own members, to preserve its leadership of markets, institutions, and movements. The working class was engaged in the preservation and expansion of the cultural, social, and economic institutions that were the pillars of survival, resistance, mobility, and creativity.

The maze of biracial political institutions created during this Second Reconstruction shared many features with the ones briefly established during the First Reconstruction: they emerged after nearly a century of devastating anti-Black violence; they were dependent on extraordinary forms of federal, state, and philanthropic intervention; they were subject to relentless legal and budgetary attacks; and they were marked by profound forms of Black political fragmentation.

As in the First Reconstruction, many of the Black organizations that emerged during the Second Reconstruction had key elements of the Blues agenda as part of their goals: the push for the fundamental democratization of all aspects of regional life, the dismantling of the political hegemony of the plantation bloc, the breakup of racial and economic monopolies, the economic redistribution of monopolized resources to oppressed and working-class communities, the creation of sustainable communities, the full recognition of human rights, and the affirmation of Black cultural and intellectual traditions. While the Bourbon bloc viewed these goals as little more than a list of heresies, in order to retain hegemony, it used federal and private assistance to selectively incorporate both elements of the Black electorate and aspects of the Blues agenda.

Federal aid, foundation support, and electoral politics relied on the optimism of the period to create a racial reform sector, an institution, organized around short-term grants and pilot projects along with promises of long-term reform. Financing was provided to support the development of new institutions organized to meet long-denied social, economic, and cultural needs. The national racial and class reform complex managed, monetized, and commodified the democratic hopes, dreams, and movements of Blacks, Latinos, Native Americans, Asian Americans, labor, and the impoverished. It also created a stratum of poverty, community development, and labor managers, workers, and entrepreneurs who increasingly played a central role in local, state, and national politics. In addition, the Great Society reform complex held out the promise of democracy and wealth to the formerly colonized nations of the world. The economic foundations of this expansion of the Fordist welfare state included mass production, mass consumption, and historic levels of profit generated from U.S. economic, political, and military interventions throughout the world. As in the First Reconstruction, the stage was prepared for hope and farce, triumph and tragedy.

Although African American, labor, antipoverty, and anticolonial movements played central roles in forcing federal, state, and local governments to create the racial and class reform complex, each was now confronted by a highly flexible institution capable of mimicking the rhetoric of reform and deploying its symbols while simultaneously blocking fundamental change. In addition, elements within the Black community were aggressively pursuing agendas that preserved existing hierarchies through programs of assimilation, gradualism, pragmatism, and uplift and selective corporate, electoral, and institutional alliances. The entry of many Blacks into public sector jobs meant that Blacks were now both the victims and beneficiaries of the reform complex.

In contrast, the Blues bloc emphasized mobilizing the most desperate section of the Black working class, *the people*. This network or grid of individuals, organizations, and communities pushed for the distribution of affordable, subsidized, and free housing, health care, education, food, heat, and water. In addition, they advocated for full employment and freedom from police abuse as basic human rights. Consequently, many of their activities were geared toward mobilizing communities to meet their subsistence needs by establishing survival programs, pushing for social reforms, holding protests, using the ballot, and developing grassroots intellectuals and leaders. Many of those working to meet the daily survival needs were also adherents of the "Freedom Now" ethic, which reflected the position of a wide array of reformist, radical, and revolutionary individuals and organizations who sought an immediate and fundamental transformation of the neo-Bourbon regime.

After the restoration of voting rights, splits emerged within the Black community over the full implementation of the Blues agenda, with some organizations beginning to distance themselves from it. Elements within the Black electoral movement faced other major challenges in addition to factionalism: the governance of increasingly impoverished and segregated cities and towns, resource blockades by other regions of the state, resource competition by white flight suburban parishes, and the transformation of the massive resistance movement from a faction of the Democratic Party into the pillar of a new conservative movement resurgent within the Republican Party. Also, the new Democratic Party's biracial political regime didn't fundamentally alter the neo-Bourbon command of the regional political economy. Finally, the mass mobilizations that gave birth to the Second Reconstruction were soon enclosed and new, autonomous mass mobilizations were blocked. By 1975 the racial populist presidential campaigns of Alabama governor George Wallace and the national Republican Southern Strategy of President Richard Nixon had fundamentally transformed the Louisiana, southern, and national political landscapes. However, in 1965 optimism abounded, except in the New Orleans region.

The Second March against Fear

Despite the devastation wrought by Hurricane Betsy on the largely African American Lower Ninth Ward, there was no blossoming of racial conciliation in New Orleans or Louisiana. The predatory practices of the Bourbon bloc continued, as did the role of Bogalusa, site of the birth of the Second Reconstruction, as the crossroads where old and new social regimes contended for power. The civil rights movement, the War on Poverty, the Vietnam War, the Voting Rights Act, and the Bogalusa movement continued to destabilize massive resistance and Bourbon rule. Although there were deep class and regional divisions among whites in the state, general agreement surrounding white supremacy, residential segregation, employment discrimination, and opposition to civil rights had made the white working class an increasingly reliable pillar of the Bourbon bloc. The restoration of African American civil rights fostered optimism that multiracial political alliances would lead to significant shifts in policy and social conditions. Yet in his often overlooked 1967 speech "The Other America,"

Reverend Martin Luther King Jr. noted that the battle for social and economic justice was actually intensifying:

> But we must see that the struggle today is much more difficult. It's more difficult today because we are struggling now for genuine equality. And it's much easier to integrate a lunch counter than it is to guarantee a livable income and a good solid job. It's much easier to guarantee the right to vote than it is to guarantee the right to live in sanitary, decent housing conditions. It is much easier to integrate a public park than it is to make genuine, quality, integrated education a reality. And so today we are struggling for something which says we demand genuine equality. . . . What I'm trying to get across is that our nation has constantly taken a positive step forward on the question of racial justice and racial equality. But over and over again at the same time, it made certain backward steps. And this has been the persistence of the so-called white backlash.[15]

King viewed the conflict in Bogalusa as a telling lesson of things to come. It provided a powerful counternarrative to civil rights triumphalism and romanticization that followed the passage of the Voting Rights Act. The older institutions of state-approved mob and random violence also persisted in Bogalusa during the mid-1960s. For example, when visiting the downtown shopping district, Black residents often required Deacons for Defense escorts just to eat unmolested at local restaurants. In a 1966 incident, a Black army officer who stopped at a local gas station to use the pay phone was murdered by a white person passing by. Even amid conflict, observers began to see the emergence of key institutional pillars of the new neo-Bourbon regime. First, in October 1965 the city of Bogalusa banned all demonstrations in order to both stop the progress of the civil rights movement and prevent further violent clashes. Intent on pushing forward, Black children launched a boycott of local schools. On October 20, 1965, "Bloody Wednesday," participants in two marches led by Black youths were beaten by the police and arrested. A judge at the time noted the emergence of one of the key neo-Bourbon institutional pillars: white mob-led racial violence was being replaced by white police violence. Second, another pillar of the emergent regime found in Bogalusa was the "officially" integrated school. At these sites, institutional and mob violence were visited on Black students, many of whom were forced to endure harassment by white administrators, teachers, staff, and students for years. A third emergent institution was partial enfranchisement. Although Blacks were one-third of the population, voter suppression efforts limited Black voter registration in Bogalusa to just 16 percent of the electorate. Voter suppression campaigns would continue to limit the Black electorate for the next four decades.[16]

The birth of the Second Reconstruction in Bogalusa and Louisiana was accompanied by a deepening social polarization rather than an era of reconciliation. Considered to be too moderate by many white voters, Bogalusa's Mayor

Cutrer was voted out of office in 1966. He was replaced by Curt Siegelin, who refused to negotiate with the Bogalusa Civic and Voters' League (BCVL). To break this impasse, A. Z. Young of the BCVL called for a march from Bogalusa to Baton Rouge to guarantee the human rights of Louisiana's Black citizens.[17] The emergent neo-Bourbon state was partially born from this crisis, as Governor McKeithen attempted to simultaneously limit organized white supremacist violence while preventing Black rebellions against mob violence and institutional oppression. Consequently, the state provided protection for the BCVL march.

On August 10, 1967, forty-four BCVL marchers, several members of the Deacons for Defense, and a small group of state troopers began the trek to Baton Rouge. In the Livingston Parish town of Satsuma, the marchers were attacked by white residents. Despite the fact that the number of marchers had dwindled to just six, their courageous attempt to claim public space as citizens was repeatedly met by violent threats and violent acts. Governor McKeithen sent an additional 150 state police to guard the marchers. After additional attacks, the security detail grew to include 825 Louisiana National Guardsmen and 170 state police officers. Lance Hill provides the following account of this massive spectacle as it reached the Amite River:

> National Guard helicopters roared overhead as a magnetic sweeper cleared the highway of roofing nails scattered by the Klan. Wilting in the 97-degree August heat, Guardsmen lined the highway with rifles and fixed bayonets. State police stood by nervously fingering submachine guns with live ammunition. Law enforcement officials discovered sections of wire under the twin spans crossing the Amite River on Highway 190, apparently intended to blow up marchers. "If they hadn't had the Louisiana National Guard, it would have been a slaughter camp," Young said later.[18]

After nine days, on August 19 the six marchers reached the capitol. They were to be welcomed by the chairman of the Student Nonviolent Coordinating Committee (SNCC), Baton Rouge native H. "Rap" Brown. According to Lance Hill, once the marchers were safely within Baton Rouge city limits, the governor was forced to address the possibility of a Black rebellion:

> Louisiana's white power structure feared a major rebellion in Baton Rouge's simmering slums. To cool passions Governor McKeithen took to the airwaves with a statewide address. When the marchers arrived in Baton Rouge on Saturday, they were greeted by fifteen hundred National Guardsmen standing by for the rally with express orders from the governor to "shoot-to-kill" if a riot erupted. McKeithen told state police officials that if any speaker made "treasonous or seditious statements" they were to "arrest them on the spot." Ignoring McKeithen's threats, several hundred blacks attended the rally which turned out to be law abiding and peaceful (Rap Brown had been arrested on a firearms charge and could not attend). Later

that night spontaneous violence did break out in the city's black neighborhoods, as gangs of youth roamed the streets breaking windows and hurling firebombs.[19]

When the BCVL promised more marches, McKeithen made a superficial effort to increase the state's Black workforce. Yet massive resistance to fair employment practices continued. The number of Blacks employed by the state increased 4 percent between 1964 and 1971. According to Fairclough, "Black clerical workers numbered only fourteen out of nearly twenty-five hundred." Those few who were employed in state and local government were confined to the most menial positions. One year earlier, the Mississippi Delta "March against Fear" had arrived in the capital of Jackson fifteen-thousand strong. The six Bogalusa marchers who reached Baton Rouge were no less heroic. In a year, the civil rights movement had changed the agenda of Louisianans. A. Z. Young of the BCVL, the Deacons for Defense, and SNCC chairman H. Rap Brown represented this shift. It was no longer the agenda of Reverend King of the Southern Christian Leadership Conference and Stokely Carmichael, the former chairman of SNCC. The Louisiana and Mississippi versions of the Black Power movement were deeply rooted in the Blues development tradition and its focus on direct action, economic transformation, collective decision making, community survival programs, cultural autonomy, and self-defense. This Deep South movement profoundly shook the Bourbon bloc, the state, the South, and the nation. It also set the stage for other movements and crises throughout the nation, the state, and the New Orleans region.[20]

The Black Student Revolt

Black college campuses continued to become radicalized after 1965. As students pushed for the realization of human and civil rights, they increasingly became the targets of state violence. This pattern was repeated in Louisiana in an intensified fashion. In October 1967 the National Guard was sent to suppress Grambling University students who boycotted classes to protest restrictive rules and an overemphasis on sports.[21] On April 2, 1969, students at Southern University's New Orleans campus lowered the American flag and raised the red, black, and green Black liberation flag. In a lecture hall they recited, "I pledge allegiance to the Black Liberation Flag and to the cause for which it stands—Black People together, indivisible for liberation, self-defense, and self-determination. I am prepared to give my life in its defense." New Orleans police chief Giarusso dared the students to swap flags again. When they did, several students were beaten, twenty were arrested, and nine NOPD officers were assigned to guard the flagpole. As rallies, class boycotts, and other forms of protest quickly spread to the Baton Rouge campus, the National Guard was deployed on campus in New

Orleans and several students were suspended, while six Southern University professors were fired. An Arab American political science professor, George Haggar, was fired and then deported. In an analysis of the state of the freedom movement, Haggar argued that several important barriers prevented future progress: "Fascist niggers, house niggers, black bourgeoisie, masochists, [and] white liberals."[22]

The gulf between student leaders and elite Black leaders continued to widen. An intense conflict occurred when President Nixon's Department of Health, Education, and Welfare launched an effort to integrate southern universities. Louisiana failed to submit a plan for integration and instead threatened Black colleges with closure. After the lead federal operative, Leon Panetta, was removed, a slightly revised federal integration and merger plan resurfaced in 1971. Although it was supported by elements within the NAACP's Louisiana State Conference of Branches, the student government association of Grambling University roundly condemned its position:

> How can you expect anyone to join an organization which is out to subject them to the grave injustices of the past, out to make them jobless, out to submerge our recent struggle for identity, and most of all, out to help the white man implement his program to keep blacks uneducated? . . . Did you not learn from the previous mistake (our Black high schools)? Or, is it just that you [want] to keep looking good to the white man and live in luxury off his donations, while keeping your black counterparts in white-made ghettos? . . . We will unite all Black colleges against merging.[23]

In a report responding to this withering attack, Raphael Cassimere Jr., chairman of the NAACP's Special Committee on University Integration, quoted W. E. B. Du Bois's response to the *Brown* decision: "Blacks must accept integration . . . in justice to generations to come, white and black. They must eventually surrender race 'solidarity' and the idea of American Negro culture to the concept of world humanity, above race and nation. This is the price of liberty."[24] Charles Payne notes that other Black leaders during this period similarly argued that institutional and individual causalities were the price of freedom:

> When some expressed fear for the future of black colleges, Walter White, the organization's [NAACP] executive secretary, replied that blacks needed to "give up the little kingdoms" that had developed under segregation. When others pointed out that integration often led black children to feel isolated and alienated, one NAACP lawyer responded that if integration led some black children to drop out, that would have to be borne since there were casualties in all social change. When it was suggested that black teachers and principals might find themselves unemployed in desegregated systems, the leadership responded that that, too, was the price of change. Robert Carter, one of the NAACP lawyers who argued *Brown*, noted that

the legal team "really had the feeling that segregation itself was the evil—and not a symptom of the deeper evil of racism. . . . The box we were in was segregation itself, and most of the nation saw it that way, too."[25]

Although Cassimere's report in favor of the merger was rejected, a new plan was proposed that would merge Southern University and Louisiana State University under a state board of higher education with significant Black representation. In October 1972 Southern University students in Baton Rouge marched on the state board, boycotted classes, and demanded both a course in Black Studies and the right to fly the Black Liberation flag. Four hundred students occupied the president's office until fifty-five sheriff's deputies hurling tear gas ejected them. In the midst of this conflict a deputy murdered two students, Denver Smith and Leonard Brown.[26]

The student revolt also took hold at secondary schools. Justin Poche documented a movement brewing among New Orleans students that would challenge racism in the Catholic Church and transform Black Catholics nationally and internationally:

At St. Joseph's Academy in New Orleans, a group of girls captured national attention with the formation of the Black Revolutionary Action among Soul Students (BRASS). The "black power" organization, one insisted, aimed to help black students find their historic cultural identity. The group demanded that black Catholics overcome their historically middle class baggage. "The only danger with BRASS," a leader declared, "is if it becomes a black middle class group. We can't forget that there are poor black men in the ghetto." BRASS reflected the desire of black youth to separate not only from white cultural and historical bonds, but also from older generations who bought into them. The group's exclusion of whites from membership produced a conflict with the high school administration. Members defended their position to "do their own thing," however. "The blacks have to separate for a while so that we can find ourselves. If we can't get together with ourselves, we can't get together with anybody." Older generations had hidden them from that identity, they insisted. While they inherited a deep faith from their parents as Christians, one explained, "my parents think 'white.'"[27]

The response to the deepening of the African American freedom movement and the emergence of multiple forms of mass mobilization was increased militarization. The Catholic student movement was also subjected to intense policing.

In May 1968 a group of 325 African Americans led by H. "Rap" Brown, chairman of the SNCC, stormed St. Francis de Sales Catholic Church when the archdiocese prohibited them from using the main building for a meeting. At a rally in Shakespeare Park, several members of the SNCC exhorted the crowd to take a stance against the governor, John J. McKeithen, and church authorities who had managed to appease Blacks for years. "You're chumps," Brown shouted.

"McKeithen tells the world that all his 'niggers' in Louisiana are satisfied, and you do nothing to show that you are in disagreement with him. You're chumps. There's a church in your community and they tell you that you can't go in it." When rain began to soak the crowd at the park, Brown declared, "I'm not going to stand in the rain and talk to you. If you want to hear me and they won't let you in that church which is in your community, then you should kick the door down." Shortly afterward a group marched to the church, at the corner of Second and Loyola Streets. Others followed in vehicles. When the police surrounded the area with riot troopers, the crowd dispersed.[28]

The freedom movement and its Blues agenda were transforming educational institutions from engines of social resignation and assimilation to a maternity ward for new movements and leaders. Old and new forms of social militarization often led to the further radicalization of these movements. The suppression of the Bogalusa movement led to the expansion of the Deacons for Defense. The Deacons served as a model for a new California movement that arose out of the Watts Rebellion. Partially led by Louisiana migrants who left the state at a young age, the Black Panther Party sought to transform African American life by creating highly organized, semiautonomous communities organized along cooperative lines. The demands and programs of this emerging shadow government mirrored many of the elements of the comprehensive Blues agenda of the First Reconstruction.[29] The organization's arrival in New Orleans was partially a return of the displaced and partially a homegrown movement attuned to the needs of local residents. In order to suppress this movement, new forms of militarization were launched in Louisiana and nationally.

Unstarving the Beast: The Black Panther Party and the Assassination of Free Grits

The Black Panther Party for Self-Defense (BPP) was created out of the turmoil surrounding the assassination of Malcolm X, the rise of the Deacons for Defense, the Watts Rebellion of 1965, the campaign of the Lowndes County Freedom Organization in Alabama in 1966, global anticolonial movements, and the war in Vietnam. Launched in Oakland, California, in 1966, the organization rapidly spread throughout the nation after the 1968 assassination of Martin Luther King Jr. and the hundreds of urban rebellions that followed. Many members of the Louisiana diaspora occupied key positions in the California chapters. A number of ideological currents pulsed throughout the BPP, from Frantz Fanon's critique of colonialism to Marxist theories of political economy and various theories of revolution and socialism. The strong presence of Blues realism was partially a product of deep family connections to the crises affecting Black communities in Louisiana, Arkansas, Mississippi, and Texas. The chairman of the national organization, Dr. Huey P. Newton, was born in Monroe, Louisiana, in

1942, while the chairman of the Chicago chapter, Fred Hampton, was born in Illinois in 1948 to parents who had recently migrated from Louisiana. By 1969 the organization had over five thousand members in a dozen chapters throughout the country. The FBI's counterintelligence program, known as Cointelpro, was used to infiltrate almost every chapter.

In August 1970 the Panthers moved their New Orleans headquarters to the Desire neighborhood. They shared a building on 3542 Piety Street with the Sons of Desire community organization. In response to the deepening poverty produced by what has been called the "second ghetto," the BPP instituted or envisioned numerous community survival and sustainability programs.[30] Community survival was at the core of the organization's ten-point platform. A partial list of demands include the following:

> (1) We want freedom. We want power to determine the destiny of our Black Community. (2) We want full employment for our people. (3) We want an end to the robbery by the capitalist of our Black Community. (4) We want decent housing, fit for the shelter of human beings. (5) We want education for our people that exposes the true nature of this decadent American society.... (10) We want land, bread, housing, education, clothing, justice and peace. And as our major political objective, a United Nations supervised plebiscite to be held throughout the black colony in which only black colonial subjects will be allowed to participate, for the purpose of determining the will of black people as to their national destiny.[31]

The BPP also launched one of the most intense campaigns against police brutality in U.S. history. One demand of the organization's ten-point platform read as follows: "We want an immediate end to police brutality and murder of black people, other people of color, all oppressed people inside the United States." On June 15, 1969, J. Edgar Hoover declared, "The Black Panther Party, without question, represents the greatest threat to internal security of the country." He pledged that 1969 would be the last year of the party's existence.[32]

The comprehensive nature of this agenda harkened back to the integrated Blues policy approach adopted during the First Reconstruction by the UNIA and by thousands of organizations and movements over four centuries. BPP chapters launched numerous survival, sustainable development, and social justice programs, including:

> the Free Breakfast for School Children Program, free health clinics, the Sickle Cell Anemia Research Foundation, the People's Free Dental Program, the People's Free Optometry Program, the People's Free Ambulance Program, the Free Food Program, the Food Cooperative Program, the Intercommunal News Service, the People's Free Community Employment Program, the Shoe Program, the People's Free Clothing Program, the People's Free Legal and Education Program, Free Busing to Prisons Program, the Free Commissary for Prisoners Program, Seniors Against a

Fearful Environment (SAFE) transportation service, the People's Cooperative Housing Program, the People's Plumbing and Maintenance Program, Free Pest Control, Community Schools, Liberation Schools Music and Dance Programs, and child development centers providing 24-hour childcare.[33]

Many of these programs were subject to immediate harassment by local, state, and federal political leaders, law enforcement officials, and the media. The anti-hunger Free Breakfast for School Children Program was launched in Oakland early in 1969. It was funded by donations and the "taxation" of local businesses. In August 1970 twenty New Orleans activists started a free breakfast program in the Desire neighborhood. Deep hunger was plaguing New Orleans, and approximately 120 children, 10 of whom were white, were fed daily at a local Catholic church. In true Bourbon fashion, Chief of Police Joseph I. Giarusso viewed the attempt to alleviate hunger with a free breakfast program as particularly dangerous because it turned the minds of the youth against white authority.[34] In his portrayal of Huey Newton, Los Angeles actor Roger Guinevere Smith recounts Newton's views on why FBI director J. Edgar Hoover designated the Black Panthers as the most dangerous organization in the United States:

> If you read the FBI files you will see that even Mr. J. Edgar Hoover himself had to say that it was not the guns that were the greatest threat to the internal security of the United States of America; . . . it was the Free Children's Breakfast Program that was the greatest threat to the internal security of the United States of America. Grits. Now why was it the Free Children's Breakfast Program? It was the Free Children's Breakfast Program because the Free Children's Breakfast Program engendered a certain following on the Black community's part, a certain respect on the Black community's part. I mean, nobody can argue with free grits. So Hoover saw it as a kind of, he saw the Free Children's Breakfast Program as a kind of, what's the word he used? He said it was a kind of, look in the file, you'll see, he said it was a kind of infiltration. That's ridiculous isn't it? Infiltration? How are Black people, who are born and raised in the Black community, who live and work in the Black community, going to infiltrate their own Black community? If anybody's infiltrating, I think it's J. Edgar Hoover.[35]

The formation of the BPP in New Orleans led to an immediate reaction from the neo-Bourbon bloc. Kent Germany notes that the local police took a similar attitude: "By mid-June . . . the NOPD in a confidential memorandum, had identified the Panthers as the 'greatest concern' of the department and the 'most dangerous' of all of the activist organizations in the city."[36] According to a 1971 BPP document, by July 1970 the local press and Governor McKeithen had targeted the Panthers for elimination soon after their founding: the reactionary press had already published the raving statements of racist Louisiana governor McKeithen to the effect that Louisiana and New Orleans would not tolerate the existence of the Black Panther Party in their city and state: "We will not let the Panthers get off the ground in this city."[37]

The response of the NOPD to the emergence of the Panthers continued the pattern of shifting white mob violence against Blacks to police violence against Blacks. The Desire neighborhood consisted of single-family homes as well as the largest public housing development in the city and one of the largest in the country constructed with federal funds. Residing in the 1,860 apartments of the Desire public housing development were over fourteen thousand residents, including ten thousand children.[38] Poorly constructed, isolated, and overcrowded, Desire was also home to a strong community ethic and numerous community organizations.

In July 1970 the NOPD's brutal response to a fight between residents threatened to turn into a major community-versus-police conflict. Aides to Landrieu, including his Black advisors from Total Community Action, Model Cities, and the Human Relations Committee, responded by placing a patrol car in the development to ease tensions. The arrival of the BPP in the Desire community occurred less than one month later. The organization attempted to build on and formalize the Blues tradition's preexisting parallel and alternative legal system and social order. BPP member Malik Rahim claimed that the organization "reduced crime to just about zero percent." The organization targeted both criminal activity and police brutality while claiming the right to community self-defense. Some viewed the BPP's approach of formally assuming powers that the Bourbon state reserved solely for itself as more dangerous than the small number of weapons the organization possessed. As Germany notes, police superintendent Giarusso became obsessed with the epistemological implications of the BPP's arrival in Desire: "With the Panthers move to Desire . . . Giarusso's concerns intensified. He worried that an 'alarming number of people' were becoming indoctrinated in the 'Panther philosophy' that taught 'hatred toward law enforcement specifically and the "establishment" in general.'"[39]

This epistemological conflict generated several violent confrontations on September 14 and 15, 1970. During the course of a BPP political education class on September 14, two of the participants were revealed as NOPD officers. According to one published account, a people's court was convened: "Henry Jerome, a Panther member, said, 'We found two pig infiltrators in our meeting. We held a trial with members of the committee. Our decision was to let the pigs go on their own and that the people would deal with them. And the people dealt with them. It was a decision of the people and not of any particular organization.'"[40]

The officers were released to fifty residents, who proceeded to beat them. Rocks and bottles followed the fleeing officers, and a house they retreated to was burned. Their vehicle was also set ablaze and dumped into a canal. One officer escaped while the other was cornered in a nearby grocery store. Store owner Clarence Broussard had reportedly overcharged residents for basic necessities during Hurricane Betsy. He was also in the process of evicting the BPP from a building he owned. After residents demanded that officer Israel Field come out of the store, Broussard opened fire and shots were returned, leaving two wounded. Additionally, two other Black NOPD officers claimed they were shot while they were investigating the burning patrol car. One of the officers had been the subject of a flyer that referred to him as a "traitor" and a tool "used to terrorize the black community." According to German, police then engaged in a midnight shootout for several hours near the BPP headquarters; thirteen persons were injured. Afterward the NOPD encouraged several hundred residents to evacuate the area before sunrise. Then, "starting around 8:30 a.m. on September 15th, 100 to 150 officers unleashed a full-scale assault with a helicopter, an armored tank nicknamed 'Bertha,' protective vests, machine guns, and assault shot guns. The Panthers fought back. The NOPD charged that the Panthers fired first and then continued to fire with 'high power rifles, automatic weapons.'"[41]

In an interview conducted years later, former mayor Moon Landrieu reached the following conclusion: "I actually had a grudging respect for the Panthers—not for what they did, not for how they did it. But they were willing to put it on the line. I often thought if I had been Black, I might have been a Black Panther myself. . . . They were willing to put their lives on the line for what they believed and what injustices they felt existed."[42]

Political Insurgency

Finally, despite the suppression of the BPP and the student movements, Black electoral movements began to make steady gains. Two new and influential Black political organizations emerged during this period. SOUL (Southern Organization for Unified Leadership) was founded after the historic, yet unsuccessful 1967 campaign by Congress of Racial Equality (CORE) attorney Nils Douglas to represent the Ninth Ward in the state legislature. According to Hirsch, "SOUL . . . embodied the heightened racial consciousness and militance of the civil rights era. . . . [It] stressed racial identity and mobilization as the best way to squeeze concessions out of the 'system.'" Robert Collins, Nils Douglas, and Lolis Elie were among those who organized SOUL to represent a base composed of "black homeowners and middle and lower middle class black citizens in the Lower Ninth Ward." Robert Collins attended Gilbert High School in New Orleans. In 1951 he became one of the first Black students to attend LSU law school. He formed a law practice with Lolis Elie and Nils Douglas on Dryades Street in New Orleans. The law firm represented CORE activists during the sit-in strikes. Collins remembers being particularly angered at segregation as it existed in the federal courthouse: "Everyone went along with the segregated system. They were blinded to what they were doing, and these were supposed to be good, Godfearing people, you know, the pillars of society. It was a lot to take."[43]

Established two years later by former SOUL members, Community Organization for Urban Politics (COUP) emerged from the Afro-Creole Seventh Ward. According to Hirsch it "coalesced around Charles Elloie's unsuccessful Seventh Ward race for state representative. Led initially by CORE affiliated attorney Robert Collins, COUP brought together young black professionals who represented the 'assimilationist' and conservative tendencies found in the downtown Creole stronghold. Its key leaders such as Henry Braden IV and Sidney Barthelemy had not been conspicuous in the civil rights movement, and indeed, as their Urban League orientation demonstrated, they were more adept at cultivating white contacts. If SOUL tried to capture the new racial assertiveness, COUP traveled the more well-worn path of accommodation and relied heavily on white familiarity and support."

The NAACP leadership was also active in seizing new opportunities. Ernest "Dutch" Morial grew up in the Afro-Creole Seventh Ward before attending Xavier University. After becoming the first African American graduate of LSU law school in 1954, he joined the law firm headed by NAACP leader A. P. Tureaud. A member of what Hirsch called the "unassimilated creole leadership of the NAACP," Morial participated in the key civil rights protests and suits of the time before becoming president of the organization from 1962 to 1965. After two unsuccessful attempts to represent the Ninth Ward on the Democratic State Central Committee, he was appointed the first Black assistant U.S. attorney in New Orleans in 1965. After changing his residence in order to run for office in the Uptown district (the First and Second Wards), in 1967 he became the first Black elected to the Louisiana State House of Representatives during the twentieth century. Uptown was also home to a new organization, the Black Organization for Leadership Development (BOLD).[44]

The political insurgency, along with the expansion of federal urban programs, led to increases in public sector employment in New Orleans for African Americans: Blacks held 20 percent of 8,219 civil service positions in 1970 and 43 percent of 10,009 civil service positions in 1978.[45] Bars and restaurants also were opened to Black patrons, but only after Black American Football League players were refused service. This incident led to a boycott of the city by the players, the league, and national conventions. As a result, in 1969 the New Orleans City Council enacted an antidiscrimination public accommodations law.[46]

However, in New Orleans and elsewhere, the development of new biracial patronage machines did not signify the full realization of the Blues agenda. Blacks were not a European ethnic group who had recently migrated to the United States. They were an ethnic group *and* a nationally racialized group. They also possessed their own institutions and intellectual traditions. Their oppression had been at the center of major regional and national transformations over the course of three centuries. It had also been foundational to the creation of land, labor, and capital, as well as resources such as housing, educational, political, and cultural institutions. Although the regional and national commitment to the fundamental reforms required wavered, this did not prevent African American electoral mobilizations from partially lifting the historic resource blockade that was maintained for many generations around Black communities. In 1964 only 28 percent of African Americans in New Orleans were registered to vote, compared to 63 percent of white residents. By 1966 Blacks represented 42 percent of the electorate, and they became the majority of the electorate by 1980.[47]

Massive Resistance in Concrete

In his speech "The Other America," Reverend Martin Luther King Jr. argued that difficult days laid ahead for communities still deprived of their human rights. Massive resistance and the white backlash movement had been organized to prevent the civil rights movement from expanding into a larger Blues reconstruction and redistribution movement. Resistance to the Second Reconstruction in New Orleans took many political, economic, and cultural forms. Neo-Bourbon urban and suburban development policies offer one example of how such resistance played out.

From the 1940s onward, cities throughout the United States were balkanized, ghettoized, and resegregated by federal and local housing, transportation, and development policies. One neighborhood after another was subjected to enclosure and displacement, concentration and dispersal. African American communities were specifically targeted for intense urban renewal and redevelopment projects that repeatedly tore asunder the fabric of neighborhoods, families, and individual lives. At the same time, completely segregated white-flight suburbs encircled the zones of disaster and disinvestment. Planned chaos, state violence, and concrete blockades were used to institutionalize a new era of spatialized racial conflicts and to defeat the numerous Blues movements that emerged to push for democratization, economic justice, and community sustainability.

The levee break during Hurricane Betsy and the Agriculture Street landfill were just two of many state-managed disasters to befall New Orleans's African American community between 1965 and 1978. During the 1960s the urban fabric of the city was destroyed to construct concrete barriers between highly politicized African American residents and the equally mobilized predominantly white residential and business districts of the city. Other barriers were constructed between Black communities and white-flight suburbs in Jefferson and St. Bernard Parishes. Despite round after round of enclosures, African American rebellions of the sort launched in dozens of other cities did not occur in New Orleans. Pierce Lewis offers several flawed cultural spatial theories as to why New

Orleans was not visited by the large-scale social turmoil found throughout the nation: Creole heritage, music making, and "New Orleans's history of good race relations." He also argues that the Bourbon strategies of limiting expectations, expulsion, and starvation combined with social, political, and neighborhood fragmentation undermined African American social movements:

> The New Orleans Bourbon elite never dreamed of holding out to blacks the expectation of better living conditions, and if the streets fell into disrepair in black areas, that was the way things had always been. Then, too, if a black felt especially aggrieved, he or she could do what millions of other southern blacks had done—get on a train and go north, more often than not to Chicago. . . . It is unprovable but quite likely that New Orleans's bitterest racial dissatisfactions were shipped off with unhappy migrants to Chicago, relieving pressures in New Orleans, but with explosive results in Chicago—a kind of differential migration of hatred. And later on, California apparently received some of New Orleans's exported racial troubles. . . . And as long as New Orleans's ghettos remained small and fragmented, there was little chance for resentment to reach a critical mass.[48]

The romanticism of "good race relations" continually masked the reality of New Orleans during a period in which several local Black communities were sealed in concrete. At the exact moment when working-class Black communities and movements hoped to improve their economic and social status through the democratization of local, state, federal, and private institutions, a countermovement was launched. A key aspect of what has been termed the urban "white backlash" involved the further monopolization of governmental and private resources. This proceeded based on the planned abandonment of many Black working-class neighborhoods, dramatic increases in the population density of others, and the valorization of business districts, institutional sites, and middle- and upper-class white residential neighborhoods. During this period, local, state, and federal resources were used to subsidize the projects launched by neo-Bourbon redevelopment planners, real estate developers, construction firms, banks, and political leaders who led the urban regime.

The marginalization of impoverished African American communities was intensified through several mechanisms: Central Business District redevelopment, urban renewal, suburban construction, the subsidization of small and large firms' hiring of suburban white workers, gentrification, monumental infrastructure projects, and massive investment in tourism, sports, and entertainment complexes. Significant investments in projects located in segregated and impoverished Black neighborhoods are missing from this list. Numerous social, economic, and physical barricades also ringed these projects. They created spatial barriers to social, economic, and cultural democratization. They guaranteed the intensification of Black destitution. While the curtain was falling on the War on Poverty and the Great Society programs of the 1960s, a new city was revealed.

It was defined by physical fortifications designed to harness civil rights, human rights, democratization, and sustainable development, in other words, the Blues agenda. To guarantee neo-Bourbon success the new socio-spatial regime was regulated by extreme forms of daily institutional racism and violence.

There were at least ten pillars of the "massive resistance in concrete" movement. First, within the city, Blacks were expelled from several neighborhoods that were being reconstructed as predominantly white islands. For example, after the campaign to block the construction of Interstate 10 (I-10) through the French Quarter, historic preservation and tourism related activities increased dramatically, as did rents. Lewis found that the Quarter was being ethnically cleansed: "As these two waves of higher rent roll downstream and lakeward, genuine residential neighborhoods are being squeezed into the northeast corner of the Quarter. . . . One can applaud the architectural results, but the continued displacements of blacks and compression of already overcrowded ghettos is disquieting, to say the very least."[49]

To save the French Quarter, I-10 was placed on top of the African American main street, Claiborne Avenue in Tremé. The historic center of old line Afro-Creole culture, North Claiborne was bisected by quadruple rows of live oaks on the neutral ground. This space was the site of an endless array of social gatherings. Additionally, the street was bordered by one of the most vibrant African American commercial districts in the nation. In August 1966 construction of the elevated I-10 Expressway on the neutral ground began. A prosperous African American business and social district was destroyed for the purpose of speeding access to the segregated suburbs.

Ronette King notes that rapid deterioration and abandonment soon followed: "The stately rows of trees were uprooted and replaced by a phalanx of concrete pylons supporting an elevated superhighway that cut through the heart of Tremé's commercial strip. . . . I-10's devastating impact on Claiborne's black business community and the neighborhood it served is a tangible reminder of how black tradespeople and business owners throughout New Orleans history have been set back time and again by changing events, discrimination and economic hardships."[50]

The chaos in Tremé was compounded in 1968 by the city's razing of nine blocks of houses, including the historic Jazz venues Economy Hall and the Gypsy Tea Room. On this site was built the Mahalia Jackson Theater of the Performing Arts and Louis Armstrong Park. "'It was a double whammy,' said [Edgar] Chase, who noted that many streets were cut off by the I-10 and park developments. . . . 'You rode over or around the black community, you didn't go through the black community. Your business had to become a destination, because nobody was going through there anymore.'"[51] In this period federal, state, and city resources were funneled away from the creation of sustainable Black neighborhoods and into massive downtown and suburban development

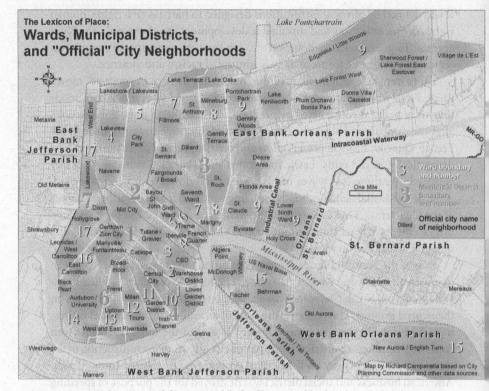

FIGURE 6. Wards, municipal districts, and "official" city neighborhoods in New Orleans. From Richard Campanella, *Bienville's Dilemma: A Historical Geography of New Orleans* (Lafayette: Center for Louisiana Studies, University of Louisiana at Lafayette, 2008).

schemes. Completed in 1968, the Rivergate downtown redevelopment project near the Mississippi River included a thirty-three-story world trade center. Housing shipping firms and the Dock Board, the project anchored the southern end of the Poydras Street corridor running through the business district. The site at the other end of the corridor became the Superdome. Created by a Louisiana constitutional amendment in 1966, this publically financed facility was opened in 1975. It has been said that the stadium was built to "Babylonian scale": seventy-two thousand seats, twenty-three stories, and an estimated cost of $160 million, nearly five times the original estimate of $35 million. Several large office buildings were also built along this corridor, including the sixty-story Shell Oil building, One Shell Square, completed in 1972.[52]

As in other cities, the language of colonialism ("discover" and "reclaim") and eugenics ("renewal," "gentrification," and "revitalization") were deployed in the effort to justify the removal of Black communities from the city's center and from architecturally prized neighborhoods. Lewis found that the "other form of pressure . . . emerges when whites 'discover' the architectural virtues of an old black neighborhood." By the early 1970s three neighborhoods were being "reclaimed": Faubourg Marigny, the Lower Garden District, and Old Algiers.[53] Increasingly, the Blacks expelled due to gentrification were forced into neighboring public housing. While those displaced from the Garden District were steered into the St. Thomas development, others found themselves seeking refuge in the Desire and Florida developments. The impact of these redevelopment projects also led to increasing levels of segregation and overcrowding in the already segregated private housing market.

The second pillar of the suburban "massive resistance in concrete" movement was the extent to which white flight negatively impacted urban African Americans. As we have seen, suburbanization in the New Orleans region was delayed due to the high cost of draining the network of swamps that surrounded and penetrated the city. The opening of these lands in the 1960s was followed by the expansion of the city westward and southward into Jefferson Parish and eastward into St. Bernard Parish. Middle- and upper-income whites began moving to Jefferson Parish in the late 1950s. Seeking to avoid school desegregation, many working-class white families with children joined the stampede to the parish during the 1960s. The populations of Metairie and Kenner on the west bank of the Mississippi River and Gretna and Westwego on the east bank grew dramatically between 1950 and 1970. By the mid-1970s, Jefferson Parish was the home of numerous single-family and multifamily dwellings, business parks, and shopping malls. The movement of residents, businesses, employees, and the taxes they generated fueled both segregation-generated wealth and the rapid decline of the city's finances and neighborhoods. New housing developments were also built in St. Bernard Parish to accommodate white flight. Although Blacks were not allowed to live in the new suburban neighborhoods, the two parishes received heavy subsidies from the Black communities of New Orleans. The lack of services, major retailers, and supermarkets in their neighborhoods resulted in many Blacks patronizing businesses in the suburbs. The blockade around Black communities established by banks, insurers, retail establishments, and grocery stores ensured that revenue generated from purchases and sales taxes were directed toward supporting spatial segregation in the region.[54]

Fueled by an increasingly segregated form of industrial development and white flight from New Orleans's slowly integrating public schools, the portion of St. Bernard Parish controlled by the political boss Leander Perez grew rapidly between 1950 and 1980, from eleven thousand to sixty-four thousand persons. Many of the white working-class residents were employed either in New Orleans or by several major firms in the parish: American Sugar Refinery, Kaiser Aluminum's Chalmette Works, the Tenneco Oil Refinery (now Exxon/Mobil), the Murphy Oil Refinery, natural gas processing plants, and shipbuilding firms. Owned by Domino Sugar and constructed in 1909, the American Sugar Refinery was one of the largest in the world. It was heavily dependent on exploited low-wage Black workers living behind the "cane curtain" in Louisiana, Texas, and the Caribbean. Built in 1951, Kaiser Aluminum's smelter at Chalmette was one of the world's largest aluminum reduction facilities. It was heavily dependent on maintaining the exploitation of bauxite reserves and neocolonial dependency in Jamaica. At its height, the firm had a workforce of three thousand before it closed during the early 1980s. Major shopping centers in the parish served the new population whose movement drained the tax base of New Orleans by removing investment in property, property taxes, and disposable income. The refusal of major retailers to locate in the city diminished the tax base even further. Similar to the institutional rents extracted in Jefferson Parish, the disposable income of the city's Black residents spent in the malls of Arabi, Chalmette, and Meraux simultaneously subsidized segregated suburban development while impoverishing the city's tax base, retailers, professionals, and so on.[55]

The third pillar of the "resistance in concrete" was the use of federal highway funds to speed commerce both in and around major cities. These funds were also used to support the massive suburban real estate boom occurring throughout the country. Uniquely organized around the question of race, these projects created a new and powerful constituency. The construction, auto, and appliance sectors and firms were key components of suburbanization. White-flight suburbs came to dominate regional politics, secured massive subsides from all levels of government, and extracted massive subsides from enclosed Black communities while simultaneously investing incomes earned in, and on, the city through the creation of new segregated spaces.[56]

The movement out of New Orleans and the creation of commuting communities and urban sprawl were accelerated by several heavily subsidized infrastructure projects. In addition to Interstate 10, there was the Lake Pontchartrain Causeway: two parallel bridges that stretch twenty-three miles across the lake from Metairie north to Mandeville in St. Tammany Parish. The first span opened in 1956 at a cost of $30 million. The second span opened in 1969 at a cost of $29 million. Taken together, the bridges are considered the longest in the world. Opened in 1958, the Crescent City Connection facilitated travel to the Westbank, the Algiers section of New Orleans, and the suburban communities of Jefferson Parish. It was the third-longest cantilever bridge in the nation when it opened and the only bridge to cross the Mississippi River south of Baton Rouge.[57]

The fourth pillar was the fact that neo-Bourbon education and its enclosure projects were inextricably tied to community enclosure projects. As implemented by majority-white school boards opposed to integration, school desegregation policies typically proved devastating to African American children, educators, and communities. White flight, smaller class sizes, and discriminatory hiring practices had resulted in a teacher corps that was disproportionately white. Instead of hiring more Black teachers, the New Orleans or Louisiana

School Board "resolved" this imbalance by implementing desegregation plans that required the mass firing of Black teachers and principals. Fairclough found that between "1966 and 1971, the number of black principals declined from 513 to 362. The number of white principals increased from 941 to 1057. Black principals were *never* assigned to majority white schools; white principals, on the other hand, were often placed in charge of majority black and even all black schools." Many of the schools were symbols of great pride in the Black community. Their principals, coaches, teachers, and staff were pillars of the Black community and role models for several generations. A study by the National Educational Association found that New Orleans's Black teachers in majority-white schools were regularly abused by white colleagues, parents, and students, whose parents told them "not to listen to no nigger."[58] Another aspect of educational resegregation was the matriculation of white students to private academies and parochial schools in the city and to predominantly white public schools in the surrounding "white-flight" suburbs. By the 1980s, 79 of New Orleans's 108 public schools were at least 90 percent Black.[59]

This rapid transition did not end the historic attack on the Black children of the region. At integrated urban and suburban schools they were subjected to pushout/dropout regimes, in which students were tracked into dead-end occupations, labeled "mentally retarded," routinely given failing grades, suspended for minor infractions, and otherwise implicitly and explicitly encouraged to drop out. By 1969, 28,000 Black children, 9 percent of the total Black enrollment, attended previously all-white schools in New Orleans, while only 241 white children attended predominantly Black schools. To address the continued resistance to desegregation, the U.S. Supreme Court ended voluntary enrollment plans in 1968 and the federal Fifth Circuit Court of Appeals ruled against delays in abolishing dual urban systems in 1969. Governor McKeithen immediately called the Louisiana legislature into a special session to pass the "freedom-of-choice" law, which provided $10 million in aid to private white academies for expansion. Although the law was eventually overturned by the Louisiana Supreme Court, white flight from the public schools continued unabated.[60]

The fifth pillar was the fact that the neo-Bourbon domination of city and state finances and taxation was not immediately affected by the Second Reconstruction. Neo-Bourbon control of state power ensured that oil revenue taxes and sales taxes would be directed primarily to maintain its monopolization of resources and political legitimacy. The city council comprised seven councilpersons, five representing districts and two elected at large. In addition, there were several boards and commissions directly controlled by elected officials. Yet the control of the city's finances was still in the hands of unelected Bourbon bankers through the Board of Liquidation of City Debt. The tax structure was equally unique. Due to reforms implemented by Huey Long, taxes were generated primarily from oil revenues and sales taxes rather than from property taxes. Similar to those in other planter-bloc-led southern states, this system minimized the taxation of large agricultural and other valuable land parcels while simultaneously severely limiting the amount of funds available for social services. Since the state controlled oil royalties, sales taxes, and the financing of local services, neo-Bourbon influence over the branches of state government often proved decisive in determining the fiscal fate of local jurisdictions such as New Orleans. In addition, firms and property owners were able to avoid taxation through several other mechanisms. The new constitution of 1972 provided five-year renewable property tax exemptions for new businesses and industries. The state also had the lowest homeowner taxation rate in the country. Since assessors rather than the Tax Commission determined fair market values, the tax rate varied greatly by parish, sometimes by block, and sometimes between adjacent houses. The commission often acted to ensure that railroad, pipeline, and utility properties were minimally taxed. This deeply embedded system of corruption and social theft defeated notions of uniformity and fairness in favor of the agenda of the dominant economic blocs. Where they existed, social services were chronically distressed and repeatedly subject to massive reductions. According to Carleton, the inequalities inherent in this system, particularly the dependence on oil and tourism, were indicators of a failed state where local government always hovered on the verge of collapse: "Since the days of Huey Long, state revenue and services have depended disproportionately upon severance taxes and royalties levied on the extraction of oil and natural gas, which are rapidly disappearing."[61]

The legacy of plantation power, oil dependency, and privatization meant that Louisiana's system of local and state finance and taxation had many cyclical crises built-in. It also resulted in heavy burdens being placed on members of the working class, many of whom did not pay property taxes but who faced high sales taxes, low levels of social service provision, and high levels of instability in social services. In the mid-1980s, Errol Laborde also noted that the system was unsustainable: "There is a $75,000 exemption on residential property tax which means that many home owners pay little or no tax on their property. The state income tax is also quite low. . . . The state which has historically been able to keep taxes low because of its oil severance revenue is finding that cow is running dry."[62]

With the formal elimination of de jure disenfranchisement and other forms of racial discrimination, the responsibility for racial management fell increasingly on the neo-Bourbon criminal justice institution, the sixth pillar of "massive resistance in concrete." Prisons, surveillance, repression, and police brutality organized an increasing range of interactions between the Black community and the neo-Bourbon bloc. For Fairclough, this complex was defined by "a multitude of sins": threatening, abusive, and racist language; the sexual exploitation of Black women; the harassment and entrapment of homosexuals; the beating of prisoners; job discrimination; and the unnecessary use of lethal force. One study found that Black working-class daily life in New Orleans was governed by institutionalized criminality: overpolicing and underpolicing, illegal detentions, illegal searches, the beating of handcuffed prisoners, arrests for the lack of identification, arrests for destitution, the shooting of fleeing suspects, false testimony, coerced confessions, torture, and false convictions. It was also the city's policy to restrict certain occupations from jury service, those occupations being work that Black workers were typically segregated into: manual laborers, domestics, service workers, truck drivers, carpenters, painters, mechanics, shipfitters, boilermakers, and plasterers. Before 1968 a Black person had never served on a New Orleans jury, and subsequently juries in death penalty cases were typically all white. In 1970 the New Orleans Human Relations Committee revealed that one policeman had killed six African Americans in eighteen months, two while off duty. Although the city attorney viewed the last death as a murder, the officer was never prosecuted.[63]

The seventh major institutional pillar of neo-Bourbon domination developed during this period was the adoption and naturalization of social science explanations of inequality. Mahoney suggests that social science and legal scholars relied on aspatial understandings to reach their conclusions. By focusing on either race or class and not their intersection, the scholarship masked the interconnectedness of institutions within the regional regime. The refusal to study regional institutions of hegemony, exclusion, disposability, and racial supremacy left available few explanations for persistent poverty. Consequently, this shift provided a "scientific" and "objective" veneer for the revitalization of the historic planter-bloc discourse of Black cultural sickness, deviancy, and inferiority:

> Housing projects became predominantly black because of the exclusion of blacks from even subsistence level employment. The shift from an upwardly mobile population to a chronically underemployed population coincided with the racial transformation of the public housing population as a whole. These shifts are not coincidental, but describe different parts of the same phenomenon: a segregatory process in which white people and jobs left the cities. . . . If we try to evaluate these developments in law as if they were entirely shaped by race, we miss a crucial part of the exclusion—the lack of opportunity in the post-industrial city that has become an exclusion from employment opportunities, not merely an exclusion from white neighborhoods, for an entire sector of the population. On the other hand, if we try to handle these complex issues entirely as economic exclusion, we fail to identify the harm we have wrought: The stigma that blames joblessness and other aspects of ghettoization on black cultural characteristics.[64]

The eighth pillar was the fact that the neo-Bourbon labor market was defined by the continued expulsion of Blacks from many sectors, particularly agriculture, manufacturing, and domestic labor. This project was accompanied by the continuation of the campaign against Black business formation, growth, and development. Ronette King found that local government spending during this period was directed away from Black businesses. "Local government contracting with black owned firms, however, was another matter. Millions of dollars in public money still was flowing almost exclusively to white-owned construction, service and supply companies." Also, the refusal of insurance and banking firms to bond them meant that Black contractors would be permanently excluded from the lucrative heavy construction business. Given that Black businesses were more likely to hire Black workers and professionals and to utilize other Black firms, the exclusion of this economic sector had a negative multiplier effect on the regional Black community.[65]

The ninth pillar was neo-Bourbon science's continued view of nature as something to be owned and mined. New Orleans was more heavily dependent on the revenue of its port than any other major city. Its relatively small manufacturing base meant that the port was dependent on the shipment of goods: Louisiana sugar, oil, gas, and chemicals; corn, grain, and soybeans from the Midwest; and tropical products and ores from Central America, the Caribbean, and Latin America. The port had found itself in an increasingly competitive environment due to several innovations: an expanding trucking industry using new interstate highways, air shipment, railroad improvements, cargo containerization, and the expansion of the ports of Houston and Mobile. According to Pierce Lewis, when "the Dock Board decided to build a new Port of New Orleans . . . the obvious location was the junction of the Industrial Canal with the Intercostal Waterway. Not only was there plenty of open space available . . . but transportation facilities were also excellent: two mainline railways, Interstate 10, and 'MR-GO' (the Mississippi River–Gulf Outlet Canal) were nearby."[66] Despite opposition from residents and environmentalists, Congress had authorized the construction of MR-GO in 1956 and it was completed in 1965. The seventy-six-mile channel was utilized by numerous container ships and barges until the late 1970s. Matthew Brown notes that that canal was also expected to lead to a manufacturing boom in "eastern New Orleans, a huge stretch of scrubbed former bottom land and swamp bordering the inter-coastal harbor way. The city's sales force has been trying to sell the area to manufacturers. There have been a few success stories, particularly among electrical assembly plants, but the conveyor belts are hardly humming."[67]

Just as the neo-Bourbon bloc expressed no remorse after the opening of MR-GO brought a devastating storm surge into the city during Hurricane Betsy, it was equally unconcerned that saltwater from the Gulf of Mexico flowed into the channel and destroyed several hundred square miles of wetlands, forests, and estuaries, along with the seafood and shellfish industry in St. Bernard Parish. Until 2007 the Army Corps of Engineers spent tens of millions of dollars annually on dredging in order to keep open the channel, at a total cost over the years nearing half a billion dollars. Having "remembered everything and learned nothing," the Bourbon bloc built a channel that eventually served as a funnel for the floodwaters that swamped St. Bernard Parish, destroyed much of the Lower Ninth Ward, and inundated most of the city during Hurricane Katrina.[68]

The final pillar of the neo-Bourbon bloc power was its maintenance through new electoral forms. Several members of the Louisiana congressional delegation were steeped in the Bourbon epistemology and its view that human rights, civil rights, and antipoverty reforms were acts of war. Initially hired by the *Times-Picayune* to expose Long family corruption during the 1930s, Felix Edward Hebert was elected to the U.S. House of Representatives representing New Orleans's First Congressional District eighteen times between 1940 and 1977. From 1971 to 1975 he served as chairman of the Armed Services Committee before being removed by a liberal Democrat revolt. A strong opponent of civil rights, Hebert viewed his friend, President Lyndon Johnson, as a regional and racial traitor: "in Louisiana he was absolutely hated because they considered him a turncoat. They considered Lyndon Johnson the most horrible man that ever lived. When he turned on the civil rights it was a 90 per cent turn to what his voting record was. In the House as a congressman he voted with the South."[69] Although he was able to secure large subsides for the Louisiana cotton, sugar, and rice blocs, U.S. senator Allen Ellender similarly was a determined opponent of the minimum wage, Social Security, Medicare, and civil rights. According to Thomas Becnel, many of these positions were articulated during Ellender's 1968 campaign for a sixth Senate term. "Calling black activist Rap Brown 'that racial troublemaker,' Ellender said, 'I would not put him in the jailhouse, I would put him under it.'" The senator was also an exponent of the policies of starving the poor and entire African American urban communities. He "refused to vote for funds for the War on Poverty. Giving money to cities, Ellender said in March of 1969, would not stop violence, which he attributed to an atmosphere of lawlessness associated with racial sit-ins and marches."[70]

"We Need a Buffer between Us and the Niggers."

After 1965 Black Louisianans were increasingly integrated into a Democratic Party whose state leadership was dedicated to ending their existing social movements. In 1985 Laborde suggested that the incorporation of Black political movements in New Orleans followed the well-traveled road of white ethnic politics: "Within that political framework the white establishment has adapted as it did earlier in the century when white ethnics gained office on the strength of classic machine politics. As New Orleans faces its municipal elections next year, various high powered whites are already being identified with major black contenders. As is common in many American cities, blacks are more likely to achieve the high public offices but the economic power remains white. Thus are the interests blended."[71] Despite this surge in Black registration during the mid-1960s, political, class, and ethnic factionalism within Black communities, incorporation by the reform complex, and the opposition to reform by large sections of the white electorate resulted in limited gains through electoral politics. Although Blacks were only 25.2 percent of the electorate during the 1965 mayoral race, the Black vote was split between Mayor Vic Schiro, who "cut deals with the old black auxiliaries in the Morrison manner," and Morrison ally Jimmy Fitzmorris, who promised to appoint a biracial human relations commission and end discrimination in city hiring and service provision. According to Hirsch, Black voters were being integrated into existing segregationist political networks: "A.L. Davis had been fired and arrested by Schiro but supported him along with the rest of the OPPVL [Orleans Parish Progressive Voters League]; so did A. P. Tureaud and Avery Alexander. Fitzmorris' ties to labor won him the endorsement of Chink Henry and the Crescent City Independent Voters League (CCIVL), and he added to that the backing of the *Louisiana Weekly*."[72] Although Schiro was a segregationist who had presided over the Hurricane Betsy crisis, he received a third of the Black vote during the election. African American political factions were selectively incorporated into existing white political networks on an ad hoc and permanent basis, much as had occurred in many other cities. Fairclough notes that even "the newer and ostensibly more militant organizations like SOUL tended to play by the old rules."[73]

However, the goals of sections of the Black leadership and the middle class were changing. Following a pattern seemingly similar to the history of ethnic politics in the United States, after 1965 southern Black politics slowly transitioned from the Blues agenda's focus on social mobilization, human rights, and economic justice to multiple and contradictory agendas organized around geographic, class, family, and generational competition. Contending blocs within the Black community competed for multiple forms of assistance, subsidies, projects, appointments, and opportunities to obtain individual and family wealth. The wide range of unmet needs in the city ensured instability in the Black factions allied with the neo-Bourbon regime, which can be seen in numerous ways. First, neighborhoods suffered differentially from hunger, unemployment, poverty, educational opportunities, and the lack of health care. Second, professionals, businesspersons, and "poor people" formed networks to push competing agendas. Third, the new citywide and statewide biracial political alliances adopted a form of pragmatism that attempted to dance between the pillars of both the Blues agenda and the "massive resistance" movement. This regional bargain or compact led to both reforms and tragedies, festivals and funerals. Some movement leaders founded new political organizations and became institutional representatives. Those who continued to protest and push for subsistence programs and direct action were slowly, and sometimes violently, weeded out by the new biracial urban regime and its "partners": the urban growth machine, the race and class reform complex, the white-flight suburban parishes, the neo-

Bourbon state government, and a federal government dedicated to harnessing further social change.

The mayoral and councilmanic races of 1969–70 marked the electoral institutionalization of neo-Bourbonism based on a new biracial political agreement between Blacks, whites, labor, and the Bourbon bloc. Maurice "Moon" Landrieu was a white Creole, Catholic Democrat who grew up in a working-class, racially mixed Uptown neighborhood. His mother operated a corner grocery store out of the family's house while his father worked in a power plant. In 1957, after completing law school at Loyola University, he opened a practice in the impoverished neighborhood bordered by Broad and Washington Streets. Reportedly, half of his clients were Black. Landrieu's tenure in the state legislature was marked by his opposition to the wave of segregationist legislation introduced during the massive resistance to voting rights and integration. During his tenure in the city council, 1965–69, he played a key role in the campaign to remove the Confederate flag from the council chambers and in establishing the city's human relations commission.

Landrieu entered the 1969 mayor's race and received the unprecedented backing of all the major Black political organizations: SOUL, COUP, BOLD, the Urban League, and Total Community Action (TCA). His platform included promises to introduce a new public accommodations ordinance and to appoint Blacks to prominent positions. The field of twelve candidates in the first primary was reduced to a runoff between Landrieu and Fitzmorris, who refused to endorse Landrieu's civil rights reforms. Although Blacks were just 30 percent of the electorate, Landrieu won based on capturing approximately 90 percent of a 75 percent Black turnout.[74]

In the general election the Landrieu campaign was aided by Morial's run for an at-large seat on the city council. Morial later blamed his loss, by 5,000 votes of 160,000 cast, on Landrieu's refusal to campaign with him in white neighborhoods. The Republican candidate for mayor was Ben C. Toledano, a member of the Bourbon bloc whose lineage stretched back to the early French and Spanish colonists and to King Louis XIV of France. He was defeated in part by the Black electorate: Landrieu received 99 percent of a 77 percent Black turnout. However, Toledano believed that he was betrayed by his own class. His compatriots in the Bourbon bloc eventually explained to him why they threw their support to Landrieu, stating that "we need a buffer between us and the niggers."[75]

Another reason for the Bourbon bloc's support of Landrieu was that he was more capable of securing and distributing new federal and state resources through selected Black patronage networks without fundamentally challenging regional hegemony. During the Landrieu administration, 1970–78, the percentage of Blacks in the civil service rose from 19.4 percent to 43 percent. Landrieu also increased patronage and appointed several Blacks as department heads. For example, COUP leader Sidney Barthelemy was appointed to head the Welfare Department. Notably, the federal contribution to the city budget rose from 7.1 percent to 23.7 percent. New investments by outside capital also increased. Hirsch argues that federal funds subsidized the stable creation of a new racial patronage system, the neo-Bourbon state, without fundamentally challenging racial, class, or political hegemony in the region: "Landrieu was able to offer new opportunities to blacks without grievously antagonizing whites because he was cutting large new slices off an expanding economic pie. . . . By providing access, he muted the call for systemic change. Black Louisiana politicians could behave as white Louisiana politicians did; indeed, those who adapted most quickly to the existing political ethos would most assuredly reap the largest prizes. [In] New Orleans' reified system of ethnic patronage, politics remained as elsewhere essentially conservative and incapable of fundamentally altering conditions for the city's poor masses."[76]

Simultaneously, the state blockade designed to limit the distribution of state and federal resources to impoverished Black communities was loosened after Black voters played a decisive role in several gubernatorial elections. First, after initial resistance and the threat of bringing in federal examiners, opposition from voting registrars waned by 1969. Black registration had increased from 30 to 60 percent, 154,000 persons, while white registration increased a quarter million by 1970, 80 percent. Consequently, while Blacks made up a third of the voting-age population, they were only 21 percent of the electorate and only 1 percent of the elected officials: 1 of 105 members of the state House of Representatives and none of the senators.[77]

In the 1968 race for governor, McKeithen defeated John R. Rarick. The latter was the legislative leader of massive resistance who received strong backing from the Citizens' Council and the Klan. McKeithen received strong support from the Black community and SOUL in New Orleans. He carried every parish and won 80 percent of the state vote. His successor, Edwin Edwards, won the office in 1972 with 57 percent of the vote and a coalition crafted out of an alliance between Black and Cajun voters.[78] The son of a sharecropper, the French-speaking Cajun graduated from LSU law school. After being elected to the Louisiana State Senate in 1965, he served in Congress from 1965 to 1971. During the gubernatorial election he defeated Democrat J. Bennett Johnson in the primary and Republican opponent and former State's Rights Party leader David C. Treen in the general election. Edwards won a second term in 1975. Edwards was from Crowly, the "rice capital of America" located in Acadia Parish. He remained formally and informally a national representative of this industry and of major agricultural blocs in the state.[79] The 1972 legislature abolished the state's Sovereignty Commission on desegregation and passed a bill introduced by its first Black woman legislator, Dorothy Mae Taylor, eliminating eleven segregation laws.[80] Edwards called a constitutional convention in 1975 to replace the Constitution of 1921 and its hundreds of amendments. He also abolished eight agencies and placed Blacks in positions throughout state government. State expenditures increased 163 percent during Edwards's first two terms. Increased tax revenues from the oil and gas sectors were generated by charging a percentage of the barrel price rather than a flat fee. These new revenues were used to increase social spending.[81]

The War on Poverty insurgency was simultaneously a Blues tradition and a valorization of the middle-class position, and it eventually became a neo-Bourbon institution. President Lyndon Johnson delivered his famous "War on Poverty" address on March 16, 1964, and the Economic Opportunity Act was signed into law in August of the same year. He described the goal of the new initiative in several different ways. On many occasions he referred to his desire to deliver economic opportunities, services, and educational resources to those who had been abandoned by the post–World War II economy. In a private 1964 conversation with the editor in chief of the Scripps-Howard newspapers, he detailed the goals of the War on Poverty in a more explicit manner:

> I'm going to try to teach these nigras that don't know anything how to work for themselves, instead of just breeding. . . . I'm going to teach these Mexicans [that] can't talk English to learn it so that they can work for themselves. I'm going to try to build a road in eastern Kentucky and northern West Virginia and a few of these places so they can get down and go to school, and get off our taxpayers' back.[82]

CHAPTER 7

The Disaster before the Disaster

Oil Regimes, Plantation Economics, and the
Southern Strategy, 1977–2005

Before the hurricane you basically had two New Orleans's. One was for the . . . white or privileged Black and [then there was] another which some accepted but most no longer tolerated. . . . If you look at the state of those in public and low-income housing, you're looking at a state of unemployment that was well over 60 percent. The dropout rate was close to 70 percent and the crime rate was one of the highest in the country. If you're talking about that segment, it was already a disaster.

New Orleans social movement leader, 2007

The hurricane had hit the inner city before Katrina ever got here. . . . There was no real attempt to address poverty. Their answer was to lock everybody up, put them in jail, and claim the problems were not systemic.

New Orleans social movement leader, 2007[1]

A familiarity with the distinctiveness of the southern economic and policy environment is required to understand the meaning of Katrina for the Gulf Coast. Much of the Deep South is defined by a history of low social investment, low wages, and racial schism. As should be clear by now, within the South and the nation, Alabama, Mississippi, and Louisiana are ranked at the bottom of many economic and social welfare indicators. In the twenty-first century there has been a concerted effort in the Gulf Coast to fundamentally erode the remaining social safety nets. The traditional tropes of Black deviancy and criminality are still used to mask poverty-generating polices. Therefore, given the upside-down world that is present-day New Orleans, this book's readers have a special responsibility. They must carefully and repeatedly investigate a reality that significantly contradicts current representations of social conditions, poverty, crime, deviancy, African Americans, and normalcy.

Ironically, the millions of tourists who flocked to New Orleans every year prior to 2005 were oblivious to the fact that they were visiting one of the greatest urban social disasters in the United States. The national political culture's adoption of social philosophies that naturalized this disaster—as well as other urban disasters during the last three decades—was perhaps the most dangerous threat to the city and the nation. Hurricane Katrina revealed both the problems in the city and fundamental weaknesses of the nation's approach to human development.

Historic patterns of racial segregation resulted in low-income African Americans being concentrated in flood-prone areas of the city and prevented from having access to the rapidly developing suburbs in adjacent parishes. A long tradition of environmental injustice concentrated low-income and predominantly African American neighborhoods in low-lying areas susceptible to flooding. The collapse of the inadequate, underfunded, and poorly designed levee system was accelerated by the presence of an underused canal that served as a storm-surge highway into the heart of the city. Additionally, evacuation planning was not targeted to these areas. Economic and racial inequality was increasingly exacerbated by the decline of manufacturing, an emphasis on low-wage service sectors, mass impoverishment, declining federal social and infrastructural support, the intensification of partisan politics, deteriorating human rights conditions, and local and national social philosophies that abandoned comprehensive approaches to addressing poverty, health, education, and other inequalities. This chapter shows how the political and economic dynamics that preceded Hurricane Katrina were directly responsible for the disaster before the disaster.

Bourbonism, Racial Republicanism, and the Roots of Neoliberalism

Our analysis begins with New Orleans municipal politics and the 1977 mayoral race, which was governed by a set of rules found in almost no other state. Introduced by Governor Edwards and approved by the legislature in 1975, the Louisiana primary system, the "jungle primary," was designed to blunt the Republican surge in the state. Held in October, the primary election pits all candidates against each other regardless of their political affiliation. If no candidate wins a simple majority of the vote, then a runoff is held in November. These runoff elections involve candidates from the same party. The October 1977 primary race for mayor involved four candidates: city councilman Joseph V. DiRosa; state senator Nat Kiefer; Chip "Toni" Morrison, the thirty-three-year-old son of the former mayor; and state representative Ernest "Dutch" Morial.

Morial was elected to the Louisiana state House of Representatives in 1967. Despite a bitter loss during a race for a city council seat in 1969, he retained his seat and went on to hold a number of prominent positions within national elite African American organizations and within the neo-Bourbon state: national president of Alpha Phi Alpha Fraternity (1968–72); first Black Louisiana juvenile court judge (1970–74); and first Black judge on the Fourth Circuit Court of Appeals (1974–78). Despite being the only Black candidate in the mayoral race, Morial did not receive the support of BOLD and COUP leaders, who were linked to Morrison by well-developed channels of patronage. After the elimination of Kiefer and Morrison, the "jungle primary" pitted Morial against DiRosa.[2] In November Morial was elected the first Black mayor in the history of New Orleans, even though Blacks accounted for only 40 percent of the electorate. As Hirsch notes, during the runoff "Morial had piled up 97% of a 78% black turnout and nearly 20% of a 75% white turnout."[3]

The new administration defied expectations when Morial created a citywide patronage system populated by middle-class Blacks and whites, professionals, appointees, firms, and individual supporters. Morial's "biracial" Louisiana Independent Federation of Electors, Inc. (LIFE), soon became a powerful electoral force that rivaled the ward-based networks of BOLD, COUP, and SOUL. Elements within the Bourbon bloc celebrated Morial for his support of their downtown, tourism, and sectoral projects. The *Wall Street Journal* declared him the "black Calvin Coolidge" for his fiscal conservatism.[4] According to Whelan, Young, and Lauria, this new stage of the neo-Bourbon regime was also marked by Morial's use of appointments, legislation, and legal action to force reluctant Bourbon leaders to include Black officials on key city boards and agencies:

> Since the turn of the century, members of the oligarchy had ruled the city from their positions on the many nonelected boards and commissions which govern major areas like the port, the lakefront, sewage and water, and the city debt. In 1979 Morial took on the Board of Liquidation, City Debt, which was self-perpetuating, by encouraging a lawsuit to end the board's "racially restrictive membership." The judge ruled against the board, nullified its last two appointments, and ordered the board to make a good faith effort in considering a nonwhite. By the time Morial left office, most of the major boards and commissions had at least one black member.[5]

Morial also tried to move the city away from its growing dependency on tourism by arguing that "we can ill afford . . . to alone remain, the hotel-keepers and waiters for well-heeled tourists." Instead, he emphasized a variety of urban development, commercial, and manufacturing projects. During his first term in office, Morial significantly increased the federal contribution to New Orleans's capital budget, from $19.5 million in 1977 to $61.3 million in 1980. This increase included Urban Development Action Grants, neighborhood revitalization grants, and other forms of assistance delivered during the administration of President Jimmy Carter. Further benefits were derived from former mayor Landrieu serving as Carter's secretary of housing and urban development from August 1979 to January 1981.[6]

This "golden age" of Black electoral mobilization and economic empowerment under Morial did not last particularly long. Two years after Morial was elected mayor of New Orleans, the massive resistance movement reemerged in the form of the election of the first Republican governor in Louisiana since the First Reconstruction. The state constitution barred Edwards from seeking a third consecutive term. The governor's race in 1979 pitted David Treen against five Democratic opponents.[7] Treen grew up in East Baton Rouge, Jefferson, and Orleans Parishes. After receiving undergraduate and graduate degrees from Tulane, he became a staunch supporter of two organizations that were pillars of the "massive resistance" movement: the Citizens' Council and the Louisiana States' Rights Party. He ran for a seat in Congress under the party's banner during the late 1950s, and in 1960 he ran as an elector for the party along with Citizens' Council leaders Perez and Rainich. Treen was at the forefront of the movement of Citizens' Council leaders into the Republican Party. As a registered Republican, he ran against Representative Hale Boggs (D) for the latter's Second Louisiana Congressional District seat, the New Orleans district, in 1962, 1964, and 1968. Treen went on to serve in Congress from 1972 to 1980, representing the Third Louisiana Congressional District, which included a wide stretch of southern Louisiana: the white-flight and massive resistance parishes bordering New Orleans (Jefferson, St. Bernard, and Plaquemines), the southeast and south central Louisiana parishes, and the heavily Cajun eastern section of Acadiana.

Treen was part of the vanguard of the national Republican Party's Southern Strategy. Combining the plantation elite and white working-class racial populists, the massive resistance movement was able to quickly dominate the minuscule southern branch of the party. This movement offered the neo-Bourbon bloc new allies among the nation's largest financial and industrial firms, which dominated Republican politics. Referred to as Racial Republicanism, this new alliance was dedicated to building the infrastructure necessary to undermine the historic gains of African Americans, organized labor, and impoverished communities that were the pillars of the new federal social contract. In Louisiana, the return of the Citizens' Council leadership to the state capitol at the head of this new movement can be understood as the partial restoration of Bourbonism. According to Joseph Dawson, the results of the open primary in 1979 left two candidates in the race, Treen and Public Service Commissioner Louis Lambert, a Democrat. After helping to pay the campaign debts of the four other Democrats in the race, Treen received their endorsement and won the general election.[8] In the face of a 12 percent state unemployment rate, Treen adopted the historic "starve the beast" government rationing policies that informed Bourbonism, the coming national Reagan Revolution, and the emergence of global neoliberalism. For Louisiana, this meant the simultaneous slashing of social spending and adoption of tax cuts and business subsidies.[9] Morial soon found himself presiding over a deepening fiscal crisis. Federal and state aid, along with increased state oil revenues, had masked the impact of the massive disinvestment that occurred during the white flight to segregated suburbs. As the city's Black neighborhoods and infrastructure began to crumble, Morial unsuccessfully attempted to expand the city's tax revenue base. This effort was defeated just as federal and state contributions to the city's operating budget were declining from 65.7 percent in 1977 to 30 percent by 1982. These reductions were followed by budget cuts that reduced the number of city employees by a third.[10] New Orleans, southeastern Louisiana, and the state entered a profound economic and political crisis that resulted in the destabilization of the neo-Bourbon bloc.

The Last Legs of Neo-Bourbonism: Legal Discrimination among Carnival Krewes

Changes accompanying the financial crisis and the reassertion of Bourbonism could also be seen in other spheres, specifically struggles around legal discrimination. On December 6, 1991, city councilwoman and human rights activist Dorothy Mae Taylor introduced legislation that would deny parade and liquor permits to Carnival krewes and their sponsoring business clubs if they engaged in discrimination based on race, creed, color, religion, national origin, ancestry, sex or sexual orientation, age, physical condition, or disability. Taylor and others argued that private clubs that practiced discrimination benefited from the $3.5 million New Orleans annually spent during Carnival for police, fire, and sanitation services. In 1988 the U.S. Supreme Court upheld a similar New York City law that banned discrimination in business-oriented private clubs. The argument was also made that the Carnival krewes and their associated clubs were sites where business deals were discussed and that excluding women and minorities put them at a professional disadvantage. The debate over the ordinance was framed in terms of race, class, and gender. Krewes such as Comus and Momus with long-established links to the New Orleans elite systematically excluded Blacks, women, and poor whites.[11]

The legislation exposed the fragile nature of the anti-Duke alliance.[12] It struck at the sacrosanct corridors of New Orleans economic power and white supremacy. The legislation was immediately attacked and the subsequent law was eventually undermined to the point of irrelevancy. The leaders of sixty-five krewes called the ordinance a "tragic mistake" and threatened to move their parades to St. Bernard or Jefferson Parishes in order to deny New Orleans part of the $480 million annually generated by Mardi Gras. Due to this economic blackmail and pressure from Mayor Barthelemy, the city council delayed its vote until December 19, at which time it voted unanimously to approve the ordinance, whose penalties included a denial of parade permits, a fine of $300, or five months in jail. A revision to the original proposal delayed enforcement until 1994 so that a mayoral commission could negotiate implementation.[13]

The krewes of Comus and Momus canceled plans to march in 1992 and were eventually joined by Proteus in 1993. Due to its central role in Mardi Gras and its quasi-official role in the year-long governance of the city, Rex reportedly decided to offer membership to several Blacks in 1992.[14] Although she voted for the ordinance, white city councilwoman Peggy Wilson promised to fight for its repeal, saying, "This has been a disaster for race relations in this city. . . . You've opened a Pandora's box and let all the little goblins fly around." Conversely, several influential African Americans were outraged. Dr. Dwight McKenna, chairman of the New Orleans School Board, stated that Mardi Gras had long been an expression of "a plantation mentality" and that "no tradition or economic loss is worth more than my dignity." Roy E. Glapion Jr., head of Zulu Social Aid and Pleasure Club, argued that segregation had always been central to Mardi Gras and that democratization was overdue. According to Xavier University professor Silas Lee, "What they are saying is that they would violate the civil rights laws to uphold the Mardi Gras tradition."[15]

Despite its having the support of thirty-five religious leaders, the ordinance was further diluted. In a five-to-one vote on February 7, 1992, the council accepted the recommendations of the mayor's commission to eliminate jail sentences for offenders and to shift the burden of proof to victims, who would now have to prove discrimination. Barthelemy supported the revisions as a way "to calm things down."[16] After six clubs pledged to integrate by 1993, on May 9 the council capitulated further by "allowing krewes to remain all-male or all-female and softened enforcement of the law. The city now must dismiss any discrimination complaint against a krewe if the club submits an affidavit pledging that it does not discriminate." According to African American lawyer Henry P. Julien Jr., "It's absurd when someone is accused of wrongdoing and can be declared not guilty by simply saying they didn't do it."[17] Yet the pressure to repeal the law continued. The Don't Mess with Mardi Gras organization collected ten thousand signatures to place an initiative to repeal the ordinance on the ballot. However, the city council blocked the initiative after the city attorney ruled that "there was precedent for invalidating voter initiatives when the issue would violate the 14th Amendment."[18]

A Black California businessman applied for membership in four of the clubs and was refused. When he filed a complaint with the Human Rights Commission, U.S. District Judge A. J. McNamara barred the commission "from looking into any discrimination complaint against the Boston, Louisiana, Pickwick and Stratford clubs" because they were not "public accommodations" as defined by the law. Susan Finch summarized the judge's assertion that the interest that the clubs' several hundred members had in keeping their identity unknown superseded constitutional prohibitions against racial discrimination:

McNamara, who was appointed to the bench by President Reagan in 1982, dismissed the city's claim that the anti-discrimination law could be constitutionally applied to the luncheon clubs because they could assert their private club status in any hearings before the Human Relations Commission. Though he agreed the city has an interest in preventing discrimination, McNamara said the clubs have "established that there is a reasonable probability that the investigation into complaints of discrimination would publicly reveal its membership lists and other intimate aspects . . . that would have a chilling effect on their members' First Amendment rights." McNamara brushed aside the city's argument that reimbursement of officers' club dues by the Whitney National Bank was proof the clubs are not purely social.[19]

Since most of the law was gutted, the leading clubs have recruited an occasional Black member. However, it is remarkable how much of the interlocking Bourbon directorate has remained untouched by the civil rights movement, as seen in membership in leading clubs, intermarriage, and attendance at select private schools and colleges.

These were men, however, of small compromises rather than strategic vision. Collectively, they wielded great power. Judge John Minor Wisdom, who knew them intimately, described them as a kind of "interlocking directorate" or "closed corporation," for the same people could be found on the governing bodies of the Hibernia and Whitney banks, Tulane University, NOPSI, the Orleans Parish Levee Board, and the Board of Liquidation of the City Debt. Many belonged to the same social clubs (Boston and Pelican), sent their children to the same private schools (Newman and Country Day) and masked in the same Mardi Gras krewes (Rex, Comus, Momus, and Proteus). This concentration of old wealth made New Orleans one of the most conservative cities in the South. More exclusive and tradition-bound than wealthy whites in other southern cities, such people were slow to change and, in Wisdom's view, "never did really assert themselves in favor of desegregation."[20]

Other works also suggest that a highly insular racial, cultural, and economic elite consciously limited new entrepreneurial activity, new professional leadership, labor mobility, and African American advancement. In a 1975 study James Bobo emphasized the dual nature of the regional political economy, in particular the extreme income polarization in the city.[21]

A present-day local leader concurred with this assessment: "Uptown whites run everything and they stood in the way of New Orleans developing in the 1960s and 1970s. It is a very narrow and insular leadership that wants to maintain the colonial setup we have here: Black people serving white people, white people having their balls and attending to their affairs, and they have a local Black political class."[22] It should be fairly obvious that such a political culture did not evolve out of thin air—rather, its development is deeply rooted in the regional political economy.

The Double Curse: The Oil Trap and Economic Crisis

Countries that depend on oil for their livelihood eventually become among the most economically troubled, the most authoritarian, and the most conflict-ridden in the world.[23] During the early 1970s, the colonial resource bargains struck by the United States and Western European firms began to collapse. Many formerly colonized countries pushed for the nationalization of critical resources and many others joined producer cartels to raise the price of their commodities. The 1973 Yom Kippur War between Israel and the forces of Syria and Egypt led to an embargo on oil exports to the United States by the Organization of Petroleum Exporting Countries (OPEC). Oil prices rose 400 percent during the six-month embargo, and prices remained relatively high after the embargo due to a cap on production. As a result, the exploitation of Louisiana's oil and gas resources intensified. Consequently, the profits of petrochemical firms operating in the state soared, as did state severance tax revenues. The Iranian Revolution of 1979 contributed to high oil prices, as did the early stages of the Iran and Iraq War (1980–88). However, Saudi production increases and price cuts, a global recession, and new energy conservation policies led to a 40 percent decline in oil prices between 1981 and 1986.[24]

The rise of oil prices between 1973 and 1981 led to a prolonged period of growth in Louisiana while other parts of the country were experiencing oil shortages, high prices, deindustrialization, and a combination of inflation and stagnation, "stagflation." As new Gulf Coast offshore wells were drilled in the biggest gas and oil field in North America, the tripling of oil prices also led to major increases in state wages and tax receipts. Coinciding with the administration of Governor Edwards, the late 1990s was marked by new state spending on education, social programs, housing construction, and downtown redevelopment in New Orleans. Profits derived from the expansion of pine plantations and soybean acreage also contributed to the overall economic boom.[25]

Despite the oil boom, Louisiana was still bound by the double curse of oil dependency layered on top of a foundation of plantation dependency. In *Development Arrested* and throughout this work, I have attempted to document the existence of and the political, economic, and social costs associated with unreconstructed plantation political economies. It is my contention that, despite numerous major and minor reforms, the resilience and scope of this complex and its institutions remain unappreciated by scholars in the United States. This situation is more than simply an intellectual curiosity; I argue that the fate of social justice and sustainable development rests on resolving the dilemmas presented by plantation-derived epistemologies, polices, and forms of social and economic dependency. According to Terry Lynn Karl and other scholars, prolonged oil dependency also creates unique and historic barriers to the attainment of sustainable development and social justice:

> Oil is a commodity with special characteristics. These include: 1) its unique role as both common natural heritage of a country and the motor of global industrialization, 2) its depletability, 3) its price volatility and consequent boom-bust cycles,

4) its especially high capital-intensity and technological sophistication, 5) its enclave nature, and 6) the exceptional generation of profits that accrue to the state and to private actors. The combination of these factors produces what has been called the "paradox of plenty" or the "resource curse." This is not due to the resource itself, which is simply a black and viscous substance, and it is not inevitable. A resource boom can be beneficial or detrimental. . . . Instead, what matters for the social consequences generated by petroleum dependence are, first, the type of pre-existing political, social and economic institutions available to manage oil wealth as it comes on-stream and, second, the extent to which oil revenues subsequently transform these institutions in a rentier direction.[26]

Karl defines a rentier direction as the product of monopoly over labor, land, and resources. This hegemony allows profits to be derived that are not reflective of social needs and costs. By definition, plantation-dominated regions are extremely rentier oriented. For example, the plantation system that evolved in Louisiana was based on a monopoly of land, resources, and capital. Another key pillar was the monopoly over, and immobility of, Black labor. The active management of impoverished and dependent African American communities included the preservation of a centuries-long competition with white labor. Slavery and sharecropping facilitated the realization of super profits by the plantations and their affiliated firms and sectors. The export orientation of this racialized system meant that the dominant bloc, the state, and local infrastructure were more preoccupied with the sale of agriculture commodities on the world market than increasing the skills, wages, and levels of consumption among Black, white, and Native American workers and communities. Wages and services were kept at near-starvation levels even during eras of reform and redistribution, that is, the Long era, the New Deal, and the War on Poverty. Numerous plantation monopolies emerged in Louisiana around the production, processing, sale, and distribution of cotton, sugar, rice, and forestry products. Related plantation monopolies were organized around the growing, importation, and processing of bananas, coffee, sugar, and rubber from severely exploited populations in the Caribbean, Central America, and South America. Mining in these regions and in Louisiana became a third pillar of the political economy. Another pillar was composed of key related sectors such as banking, insurance, commodity exchanges, and shipping. Monopoly super profits generated by these plantation- and mining-related sectors are the institutions on which the Bourbon regime was built, and they partially explain its historic domination of state politics, institutions, and policies.

The plantation complex differs from the petrochemical oil complex in several ways. First, agriculture is vastly more physically extensive than the petrochemical enclaves. However, there is a vast physical network of oil-, gas-, and chemical-drilling platforms, pipelines, storage facilities, refineries, and processing plants that run throughout southeastern Louisiana and into the Gulf of Mexico. This complex also extends westward to the refining, shipping, management, and financing center of Houston, Texas, including thousands of leases, pipelines, wells, and platforms covering over thirty thousand acres of offshore Louisiana, Texas, and Alabama. This massive zone is perhaps the largest mining region in the world and the largest oil plantation.[27]

The region also includes an enormous zone of environmental devastation and compromised health running along the Mississippi River from Baton Rouge to New Orleans, which has been designated "Cancer Alley." In addition, the policy of dredging wetlands to lay pipelines and carving channels to speed shipping has made New Orleans, the surrounding region, and the state more vulnerable to hurricanes. Petrochemical production and agricultural runoff have also created large dead zones within the Gulf of Mexico. Finally, the argument can easily be made that the footprint of hydrocarbon dependency in the region is larger than that of any other exploited resources due to its impact on air quality, water quality, and global climate change.

A second distinction between oil and agriculture is that plantation agriculture is not as subject to depletion or as capital intensive. Although monopolies dominate both complexes, a greater variety of producers, institutions, and communities are involved in the politics of agricultural production. Yet the brutal sugar plantation tradition of militarized agriculture provided a comfortable home for the oil, chemical, and gas industries that located along the Mississippi River's Chemical Corridor. Craig Colten describes the evolution of the complex created by the intersection of the plantation and oil sectors in the following manner:

> The construction of Standard Oil's Baton Rouge refinery in 1908 signaled the beginning of development in the lower Mississippi River chemical corridor; its flood-proof site, on high terraces near the head of navigation for ocean-going ships, offered ready access to crude oil and natural gas, ample water for industrial processes, and a giant sink for wastes, in addition to the favorable winter climate. Other refiners and chemical manufacturers quickly followed Standard Oil's lead, and there was an accelerated program of federal investment during World War II. By 1947 there were 117 refineries and chemical plants in Louisiana, and their numbers continued to grow: 211 in 1962, 284 in 1981, 320 in 2002. Along the lower Mississippi River, the number of oil-refining and chemical-processing plants rose from 126 in 1962 to 196 in 2002. A landscape once dominated by sugarcane fields had been thoroughly transformed.[28]

Most of the oil and gas facilities were owned by out-of-state and, later, foreign corporations. The firms and their personnel were quickly integrated into the plantation bloc. Composed of agricultural, import, and mining monopolies, the Bourbon regime was exponentially strengthened by the arrival of the petrochemical monopolies. As Louisiana became more rentier oriented, obtaining and preserving windfall profits became the defining goals of state institutions.

Karl argues that once the oil rentier state is established, private and public institutions become increasingly dependent on maintaining windfall profits. Additional governmental resources are devoted to preserving and expanding the petrochemical sector at the expense of other segments of society. Falling rates of profit due to competition, technological change, market instability, and demands for social justice and sustainability are faced by all regional political economies. During periods of crisis, like the present period, contending blocs in a region each attempt to implement their vision of transformation. Demands to maintain windfall monopoly profits significantly constrict the solutions offered by the existing leadership. During periods of crisis, rentier states often exhibit a decreasing concern for a wide range of social relations: social conditions; labor; the rights of historically oppressed racial and ethnic groups, women, and children; health; the environment; and local industry. "[The] consequences of oil-led development tend to be negative, including slower than expected growth, barriers to economic diversification, poor social welfare performance, and high levels of poverty, inequality and unemployment. Furthermore, countries dependent on oil as their major resource for development are characterized by exceptionally poor governance and high corruption, a culture of rent-seeking, often devastating economic, health and environmental consequences at the local level, and high incidences of conflict and war."[29]

This description captures many of the neoplantation and petrochemical fault lines present in Louisiana prior to the mid-1980s. The Bourbon tradition of minimal investment in education was reinforced by the oil sector's ability to import highly skilled workers without making major investments in public education. This led to the creation of a highly mobile labor aristocracy and a corporate leadership that had a marginal commitment to the long-term well-being of the region. Additionally, the Bourbon scientific and legal community worked hard to protect the agriculture, oil, gas, and chemical sectors from the astronomical health costs associated with decades of human and environmental degradation: water and soil contamination; toxic emissions; the destruction of wildlife habitats, forests, and wetlands; the creation of hazardous waste sites; the decimation of fishing and the seafood industry; the creation of dead zones; and, in 2010, the apocalyptic destruction of Gulf Coast waters, lands, wildlife, and communities due to oil-industry negligence.[30] Karl concludes that, similar to plantation-based development, oil-based development is a form of enclosure that decimates ethnic groups physically, economically, socially, and culturally while simultaneously militarizing ethnic and race relations. This "disruption is most profound among ethnic minorities and indigenous peoples who live off the land and whose customs and traditions may also be threatened."[31]

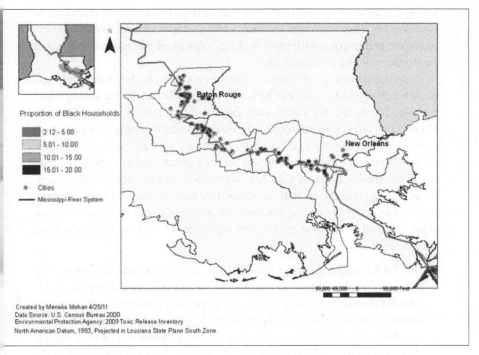

FIGURE 7. Proportion of Black households earning $15,000 to $19,999 (1999) within a one-mile buffer of chemical facilities in Cancer Alley. Menaka Mohan.

The targeting of Black communities by the state and by petrochemical sectors severely compromised both the health and culture of those living in the towns and on the plantations along the Cancer Alley Chemical Corridor prior to the 1970s oil boom. By the late 1980s, the Cancer Alley Chemical Corridor of Louisiana had come to symbolize the very definition of environmental racism in the national imaginary. According to activist Vera Brooks, by 2001 the predominantly Black towns of Convent, Diamond, Ella, Oakville, Mossville, Myrtle Grove, Morrisonville, New Sarpy, Norco, and Reveilletown had been turned into "toxic prisons."[32]

This historic enclosure devastated Afro-Creole, African American, and Native American communities and culture. This physical imposition of the chemical and gas industries upon these plantation, former plantation, and plantation-adjacent communities resulted in the physical destruction of one of the most vibrant centers of culture, consciousness, and plantation resistance in the Americas. Those communities not leveled by the construction of refineries and plants found themselves slowly poisoned by the air, water, and soil contamination. These communities suffered, and continue to suffer, enormous losses. Yet these communities also continued their three-century resistance to Bourbonism. They were both the source of a global movement to end their exploitation and major contributors to the emergence of the national and global environmental justice movement.

Despite their multiple ills, oil blocs have access to rents—institutionally organized windfall profits—that can be widely and rapidly distributed during boom periods. The Louisiana welfare state expanded dramatically under Edwards. His first two terms were marked by the establishment of a huge state patronage network within the Black community, continued African American political factionalism, and a decline in support for the fundamental reforms embedded in the sustainable Blues agenda. An understanding of the neoplantation/neo-Bourbon state and the oil state as outlined by Karl is necessary to understand several aspects of the fragile, fractured, demobilizing, and debilitating nature of oil-financed progressive reforms and repression in Louisiana from the Long era to the present:

> Oil wealth produces greater spending on patronage that, in turn, weakens existing pressures for representation and accountability. In effect, popular acquiescence is achieved through the political distribution of rents. Oil states can buy political consensus, and their access to rents facilitates the cooptation of potential opponents or dissident voices. With basic needs met by an often generous welfare state, with the absence of taxation, and with little more than demands for quiescence and loyalty in return, populations tend to be politically inactive, relatively obedient and loyal and levels of protest remain low—at least as long as the oil state can deliver. Thus for long periods an unusual combination of dependence, passivity, and entitlement marks the political culture of petroleum exporters.[33]

Historically, the Bourbon bloc has been able to severely limit regional, parish, and local autonomy through a double dependency formula that has made working-class communities exceedingly vulnerable. Historic and widespread state property tax exemptions represent a major transfer of wealth to agricultural, business, and large property owners. The history of levying minimal property taxes stretches back to the antebellum period and the domination of the state by large plantation owners. This was their recipe for accelerating their accumulation of wealth—guaranteeing a weak state along with generalized poverty and dependency. The collection of property taxes was further undermined by the plantation bloc's efforts to undermine the generation of tax revenues to support Reconstruction-era governments and social reforms.

With the lowest property tax rates in the nation, local governments in Louisiana have remained heavily dependent on the state for funds to support basic social services, health care, and education. Furthermore, when social reforms did emerge under the Long regime, funding for these necessities was tied directly to severance payments generated by oil and gas production. When Long threatened additional taxes, the oil industry responded by organizing its own militia and threatening to launch a coup. When the civil rights movement threatened to reorder Deep South economies, the oil and gas sectors funneled resources to Leander Perez and the populist, elite-led White Citizens' Council movement.

This pattern of reform and repression ensured that impoverished communities, particularly impoverished urban and rural Black communities, would have a very limited role in social service decision-making processes even after they regained the right to vote. Even during oil boom periods, high levels of rural and urban African American poverty were maintained by racially discriminatory budget, employment, education, housing, health care, and environmental policies. The layers of the classic Bourbon antireformist state were preserved and repeatedly reinforced by the windfall profits derived from the oil and gas industries. Only large-scale statewide coalitions were capable of affecting local reforms. Despite these efforts, deep political, regional, class, and racial divisions, along with corruption and co-optation, made such movements exceedingly difficult to assemble.

Although oil-dominated states are said to exhibit a great degree of stability, plantation-dominated states tend be crisis ridden. The unstable oil- and federal-funding-dependent neo-Bourbon state defined by the Edwin Edwards coalition of Blacks, Creoles, Cajuns, and other Democrats began to fracture when confronted by the oil crisis in 1986 and by the movement for Bourbon restoration.[34] The OPEC cartel's limits on production collapsed by the mid-1980s. Saudi Arabia significantly increased its production, and this contributed to a rapid decline in the price of oil, from a high of fifty dollars a barrel in 1980 to ten dollars a barrel by 1986. According to Roberto Suro, for Louisiana the "collapse of exploration and drilling was only one point of pain in the demise of an entire economy based on heavy borrowing and a belief that the boom could never end."[35] Numerous major short-term impacts flowed from the oil trap crisis. First, the state's unemployment rate reached 13.1 percent, double the national average. "In Louisiana employment in oil and gas extraction dropped by more than half from 1981 to 1987 as the state lost about 9 percent of all its nonagricultural jobs."[36] In New Orleans in 1986, a newly elected Mayor Barthelemy noted that estimates of Black unemployment had reached 25 percent.[37] Major oil firms laid off numerous workers before moving their offices to Houston. Also, many hotels and downtown retailers in New Orleans went bankrupt as the tourism industry declined. Finally, office vacancies increased dramatically, as did the number of property foreclosures.[38]

The oil bust led to a profound crisis in all the oil-dependent states: Louisiana, Texas, and Oklahoma. It also set off a round of intense competition between states and regions within states to recruit new firms. Governments also increased subsidies for existing petrochemical firms while decreasing the regulation of their environmental impacts. There were major efforts to reorganize the workforce when tens of thousands of workers, from professionals to recent high school graduates, began to flee the region: "Adm. Bobby R. Inman, who has headed two major Texas-based computer firms since he left the Central Intelligence Agency in 1982, said there is a serious risk that 'if we do not make some tough decisions or we make the wrong decisions, this region could end up like a very large Mississippi.'"[39]

By the late 1980s Governor Buddy Roemer of Louisiana noted that the "downside to this situation is that we'll never get our kids back. If the price of oil shoots up and we decide we don't need reform because things are OK. Again, we'll never see all those people who have left, especially the young people, because they've realized there is no future here without fundamental change." He also argued that there had to be a break with the rentier neo-Bourbon epistemology. "We can't settle for just being cotton pickers anymore. . . . Our natural resources were so plentiful that all we had to do was harvest them to get rich, whether it was cotton or oil and gas or lumber or cattle. But in this world today it is no longer enough to be asset-rich unless your No. 1 asset is human beings." According to one Texas corporate executive, during the crisis the historic underfunding of education suddenly became "an economic time bomb." Suro notes that while other oil states launched major reforms, Roemer's attempted "Revolution" of the late 1980s, an attempt to reduce taxes on businesses while increasing them for homeowners, was initially unsuccessful:

> Traditionally a region where individuals paid low taxes, the oil states have had to defy the national trend during the era that made "no new taxes" a rallying cry to make up for lost revenues from the oil industry. Texas and Oklahoma have enacted substantial tax increases since the oil busts that have brought their levies close to the national average. Now there is talk of raising taxes some more. . . . In Louisiana, Governor Roemer, a liberal Democrat, has been trying to wean the state from the populist largess instituted by Gov. Huey Long in the 1930's. Governor Roemer insists that fiscal luxuries like a homestead exemption, which frees most homeowners from property taxes, were viable only when the oil industry made vast contributions to the state treasury. So far, however, he has had only limited success in overhauling the tax system to transfer some of the burden from businesses to ordinary citizens.[40]

In Louisiana, the double curse of the plantation and oil imperatives led the state down a development path that intensified the impoverishment of its residents. During the oil crisis, conflicts within the increasingly unstable neo-Bourbon bloc would repeatedly shock the nation for the next two decades.

Consequently, on the eve of Hurricane Katrina the double curse of plantation and oil economics had already created a major social disaster. What the failure of the levees in 2005 revealed was triply shocking: the restoration of Bourbonism locally; its restoration nationally under the guise of Reaganism, devolution, starve the beast policies, and so on; and its restoration internationally under the guise of structural adjustment and neoliberalism. These elite responses to social and economic crises have led to a broken region, a broken nation, and a broken world system.

Bourbon Neoliberalism and the Southern Strategy

Edwin Edwards faced several political challengers, including Congressman Robert L. "Bob" Livingston, a Republican who spent part of his childhood in New Orleans and represented the adjacent community of Metairie. His core constituency included the white-flight suburbs located in Jefferson Parish, the Florida Parishes, and other parts of the state. Another major challenger to Edwards was Congressman Wilbert J. "Billy" Tauzin III. A Democrat from just outside of Thibodaux, in La Fourche Parish, Tauzin was also a Cajun and Edwards's former floor leader in the state legislature. He was also a representative of the sugar plantation bloc located in the southern and southwestern sections of the state. Later he went on to found the conservative Blue Dog coalition among congressional Democrats before becoming a Republican in 1995.[41]

Although Edwards and Roemer made it to the runoff, Burk Foster argues that the transition of power began before the general election:

> When he ran a weak second to Democratic Congressman Buddy Roemer in the September open gubernatorial primary, Edwards capitulated the office to Roemer and then virtually dropped from sight, spending a good part of his last six months in office on his ranch outside Junction, Texas. Now it was his turn to play caretaker, and he demonstrated that he was not well-suited to the role. When Roemer's transition government wanted to start early with deep budget cuts to reduce deficits, Edwards made some cuts, refused more, and hinted that he would be available in four years to save the state from calamities of the "Roemer Revolution."[42]

Roemer promised to bring revolutionary change in order to meet the multiple crises of Louisiana's political economy. During his term as governor, he cut numerous social programs in addition to pushing for business tax breaks, increased taxes on middle-class homeowners, increased teacher pay, and new environmental regulations. The legislature defeated many of his educational reforms. Instead of accepting reductions in the property tax exemption, which would require greater contributions from the middle and upper classes, the body chose to further burden impoverished citizens with new sales taxes. Although a Democrat, Roemer admired the Reagan agenda and switched parties just before the gubernatorial election of 1991.[43] Roemer was one of many Southern Democrats who joined the national Reagan Revolution during the 1980s and 1990s. The devastation of limited social spending, civil rights enforcement, and the labor movement were combined with "Southern Strategy" political tactics during the Reagan era to pave the road for the Bourbon restoration in Louisiana. During multiple crises of the 1980s, the movement to restore Bourbonism in Louisiana was strengthened by federal policies adopted during the Reagan administration.

Federal Political Institutions

After 1965 the nationalization of massive white resistance was combined with some concessions around efforts to integrate employment, housing, education, labor, the professions, and electoral politics. The massive resistance and "white backlash" movements of the 1950s and 1960s was the result of a revitalized Republican Party whose "Southern Strategy" relied on growth through the reproduction and expansion of Bourbon neoliberalism. A 1962 article in the *Louisville Courier Journal* heralded the birth of "Racial Republicanism": "The truth is that this Republican upsurge, if that is the word, owes much of its momentum to the very thing that has kept the South in one party bondage for nearly a century—an unreasoning passion to maintain 'white supremacy.'" The Southern Strategy of the Nixon and Reagan campaigns crafted a southern, western, and northern national compact based on white economic and racial fears. Throughout the South during the 1970s, elements within the "massive resistance" movement were changing their registration from the Democratic Party to the Republican Party. The national Republican Party's Southern Strategy crafted an alliance composed of plantation blocs, major business sectors, white-flight suburban residents, rural whites, working-class white urban Catholics, several unions, and White Citizens' Council leaders. The new electoral alliance also supported a restructuring of urban, rural, regional, gender, and class relations. The institutions of national and global capitalism were also reformed under the banners of privatization, deregulation, and neoliberalism. The Southern Strategy involved more than just organizing a new electoral constituency; it also marked the revitalization of the plantation bloc epistemology and its emphasis on social fragmentation, impoverishment, dependency, militarization, and racial schism in order to guarantee the redistribution of wealth upward.

> In 1981, Lee Atwater explained the movement's rhetorical evolution as a series of "Black magic" incantations: "You start out in 1954 by saying, 'Nigger, nigger, nigger.' By 1968, you can't say 'nigger,' that hurts you. Backfires. So you say stuff like forced bussing, states' rights and all that stuff. You're getting so abstract now [that] you're talking about cutting taxes, and all these things you're talking about are totally economic things and a byproduct of them is [that] blacks get hurt worse than whites. . . . [It] is getting that abstract that coded that we are doing away with the racial problem one way or another. You follow me."[44]

Relying on the tactics of racial schisms to achieve new majorities, the Southern Strategy was supported by younger and older activists linked to the Citizen's Council movement. For example, in the U.S. Senate, between 1981 and 1987 South Carolina's Strom Thurmond simultaneously served as president pro tempore and the chair of the Committee on the Judiciary. Likewise, during the same period, North Carolina's Jesse Helms chaired the Senate Committee on Agriculture, Nutrition and Forestry.

During the multiple crises of the era, the Reagan administration and the Southern Strategy movement supported the revitalization of the historic Bourbon disenfranchisement institution. This can be seen in several processes, including voting disenfranchisement, the upward redistribution of wealth, and community destabilization. Although Blacks made up 30 percent of the state's population in 1980, when the legislature hinted at creating a majority Black congressional district, Governor Treen promised a veto. The district drawn to split the Black electorate was approved by President Reagan's Justice Department. In 1983 it became the first congressional redistricting plan approved by the Justice Department to be struck down by the federal courts since the enactment of the Voting Rights Act in 1965. Additionally, during the 1986 U.S. Senate race, the Republican National Committee (RNC) tried to reduce the Black electorate in Louisiana by as many as eighty thousand voters in order to enable Republican congressman W. Henson Moore of Baton Rouge to defeat Democratic congressman John B. Breaux of southwestern Louisiana.[45] According to a 2004 study by Chandler Davidson and colleagues, the national Republican disenfranchisement program deployed in Louisiana was patterned on a similar project launched in Arizona during the 1950s by William Rehnquist, the Reagan-appointed chief justice of the Supreme Court:

> As part of its 1986 ballot security program, the RNC had hired a private contractor to conduct operations nationwide. One such operation focused on Louisiana. Run by Ballot Security Group out of Chicago, it followed a pattern Republicans had used at least since the 1950s. . . . Nonforwardable letters were sent to 350,000 registered voters across the state. About 30,000 were returned. Most of the returned letters had been addressed to blacks. . . . The head of Ballot Security Group denied his company was targeting blacks, although he acknowledged the returned envelopes primarily came from their addresses, "That's to be expected," he said, "because more of them are renters and they move more often."[46]

Other evidence suggested that the targeted districts were the same ones in which Reagan received less than 25 percent of the vote during the 1980 presidential campaign:

> The fact later emerged that the letters had been targeted at districts voting over 75 percent for Democratic Presidential candidate Walter F. Mondale in 1984, a pattern

that seldom occurred outside heavily black districts. As the attempted purge began to attract attention, assertions that candidate Moore's money had helped subsidize it were initially denied but later turned out to be true. Democrats went to court to obtain a restraining order and succeeded. Had the Republicans not been prevented from continuing their program, their next step would have been to send challenged voters a registered letter notifying them of the action. If there was no reply, a notice would be placed in the parish (i.e., county) official journal, and if there was still no response, the voter's name would be . . . purged-from the registration list.[47]

As Davidson and others note, the documents that emerged from the scandal revealed a historic shift. The disenfranchisement institution had once again become a national movement, a rehearsal for the demise of the Second Reconstruction:

> Voters in affected areas brought suit. In the discovery phase, a particularly damning memo came to light, which spelled out clearly the motive behind this ballot-security program and suggested as well the motive behind many other programs which had used this purging tactic. The memo was from Kris Wolfe, the RNC midwest political director, to Lanny Griffith, the RNC southern political director. "I know this race is really important to you," Wolfe wrote. "I would guess that this program will eliminate at least 60–80,000 folks from the rolls. . . . If it's a close race . . . which I'm assuming it is, this could keep the black vote down considerably." After considering the evidence, the trial judge called the Louisiana ballot security program "an insidious scheme by the Republican Party to remove blacks from the voting rolls. . . . The only reasonable conclusion is that they initiated this purge with the specific intent of disfranchising these blacks of their right to vote." He prohibited use of the tactics in the future.[48]

The federal support for a new era of "massive resistance" helped to break the remnants of the racial and class reform complex and efforts designed to build an urban consensus centered on social justice and sustainable development.

The reemergent Bourbon bloc used these multiple crises to launch a massive redistribution of wealth. In 1981 Louisiana was considered one of the wealthiest states in the nation. Yet approximately 40 percent of state revenues were dependent on oil and gas severance taxes. During the oil boom, a massive tax cut initiated by Governor Edwards removed an estimated $600 to $700 million from the treasury annually. One of Governor Treen's first acts after taking office was to push for the passage of a $1 billion tax cut in 1980 that primarily benefited wealthy residents and firms. Both actions increased the state's dependency on oil severance payments. When oil prices fell in 1981, the Treen tax cut alone effectively decreased state revenues by 25 percent. The movement to cut corporate taxes was institutionalized and served as a pillar of Bourbon neoliberalism.[49]

In addition, petrochemical plant layoffs and closures led to dramatic decreases in sales tax revenues and dramatic increases in unemployment. The state's 11.5 percent unemployment rate in 1982 pushed the unemployment compensation fund into bankruptcy. The legislature responded by passing a bailout plan that capped both the amount of unemployment benefits distributed and the number of weeks for which support was provided. The next Treen budget further destabilized impoverished working-class communities. When the $5.3 billion 1983 state budget ran a deficit of nearly $300 million, Treen imposed a 4.4 percent statewide budget cut targeting state agencies and state-supported local services. The movement to create and preserve high rates of unemployment as a means to reduce the deficit became an institution, as did the related movement that unleashed a perpetual assault on government subsidies for working-class communities. Collectively, the deficit, budget cuts, tax cuts, and high unemployment combined to create a fifth institution with its own internal dynamic and trajectory: the perpetual destabilization of impoverished communities.[50]

A similar destabilization was being created at the federal level. The decline in state income and economic activity was compounded by a national economic recession beginning in 1979. It was defined by severe deindustrialization, massive layoffs, high rates of unemployment, and the economic and social collapse of many regions, cities, towns, rural areas, and inner-city African American communities. The Reagan administration used these crises to build a multiregional alliance capable of dismantling key components of the national welfare state. Electorally and financially supported by white-flight suburbs, regions opposed to civil rights, and economic sectors opposed to unions, regulation, and existing tax rates, this movement destabilized national, regional, and local political alliances along with the economic foundations of regions and communities. Organizations, policies, and programs that supported family and community sustainability were severely undermined or eliminated. Federal aid to New Orleans fell from $123 million in 1980 to $65 million by 1982.[51] Targeted reductions in federal and state funding between 1984 and 1989 resulted in the city's budget declining by a third, from $324.9 million to $213.0 million.[52]

A final institution created during this period emerged from the adoption of urban triage as public policy and its naturalization. While intensifying his close cooperation with private sector groups, corporate boards, and Bourbon-dominated commissions, Mayor Barthelemy chose to pass along the crisis to the most vulnerable Black working-class communities. White flight resulted in a city that was increasingly Black while massive disinvestment, redlining, and increased regional occupational competition resulted in a city that was increasingly impoverished. In 1986 the city deficit of $30 million was compounded when the state legislature, facing a deficit of between $600 million and $800 million, decided to reduce funding for New Orleans by $25 million. Subsequently, Barthelemy launched an effort to reduce the size of city government by canceling contracts, downsizing agencies, and eliminating city employees. Approved by the city council, this plan involved "nearly seven hundred layoffs, seven million dollars in new temporary taxes and fees, and 7.6 million dollars in other cost-cutting measures. The budget prescription even extended to vital city services. Barthelemy detailed plans to lay off 195 of the city's approximately 1,000 Fire Department employees and 184 of the Police Department's 1,700 employees."[53]

After a plan to create a $195 annual property service charge failed at the polls,

> the City Council [chose] to reduce the workweek of the city's 5,600 employees to four days. City Hall and other municipal buildings closed on Fridays, and Barthelemy also ordered the closure of one-third of the city's fire stations. In addition to these drastic measures, 200 additional city workers were laid off. And all city workers who retained their jobs suffered a 20 percent pay cut for the remainder of the year. The Council also approved a 1.5 percent tax on the earnings of anyone who worked in the city, although court challenges to the legality of the earnings tax negated that potential revenue stream.[54]

The 1986 unemployment rate of 11.1 percent was amplified by layoffs of twelve hundred employees in the city workforce. Historic and existing patterns of racial discrimination meant that Black city employees' incomes supported far more persons and businesses than was typical in a nonsegregated environment. Therefore, targeting the city workforce had a negative multiplier effect throughout Black New Orleans. Another negative consequence was that the Black community, businesses, and professionals became even more dependent on the patronage positions and contracts distributed to COUP and SOUL.[55] By 1989 the state was facing a budget of $1.3 billion and Governor Buddy Roemer was threatening to further cut state funds allocated to the city. The New Orleans Business Council intervened and helped negotiate a deal that appropriated $19 million for the city's budget.[56]

The Carceral State

Man is born free, and everywhere he is in chains.
Jean-Jacques Rousseau, *On the Social Contract*, 1762

Asked for bread, received
a stone
Asked for fish, received
a snake
Asked
and was not given

Sought
and was lost
Knocked
and was knocked out
    Joe C. Ireland, poem found scratched into a cell wall at Orleans Parish Prison[57]

The oil crisis and Bourbonism combined to make New Orleans one of the primary modern incubators of the national and global prison-industrial complex, an institution that demonized, destabilized, trapped, and captured working-class Black communities, the most ardent supporters of the Blues agenda. The torture of Black citizens by the New Orleans Police Department continued during this period. Defined by mob violence and a sense of impunity, the police department's actions repeatedly shocked the nation. For example, nine citizens were shot, seven fatally, by NOPD officers during the fall and winter of 1980–81. The victims included an unarmed mentally disturbed woman, an unarmed and cornered robbery suspect, and an unarmed high school band member shot by a drunken on-duty police officer during a Mardi Gras parade. According to Human Rights Watch, there were also incidences of collective punishment: "[After] a white officer was killed in November 1980, mobs of police officers went on a rampage in Algiers, a black section of town, killing four and injuring as many as fifty residents. Some of the victims were tortured, including two who were dragged to swamps where the officers carried out mock executions. The violence led to the resignation of the police superintendent. . . . Three homicide detectives were convicted on federal criminal civil rights charges."[58] Despite numerous protests, both Mayor Morial and Orleans Parish district attorney Harry Connick resisted the creation of a civilian review board for the 75 percent white department.[59] Morial did appoint Warren Woodfork as the city's first African American police chief in 1984. He was later retained by Barthelemy until he retired in 1991.[60] During his tenure, Woodfork was not able to quell the NOPD's rampant brutality and corruption. For example, a March 22, 1990, downtown shootout resulted in the death of a white officer, Earl Hauck, and the arrests of an African American suspect, Adolph Archie. Hearing death threats being broadcast on their radios, the officers transporting Archie to a local hospital for treatment were met by a lynch mob of one hundred fellow officers. Claiming they feared a lynching, they delivered Archie to a police station, where he was promptly beaten to death. Even the coroner was forced by the evidence to conclude that Archie's cause of death was "homicide by police intervention."[61]

According to a 1992 U.S. Department of Justice report New Orleans ranked first nationally in complaints of police brutality between 1984 and 1990. A 1998 Human Rights Watch study concluded that "despite its abysmal record, the police department has avoided the widespread community protests or other sustained external pressure that are often necessary for reforms to take hold permanently." The fragmented political structure, competitive patronage networks, deepening poverty, rising number of crises of desperation, and terror muted demands for police reform. Widespread racial and ethnic repression define plantation regimes and, according to Karl, they are also common features of oil regimes: "But the spending of oil rents supports repression as well as cooptation to keep authoritarian rulers in power. Not surprisingly, then, oil dependence is closely associated with military spending and the creation of extensive repressive apparatuses. . . . While all states may use their fiscal powers to reduce dissent through coercion or cooptation, oil wealth provides states with exceptional possibilities to do so."[62]

The toxic mix of the oil crisis, layoffs, a national recession, and cuts in educational and job-training programs began to dismantle social networks in one neighborhood after the other. Crack cocaine fueled a large population of addicts, a major health crisis, and a competitive drug trade defined by organizations and individuals with unprecedented access to automatic weapons. According to Lyle Perkins, "NOPD statistics reflected a 127 percent increase in the city's murder rate between 1985 and 1991. During that period, robberies escalated by 44 percent and total violent crimes increased by 33 percent."[63]

The oil crisis also reopened the door that allowed remnants of the "massive resistance" movement and Bourbonism to redesign the regional, national, and global criminal justice system. Pseudoscientific theories were provided by leading academics to restore the legitimacy of Bourbon logic. Increasingly, Black workers unemployed due to the intersection of a deepening recession and increasing employment discrimination were viewed as threatening, genetically predisposed toward violent crime, the products of vicious mothers and absent fathers, and generally disposable. According to Foster, as the rate of African American incarceration and the length of sentences grew exponentially, parole, probation, and rehabilitative programs declined dramatically:

> Before the 1970s, Louisiana was not a particularly punitive state. It ranked 13th nationally in 1965, with a rate of 109.1 prisoners per 100,000 population. . . . Until 1972, the standard was: any inmate who behaved himself in prison would be let go after ten-and-a-half years—the so-called "10–6 rule." What happened in the seventies was that the state stopped letting people go. . . . Existing alternatives were de-emphasized. The 10–6 rule was disallowed, good time was cut back, parole and sentence commutations became less frequent. At the same time, the state jumped heavily into mandatory sentencing for violent crimes and drug offenses and judges began to apply longer sentences to repeat property offenders. . . . The number of state prisoners has tripled, from 5,300 in June 1975 to 15,329 at the end of June 1987 (This is close to the same prison population as Louisiana's mother country, France, a nation of 55 million people).[64]

The Reproduction of Criminalization

Although often ignored by scholars and community development practitioners, human rights is a critical component of sustainable community development. Examining the production and manufacture of bondage is central to comprehending the social disasters prior to, during, and following Hurricane Katrina. After three decades of major social movements, protests, lawsuits, institutional reforms, individual sacrifices, and electoral successes, during the 1990s, human rights in the New Orleans region experienced significant reversals. As previously mentioned, New Orleans had the highest ranking of citizen complaints of police brutality in the country. Although the city's crime rate began to drop between 1995 and 1996 due to the national economic recovery, aggressive policing and zero-tolerance policies led to a 27 percent increase in citizen complaints between 1996 and 1997. Police abuse expert James Fyfe notes that "some cities' police departments have reputations for being brutal, like Los Angeles, or corrupt, like New York, and still others are considered incompetent. New Orleans has accomplished the rare feat of leading nationally in all categories."[65]

For example, during this period New Orleans claimed the unprecedented achievement of having two of its officers sentenced to death. NOPD officer Len Davis terrorized the Desire public housing development for years. Over twenty complaints were filed against him between 1987 and 1992, including one for an incident where he beat a woman in the head with a flashlight. A federal court sentenced Davis to death in 1996 for the slaying of Kim Groves, who was murdered soon after filing a brutality complaint against him in 1994. Davis and six former officers were also convicted of running a major cocaine ring. Antoinette Frank was another NOPD officer sentenced to death. Engaged in an attempted 1995 robbery, she murdered a Vietnamese brother and sister whose family owned the store and an off-duty NOPD officer working as a security guard. Morial appointed Richard Pennington as police superintendent in 1994 and he attempted to lessen abuses through "firings, reprimands, background checks, a ban on hiring known criminals, the monitoring of repeat offenders, and limits on off-duty employment."[66]

Although the U.S. attorney for the Eastern District of Louisiana, which includes New Orleans, stated that corruption in the NOPD was "pervasive, rampant, [and] systemic," New Orleans district attorney Harry Connick Sr. rarely prosecuted officers. Similarly, federal prosecutors prosecuted only 9 of 819 potential cases of abuse and corruption between 1992 and 1995. Prior to the Davis case, the U.S. attorney's office under Presidents Bush and Clinton had refused to convene a federal grand jury to investigate the multiple complaints. Afterward, between 1994 and 1997, fifty-four officers under investigation were dismissed and another seventy-three resigned. Also, the U.S. Justice Department was finally forced to launch a systematic investigation of NOPD abuse in 1996. In

1998 Superintendent Pennington directed a case involving two officers beating a handcuffed man to Eddie Jordan Jr., who in 1994 had been appointed as the first African American U.S. attorney in Louisiana. Jordan brought an indictment against the officers on federal civil rights charges.[67]

The modern Louisiana prison-industrial complex is an engine fueling African American impoverishment, confinement, plantation labor, human rights violations, disenfranchisement, and the Bourbon restoration. Desperation in the cities was fueled by a raft of legal traps reminiscent of the Black Codes: mandatory minimum sentences, the elimination of parole, and "three strikes" laws—lifelong incarceration—for nonviolent offenders. In 2000, Blacks represented 32.5 percent of Louisiana's population and yet they made up 72.1 percent of those incarcerated. By 2003 Louisiana ranked second among all states in the number of youth sentenced to life without the possibility of parole and first in the percentage of youth aged fourteen to seventeen serving such sentences. Not only was the rate of white youth serving the sentence the highest in the country, but the Black rate was nearly five times higher.[68] With eight hundred inmates per one hundred thousand residents in 2003, the state had an incarceration rate that professor Burk Foster describes as "the highest rate in the universe."[69] In the early 1990s Fairclough observed that "Louisiana has executed more prisoners than any other state except Florida and Texas; in proportion to its population, it is America's leading executioner."[70] The construction of the Louisiana prison-industrial complex would serve as a model for the nation as Bourbon leadership created a new era of bondage.

New Institutions in the Late Twentieth and Early Twenty-First Centuries

As we have seen, there was a social disaster of immense proportions occurring in New Orleans before Hurricane Katrina struck the city. The Bourbon restoration was defined by the disposability of Black working-class lives and a predatory economy laced with numerous institutional traps. These institutions are more than just social constructs. They involve centuries of investment, billions of dollars of fixed capital, and forms of social regulation enforced by numerous rules, laws and courts, academic institutions, and distinct systems of representation of fixed capital.

EMPLOYMENT

A key institutional pillar of the Bourbon restoration was the expansion of the low-wage economy and the numerous forms of dependency and desperation associated with it. A 2005 study by Total Community Action found that there was a significant downturn in the New Orleans metropolitan economy between

1969 and 1999. The response of local government and the private sector was to increase the city's dependence on low-wage services:

> Services, which include the hospitality sector, show a dramatic gain, rising from 22% to 34% of all jobs. Manufacturing showed a large drop, falling from 12.6% to 6.3%. Other significant declines occurred in transportation, mining, and wholesale trade. The reduction in transport reflects the contraction of port activities, which also influences the wholesale trade sector. The decrease in mining is a consequence of the meltdown of the U.S. oil and gas industry during the 1980s. Taken together, these decreases accounted for 14.4% of all jobs, and most of these are in relatively high-paying activities. The job decreases were offset by gains in services and retail trade. [Approximately] 78% of all job growth occurred in these two low-paying sectors.[71]

The fight to preserve the cheap labor economy and to maintain a racially organized workforce took many forms. One of Governor Foster's first acts in office was to eliminate state set-asides and affirmative action programs for people of color and women. In response Representative Reverend Avery Alexander (D-New Orleans) led protests at the governor's mansion and at Foster's plantation in Franklin. Surprisingly, Foster asked Alexander to deliver the opening prayer at a special state legislative session in 1996. Alexander prayed,

> O Lord our God . . . save us from all who persecute us. . . . Visit Gov. Foster, please Lord. Show him the path toward justice. Give him the courage to do what is right for the oppressed. Put love in his heart instead of hatred. May he be the kind of leader we need and want in the state. . . . [Alexander asked God to] rise up in anger because of the rage of the enemies of the black, poor, women and working people of Louisiana. Our enemies have encircled these legislative chambers and seek to erase more than a century of [civil rights] progress.[72]

There were other consequences related to the increased dependence on and power of low-wage sectors such as tourism, entertainment, sports, gaming, and services. High levels of unemployment and poverty were intensified by declining real wages. And as previously discussed, a uniquely traumatic desegregation crisis during the 1960s led to the creation of white-flight constituencies in neighboring parishes. These trends and policies combined to create significant barriers for Black city residents seeking either jobs with the potential for upward mobility or suburban employment opportunities. In other words, the poverty-reduction strategies of individuals, families, and local government were uniquely constrained by the type of jobs available and by continued racial discrimination.[73] Leaders of the low-wage sectors and their allies strongly resisted any changes in the opportunity structure and sought to preserve their trapped labor force at every turn. For example, families in the Black neighborhoods that were flooded in 2005 had a median income of only $25,759 in 2004, barely more than half the national average. The wages of many workers in the city were so low that they qualified for both public housing and food stamps. Although New Orleans voters approved a citywide living wage measure in 2002, it was later overturned by the courts. Additionally, public and private affirmative action initiatives were defeated.[74]

By 2004 the New Orleans population and its employment base were declining and the city had some of the nation's highest rates of unemployment, drug abuse, crime, incarceration, and racial segregation.[75] Harry Holzer suggests that on the eve of Katrina many young African American men were trapped in an institutionally organized downward spiral: "In August 2004, the unemployment rate for black teenagers nationally was just over 35%. The percentage of the population employed was only about 20%, which is only about half the rate observed for whites. Among young black men in New Orleans aged 16–24 who were not enrolled in school, fully 40% were not even in the labor force . . . one of the worst rates of nonparticipation in the nation."[76]

POVERTY

Throughout this work I have argued that poverty in Louisiana is not a natural disaster. It is a human-made disaster. Hence I use the term *impoverishment* to encourage an examination of the disastrous choices that were made to create community, racial, class, and gender destitution in the region. Impoverishment is a highly organized institution. As discussed earlier, falling oil revenues, a national recession, and federal budget cutbacks sent the region into crisis. The regional Blues agenda was defeated in favor of the draconian Bourbon impoverishment agenda.

By 1992, a comparison by the Annie E. Casey Foundation of states and the District of Columbia found Louisiana and Mississippi once again competing for the most disastrous rankings: for the percentage of low-birth-weight babies, forty-ninth and fiftieth, respectively; for infant mortality, thirty-seventh and fiftieth; for child death rates, ages one to fourteen, forty-ninth and fiftieth; for births to unmarried teens, forty-seventh and forty-ninth; for juvenile violent crime, forty-third and sixteenth; for teens who drop out of high school, fifty-first and twenty-eighth; for percentage of teens not in school or working, fiftieth and forty-fifth; for teen violent deaths, forty-seventh and forty-eighth; for percentage of children in poverty, fifty-first and forty-ninth; and for the percentage of families with children headed by a single parent, fiftieth and forty-ninth. In the same year, a survey found that the median family income of African Americans in Louisiana stood at 58 percent of the white median income. Not only was this gap wider than it had been in 1968 but the assets of white households were "*ten times* the net assets of the median black household. In New Orleans, one of the poorest cities in the nation, 37 percent of the black families were below the poverty level compared with 9 percent of white families. Only Mississippi had a greater percentage of poor people than Louisiana."[77]

After President Clinton introduced the Temporary Assistance to Needy Families program in 1996, states were enabled to experiment with welfare. Louisiana adopted one of the most draconian programs in the nation. Launched in 1996, Louisiana's version of federal welfare reform, Family Independence Temporary Assistance Program, reduced state welfare rolls by two-thirds. According to a recent study by Sheila Zedlewski: "[Two] years after leaving welfare, 41 percent of former welfare recipients were not working and had not returned to welfare. . . . In short, single mothers with little or no employment experience could only get a small cash benefit for two years at a time in New Orleans. They had limited access to job training, and many who lost benefits as time limits expired were living without earnings or government cash assistance. Other research shows that these 'disconnected families' rely on noncash government assistance and family members to survive."[78]

By 2004 the child poverty rate in New Orleans stood at 40 percent, the highest in the nation. The city was still the epicenter of urban poverty in the United States while Louisiana had become the second most impoverished state in the nation. In the same year, Louisiana governor Kathleen Blanco called an emergency governor's "Summit on Solutions to Poverty" to address the growing crisis.[79]

The Bourbon restoration was defined by the elderly, children, women, low-income families, and entire communities being caught in a poverty trap governed by numerous types of predators. The Center on Budget and Policy Priorities found that in New Orleans more than 54 percent of impoverished households and 65 percent of impoverished elderly households did not possess a car, truck, or van in 2000. Poverty, low wages, insurance redlining, and predatory auto lending had left many residents without the means to evacuate the city in 2005.[80] Approximately one in five elderly residents of New Orleans was impoverished in 2004, nearly twice the national average.[81] As noted in the Annie E. Casey Foundation's *Kids Count Databook 2003*, the cost of being impoverished in New Orleans and Louisiana was uniquely dangerous: "The simple fact is that many low-income families, especially those living in high-poverty communities, end up paying too much for many of life's necessities: food, shelter, transportation, credit, and financial services. Not only are the prices they pay routinely more costly, but they are often downright predatory as well. . . . [Examples of these costs] include interest on prime-rate new car loans. . . . Drivers from inner-city neighborhoods often are charged higher rates despite state laws barring car insurance redlining."[82]

HUNGER

To rebuild New Orleans on a more equitable and socially just foundation, the Bourbon institutions of impoverishment constructed prior to Hurricane Katrina must be studied carefully. Such an analysis leads us to another trap economics institution that reemerged during this period: hunger. In the region and the state, the proportion of families and children facing hunger grew. More than 10 percent of the families in New Orleans and Louisiana received food stamps in 2003. In the city, approximately 40 percent of low-income children under age six received Women, Infants and Children program benefits. A 2002 survey found that federal and state antihunger efforts had erected a blockade around the city in the midst of a crisis. It found that New Orleans residents were more impoverished and received less assistance than the rest of Louisiana and the rest of the South. Despite the fact that 83 percent of school-age children received free or reduced-price lunches, over one-fifth of low-income families with children went hungry and over a quarter were food insecure.[83]

Early in 2005 Mathematica Policy Research organized a survey of hunger in the twenty-three parish regions serviced by the Second Harvest Food Bank of Greater New Orleans and Acadiana. The survey found that the network of agencies and organizations associated with the food bank served 248,000 different individuals annually and 62,000 individuals in a given week. Many of those receiving assistance were youth: 31 percent of household members were children under eighteen years old; 7 percent were children aged zero to five years; and 8 percent were elderly. Although 35 percent of the households had an employed adult member, 75 percent of households served had total incomes below the federal poverty level and 34 percent of the households were homeless. Additionally, Blacks made up 68 percent of the recipients, whites 22 percent, and Latinos 7 percent. The survey also found that 82 percent of the client households were food insecure and that 52 percent were experiencing hunger. Despite the national celebration of Louisiana cuisine, nearly two hundred thousand African Americans in the urban and rural areas of southeastern and southwestern Louisiana were experiencing significant levels of hunger before the arrival of Hurricane Katrina.

HOUSING AND HOMELESSNESS

This same study found that households receiving assistance reported having to make life-threatening choices between purchasing food and paying for other necessities: 44 percent had to choose between food and utilities or heating fuel; 35 percent chose between food and rent or mortgage payments; and 47 percent chose between food and medicine or medical care. Households relied on the food bank network despite the fact that 47 percent of the households received food stamps and 80 to 85 percent of the households with children participated in the federal school lunch and school breakfast programs. Faith-based organizations stepped in to meet gaping holes in the regional safety net: "74% of pantries, 87% of kitchens, and 66% of shelters are run by faith based agencies affiliated with churches, mosques, synagogues, and other religious organizations." Finally, between 2001 and 2005, "71% of pantries, 87% of kitchens, and 56% of shelters reported an increase in the number of people served." Despite the devastating impact of growing rates of hunger, particularly within African American communities, the Bourbon bloc continued to push for policies deeply embedded in both its own "starve the beast" tradition and in the related philosophic tradition of modern conservatism.[84]

Another Bourbon trap institution that took a new form during this period was the manufacture of residential enclosures and homelessness. According to an Urban Institute study completed prior to Hurricane Katrina, although families in New Orleans faced a severe affordability crisis, they were less likely to receive housing assistance than other citizens in Louisiana and the South:

> Nearly half of low income families with children paid rent without assistance compared with 35 percent in the southeast and 34% in Baton Rouge. Consequently families in New Orleans faced higher housing costs relative to their incomes before the storm hit. Rent or mortgage costs equaled or exceeded 40% of household income for over one-third of New Orleans' low income families in 2002, compared with 16% of similar families in the Southeast region. The survey showed almost 12% of low income families with children in New Orleans lived in overcrowded housing, and about 42% reported at least one major housing defect such as faulty plumbing or rodent infestation. About 27% of the families had fallen behind in their housing payments in the past year, and 16% had their heat, electricity or water cut off at some point.[85]

Despite a long history of criminal neglect and corruption and a severe housing affordability crisis, the Housing Authority of New Orleans plunged ahead with a public housing demolition campaign. Designed during the late 1990s, President Clinton's Hope VI program was used in New Orleans and throughout the country to sell public housing sites to private developers hoping to create middle-income and luxury housing. Although HANO promised that the demolition of the St. Thomas development was to be followed by construction of a mixed-income complex, the largest federal Hope VI project in the nation, former residents complained that the mixed-income formula systematically excluded them. Once the new River Garden development was completed in 2004, only seventy of its eight hundred units were reserved for former public housing residents. Approximately 1,300 units of the 1,440-unit Magnolia Public Housing Project in the Third Ward were demolished in 1998. Despite the growing housing affordability crisis, demolitions accelerated between 2003 and 2004. The hundred-building Desire development was demolished in 2003. The following year four of the six low-rise buildings in Melpomene Projects in Central City (Third Ward) were demolished. The thirteen-story, one-thousand-unit William J. Fischer housing development in Algiers (Fifteenth Ward) was demolished in the same year. The Lafitte Projects downtown in the Sixth Ward were scheduled for demolition in 2005. On the eve of Katrina, only fifty-one hundred public housing units remained in the city.

A Unity for the Homeless survey in 2004 estimated the greater New Orleans homeless population at 6,450 persons. They were found to be living in a variety of situations: 13 percent lived on the streets, 25 percent in emergency shelters, 39 percent in transitional housing or treatment facilities, and 16 percent in permanent supportive housing, while 5 percent had been evicted or discharged in the past week. Families represented 35 percent of the homeless population, unaccompanied men 42 percent, unaccompanied women 14 percent, and youth 7 percent. Approximately 76 percent of the population had some sort of disability or chronic illness: mental illness, substance abuse, HIV/AIDS, and physical or developmental disabilities. Additionally, 25 percent were veterans, 45 percent reported no income, and 67 percent lacked health insurance.[86] Uncounted were the tens of thousands living in overcrowded homes with families and friends.

The homeless and their advocates charged that the zero-tolerance campaign launched by the city in 2001 was an attempt by the Morial administration to criminalize homelessness. Many were arrested and given thirty-day jail sentences for obstructing the sidewalk and public drunkenness if they chose to reside, congregate, or work in corporate, redevelopment, or tourist areas (that is, the Central Business District, the Warehouse District, or the French Quarter). A complaint alleging civil rights violations was filed with the FBI in 2002.[87]

HEALTH CARE AND ENVIRONMENTAL JUSTICE

Another trap institution is the region's health care system, which daily reproduced health disparities. Child mortality was a major concern of the participants in a 2005 governor's summit, with findings echoing those of the 1992 Annie E. Casey Foundation study: "Louisiana ranked in the bottom 20% of states in the following health-related categories (2001 figures): percent of low birth weight babies: 10.4%, state rank 49th; infant mortality rate, 9.8 deaths per 1,000 live births, 48th; child death rate, 33 deaths per 100,000 children aged 1–14, 47th."[88] Louisiana reported 16,066 cumulative AIDS cases to the Centers for Disease Control (CDC) as of December 2004. With more than seventy-two hundred HIV/AIDS cases in 2004, the New Orleans metropolitan area ranked thirteenth in the nation, while the state ranked sixth. An estimated 7,194 persons with HIV/AIDS lived in the New Orleans metropolitan area in the same year.[89] According to the CDC, HIV/AIDS surveillance report, the "rate for African-Americans is over seven times higher than those among whites." In 2004, 76 percent of newly diagnosed HIV infections statewide were in African Americans. "Overall," the report states, "HIV/AIDS rates have declined in both white and African American men since 1994." However, the rates among "both white and African American women have remained stable."[90]

Closely related to health and well-being is another trap institution—the manufacturing of toxic communities. The zone alternatively known as the Chemical Corridor and as Cancer Alley was also the home of one of the most impoverished and heavily African American communities in the country. This heavily subsidized and protected eight-mile-long human-made disaster between Baton Rouge and New Orleans continued to produce the highest rates in the world of several forms of cancer. Across the river and immediately south of New Orleans, a thirty-three-acre site in the town of Harvey was used for decades by Exxon/Mobil Corp. as a dump for radioactive material. The company never informed the property owner of this use nor did it inform the impoverished African American communities that surrounded the site, even though a playground was located fifty feet from the dump. The residents were not tested for the brain and lung cancers that often take twenty years to manifest. The $1 billion in punitive damages awarded to the property owner in 2001 was reduced to $124 million by the Louisiana Fourth Circuit Court of Appeals before the ruling was vacated by the U.S. Supreme Court in 2007.[91]

Opened in 1956, the Desire public housing development was located on an isolated Ninth Ward peninsula that was surrounded by a shipping canal, railroad tracks, and an interstate highway. In addition to being near the Florida public housing development, Desire was built adjacent to the seventeen-foot-deep Agriculture Street Landfill. The pipes and the plumbing in the 1,832-unit complex's apartments began to crumble almost immediately due to soil subsidence. A former swamp, the Agriculture Street Landfill was used as an open dump beginning in 1910 and became the repository for much of the debris from Hurricane Betsy in 1965. Although it repeatedly caught on fire, in 1967 Mayor Schiro and HANO decided that the ninety-five-acre landfill was the perfect site for housing working-class African Americans.[92] After the initial 167-unit public housing development was constructed, between 1975 and 1981 sixty-nine single-family homes, townhomes, and senior housing units (Gordon Plaza Elderly Housing Apartments) as well as a community center were placed on the landfill. In 1994 the federal government added the landfill to the Superfund list, which marks the thirteen hundred most dangerous toxic waste sites in the nation, after surface and subsurface soils were found to contain metals, pesticides, and polycyclic aromatic hydrocarbons. An investigative report by Craig Flournoy noted the devastating consequences of this development path:

> A joint federal-state study in 1997 found that those who lived on or near the landfill had a 60 percent higher incidence of breast cancer than residents in a surrounding three-county area. Elodia Blanco knows this all too well. She and her husband bought a home on the landfill almost 20 years ago. In 1986 her daughter, then 12, developed breast cancer. She said her family has no history of breast cancer. Melika Thornton, now 26, survived. But Ms. Blanco said she is stuck with a worthless

home. . . . According to schoolteacher Pat James the "government has trapped us in a toxic ghetto." In 1996, Chris Hornig, a former public housing official with HUD, classified Desire as a "public housing sin."[93]

By 2000 Desire had just two hundred residents. In 2003 it was demolished and then partially rebuilt. Although racism was denied, Flournoy's research revealed a long history of racial targeting:

> [Desire residents] are virtually all black, as are the residents in the city's other 7,300 public housing apartments. A computer analysis by the *Dallas Morning News* found that three-quarters of the public housing in New Orleans is within a mile of one or more toxic dumps. A few hundred whites live in housing built or renovated under the federal Section 8 program. None is within a mile of a toxic dump, the analysis shows. Blacks constitute 62 percent of the city's population and whites 35 percent. Deborah Davis, the project's resident council president, has lived in Desire for 40 years. She said government sanctioned neglect—driven by race—turned Desire into a "sick community. There's no place more hopeless than Desire."[94]

After the designation of the area as a Superfund site, residents sought a buy-out and relocation. The U.S. Environmental Protection Agency refused and launched a $20 million cleanup in 1998. Arguing that the cleanup was insufficient, the Concerned Citizens of Agriculture Street Landfill filed a class-action lawsuit against the city of New Orleans for damages and relocation costs. By 2000 the school board had closed the new elementary school due to fear of toxic exposure. Suits were brought by dozens of former teachers, hundreds of students, and hundreds of residents against the city and the housing authority to compel them to pay for medical checkups, medical treatment, ruined property, and relocation costs. However, Mayor Morial was still advocating for a Hope VI rebuilding plan worth $125 million for a mix of eight hundred townhouses, apartments, and single-family homes on the Desire site. Resident Elodia Blanco referred to the proposal as a "complete disaster. It's a way of keeping black folks in toxic black neighborhoods. . . . I call it the new racism." Peggy Grandpre noted that the "government will drive African Americans into this area if it kills them."[95]

Life along the Bourbon Chemical Corridor came to define the meaning of environmental racism and trap economics for the nation. Terms such as *kill zones* and *toxic prisons* have also been used to describe this monumental disaster. Particularly targeted by oil and chemical plants were Black plantation communities and unincorporated Black towns along the Chemical Corridor and in the southwest part of the state. Clusters of plants were constructed around these communities as early as the 1930s and the practice continues into the present period. The residents of these Black towns and communities were denied participation in the siting process before 1965 due to their disenfranchisement. Even after the right to vote was restored the wishes of residents in the unincorporated towns were ignored by parish councils and the state. A 1993 report issued by the Louisiana Advisory Committee to the U.S. Commission on Civil Rights found that Black communities in the state were "disproportionately affected by the state government's system for issuing permits." According to Juanita Marie Holland, "These African Americans, whose ancestors suffered the horrors of slavery, now find themselves once again disenfranchised and oppressed—prey to the commercial interests of large, powerful industries who are willing to risk the health and futures of communities of color and other citizens whose political voices were not loud enough to be heard over the din of industrial greed."[96]

A 1998 tour of Cancer Alley towns was organized by the Black Church Environmental Justice Program. The program was a joint project of the National Council of Churches Eco-Justice Working Group and the ecumenical Black Church Liaison Committee, which was a joint initiative of the National Council of Churches and the U.S. Conference of the World Council of Churches. Tour participant Reverend Dr. Willie T. Snead Sr., president of the 2.5-million-member National Missionary Baptist Convention of America, concluded that "these people are in prison and there's poison loose."[97]

Another tour along the corridor was organized in 2001 for prominent political and cultural leaders such as writer Alice Walker, Congresswoman Maxine Waters, actor Mike Farrell, and poet and publisher Haki R. Madhubuti. The tour rolled past the towns of Reveilletown and Morrisonville, which had ceased to exist after prolonged exposure to toxics and prolonged community battles.

> "The people literally started dying out when the plant came around us," said Linda Turner. In 1987, the residents of Reveilletown sued Georgia Gulf, claiming serious health problems and property damage from the company's vinyl manufacturing. In a settlement sealed by the court, Georgia Gulf relocated the families and bulldozed every building in the town. Soon after, residents of nearby Morrisonville threatened action against Dow Chemical for creating similarly toxic conditions in their town. To avoid a potentially massive liability, Dow relocated residents to a new subdivision. Now nothing remains of Morrisonville but the cemetery where the town's people had been buried for more than 100 years. When residents moved into Morrisonville Acres, the new community built for them, many died of illnesses before they could enjoy their new homes.[98]

Holland provides the following description of the tour in the town of Ella:

> In Ella, Myrtle Grove [Iberville Parish], Norco and New Sarpy [St. Charles Parish], delegates stopped to listen to the imperiled and angry residents of these small country towns. They watched children on playgrounds framed by factory smoke, and listened to tales of toxic contamination, abandoned towns, cancer, respiratory illness and genetic defects. They heard condemnations of a corrupt government

that serves the chemical industry rather than the people. . . . At their first stop, less than two miles from the Georgia Gulf chemical plant, the town of Ella's water supply is contaminated by vinyl chloride and arsenic. Ella, also known as Ella Plantation, derives its name from the slaveholding plantation that once occupied the site. . . . Brooks described Ella's deterioration, how death and illness had cut their community by two-thirds, how toxic contamination made it almost impossible to keep animals or harvest a vegetable garden. "We're in an awful place here," she said, "and we're just like dogs waiting to be gassed."[99]

In the towns of Norco and New Sarpy, residents live only a few feet from the Shell Chemical, Orion, and Motiva chemical plants. Just one day before the tour arrived, lightning struck a nearby gas-storage tank, sparking a fire that burned all night. Residents of Cancer Alley have complained for years of the frequency of such dangerous events. Tour attendees gathered on the children's playground, just yards away from the immense chemical complex: a metal maze of girders, catwalks, and smokestacks that belched clouds of thick, dark smoke and flared with the burnoff of chemical wastes. They listened as residents spoke of their struggles negotiating with the chemical companies for funding to help them relocate. Local children stood holding signs reading "Give us a Safe Playground," "Too Many Explosions," "Shell Is Choking us," "Relocation NOW," and "Life, Not Early Death."[100] Tests found that the residents of the African American town of Mossville near the southwestern Louisiana city of Lake Charles had "dioxin levels in their blood three times the national average." At the southwestern end of the state, the cities and towns of Calcasieu Parish, some of them founded by freed slaves in the nineteenth century, sit next to more than fifty-three industrial factories, forty of which are clustered within a ten-mile radius of the factories. The communities these plants loom over, most of them made up of poor African American families, have complained for years of "the contamination of their land, water and air, and the attendant cancers and other life threatening illnesses that have been so prevalent since the chemical factories moved in. Their environment, with its intense concentration of vinyl chloride plants—the chief producers of dioxins—has earned the title 'Global Toxic Hotspot,' while the state of Louisiana as a whole has been labeled a 'polluter's paradise' by Greenpeace."[101]

EDUCATION

The education institution was also transformed during this period. Students, families, neighborhoods, and schools have been trapped by underfunding, chaos, and conflict since the 1960s. Under the Bourbon regime the entire public school system began to be enclosed and historic African American schools began to be extinguished. In 2005 New Orleans had 128 public schools, four thousand teachers, and sixty thousand students. The public school system had been in a deep state of crisis during the previous decade: ten superintendents in the previous ten years; 73.5 percent of the schools received academic warnings or were deemed academically unacceptable by the state in 2004; 35 percent of the schools did not meet the progress requirements of No Child Left Behind; and the Orleans parish school district had a deficit of at least $30 million. Also, three-quarters of eighth graders failed to score at the basic level on state English assessments. The system in many ways continued to reflect the integration crisis of the 1960s. Not only were the schools in the white-flight suburbs overwhelmingly white, in the city suburban districts and in the city, half of all school-age children were attending private or parochial schools. Despite the heroic efforts of many parents, teachers, and administrators, several educational advocates characterized the public school system as a warehousing program for working-class Black youth.[102] Other advocates and scholars have suggested that public schools were transformed from an alternative to crime into a pipeline into the prison-industrial complex.

As can be seen, life for New Orleans's Black working class had been in a state of crisis long before Katrina hit. Indeed, these patterns are emblematic of adjacent regions as well, including the Black Belt of Alabama and the Mississippi Delta. Together they have been a generative source for national social policy innovations for nearly two centuries. Louisiana Bourbonisms and the Delta plantation-bloc epistemology have been the breeding ground for national schisms on many occasions. The above discussion has examined the impact of the collapse of Longism and Fordist welfare in Louisiana on the daily lives of the African American working class. Typically, Louisiana and Mississippi have competed with each other to be the worst state in terms of health, education, and welfare. Consequently, to better comprehend the movement that created the social disaster between 1992 and 2005 and the Katrina social disaster it is necessary to briefly examine the mobilization and plan of the Mississippi Delta plantation bloc.

The Mississippi Delta Plan

Way down in Mississippi
Down in Mississippi where I come from
Down in Mississippi where I was born
Down in Mississippi where I come from
They had a huntin' season on the rabbit if you shoot him you went to jail
The season was always open on me
Nobody needed no bail!
Mavis Staples, "Down in Mississippi," 2007[103]

We begin with the story of Haley Barbour, who was born in 1947 to a prominent family of Mississippi Delta plantation-bloc lawyers based in Yazoo City. Upon entering politics, he quickly obtained several key political positions at a very young age as part of the Southern Strategy. These included serving as a member of Nixon's presidential campaign staff in 1968 and 1972; as executive director of the Mississippi Republican Party and of the Southern Association of Republican State Chairmen, 1973–76; as a candidate for the U.S. Senate, 1983; as director of President Reagan's White House Office of Political Affairs, 1983–87; as senior adviser to George H. W. Bush's presidential campaign, 1988; as Republican National Committee chairman, 1993–97; and as senior advisor to George W. Bush's presidential campaign, 2000. In 1991 Barbour cofounded the highly partisan K Street lobbying firm Barbour Griffith & Rogers, LLC, with allies from the Southern Strategy movement. Designated by *Fortune* as the nation's most powerful lobbying firm, its client list included cotton, tobacco, oil, and energy giants such as the Delta Pine & Land Company, Lorillard Tobacco Company, the Southern Company (Alabama Power, Georgia Power, Gulf Power, and Mississippi Power), Citigroup, Qatar, and the nascent republic of Kurdistan. Several environmentalists have claimed that Barbour personally engineered the demise of the Kyoto Protocol on global warming, the retreat from CO_2 regulations, and the elimination of Mississippi's antitobacco campaign, the most successful in the country.[104]

Barbour entered the 2003 race for governor of Mississippi having participated in numerous electoral campaigns won through the creation of racial schisms. The 2003 race served as a platform for launching a Mississippi Delta Plan imagined by the Delta Council in the late 1980s. As discussed in *Development Arrested*, this plan involved creating a new enclosure and new forms of dependency based on eliminating social services, housing and educational assistance, infrastructure funding, and labor rights. Partially delayed by the efforts of Bill Clinton and the Democrat Leadership Council to build a new electoral alliance in the region, the plan was fully supported by President George H. W. Bush in 2001. In the fall of 2003 Barbour attended a fundraiser for a segregated white academy organized by the modern version of the White Citizens' Councils, the Council of Conservative Citizens. When challenged, Barbour refused to demand that the group take his picture down from its website. Also, after a visit to a predominantly African American Head Start program in May, he stated, "Some of those kids in it would be better off sitting up on a piano bench at a whorehouse than where they are now."[105]

During and after his successful campaign against Democratic governor Ronnie Musgrove, Barbour used other racial codes to launch an offensive against Medicaid, a program that served 780,000 of the impoverished state's 2.1 million residents. He objected to the state paying for "health care for people who can work and take care of themselves and just choose not to." The majority Democrat legislature capitulated and approved cutting the benefits of sixty-five thousand of the most impoverished recipients: the elderly, the disabled, cancer patients, and the mentally ill enrolled in the Poverty Level Aged and Disabled program.

Previously those eligible for the program had to have an income of $12,600 or less per year. In 2004 Barbour attempted to eliminate all those whose income was above $6,800 annually. Protests and an injunction delayed implementation of this draconian legislation. His attention was then turned to eliminating an estimated fifty-five thousand children from the Medicaid rolls.[106]

Simultaneously, after years of steady declines, Black and white infant mortality rates in the state began to rise:

> To the shock of Mississippi officials, who in 2004 had seen the infant mortality rate—defined as deaths by the age of 1 year per thousand live births—fall to 9.7, the rate jumped sharply in 2005, to 11.4. The national average in 2003 . . . was 6.9. . . . Most striking . . . is the large racial disparity. . . . Infant deaths among blacks rose to 17 per thousand births in 2005 from 14.2 per thousand in 2004, while those among whites rose to 6.6 per thousand from 6.1. (The national average in 2003 was 5.7 for whites and 14.0 for blacks.) The overall jump in Mississippi meant that 65 more babies died in 2005 than in the previous year, for a total of 481.[107]

The increase in infant mortality was directly attributable to Barbour's polices. During the 2004 election campaign he promised to cut Medicaid:

> Face-to-face meetings were required for annual re-enrollment in Medicaid and CHIP, the children's health insurance program; locations and hours for enrollment changed, and documentation requirements became more stringent. As a result, the number of non-elderly people, mainly children, covered by the Medicaid and CHIP programs declined by 54,000 in the 2005 and 2006 fiscal years. According to the Mississippi Health Advocacy Program in Jackson, some eligible pregnant women were deterred by the new procedures from enrolling. One former Medicaid official, Maria Morris, who resigned last year as head of an office that informed the public about eligibility, said that under the Barbour administration, her program was severely curtailed. "The philosophy was to reduce the rolls and our activities were contrary to that policy," she said. . . . The state Health Department has cut back its system of clinics, in part because of budget shortfalls and a shortage of nurses. Some clinics that used to be open several days a week are now open once a week and some offer no prenatal care.[108]

The southern regional director of the Children's Defense Fund, Oleta Fitzgerald, observed that when "you see drops in the welfare rolls, when you see drops in Medicaid and children's insurance, you see a recipe for disaster. Somebody's not eating, somebody's not going to the doctor and unborn children suffer."[109] After years of being deemed one of the most deadly child protection services agencies in the country, Mississippi's Department of Human Services had, in Barbour's own words, "collapsed" under his administration. A study conducted by Children's Rights found that the state "deliberately (and unlawfully) diverts children from the child welfare system by failing to investigate reports of abuse and neglect." When confronted with this ongoing tragedy, Barbour decided to cut the agency's budget in 2004.[110] The chairman of the Mississippi House Public Health Committee, Steve Holland (D) of Plantersville argues that the state under Barbour was engaged in a full-scale assault on its own people: "These are truly our sickest, most vulnerable, most disabled citizens, who must rely on the state for help. This is the good of government right here. And yet, he wants to do away with it. So, starving the beast of government in this case is starving people's lives. And that's not right in any state in the nation."[111] It was this kind of planning that laid the groundwork for Katrina being such an utter disaster.

CHAPTER 8

The New Urban Crisis

Katrina Time and the Planned Abandonment Movement

Five damn days, five long days
And at the end of the fifth he walking in like "Hey!"
Chilling on his vacation sitting patiently
Them black folks gotta hope, gotta wait and see.
Niggas starving and they dying of thirst
I bet he had to go and check on them refineries first
Making a killing off the price of gas
He would have been up in Connecticut twice as fast
After all that we've been through nothing's changed
You can call Red Cross but the fact remains that . . .
I ain't saying he's a gold digger, but he ain't messing with no broke niggas (2x)
George Bush don't like black people (4x)
The Legendary K.O., a hip-hop group from Houston[1]

Numerous works provide excellent minute-by-minute chronologies of the disastrous progress of Hurricane Katrina, from the formation of the hurricane in the Atlantic Ocean to its Mississippi landfall on August 29, 2005. A massive outpouring from global media outlets still struggles to explain how after two decades of national triumphalism the sole global superpower could experience such a monumental structural collapse of federal institutions in the Gulf Coast. The Katrina crisis reverberated from the Lower Ninth Ward to the global arena. As many international observers looked on in disbelief, the Blues agenda once again congealed, this time under the thirty feet of water that covered parts of the Ninth Ward and other parts of New Orleans.

After the levees collapsed, there were several types of relief efforts occurring in New Orleans simultaneously. Most of the global witnesses to the tragedy observed the fragmented response of the federal government to the immediate needs of those who were abandoned in the city. Another, more coordinated and efficient rescue operation proceeded beyond the spotlights. The extremely well-coordinated effort to rescue the New Orleans Bourbon bloc by the federal and state governments is not completely understood. Analysts who investigate the federal government as an autonomous entity miss several key features of the American political structure. Federal policies are heavily influenced by class, sectoral politics, and race. Yet what is often overlooked in the present period is that the federalist structure is organized to accommodate the demands of alliances formed by regionally dominant blocs. In general, the federal government is a product of regional compacts. George W. Bush's regional alliance, which includes the Bourbon bloc of Louisiana and the Mississippi Delta plantation bloc, occupied positions of economic, political, and intellectual power far beyond what their population size would suggest. These blocs are the cornerstones of the modern Republican Southern Strategy, the intellectual hearth of the "starve the beast" epistemology, and paradigms for the future of national neoliberal urban and rural social policy. Additionally, in an extremely competitive national political environment, the composition of the congressional delegations from these states was decisive in determining which party would hold the Senate and the House.

These states had the first- and second-highest concentrations of African Americans in 2006: Mississippi with 37.1 percent and Louisiana with 31.7 percent. Historically as well as in the present period, both states have framed the national confrontation with racism. Simultaneously, both states are fountains of the Blues epistemology and the Blues development agenda. Consequently, it is little wonder that the first mission of the federal government after Katrina hit and the levees collapsed was to rescue the Bourbon bloc, its infrastructure, and its personnel. The second mission was to restore it to a functioning level. The third mission was to ensure that the Blues agenda did not take hold in the city, the region, and the state.

While the federal government coordinated much of the national polices to preserve the Bourbon bloc, it was also working at the behest of the regime. The local, state, and federal agenda for reconstruction was not hard to find, since so many key elements were torn from the pages of classic Bourbonism. This movement rapidly transformed one of America's great cities. The disaster was then held out as the model for the future of urban America. Tens of thousands of concerned global citizens came to rebuild New Orleans only to leave disgusted by Bourbon immorality.

□ □ □

Some students considered my first book, *Development Arrested*, as an obituary for forgotten African American communities and movements that expired at the hands of an ever-expanding plantation regime. By the 1990s, many students had witnessed collapsing urban Black communities firsthand. Many also accepted this historic collapse as inevitable and almost natural. They felt defenseless before political and economic forces that were enclosing their communities, and they imagined rural Black communities to be either more passive then they were or more heroic than they could become. Others believed that since class was the determinant of success, as future members of the middle class they had no inherent responsibility to improve conditions faced by the Black working class. Such a cynical reading ignores the most important arguments undergirding the work. First, hegemonic blocs face crises, both short-term and prolonged, more commonly than is typically understood. Second, the African American working-class traditions of resistance, affirmation, and development were also expanding. Both of these concepts run directly counter to the deeply eugenic narratives of urban revitalization and underclass deviancy used to support the four wings of the current urban enclosure movement, initiated in the 1970s: racially organized inner-city gentrification, racially organized suburbaniza-tion, the defunding of social welfare programs, and racially organized mass incarceration. Similar to the philosophy behind the "Road Home" program, the government's housing response to Hurricane Katrina, these narratives are rife with imagined landscapes designed to mask powerful institutions and traditions dedicated to the preservation of inequality. They also hide the foundations of a new society dedicated to social justice.

Older than the republic, the Blues development agenda has repeatedly broad-ened the meaning of American justice and democracy. After Hurricane Katrina's landfall, and after the levees failed, African American communities in Louisi-ana, Mississippi, and Alabama experienced assaults on all indigenous Blues in-stitutions. Black, Native American, Vietnamese, Latino, and white communities all suffered soul-shattering tragedies that can never be forgotten. The tragedies faced by African American communities were exponentially compounded by the disastrous social attacks and enclosures launched before, during, and after Hurricanes Katrina and Rita.

What I call the "post-Katrina New Orleans enclosure plan" has remained in a state of crisis from its inception. Yet despite widespread and historic failures, its corpse is repeatedly resurrected, costumed, masked, perfumed, and paraded once again before an adoring public. This carnival of death is led by an alli-ance between neoplantation, New South, petrochemical, and new urbanism blocs. These blocs seem oblivious to issues beyond the preservation of their economic, class, racial, and neighborhood monopolies. Members of this alli-ance were suddenly asked to rebuild a political economy they had spent the last three decades systematically cannibalizing. Unremarkably, they chose to enrich themselves while simultaneously launching a campaign to ensure the permanent displacement of African American communities, the further impov-erishment of working-class communities, and the undermining of the regional and national remnants of the New Deal, the Great Society, the War on Poverty, the civil rights movement, and the Second Reconstruction. Still, this enclosure movement and its unending series of plans have faced monumental challenges from the region's African American communities and their local, national, and international allies. What has been referred to as the "Third Battle for New Orleans" can also be conceptualized as the beginnings of the Third Reconstruction, a Blues Reconstruction.

Hurricane Katrina collapsed the Potemkin Village façade of Louisiana as a "New New South state." It revealed a region whose African American communities were always subject, in one form or another, to the plantation and neoplantation development tradition of preserving racial and class inequality, social militarization, and a disarticulated economy geared toward cheapening the value of labor. Despite the celebration of Black middle-class achievements, most working-class urban and rural communities have been systematically withered for two decades by the neo-Malthusian socio-spatial enclosure movement known as "starve the beast." Three years after the August 29, 2005, landfall of Katrina, federal, state, local, and African American institutions continue to fall like dominoes. In this endless swamp of man-made disasters is the lifeless carcass of the American welfare state: upended, abandoned, and unmourned. From this torrid sea of nightmares and funerals has emerged the shadows of a new social order.

The historic and epic struggle of African American communities in Louisiana, Mississippi, and Alabama to create a world based on social, economic, and cultural justice must be the cornerstone of the Third Reconstruction. The Blues social vision permeates the South, the United States, and the modern world. The fear of this vision fostered the creation of numerous institutions designed to perpetuate social, cultural, economic, and psychological violence. During his travels through the South in the 1830s, the French social theorist Alexis de Tocqueville discovered that the Gulf Coast region was the crucible of U.S. race relations and that the South was haunted by its future: "In the southern states there is silence; one does not speak of the future before strangers; one avoids discussing it with one's friends; each man, so to say, hides it from himself. There is something more frightening about the silence of the South than about the North's noisy fears."[2]

What is this future, this dawn, that is so resolutely feared? Although all the nations of the world heard the screams emanating from New Orleans, they were not heard by their own government. Its first response was to silence those voices and their Blues social vision in order to quickly establish a new, far more deadly, normalcy of daily life. Many of those efforts were exposed, resisted, and defeated by Louisianans and Mississippians who had nothing more than the clothes on their backs and an unquenchable thirst for justice. They were quickly denounced as looters, as violent, as irrational, and as insurgents. This perspective could be pitied if it were not for its wholesale adoption by politicians, law enforcement officers, the media, and religious leaders. Still, they pressed forward. Their heroic efforts were rewarded by wave after wave of new plans with the same objectives: the dissolution of local democratic institutions and the deepening of working-class impoverishment and African American displacement. Day after day, month after month, the effectively homeless refused to be silenced as they wrestled with the most powerful institutions in the world's most powerful country. While this epic struggle can never be fully told or comprehended, this discussion is an initial attempt to outline the parameters of the conflict between the Bourbon, New South, and Blues development traditions emerging from the deepening crisis in Louisiana after Katrina. The first section provides an overview of some key social and economic indicators that suggest the meaning of Katrina time. It is followed by an exploration of the New Orleans enclosure movement. Before Katrina, the neoplantation public policy known as "starve the beast" was used to reorganize the national political economy in a manner that guaranteed the failure of the levees, bringing institutional collapse and thousands of unnecessary deaths. The tragedy was then used as a pretext for launching a new movement designed to accelerate the dismemberment of the welfare state in the region and in the nation. These national movements find both their origins, and their most concrete post-Katrina expressions, in the Bourbon-bloc movement of New Orleans and that of the Mississippi Delta plantation bloc. Combined, these national and regional movements have created new institutions that daily reproduce mass destitution, displacement, disempowerment, racial inequality, and new disasters.

What Is Katrina Time?

That old muddy river's rollin'
right above my baby's
head. That old muddy
river's rollin' right
above my baby's head.
Yesterday, I kissed her
lips,
But now today my baby's
dead.
    Amin Sharif, "Big Easy Blues"[3]

You lay on the ground in excruciating pain
Cameras rolling
Revealing to the world yet again
The History
The Truth

that lies in the darkness of New Orleans streets
The forgotten story our ancestors wanted told
Another beating of our own
Another attempt to wake us up
Our ancestors restless journey from dust to dust.

Claire Carew, "It Ain't about Race"[4]

Let us begin by providing a brief overview of post-Katrina New Orleans. The uninsured property losses from Katrina were estimated to be in excess of $60 billion. Residential damage in New Orleans alone was $14 billion. According to U.S. Census and other estimates, by 2007 the population of New Orleans was nearly 60 percent of its pre-Katrina size.[5] Between 2005 and 2006 the Black percentage of the total population fell from 68 to 59 percent, while the white population rose from 27 percent in 2005 to 34 percent in 2007. Numerous barriers have prevented the return of impoverished residents heavily dependent upon spatially specific social and institutional networks. For example, at the end of the 2006–07 school year, public school enrollment for African Americans had declined from approximately sixty thousand during the 2004–05 school year to twenty-six thousand.[6] Displaced families with school-age children, families needing day care, the elderly, those in need of constant medical care, renters, public housing residents, the unemployed, and many homeowners in need of assistance have been unable to return. No system has been established to track the fate of displaced persons once they are no longer receiving direct assistance from the state or the federal government.[7]

THE MANUFACTURE OF UNEMPLOYMENT

Although the region experienced a construction boom, many employers and employees have not returned. The *Metropolitan Report* issued by the University of New Orleans's Division of Business and Economic Research suggests that the economic recovery in the metropolitan region began to stall as firms and professionals sought more desirable places to live and work. For example, Chevron moved five hundred jobs to St. Tammany Parish and Freeport-McMoRan Copper & Gold Inc. moved its headquarters to Phoenix. By July 2007 three major sectors of the economy still had a combined total of sixty thousand fewer jobs than in 2005: government, 75,300 jobs compared to 104,000 in 2005; health care, 45,800 of 61,700 jobs; and the low-wage, $9.6 billion tourism industry, 65,800 of 85,000 jobs.[8] Although there was growth in the construction sector, the rate of job growth may have peaked in 2007. "From November 2005 to June 2006, the area added 7,400 jobs a month, then slowed by December 2006 to 2,000 monthly. In June 2007, the gain was only 300."[9] The authors of the *Metropolitan Report* of July 2007 suggest the slowed recovery is due to the failure to focus on the immediate reestablishment of the social safety net, among other reasons: "Some of the causes for the slowdown in local growth in the second year are: a shortage of affordable housing has resulted in a labor shortage and substantially higher wages for low-skilled workers; high insurance costs; uncertainty about the safety of levees; slower than expected flow of insurance and Road Home money; and quality of life issues such as inadequate availability of medical care, and limited public school availability in Orleans Parish."[10]

There are generational repercussions to the enormous Katrina-related job displacement: loss of wages, benefits, seniority, and mobility; loss of dual incomes; increased travel time and costs; the destruction of support and information networks organized around neighborhoods, schools, workplaces, professions, and recreation; the elimination of entrepreneurial networks; and the elimination of multiple systems of information, exchange, and redistribution. There were also thousands of jobs in the informal sector. Untaxed cash and barter transactions permeated this extremely impoverished city and were central to the survival of tens of thousands of residents. The employment situation is particularly difficult for older and retired workers, many of whom were left without homes.[11]

Starve the Beast I: National Neoplantation Planning and Trap Economies

I don't want to abolish government. I simply want to reduce it to the size where I can drag it into the bathroom and drown it in the bathtub.
  Grover Norquist, Americans for Tax Reform[12]

How do we understand the specific and unequal ways in which dominant power blocs in New Orleans responded to Katrina? On the one hand, one could argue that it is just racism as usual. On the other, if we place this set of responses in a larger historical and political context it becomes apparent that something much larger is afoot. Specifically, I argue that Katrina embodies the convergence of neoplantation planning at the national, regional, and local levels—a project that has been many years in the making.

The U.S. welfare state drowned on August 29, 2005, in the toxic flood that washed away lives, homes, and neighborhoods in New Orleans, Louisiana, Mississippi, and Alabama. A tombstone placed at the Claiborne Avenue entrance to the Lower Ninth Ward marks its final resting place. It was starved and then drowned by the national neoplantation planning tradition and the restored Bourbon regional planning tradition. Before examining key hegemonic movements and institutions, pre- and post-Katrina, it is necessary to briefly note several of the development traditions that are shaping national public policy in the region.

Paul Krugman notes that two policy prescriptions emerged during the early days of the Reagan administration:

> One of those doctrines has become famous under the name "supply-side economics." It's the view that the government can cut taxes without severe cuts in public spending. The other doctrine is often referred to as "starving the beast," a phrase coined by David Stockman, Ronald Reagan's budget director. It's the view that taxes should be cut precisely in order to force severe cuts in public spending. Supply-side economics is the friendly, attractive face of the tax-cut movement. But starve-the-beast is where the power lies. . . . The other camp in the tax-cut crusade actually welcomes the revenue losses from tax cuts. Its most visible spokesman today is Grover Norquist, president of Americans for Tax Reform. . . . And the way to get it down to that size is to starve it of revenue. "The goal is reducing the size and scope of government by draining its lifeblood."[13]

Although this social philosophy has been characterized as devolution, privatization, and neoliberalism, its true origins lie in the 1870s and the effort to eviscerate Radical Reconstruction in favor of the restoration of destitution, dependency, and African Americans' bondage. The pillars of the neoplantation bloc's movement to overthrow the southern Reconstruction governments were the demonization of the pillars of the Blues tradition: African American communal life, human rights, public spending for comprehensive social services, racial justice, the sanctity of ethnic cultural communities, economic redistribution, cooperative sustainable development, and the philosophy of and movement to attain regional and global justice. A similar movement was launched to undermine the expansion of federal social policy during the New Deal. Its leading intellectuals, the Twelve Southerners, published an attack on industrialization in 1930, *I'll Take My Stand*. One of the twelve, Donald Davidson, attacked the New Deal directly in his 1938 work *Attack on Leviathan*. These works described the New Deal as a criminal activity that promoted centralization, industrialization, urbanism, Marxism, Freudianism, Easternism, futurism, Darwinism, and so on. This epistemology informed the plantation bloc's "states rights" movements launched against federal authority, the civil rights movement, and the War on Poverty during the 1940s, 1950s, and 1960s. According to Krugman, this attack on federal power, economic justice, and human rights was revived by elements within the Reagan administration and the Heritage Foundation, an influential think tank:

> the Heritage Foundation, ideological headquarters for the movement, has made it pretty clear. Edwin Feulner, the foundation's president, uses "New Deal" and "Great Society" as terms of abuse, implying that he and his organization want to do away with the institutions Franklin Roosevelt and Lyndon Johnson created. That means Social Security, Medicare, Medicaid—most of what gives citizens of the United States a safety net against economic misfortune. The starve-the-beast doctrine is

now firmly within the conservative mainstream. George W. Bush himself seemed to endorse the doctrine as the budget surplus evaporated: in August 2001 he called the disappearing surplus "incredibly positive news" because it would put Congress in a "fiscal straitjacket."[14]

Conflicts between the plantation-bloc, New South, and Blues development traditions have produced a chaotic social policy landscape in the South. Distinctive class, race, and gender regulations are found in regions of each state. These semiautonomous regions also exhibit different forms of social, environmental, and economic planning and development. Regional relations sometimes become combustible when attempts to preserve autonomy and hierarchies clash with the desire to secure national and global investments. Consequently, a crisis in one multicounty region can rapidly take on national and international proportions. For example, the modern "starve the beast" strategy was historically informed by the Delta crisis of the 1930s. The local plantation bloc successfully starved African Americans out of the region using New Deal subsidies.[15] This movement was supported by both major political parties until the civil rights movement and the Poor People's Campaign forced the restoration of civil and economic rights. Crafted during the Johnson, Nixon, and Reagan administrations, the current federal "starve the beast" movement is designed to reestablish numerous forms of domination by comprehensively transforming key institutions within the national and international political economy, that is, "devolution" at home and "neoliberalism" abroad.

There are several goals associated with the "starve the beast" philosophy. First, it solidifies an economic alliance between regional blocs and national elites by using tax cuts to redistribute wealth upward toward the rich. Second, fragmentation, privatization, and devolution enable dominant regional blocs within states to eliminate economic, political, racial, and human rights guarantees that served as barriers to their further monopolization of regional labor, land, capital, and other resources. Third, one of the principal goals of this alliance is to create dominant political coalitions opposed to guaranteeing affordable housing, subsistence, livable wages, full employment, quality education, and health care as economic and human rights. Consequently, embedded in this project is the defeat of sustainable development.[16]

A fourth goal, initially deployed to destabilize the First Reconstruction, is to undermine welfare state institutions and programs through tax cuts, program cuts, and deficit spending. Krugman notes that war is "almost always accompanied by tax increases. But not in 2003. 'Nothing is more important in the face of a war' declared Tom DeLay, the House majority leader, 'than cutting taxes.' And sure enough, taxes were cut, not just in a time of war but also in the face of record budget deficits." These policies created a perpetual crisis in federal, state, and local budgets.[17]

Fifth, this movement has deployed several strategies to undermine the working class and organized labor. Krugman notes that to "starve the beast, you must not only deny funds to the government; you must make voters hate the government. There's a danger that working-class families might see government as their friend: because their incomes are low, they don't pay much in taxes, while they benefit from public spending. So in starving the beast . . . you must raise taxes on working-class Americans in order, as *The [Wall Street] Journal* said, to get their 'blood boiling with tax rage.'"[18]

Sixth, core democratic rights and practices such as voting and the right to be free of government surveillance are devolved to the status of debates rather than guarantees.

Seventh, this project also demands the silencing of African American communities and the Blues tradition of sustainable development. As it was during the collapse of the First Reconstruction, African American demonization is a central organizing principle of the collapse of the Second Reconstruction. A representative of the oil and plantation-bloc alliance, George H. W. Bush relied heavily on strategist Lee Atwater during his successful 1988 campaign for the presidency. Atwater is widely credited with using the demonic icon of the Black rapist in a television commercial that swung many white voters to the Bush column.

During his term, the senior Bush vetoed the Civil Rights Act of 1990, nominated Clarence Thomas to the U.S. Supreme Court, and helped eliminate bussing aimed at achieving school desegregation.[19] As the governor of Texas from 1996 to 2000, George W. Bush gained notoriety for the assembly line–like regularity of the state's execution of Blacks, Latinos, women, the impoverished, the mentally ill, and the innocent. His victorious presidential campaign in 2000 was marked by a historically unprecedented electoral crisis centered around the disenfranchisement and intimidation of African American, Caribbean American, Jewish, and white Democratic voters in Florida. Once in office, he immediately supported several racial campaigns: to eliminate affirmative action, to eliminate Black and Latino congressional districts in Texas, and to eliminate progressive senior lawyers in the Civil Rights Division of the U.S. Department of Justice. National and international racial schisms also became more commonplace: the racial profiling of Arabs, the mass deportation of Mexicans, wholesale urban gentrification, the colonization of Haiti, the crises in Darfur and Palestine, and ethnic cleansing in Iraq.[20]

One year before Katrina struck, the relationship between the Bush administration and the Black community had reached a new low. In June 2004 NAACP chairman Julian Bond accused the administration and the Republican Party of deliberately appealing to the "dark underside of American culture. . . . They preach racial equality but practice racial division. . . . Their idea of equal rights is the American flag and Confederate swastika flying side-by-side." After Katrina, during the Congressional Black Caucus's Town Hall meeting on September 26, 2005, Congressman Charles Rangel of Harlem proclaimed President Bush "our Bull Connor," while Congressman Major Owens of Brooklyn argued that there was an important difference between the president and the violently brutal Alabama sheriff. "Bull Connor didn't even pretend that he cared about African-Americans. . . . You have to give it to George Bush for being even more diabolical. . . . With his faith-based initiatives, he made it appear that he cared about black Americans. Katrina has exposed that as a big lie. . . . This is worse than Bull Connor."[21]

Finally, another goal of the national neoplantation movement is planned crisis. Sustainable political economic alternatives are made to appear irrational, while the descent into peonage and chaos, to Bourbonism, is made to seem rational and even patriotic. Krugman concludes,

> In short, everything is going according to plan. For the looming fiscal crisis doesn't represent a defeat for the leaders of the tax-cut crusade or a miscalculation on their part. Some supporters of President Bush may have really believed that his tax cuts were consistent with his promises to protect Social Security and expand Medicare; some people may still believe that the wondrous supply-side effects of tax cuts will make the budget deficit disappear. But for starve-the-beast tax-cutters, the coming crunch is exactly what they had in mind. . . . The astonishing political success of the anti-tax crusade has, more or less deliberately, set the United States up for a fiscal crisis. . . . If Grover Norquist is right—and he has been right about a lot—the coming crisis will allow conservatives to move the nation a long way back toward the kind of limited government we had before Franklin Roosevelt. Lack of revenue, he says, will make it possible for conservative politicians—in the name of fiscal necessity—to dismantle immensely popular government programs that would otherwise have been untouchable.[22]

In a 2003 Democratic Leadership Council publication, Ed Kilgore argued that "the 'starve the beast' theory offers Republicans the political equivalent of a bottomless crack pipe. Tax cuts no longer have to be rationalized by any particular theory of economic growth, efficiency, consistency, or fairness. Politicians are free to defend or extend corporate or other narrow tax subsidies; free to target tax cuts to their favored constituencies; and entirely free from the constraints normally supplied by budgetary arithmetic." Once-untouchable iconic communities and infrastructure have already been "touched," hollowed, and fragmented. New Orleans and the Gulf Coast were still being victimized by the neoplantation and New South development traditions when the restoration of the national plantation development tradition began in earnest during the 1980s. As it has so many times in the past, the infrastructure ignored during this movement not only collapsed, it killed. Although sixteen hundred persons died in New Orleans, neoplantation planners were anticipating another eight thousand to twenty-three thousand victims.[23]

During Hurricane Katrina, key links within the vast network of levees collapsed under the weight of the fatal contradictions inherent within this development tradition. The historic channelization of the Mississippi River by the U.S. Army Corps of Engineers intensified pressure on the levees while accelerating the subsidence of adjacent land. In addition, while the corps built substantial levees to protect agricultural lands, it built inferior levees with fatal design flaws on poor soils to protect below-sea-level urban neighborhoods. The dredging during the construction of the vast network of oil pipelines fatally undermined the wetland storm buffer. This hurricane highway fed directly into another hurricane highway aimed at the heart of New Orleans via St. Bernard Parish. Used by only a few firms after it was opened in 1968, the MR-GO, as previously explained, operated as a funnel for the storm produced by Katrina. Despite the united pleas of political leaders and scholars, the Bush administration consistently refused to fund hurricane-protection projects in New Orleans. A 2005 request for $27 million for a Lake Pontchartrain project was met with a $3.9 million counteroffer. The historic Bourbon bloc planning and the national neoplantation straitjacket of tax cuts, budget cuts, deficit spending, and the Iraq abattoir have turned every hurricane season into a version of urban Russian roulette.[24]

A final example of the consequences of "starve the beast" planning is the Federal Emergency Management Agency (FEMA) evacuation plan for New Orleans. FEMA was established by an executive order signed by President Jimmy Carter soon after the core meltdown at the Three Mile Island nuclear power plant in 1979. The new agency centralized the activities of more than one hundred federal agencies and programs. Although it was elevated to a cabinet-level department during the Clinton administration, after 9/11 it was devolved into the Department of Homeland Security by the Bush administration. FEMA was soon hollowed out by intellectual and logistical gaps, fragmented lines of authority, the constant shifting of resources to antiterrorism initiatives, and an ever expanding array of privatization schemes that directed critical resources and responsibilities to an army of inefficient, politically connected, and unqualified consultants, contractors, lobbyists, and former officials.[25]

FEMA director Michael Brown identified the threat posed by a major hurricane striking New Orleans as a priority for the agency. In July 2004 FEMA spent $80 million for an eight-day planning scenario in which a Category 3 hurricane named Pam struck the city and left between twenty-five thousand and one hundred thousand persons dead. After this exercise, which involved three hundred federal, state, and local officials, the parish governments and the state prepared mandatory evacuation plans. Designed to reduce the number of potential casualties, the plans placed emphasis on a mass bus and automobile exodus. Yet the likelihood of thousands of deaths was still anticipated in New Orleans and accepted. The "Hurricane Pam scenario teams did not determine strategies for evacuating people ahead of time. Instead, officials predicted that only one-third of the city's residents would make it out in time and designed their response plan around that assumption."[26]

Despite planning for temporary housing and for reopening schools and firms after a disaster, the abandonment and death of tens of thousands among the elderly, the disabled, the sick, and impoverished African Americans was expected.[27] According to written testimony submitted to the U.S. Senate by Johnny B. Bradberry, secretary of the Louisiana Department of Transportation, the state had an evacuation plan in place by the beginning of the 2005 hurricane season. However, no part of this plan was designed to evacuate those groups identified above or others who lacked transportation. He received a request from the governor to plan for this population just seven weeks before Katrina, and still no immediate action was taken. "I should have charged my people with ensuring that officials on the local and/or federal levels were performing that function if we were not prepared to fully execute that duty."[28]

Claiming a lack of resources, the city said it could not evacuate 134,000 residents who were without transportation. In the face of a potentially massive death toll, Mayor Nagin offered the following: sixty-four buses and ten lift vans for evacuation; verbal support for a faith-based evacuation planning effort; and financial support for the production of hundreds of DVDs scheduled to be released in September 2005. The DVD project was partially coordinated by Reverend Marshall Truehill of Total Community Action. He noted that the "primary message is that each person is primarily responsible for themselves, for their own family and friends."[29] In the immediate aftermath of Katrina, FEMA officials still believed that the wholesale destruction of human life they had planned for had occurred. On September 9, 2005, CNN noted that FEMA "ordered 25,000 body bags for the New Orleans area. They were delivered to the Louisiana Department of Health and Hospitals, the agency charged with handling the remains."[30]

Although the car evacuation and the body bag delivery logistics were flawlessly planned, there was no plan to sustain the survivors. In 2006 former FEMA director Michael Brown testified before Congress that the agency was increasingly dysfunctional under the leadership of Secretary of Homeland Security Michael Chertoff. Resources had been shifted away from disaster and relief planning and toward antiterrorism projects:

CHAIRMAN REP. TOM DAVIS: "We had contracted, and then they just never came?"

MR. BROWN: "They just never came I know I've said Louisiana and New Orleans was dysfunctional, but you know what? We were dysfunctional, too, because the things that I was asking for wasn't occurring. And so the whole thing became this dysfunctional mess."

REP. WILLIAM JEFFERSON (NEW ORLEANS): ". . . Finally, Secretary Chertoff came here and he said, 'I think Katrina tested our planning and our planning fell short.'"

MR. BROWN: "I would ask, What planning?"[31]

True to neoplantation logic, African American victims were blamed for their own demise. In March 2007 former Georgia congressman and former Speaker of the House of Representatives Newt Gingrich delivered a speech before the Conservative Political Action Committee. In condemning the victims of planned abandonment, he called for an investigation of their failures. "How can you have the mess we have in New Orleans, and not have had deep investigations of the federal government, the state government, the city government, and the failure of citizenship in the Ninth Ward, where 22,000 people were so uneducated and so unprepared, they literally couldn't get out of the way of a hurricane?"[32]

In an era when planned abandonment and "starve the beast" policies dominate the regional landscape, many social scientists continue to deny the very existence of racially conscious planning. They ignore the role of regional variations of "massive resistance" in the social construction of white-flight suburbs, urban renewal, "benign neglect," and gentrification. The "inconvenient truths" of planned abandonment and urban triage have been surgically excised from the discourse surrounding new planning movements such as mixed-income development, new urbanism, and smart growth. Planners, developers, public officials, social scientists, and elements within the Black leadership prefer to discuss Black moral failings rather than the necessity of the Blues development agenda. The latter is considered either nonexistent, irrelevant, disposable, or dead. There is strong resistance to discussing racially organized social and policy movements in general, as well as the impact of these mobilizations on their own discourse, theories, professions, and fields in particular. This luxury is not sustainable. In addition to enabling neoplantation planning and its system of representation to enter in through the back door, they are contributing to the fragmentation and failure of local governance. Although treated as paradigmatic anomalies by these schools and institutions, the regional and global trajectory of racial, class, and gender mobilizations within distinctive regions must be understood as central to the Blues epistemology, just as the Blues development tradition is central to the construction of truly sustainable communities with leadership dedicated to cooperative development and social justice.

Some "progressives" have even argued that majority-Black working-class communities themselves are inherently dangerous to Black working-class people. The historic discourse on Black immorality was reintroduced after the War on Poverty. It demonized Black working-class communities while naturalizing "massive resistance" and related impoverishment. This morality discourse simultaneously denied the progressive role played by racial, ethnic, gender, and labor movements in creating a wide range of political, cultural, social, and economic guarantees. Far from being "particularistic," the African American working-class Blues tradition has informed transformative movements from one end of the earth to the other. To deny this tradition, its goals, and its organic leadership places African Americans, the nation, and the world in harm's way.

One of the critiques of the first edition of *Development Arrested* was that the book was not about planning. Critics argued that social movements, racial discourse, and human rights concerns are peripheral to the theory and practice of planning and development. By implicitly accepting and using hegemonic determinations of rationality and efficiency, this technocratic essentialism is used daily to condemn hundreds of communities to prolonged crisis. Once shed of concerns for community sacredness, human rights, democratic participation, and racial, class, and gender justice, social policy and planning devolves into a form of naked aggression. As I have argued throughout this study, the massive loss of life and abandonment for days in New Orleans at the time of Hurricane Katrina was the result of planning developed by officials in federal, state, and city governments. Unfortunately, this abandonment plan, this plan for a gross violation of basic human rights on the basis of race, age, and income, worked perfectly.

Some would argue that this form of neo-Malthusian planning and its acceptance of massive casualties is solely a product of class hierarchy and that race was inconsequential. Such an argument is not only ahistorical, it is dangerous. It fails to understand how centuries-old racial hierarchies are able to naturalize African American lives as inconsequential. It ignores the process regional institutions use to render African Americans invisible. Neoplantation planning also renders African Americans as threats to the body politic. Several centuries of racism placed African Americans on the most flood-prone lanes behind inferior levees and then abandoned them. While Bourbonism presents a unique dilemma for the body politic, African American communities throughout the nation discovered that the bell that tolled for the victims of Katrina was tolling for them. This is the argument put forward by former New Orleans mayor Ray Nagin, one of the most contradictory public officials of the new century. Despite this fact, his opinions based on his intimate knowledge of the events surrounding Katrina never cease to shock the region and the nation. In a March 15, 2007, speech before the National Newspaper Publishers Association, Mayor Nagin argued that New Orleans suffered a triple tragedy: the first human-made disaster was followed by a second human-made disaster. Furthermore, the second planned disaster is being used as a model to devastate historic Black communities throughout the nation:

> Because see they had dispersed all our people across 44 different states with one way tickets out. They thought they were talking about a different kind of New Orleans and they didn't realize folk were awake. And they were paying attention. And they weren't going to let a plan unfold that changed all the history of what we have fought for over many many years.... Because Ladies and gentlemen, what happened in New Orleans could happen anywhere. They are studying this model of natural disasters, dispersing the community and changing the electoral process in that community. You need to really understand what is going on.[33]

Massive Resistance Meets Starve the Beast: The Bush/Heritage Foundation Plan

Our third commitment is this: When communities are rebuilt, they must be even better and stronger than before the storm. Within the Gulf region are some of the most beautiful and historic places in America. As all of us saw on television, there's also some deep, persistent poverty in this region, as well. That poverty has roots in a history of racial discrimination, which cut off generations from the opportunity of America. We have a duty to confront this poverty with bold action. So let us restore all that we have cherished from yesterday, and let us rise above the legacy of inequality.

President George W. Bush, Jackson Square, New Orleans, September 15, 2005[34]

And I, to this day, believe that if that would have happened in Orange County, California, if that would have happened in South Beach, Miami, it would have been a different response. . . . Very little of those dollars have gotten to the local governments or to the people themselves. . . . We are being strangled, and they're using the money to set local policies to try to take control of the city to do things that they had in mind all along, and that's to shrink the footprint, get a bunch of developers in the city, and try to do things in a different way.

Mayor Ray Nagin, August 20, 2006[35]

By 2005 the starve the beast strategy had become the central organizing principle of the Bush administration's political and economic planning. Despite the strongest warnings possible from the most informed scientists and administrators, President Bush failed to lead preparations for the massive Category 5 hurricane barreling toward the Gulf Coast. By some accounts nearly one hundred thousand people were trapped in New Orleans: thirty thousand at the Superdome, an estimated ten thousand to twenty thousand at the Morial Convention Center, and more than eight thousand in the Orleans Parish jails. Another seventeen hundred perished under the most horrifying circumstances. Their cries for assistance were ignored by the Bush White House. The administration awoke from its five days of studied indifference after Mayor Ray Nagin and Hip Hop artist Kanye West used the national media to denounce its starvation policies. West suggested that Bush, the state, and elements with the media demonized Blacks as beasts in order to give "them permission to shoot us." In response, Bush delivered a speech at Jackson Square in New Orleans on September 15. Uncharacteristically, he acknowledged the debilitating effects of racism and promised what initially appeared to be a return to elements of the New Deal and the War on Poverty.

In reality his speech signaled the beginning of a mobilization designed to apply an accelerated version of the starve the beast paradigm. The plan implemented was based on the Heritage Foundation's idea of utopia. Prostrate, New Orleans and its diaspora would now become the victims of a third manmade disaster. To expect that during a disaster, when desperation is the norm, institutions created to defend and reproduce race-, class-, and place-based inequality would suddenly abandon their missions and proceed on the basis of social equality is both delusional and dangerous. Yet the lives of regimes are dependent on such legitimating narratives. Therefore, the Bush administration's first coordinated action in response to the growing crisis in New Orleans was to deny that racism played a role in the evacuation, the delivery of assistance, and the reconstruction projects. Simultaneously, the administration was engaged in several other racial projects: silencing independent Black voices; creating new institutions designed to intensify racial, economic, and gender inequality; and securing the enclosure of the city and the permanent expulsion of nearly 210,000 African Americans. Approximately forty thousand whites and nearly ten thousand Latinos and Asian Americans found themselves outside of the quickly fortified city. Yet their road home was not the dead-end experienced by many African Americans. The plans and institutions associated with the New Orleans blockade were crafted based on a fanatical hostility toward the assertion of the right of return demanded by more than eighty thousand, overwhelmingly African American, working-class households earning under $35,000 annually.[36]

As has happened so often in the last several decades, the failure of the federal state was used to justify further devolution, fragmentation, and the further concentration of wealth, resources, and responsibilities in the hands of the dominant regional blocs. The looting of Black, white, and Native American communities has been the principal sport of the New Orleans Bourbon and Mississippi Delta blocs for generations. After Katrina regional leaders were joined by a national network of predatory firms, institutions, consultants, experts, and politicians to loot New Orleans, the Gulf Coast, their welfare states, their social justice organizations, their unions, their civil rights, new federal disaster relief appropriations, and billions of dollars in charity sent from throughout the world. One of the centers of national neoplantation thought and policy provided the blueprint— Mississippi and Louisiana.[37]

Regional Planning: The "New South" versus the Neoplantation Bloc

My father predicted this would happen.
    Julia Wright, daughter of Richard Wright[38]

The hegemonic regimes of the Mississippi Delta and New Orleans have remained at the political, economic, and intellectual center of the global neoplantation complex. Cotton, oil, sugar, steel, auto, timber, banking, shipping, the legal sector, educational institutions, and real estate are all inextricably linked through a series of regional, national, and international movements and compacts. The reemergence of the Bourbon/neoplantation/neoliberal philosophy of governance was accompanied by the accelerated cannibalization of critical sections of the Fordist welfare state. Under the banner of neoliberalism and structural adjustment, the neoplantation development tradition has been globalized. Its features are the trademarks of Katrina: hollowed states, community abandonment, mass impoverishment, displacement, ethnic schisms, and the relentless upward redistribution of wealth. While many of the roots of the philosophy are deeply embedded in the soils and substratum of Louisiana and Mississippi, it has come to fruition, once again, under the auspices of the Bush administration. It favors the creation of privatized social-spatial zones maintained by high levels of state-organized destitution, dependency, and incarceration and low levels of continual communal violence.[39]

The New South development tradition contributed to the demise of the welfare state and the restoration of the Delta neoplantation and Louisiana Bourbon epistemologies. Its attempt to preserve a governing coalition in an increasingly conservative South led its leaders down the road backwards. After 1965 the New South bloc's attempt to preserve social and economic stability in the nonplantation regions of their states rested on several pillars: a compact supporting continued subsidies for the plantation bloc; a compact with the Black political leadership to support civil rights, minimal social programs, and Democratic candidates; and a compact between the New South Democrats, manufacturers, and a segment of working-class whites outside the plantation regions. By the 1980s the New South's economic, racial, and political agreement was increasingly destabilized by plant closures, the oil crisis, a regional Republican insurgency, and the institutionalization of Reaganism in the three federal branches.

Founded in 1985, the Democratic Leadership Council (DLC) emerged from the New New South development tradition. Although still organized around industrial and corporate recruitment and preserving racially uneven development patterns, the new iteration of this tradition sought national power at the height of a southern and national conservative mobilization. Referred to as the corporatist or Clinton wing of the party, the DLC national movement set a goal to maintain the support of a mobilized Black electorate while slowly abandoning the party's progressive agenda. To capture white southern, northern, and western moderates, conservatives, populists, and labor, it consciously chose to undermine several Fordist welfare state institutions that have been defined by racial supremacists as the hearths of African American "depravity": affirmative action, employment programs, public housing, Aid to Families with Dependent Children (a welfare program), and historic inner-city Black neighborhoods. Similarly, this leadership bloc supported the massive expansion of the prison-industrial complex. The DLC counted among its Louisiana members former U.S. senator John Breaux; U.S. senator Mary Landrieu; former governor Kathleen Blanco; Ray Nagin, the former mayor of New Orleans; and former state representative Karen Carter. In 2007 two of the fifty-three members of the DLC's New Democrat Coalition in the U.S. House of Representatives were from the region, Representative Charlie Melancon of Louisiana and Representative Arthur Davis of Alabama. The former is a plantation-bloc leader who previously served as the president and general manger of the American Sugar Cane League in Louisiana for eleven years. In the region, only Representative Bennie Thompson of Mississippi was part of the seventy-two-member, social justice–oriented Congressional Progressive Caucus.[40]

In the early 1990s the Delta neoplantation bloc began a planning process to reorder the region. It was interrupted by the New South bloc of the Delta states, headed by governors Clinton of Arkansas, Roemer of Louisiana, and Mabus of Mississippi. They helped to launch the Lower Mississippi Delta Development Commission (LMDDC) in order to create a consensus-building process and a ten-year plan that were designed to stabilize existing agreements while thwarting the neoplantation political and economic insurgency. The fear of potential disinvestment resulting from the growing David Duke movement also propelled this bloc to act. Although the LMDDC spawned several enterprise and empowerment zones under the Clinton administration, the regional agency received little funding. On the other hand, the conflict between the neoplantation bloc and the New South bloc intensified. In its first term, 1993–96, the Clinton administration was trapped in a net of continuous attacks. Launched in 1994, the "Contract with America" movement promised a Republican "Solid South," a "permanent" Republican majority in the U.S. House and Senate, and a massive shift of resources from impoverished families to corporations and to the wealthy.

The Lower Mississippi Delta Development Council

They want the oil / But they don't want the people (16x)
    Jayne Cortez, "U.S./Nigerian Relations," 2009[41]

The national expansion of the neoplantation development tradition also benefited from conservative Democratic supporters, including the Boll Weevil Democrats, who consistently supported the Reagan agenda. Their successors, the Blue Dog Democrats, were also formed in 1994. The Blue Dogs' name originated from a member who claimed that liberals had choked conservatives in the party until they turned blue. Others claim the caucus was named for the ubiquitous blue dog found in the paintings of Cajun artist George Rodrigue. Most of the forty-eight Blue Dog members in Congress in 2007 were from the South and California. Gulf Coast representatives included New Orleans–born U.S. representative Gene Taylor of Mississippi and U.S. representative Melancon.[42]

The conflict between the New South and the neoplantation bloc defined the crisis of Clinton's second term and the effort to impeach him. Furthermore, this conflict threw the nation into crisis during the contested defeat of Vice President Gore, a DLC leader, during the 2000 presidential elections. Although they combined moralistic attacks against their African American supporters with punitive social policies, New South leaders increasingly failed in their efforts to block the institutionalization of the neoplantation agenda. This happened in two ways. First, the institutionalization of massive resistance at the federal level reopened the federal vault of power and resources. Second, the neoplantation bloc remained committed to many of the same in-state subsidies supported by the New South bloc. A central part of the original New South bargain crafted during the Great Depression was that the plantation bloc's control over its regions would remain unchallenged. African Americans living in the plantation regions, the Black Belt, faced wave after wave of impoverishment and enclosure projects. By the late 1990s, New South leaders were attempting to perform the "tap dance of death." They were engaged in adopting elements of the massive resistance agenda while attempting to secure office based on Black votes. To maintain legitimacy, both blocs agreed to provide massive local, state, and federal subsidies to corporate agriculture, the plantation bloc, manufacturers, the forestry industry, large property owners, relocating firms, existing firms, and predominantly white regions, communities, and workers. Although several analysts believed that this tradition of unending giveaways, the "buffalo hunt," had reached a point of exhaustion in the 1980s (see *Development Arrested*), southern states spent billions of dollars to underwrite sports, entertainment, gambling, and tourism firms at the expense of impoverished communities in general and working-class African American communities in particular. Additional billions were devoted to securing and supporting the plant construction projects of Japanese and German auto and steel manufacturers. Encompassing rural Alabama, Arkansas, Florida, Georgia, Kentucky, Louisiana, Mississippi, North Carolina, South Carolina, Tennessee, and Virginia, the fifteen-year-old "Southern Auto Corridor" now bills itself as the "World's Fourth Largest Economy." These projects have repeatedly been embroiled in conflicts with African American communities for several reasons: the seizure of property and communities, environmental degradation, and employment discrimination.[43]

A related development tradition masked by Katrina scholarship is another point of unity between the neoplantation and New South blocs: the demands of the oil, gas, and chemical sectors. Mining and plantation regional regimes, as discussed in the previous chapter, exhibit pronounced similarities. Within the development literature, the "oil curse" has been described as being partially predicated on the disposability of human rights and human life. According to Samuel Schubert,

Studies undoubtedly show that oil dependence leads to a skewing of political forces. It concentrates production to geographic enclaves and concentrates power in the hands of a few elites. It becomes a fisherman's market for rent-seeking behavior, where those with money jockey for positions and influence to acquire lucrative contracts, the revenues from which are used to further bribe and manipulate those in power. Consequently, those in power secure their positions of their benefactors, creating a vicious circle of corruption and patronage, secured from open inspection of a free press, public accountability, or standards of international business and po-litical practice. . . . Leaders accustomed to oil wealth have no need for taxation. Thus they have no need for the population, or their property, political, or civil rights.[44]

As we have seen, Louisiana's "plantation curse" was compounded by its "oil curse." According to Frederic Billings, "Louisiana produces approximately one-quarter of the nation's bulk commodity chemicals and leads the United States in release of toxic chemicals into the environment. The seven parish industrial corridor has the highest density of petrochemical industries in the nation and possibly the world." Yet he goes on to argue that cancer rates in "Cancer Alley" are not elevated beyond normal national and state levels. Conveniently ignored by Bourbon science are the clusters of rare cancers wreaking havoc on Black and other communities. Major petrochemical plants have intentionally chosen to locate in these places because they are marginalized by historic and active patterns of racial discrimination and electoral disenfranchisement. Bourbon science is a mask linking neoplantation, New South, and neoliberal regimes throughout the world. They serve to mask the resilience of institutionalized social and environmental violence.[45]

Often ignored in the debate on environmental degradation and wetlands restoration is the decades-old practice of constructing oil pipelines through the coastal wetlands. This network links onshore pipelines, storage facilities, and refineries to oil platforms in the Gulf of Mexico. Subsequent erosion has created a hurricane highway leading directly to the doorstep of New Orleans. Not only did this complex receive federal assistance before the people trapped in the city did, it was offered new subsidies by state officials as well as by federal officials who also happened to be industry leaders, the president and vice president of the United States.[46]

Hegemonic blocs in Louisiana and Mississippi also benefited from the South-ern Strategy/Racial Republicanism movement that emerged in the 1960s as part of the backlash against the civil rights movement and the War on Poverty. The social disasters maintained in the Deltas of the Lower Mississippi Valley were global disasters from their inception. Nineteenth-century observers noted an indifference to humanity characteristic of a society simultaneously at war with nature, itself, and unseen global forces. Yet every generation of Americans has been forced to relearn this enduring lesson, to relearn the Blues. The loss of life and community that occurred in New Orleans and the Gulf Coast region did not have to occur. The vulnerability of New Orleans to hurricane-induced flooding was well known, documented, and anticipated. It was the product of a centuries-long war against nature and working-class and African American communities. The beneficiaries were a hegemonic bloc led by plantation agriculture, banking, shipping, petrochemicals, real estate, and tourism.[47]

The national institutionalization of Racial Republicanism with a neoplantation Southern base combined with deep philosophical divisions within the Democratic Party to ensure that comprehensive federal social policies would not follow Katrina. Instead of sustainable development policies premised on social justice, the region was subjected to a massive experimentation with the radical federal policies of fragmentation and devolution. The effort to intensify class hierarchies meant that working-class communities and labor were subjected to a third disaster. Years after Katrina, national and state politicians rarely mention the multiple tragedies visited upon New Orleans and Mississippi by human-made disasters. The state violence perpetrated by the resilient neo-Bourbon planning tradition of the region remains unassailed, in part due to regional, national, and international instability. Growing challenges to Racial Republicanism and neoliberalism have led to an intensification of conflicts at the federal and state levels of government. Similarly, the stability promised by the Clinton-led DLC and its pragmatist philosophy of triangulation is increasingly less appealing in a nation riven by Katrina, war, and deep economic, regional, international, immigration, and class conflicts. The collapse of the national DLC and the national New South development agenda resulted in some of its leading members forming alliances with the neoplantation bloc, that is, the George H. W. Bush–Bill Clinton fund and the John Breaux–Trent Lott lobbying firm. On the other hand, these collapsing structures unleashed a new era of southern, western, and midwestern populism on the left and the right, marked by the presidential contenders Barack Obama, John Edwards, Mike Huckabee, Ron Paul, and Tom Tancredo in the 2008 presidential elections. The search for a new interregional compact and a new national economic agreement—sociospatial fixes—in the midst of the Gulf Coast disaster promises to exponentially intensify the crisis of the region. On the other hand, out of necessity, more and more Americans have rededicated themselves to the construction of regional, national, and global governing bodies that guarantee social justice and community sustainability. For this national movement, Katrina has been the banner.

Local Recovery Planning

Post-Katrina, local and state entities were preoccupied with the restoration of key sectors: oil, tourism, gaming, and sports. This was compounded by an economic leadership increasingly focused on new tourism development and the tangible benefits of real estate appreciation and speculation. A conservative conclusion is that many aspects of regional life will remain in a state of chaos for years to come even if there is national economic stability. These economic problems were exacerbated by endless conflicts between the federal government, Louisiana, and the city of New Orleans over who would oversee disaster relief security and the distribution of governmental funds. Conflicts also occurred within and between charitable organizations, distressing families over the pace and direction of donations totaling several hundred million dollars. Traditional industrial recruitment shaped the Gulf Opportunity bonds being used to pursue steel and auto plants along with oil, tourism, professional sports, and luxury real estate projects.

The initial local recovery plans advocated permanent rebuilding moratoriums for predominantly low-income Black neighborhoods and public housing developments. The "shrunken footprint" plans advocated by the Heritage Foundation, the Urban Land Institute, and environmental organizations during the first eighteen months after the hurricane continue to fuel numerous racial, class, and neighborhood conflicts. With little input from the city council, the mayor created the Bring New Orleans Back Commission (BNOB) in January 2006. The BNOB's March 2006 recommendations sought to transform the Lower Ninth Ward and New Orleans East into parks, greenspaces, and wetlands while transforming the rest of the city into a large tourism, gaming, resort, retirement, entertainment, and recreational complex. This proposal to shrink the city's footprint was predicated on abandoning the predominantly African American neighborhoods of Gentilly, the Lower Ninth Ward, and New Orleans East. The attendant real estate speculation accelerated demolitions and drove dramatic rent increases in a severely truncated rental market. This policy sparked an intense conflict that continues into the present period. It also expanded the "right to return movement" that spans several states.

Established in October 2005, the Louisiana Recovery Authority used $4.6 billion in federal funds to create the largest housing recovery program in U.S. history in May 2006. Although the vast majority of funds were dedicated to providing grants to homeowners, the distribution of funds has been plagued by monumental delays. Also, the average grant is often too small to allow rebuilding. Incomplete levees and the doubling of homeowner insurance rates have prevented rebuilding and fueled widespread conflicts. Approximately $892 million was reserved to assist the production of 51,000 affordable rental units in the state and 1,870 housing units for those with special needs. Although 60 percent of the households displaced were renters, little direct assistance was offered to cover their property losses, moving costs, and new rental expenses. Funds eventually allocated for this purpose were not widely announced and did not meet the needs of renters without incomes or in low-wage jobs.[48]

Legislative bodies in neighboring parishes and the city have created various ordinances and policies designed to prevent the creation of FEMA trailer parks, the construction of rental housing, and renting to displaced African Americans. Simultaneously, the federal government has sought to demolish all of the existing public housing stock in New Orleans. After the failure of the BNOB Commission, the city council, along with various neighborhood associations, community organizations, universities, professional associations, and private sector groups launched their own planning initiatives. This movement fostered a community environment defined and redefined by personal tragedies, uneven neighborhood development, outrage, perpetual stress, depression, and countless protests. Additionally, it has served to pit renters against homeowners, those with savings against those without, neighborhoods against neighborhoods, and organizations within neighborhoods against each other. In this highly segregated city, it has also pitted Asian Americans, Blacks, Latinos, whites, and immigrant communities against one another.

Urban development models such as new urbanism, smart growth, and mixed-income developments do not address the question of how hundreds of thousands of low-income residents can return to the city. The lack of concern with this question raises other concerns about the undemocratic process of imposing a predetermined development agenda on a prostrate city whose residents are absent. During several planning iterations, the models presented were not the ones that residents were most concerned with. All of the previous planning projects were consolidated in June 2007 under the United New Orleans Plan. So far the city has been unsuccessful in seeking $1 billion in public and private financing. Another $1 billion is expected to be secured from existing FEMA commitments. The plan envisions a slow pace of development organized around targeted investments at several key nodes in each of the seventeen neighborhood districts. The Lower Ninth Ward and New Orleans East have not been designated as major investment areas. These planning processes often ignored the desire to reestablish neighborhoods and for social service integrity and human rights as the foundation for redevelopment. According to a women's services provider, "The least successful redevelopment activity has been the planning process. The lack of a plan and true community engagement. . . . The lack of acknowledgment that people are displaced. . . . The lack of acknowledgment that peoples' human rights have been violated."[49]

Children have also been left out of the development debate. Their needs have not been prioritized by policy makers. Indeed, some have expressed open hostility to their return:

The great sin is the disconnect of Black children from the city. That means that Katrina is not post, it is present because of the emotional weight it is having on children disconnected from the city. It cannot be measured and they are not on the agenda.... You don't hear no politician.... I mean you don't expect it from the president but you don't hear nobody saying anything about the emotional hardships of these children. This spiritual drain in terms of the absence of children is not only detrimental to their person but it [is] also destructive to the whole New Orleans culture.... When you have a disconnect of kids and it is not put on the agenda and they become trapped in a depression, so that's it's like a double deck. You lose their presence and also that potential.... There is a total indifference, a great sin, it has to do with institutional racism.[50]

The decision to fragment the educational system is also fueling numerous controversies. In October 2004 there were 66,372 students enrolled in New Orleans public schools, 90 percent of whom were African American. When schools reopened in January 2006 there were 6,242 students; 12,103 by May 2006; 26,165 by February 2007, and an estimated 30,000 students in September 2007. Most of the 128 schools were under the jurisdiction of the Orleans Public School Board (OPSB) prior to Katrina. By 2004 several public schools were beyond the board's direct control: two independent charter schools and one school that had been taken over by the state for poor performance and placed in its Recovery School District (RSD). After Katrina the state took over 112 of the public schools and placed them within the RSD before chartering some out to various organizations. With eighteen schools left, the OPSB also chartered out several of the schools that remained under its jurisdiction. By February 2007 control of the public schools was distributed as follows: OPSB, five; OPSB charters, thirteen; RSD, nineteen; RSD independent charters, eleven; RSD Algiers charters, six; and independent charters, two.[51]

New Orleans's public schools were transformed into a massive experiment based on the free-market ideologies underlying the charter school movement. This was accomplished by the U.S. Department of Education pledging $20 million to support charter schools while offering little in the way of new funds for traditional public schools. In October 2005 the governor issued an executive order allowing the state to create charter schools without previously required parent and teacher approval. Soon after, the legislature voted to place 87 percent of Orleans Parish under state control and voided the collective bargaining agreement. Without a budget, the OPSB fired its entire workforce of four thousand teachers and thirty-five hundred staff members in February 2006. The new charter schools are distinguished by special admissions criteria, enrollment caps, differential wages and hourly rates, outside funding, and other practices. In this fragmented system students are segregated by special needs, class, test scores, school resources, family, and race. The "left over" children have been blocked from entering the charter schools and the RSD system. Their schools are defined by market boundaries, a lack of resources, a heavy security presence, large class sizes, the absence of veteran teachers, and racial segregation. Veteran former teachers claim that the RSD is plagued by the exclusion of teachers in decision-making processes, high teacher turnover, poor working conditions, longer hours, a lack of collective bargaining rights, precarious job security, and a lack of respect.[52]

The transformation of public education has fueled a deep schism in the city. Declining test scores have contributed to this frustration. Several leaders I interviewed saw the fragmentation of the schools as part of the larger effort to disempower African Americans.[53] One youth service provider observed, "[I] think it is garbage. . . . It is about white folks raiding the cash register. Special educational needs are not being served. Then you insist [that] what is there is better tha[n] what was before. . . . This is not happening to white children. How can you fire 7,000 teachers? There is a massive takeover of anything of value. The failure of the schools is based on institutional racism. There is no community where white children are forced to endure what black children have to."[54]

The Nonprofit Model of Assistance

Before Katrina, few nonprofits existed in New Orleans and philanthropy was limited. Several of the existing foundations adhered to the southern model of philanthropy, with its emphasis on small grants and administration dominated by a small elite. After Katrina, the problems of this very hierarchical model were compounded by the entry of foundations with neither an understanding of local realities nor clearly articulated goals for how to empower communities in New Orleans's schismatic environment. In addition, many of the nonprofits, which raised tens of millions of dollars, have spent more on administrative costs, media, preserving elite institutions, and counseling than they have on meeting the basic needs of the impoverished and empowering local residents. A women's service provider suggests,

> One thing that has been unfortunate [is that] before Katrina you didn't have a lot of organizations or people employed by organizations, mostly nonprofits, to engage in organizing or activist-based work. And since Katrina you have a lot of organizations that have developed as [a] result of the storm. A lot of community-based organizations have been pressured to become nonprofits. A lot of nonprofits modified their mission to capitalize on dollars that are coming down or supposed to come down. Unfortunately, what I've experienced is that a lot of organizations that didn't exist before or some that did exist before, most of the people they are hiring are not people from this area. They say there is a lot of money, I don't know where it is. . . . One organization's whole staff wasn't here before Katrina. They feel there are no qualified people here and that not being from here qualifies you for funding. . . . Development is not coming from the people but from the institution. . . . The foun-

dation donors, some that have never done work in the South, are asking, "what are you doing in the South?" so they throw money at it but there are no results.[55]

The nonprofit model preserves and increases dependency among recipients, staff, and organizations without directly addressing fundamental and historic problems.

Residential Enclosures and Homelessness

Approximately sixty-five thousand, or 76 percent, of the city's owner-occupied homes suffered significant damage from the hurricane.[56] According to Policy-Link, much of the rental housing stock was significantly damaged or destroyed: 70 percent of low-cost rental housing (60,351 out of 86,520 units); 81 percent of public housing (4,144 out of 5,156 units); 80 percent of units rented using housing vouchers (7,166 out of 8,981 units); and 80 percent of Section 8 units (3,314 out of 4,122 units).[57] Although housing has occupied a central place in post-Katrina development debates, compensation for homeowners and real estate speculation have dominated much of the official policy discourse. Low-income residents, youth, the elderly, parents of schoolchildren, unions, renters, public housing residents, and those who lived in the most devastated neighborhood (the Lower Ninth Ward and New Orleans East) have had to stage thousands of local, state, national, and international protests to have their concerns heard. Those facing doubled and tripled rents or who are living three families to a single apartment have not been heard. Also often left out of policy debates is the dramatic rise in homelessness in the city and the simultaneous decline in the number of shelter beds available, which dropped from 1,100 before Katrina to 450 in 2006.[58] "One of the main challenges is low income housing," a youth cultural worker teaches us. "They changed the definition of affordable housing. . . . It used to be $300 to $400 in New Orleans. . . . Now the definition is $800 to $1,200. We need low income housing to get the people back . . . because the wages are still the same. The wages are still $6 or $6.25 but everything else went up—gas, food and housing."[59]

At the same time, Louisiana and Mississippi have become the epicenter of the subprime mortgage crisis: "About 21 percent of the state's 60,000 subprime mortgages were at least 30 days past due in last year's fourth quarter, up from 15 percent in 2004, the year before the storm. Only Mississippi and Michigan had higher delinquency rates for home loans to borrowers with weak credit or heavy debt, according to the Washington-based Mortgage Bankers Association."[60]

These housing problems are exacerbated by an infrastructure crisis that is plagued by conflict. For example, the future of the levees still remains in the hands of a federal government that has underfunded levee projects for decades.

Additionally, it is in the hands of the Army Corps of Engineers, which, as has been previously discussed, is blamed for the flooding because it constructed a storm-surge highway, the Mississippi River–Gulf Outlet, and then tried to keep it open after Katrina. Moreover, the failure of the Corps' severely defective levees contributed to the destruction of large parts of the city. According to one interviewee, the cost of the Corps' actions are incalculable and it is doubtful whether the public trust can be restored:

> The breeching levees caused the flooding which wiped out the city. The Corp should be sued for intentional murder because they withheld the information about the actual conditions of the levee which influenced how much insurance you got. [In turn,] insurance was saying [that] if you're in certain areas it's not going to flood, so you don't need insurance. . . . That has created untold financial havoc for people, everyone, Black, white, green, or polka dot. Without insurance you lose a lot of options with FEMA, with the Road Home money, or the No Road Home money, and it set up a whole precedent of policies that are actually discriminatory, not just to Blacks but to anybody who believed what the Corp said. They're liars. They lied about it. They continue to lie about it. They enacted legislation on the lie and all of that has caused all the havoc you have. Now your president does not want to come to our aid.[61]

Finally, the ACLU suggests that New Orleans's role as the center of Black and progressive politics in the state was undermined by complicated state voting requirements and efforts to limit access to the ballot by displaced residents: "In erecting barriers to voting, Louisiana officials have locked doors many believed were closed only temporarily by Hurricane Katrina. These barriers have resulted in the creation of a second class citizenry, scattered throughout the Gulf Coast and connected only by the tragedy that defines the post-Katrina experience. In addition, it has deepened the continued suffering of Louisiana's 'abandoned and abused,' who increasingly find themselves homeless and harassed in places like Texas and Mississippi. Indeed, many of Louisiana's displaced persons are not only *persona non grata* in their adopted communities, but also in these communities' political and criminal processes."[62]

The Manufacture of Racial Bondage

In *Broken Promises: Two Years after Katrina*, the American Civil Liberties Union reached the following conclusion:

> In the two years since Katrina, countless race-based attacks on the civil and human rights of people in Louisiana and Mississippi have tainted the recovery process. Although authorities have adopted few policies that explicitly discriminate against

people on the basis of race, the effects of many new policies have fallen disproportionately on people of color. While trying to rebuild their lives and regain a sense
of normalcy, African-Americans in the region have faced problems stemming from
police abuse, over-policing and racial profiling, housing discrimination, and voter
disenfranchisement. Latinos have also borne the brunt of excessive law enforcement techniques and racial profiling.[63]

Not only can the slowness of relief efforts be seen as a human rights violation,
but many abuses occurred in the midst of the crisis, including at the Crescent
City Connection bridge and the Danziger Bridge when African Americans were
prevented from entering Jefferson Parish. These cases, along with vigilantism
and abuses visited on Orleans Parish Prison inmates, continue to generate turmoil in the region's courts and communities. Presently, police checkpoints directed at African American mobility and a state "driving while undocumented"
law speak to the danger faced by residents who return. In St. Tammany Parish, young African American men wearing dreadlocks have been equated with
"trash" by the sheriff and routinely harassed. New Orleans ordinances have attempted to limit the construction of trailer parks and rental housing. In the case
of St. Bernard Parish, an ordinance limits the tenant population to those related
to parish homeowners, 93 percent of whom are white. "A recent report by the
Greater New Orleans Fair Housing Action Center revealed that nearly 60% of
the landlords they investigated discriminated against African-American testers
searching for rental housing in the Greater New Orleans area." Residents of the
trailer parks are being used by farmers and other local employers as the most
disposable forms of labor. Residents are also subjected to numerous restrictions
on their mobility and constant raids. "We had to get the Justice department
to investigate the trailer camps because the owners were threatening African
American males," reports one senior service provider. "[They said that] they
better not come out of the park."[64]

In 2002 the murder rate in New Orleans was nearly nine times the rate for the
United States as a whole, 53 persons per 100,000 compared to the U.S. rate of 6
per 100,000. When compared to national figures, New Orleans crime appears
significantly higher. Moreover, once the data underlying the aggregate statistics
is revealed, a different picture emerges. The murder rate in the city of New
Orleans exceeds that of its closest competitor by a factor of two and that of its
most distant competitor by a factor of five. The situation for the robbery rate is
somewhat better, but New Orleans still ranks second in the nation. Murder and
robbery tend to be associated with drug activities. In turn, the latter is closely
related to the lack of significant employment alternatives in the mainstream
economy. Viewed from this perspective, murder and robbery rates are key indicators of the extent of poverty in a community. Depending on which population
estimates are relied on, New Orleans either experienced a downturn in the rate

of homicides in 2006 or it has an exploding homicide rate, the highest in the nation, placing it among the most dangerous cities.[65] The crime panic that has gripped the city and state has not been matched by a similar concern for impoverishment and widespread human rights violations. Another cultural leader in New Orleans viewed the panic as a human rights issue:

> Young people see the violence on the news and the media, we also understand the conditions that were made to create the violence that we see. . . . These situations were made for us. . . . They only put [out] so many jobs. They put all of our people in this one confined area with no money. . . . You got a lot [of] people in the city living in abandoned houses. You gotta lot of people that got three or four families living with them. You got a lot of people living in cars. You got a lot of people homeless. You got a lot of people that don't have no income, no jobs, no health care. . . . So with all this and no aid being put . . . into the hands of the people that need it, two years after one of the biggest disasters in this country, some of those situations will breed themselves. . . . You have some beef. You have some drug stuff but you got basic needs not being met. . . . Some people don't have a lot of education so they resort to the ways they know how to get money and take care of their families.[66]

As poverty and hunger intensify due to the lack of employment and the high cost of living, individuals and the communities that support them face dangerous dilemmas without assistance from local government. It was in this context that a leader of grassroots social movement observed,

> Too many people skip a meal to make sure they got a roof over their head [or] to make sure they got lights. We just helped a lady. She get $500 a month, that's her income. . . . She got Section 8 so she's paying 30 percent for rent. . . . Now, she's got to pay lights, gas and water. We met her because she fell behind on her electricity bill. We raised money to help . . . but we know she will need help two or three months from now. . . . Somewhere down the line she will be caught in that same dilemma and it would be the same dilemma for many people since the hurricane and nobody is talking about helping.[67]

In terms of hunger, severe food shortages are being experienced in northeast, central, and northwest Louisiana due to the displacements caused by Hurricanes Rita and Katrina. Working families in New Orleans who have never before requested aid are now relying on free food distribution networks. A food and nutrition crisis is growing due to several factors: the rising cost of living, the lack of medicine and medical care for the elderly, and school breakfast and lunch programs serving inedible food. In June 2007 the state legislature provided $5 million to support the efforts of the Louisiana Food Bank Association in the face of a tripling of demand. According to Natalie Jayroe, president and CEO of the twenty-three-parish Second Harvest Food Bank of Greater New Orleans and Acadiana, the "food system of south Louisiana is severely compromised, recovering school systems are having trouble providing school lunches, Meals on Wheels programs are coming back slowly, community centers serving seniors have been destroyed, retail grocery stores have not returned to all neighborhoods, only a fraction of the hundreds of faith-based agencies serving the poor have reopened, and food stamp offices are closed."[68]

The Abandoned

Stuck in the hood like they poured cement on us.
Ghetto birds still shittin on us, government still quittin on us.
lost a few homies and the grief still sittin on us.
so we got the names writtin on us, white folks still spittin on us.
and them bitch ass police k-9's teeth still grittin on us.
    Lil Wayne, "Cry Out (Real Rap)," 2014.

President Bush failed to mention New Orleans in his January 23, 2007, State of the Union address. Similarly, in her May 2007 address opening the state legislature, Governor Blanco failed to mention the city or the region. At a June 14, 2007, rally at the capitol, regional leaders questioned her leadership, the Road Home program, and historic regional biases in the legislature. Mayor Nagin asked, "What's the difference between someone who lives in north Louisiana and someone who lives in south Louisiana?" Aaron Broussard, president of Jefferson Parish, also pleaded with the legislature: "If this Legislature from north of (Interstate 10) does not see the need south of I-10, then the Lord is going to tell them, 'When you did not help the least of your brethren south of I-10 you did not help me.'" Demographic shifts wrought by Katrina and Rita will more than likely lead to a fundamental political and regional power shift in the state and the city over the next decade. Southeast Louisianans feel they have been abandoned by the president and by Governor Blanco and her successor, Governor Bobby Jindal. The intersection between race and political affiliation could exacerbate regional, racial, and political tensions throughout the state. According to a public official,

> The first failure was that the leadership was in shock. Getting organized was agonizing. Then the turfdom, people held onto things with the last breath of their body. The leadership was disengaged and dysfunctional. The racism is alive and well. Part of the mayor's situation was that he's done very well. . . . [He is] part of the leadership. Then, when he realized what was happening with his people . . . Chocolate City, etc. . . . He went ballistic. He came to realize that they didn't want us back and that the governor was not going to get us any money at all. In fact she said as recent[ly] as June of this year [2007], "Actually I don't care if New Orleans ever gets

out of trailers. Maybe they ought to live in trailers." She said that to the audience from New Orleans who were there at the first opening of the legislative session. . . . Nobody challenged her. . . . Nobody. . . . Blacks and whites were aghast.[69]

The Louisiana Recovery Authority exhausted the $6.2 billion dedicated to residential rebuilding by June 2007. A *Times-Picayune* article described the confusion on the eve of the Road Home Program's July 31, 2007, deadline: "At the close of business Friday, 142,925 homeowners had applied for Road Home grants, with 121,037 having completed in-person consultations. Almost 85,000 grants, totaling $6.39 billion, had been calculated. That leaves about 58,000 applicants—a figure that does not include any new applications filed before the program's July 31 deadline—awaiting a benefit calculation. Of those who have received letters, 44,655 have returned the document and selected an award option; about 25,000 have closed. More than $1.4 billion actually has been disbursed. The impending shortfall ranges from $2.9 billion to $5 billion, according to various projections."[70]

By September 2007 the total number of applicants for the Road Home Program reached 184,000. Given the slowness of the process, low settlements, and rising insurance rates, many who received payments were not able to rebuild. According to Andy Kopplin, executive director of the Louisiana Recovery Authority, "Those who were able to rebuild were those who possessed resources [and] received funds. So far, the folks who have been most successful rebuilding are those who could borrow more money, who had large insurance settlements, or who had sufficient savings to get underway." Approximately thirty thousand applicants have been denied assistance and there are no funds to address the needs of another forty thousand applicants. Additional funds were sought from Congress and some were generated within the state by shifting $277 million from state building repairs and $300 million from the new Charity Hospital building fund. Despite channeling massive funds from health care institutions, infrastructure projects, and building repairs to homeowners, the state discovered in late September 2007 that another $1 billion was needed. In sum, the future of federal, state, and regional support for the rebuilding of southeastern Louisiana, for its impoverished and displaced residents, and for its African American community is tenuous.[71]

Seniors on fixed incomes have been scattered all over the country and no specific provisions have been made to assist their return or address the increased rents they face. The experiences of seniors living alone in trailer parks without families, friends, ministers, or doctors constitutes another hidden human disaster. In the words of another senior service provider,

Many of the elderly didn't have transportation. So they were stuck thirty or forty miles from nowhere. So they could not get to and from stores, they could not get medical treatment. Even the way they were set up they could not get their mail. So if FEMA were to send $2,000, there was no way they could get their $2,000. People

were coming out the woodwork to assess their needs, but there w[as] no money
to meet their needs. . . . Separated from support system friends, church members
and . . . families . . . they were scattered. . . . A lot of senior centers haven't opened
since the storm. . . . You had some people who were very active, very socially conscious. So they went to public meetings, they participated in the electoral process.
They went to church every Sunday. My seniors, eighty and ninety years [old] still
going camping with youth. . . . After the storm they became a lot more fragile and
we've lost many of our seniors.[72]

Another invisible and silenced population is the enormous effectively homeless population residing outside the city. The lack of federal documentation
on still-displaced residents can be read as part of a larger effort to deny these
residents a role in the future of the city. According to Donald Powell, federal
coordinator for Gulf Coast rebuilding, by April 2007 FEMA was still supporting
a large number of displaced residents in apartments and trailers. "About 17,000
are in Texas and about 13,000 in Houston alone. . . . And the majority . . . the
balance, are in Louisiana with some small amount in Mississippi and Alabama.
In the trailer population, there's about 85,000 that are located in trailers, and
the majority of those are in Louisiana; about 55,000 in Louisiana and 26,000
in Mississippi and then some scattered in other states."[73] An August 2007 article suggests that approximately eighty-two thousand trailers are still occupied:
forty-five thousand in Louisiana, twenty thousand in Mississippi, seventeen
thousand in Texas, and four hundred in Alabama.[74] A New Orleans community
leader who has spent the majority of his time working with the displaced offered
the following estimates in July 2007: "There are 175,000 in trailer parks, 30,000
in homeless shelters, 8,000 in New York (many of whom are in homeless shelters), and 65,000 in Houston living worst than they lived here."[75]

   According to a comprehensive sample survey conducted by the Texas Health
and Human Services Commission, in August 2006 251,000 Katrina evacuees
remained in Texas and 135,000 lived in homes receiving housing subsidies. African American households headed by women were particularly at risk: 80 percent of those surveyed were African American; 61 percent were adults; 60 percent were female; and 54 percent of the households had at least one child. Many
of the evacuees were trapped by poverty before the hurricane: 61 percent of the
households earned less than $20,000 per year. After the tragedy the evacuees
found themselves in an economic netherworld: 59 percent were unemployed;
41 percent had a monthly household income of less than $500; 54 percent of the
households received federal housing subsidies; 39 percent received food stamps;
and 32 percent received unemployment benefits. Approximately 39 percent of
the respondents reported their health status as poor and 40 percent reported
their mental health status as poor. Simultaneously, the share of evacuees without health insurance increased from 18 percent to 36 percent, while the share

of children uninsured rose from 8 percent to 30 percent. Half of the evacuees said they expected to be living in Texas a year after the survey, and 40 percent expected to remain in the state at least two years.[76]

The displaced persons in Louisiana's FEMA trailer parks were surveyed in the spring of 2007. Among the findings from the sample population: 29 percent of the respondents had owned their residence prior to the hurricane. "Nearly half the sample were either unable or unwilling to speculate as to how much longer they would stay at their current location." Although 55 percent were employed full-time before the storm, more than two-thirds were currently unemployed. On average three people lived in a trailer. Many reported the deterioration of their health since the evacuation. High levels of diabetes and depression were found throughout these camps.[77] One New Orleans community leader argued that private sector and governmental policies exacerbated the growth of the rural trailer parks:

> In October 2005 there was a moratorium on evictions and still people's shit was being thrown out on the street. We arranged with a judge to stop this. . . . We have people in St. Charles Parish and East Baton Rouge Parish in what I call "gulags." There is plenty of land on high ground in New Orleans that could have been used to build trailer parks to bring people home. The mayor and the governor could have used their emergency powers to put trailer parks in the city. They refused. Therefore, there is no affordable housing in the city.[78]

Challenging the neo-Bourbon/neoliberal path has proven exceedingly difficult. Short-term gains based on social cannibalism have proven seductive to movements across the political spectrum. Controlling asset stripping requires a comprehensive approach to policy reform that ensures the sustainability of working-class communities and social justice. Although resistance to this Blues agenda has taken many forms, so have the efforts to reshape society on equitable foundations. David Harvey and others have identified several of the alternatives to neoliberalism emanating from movements throughout the world: campaigns against racism and intolerance; wide-ranging democratic, economic, political, and cultural reforms; expanded labor rights; a new rhetoric of rights; electoral campaigns; campaigns for cultural dignity; gender equality; regional equity; campaigns for guaranteed standards of living, including health care, income supports, and full employment; "right to the city" efforts to preserve working-class access to enclosed spaces; promoting working-class leadership; environmental sustainability; crafting sustainable histories; truth and reconciliation commissions; mass demonstrations; a more interventionist federal state; social-spatial and political delinking; reclaiming the commons; seizing assets; and building new public rights and assets.[79]

The thousands upon thousands of social actions launched by New Orleans residents since Katrina are numerically surpassed only by the actions of the millions of citizens from around the world who have come to their aid. All have worked collectively to reunite families, restore communities, and replace private property. Despite these efforts, firms, sectors, and local, state, and federal officials have been engaged in a relentless campaign of asset stripping. Yet deeply at the core of the residents' campaign against asset stripping is the right they have given themselves, the right to return. Not only can this right not be stripped from them, but it is the foundation of the centuries-old campaign to build a new commons in New Orleans, Louisiana, the South, and the nation. Not all assets are visible and not all assets can be stripped. New Orleans is the birthplace of many tragedies. It is also home to many miracles, including the beginnings of the Third Reconstruction, a Blues Reconstruction.

CONCLUSION

The Cornerstone of a
Third Reconstruction

JORDAN T. CAMP AND LAURA PULIDO

> After the . . . landfall of Katrina, federal, state, local, and African American institutions
> continue to fall like dominoes. In this endless swamp of man-made disasters is the
> lifeless carcass of the American welfare state: upended, abandoned, and unmourned.
> From this torrid sea of nightmares and funerals has emerged the shadows of a
> new social order. The historic and epic struggle of African American communities in
> Louisiana, Mississippi, and Alabama to create a world based on social, economic,
> and cultural justice must be the cornerstone of the Third Reconstruction. The Blues
> social vision permeates the South, the United States, and the modern world.
>
> Clyde Woods, *Development Drowned and Reborn*, chapter 8

The post-Katrina enclosure movement, as Clyde Woods conceptualized it, represented a neoliberal political project of upward wealth distribution. According
to Woods, the displacement of Black working-class communities from inner cities, the deployment of policing and military strategies to support asset stripping,
and the political attack on institutional victories of the Second Reconstruction
were the essential elements of the Bourbon strategy of development. Yet, as he
anticipated, this project also provoked resistance and criticism by grassroots
social struggles engaged in the "Third Battle for New Orleans," or what he described as the cornerstone of a "Third Reconstruction."[1]

As we write this conclusion we are struck by how prescient Clyde was. So
much of what he described and anticipated has become reality. Indeed, in
Woods's hometown of Baltimore in April 2015 one could see how the Reconstruction agenda identified in *Development Drowned and Reborn* has once again
become a national and global imperative. The spontaneous uprising by Baltimore's Black working class in response to the police killing of Freddie Gray, a
twenty-five-year old African American, and the rise of the Black Lives Matter
movement underscores the stakes in his intervention.[2] Indeed, Woods witnessed
uprisings in Baltimore before, when he "saw major sections of my hometown . . .
burned to the ground" in the aftermath of Dr. Martin Luther King Jr.'s assassi-

nation in April 1968. In turn, he saw how the economic crisis of the 1970s led to "the demolition of the homes of ten thousand neighbors in order to build a one-mile freeway to nowhere." "For at least thirty years," Woods noted, "toxic fumes have spewed forth from factories located across the street from nearby residential blocks." These material conditions were only exacerbated by, in his words, "rampant police brutality, and mass imprisonment," as well as the "demolition of hundreds of units of public housing."[3]

Yet *Development Drowned and Reborn* demonstrates that scholars have largely been unable to listen to "the cries emanating from the soul of this nation." That is why this book seeks to directly engage with the voices of poor and working-class communities. It forcefully argues against the hegemonic racial narrative that purports "different racial/ethnic communities have no similar needs and desires." Woods spent his professional life illustrating that the study of social movements among working-class communities was the key to understanding the problems they faced due to structural and environmental racism, labor exploitation, gentrification, mass incarceration, police violence, and poverty. Black freedom and labor movements have, as Woods argues so forcefully in *Development Drowned and Reborn*, drawn on the "memory of the Blues agenda which gave birth to the First and the Second Reconstructions."[4]

Like W. E. B. Du Bois in *Black Reconstruction in America* (1935), he was determined to show how the overthrow of the Second Reconstruction led to the rise of a new imperial Bourbonism. This historical and geographical context is the key to understanding Woods's contention that U.S. elites have been "celebrating a freedom agenda that was only partially realized." "Yet," Woods observed, "through the eye of Katrina we see the old dry bones of both the Freedom Movement and the plantation oligarchy walking again in daylight."[5] Much of what Clyde anticipated has become reality. Of particular note are the connections between the changes in the political economy in the South, the United States, and the world. Clyde had argued for decades that the region's elite sought to export plantation politics. It was precisely the power of a "hegemonic bloc led by plantation agriculture, banking, shipping, petrochemicals, real estate and tourism" that led Clyde to refer to the South as "the tail wagging the dog." To be sure, the entire United States and the planet are subject to the immiseration, enclosures, and denial of fundamental human rights that he spent much of his life writing about.[6]

While Clyde did not wish to imply that the region was solely responsible for the neoliberal turn and growing economic and political inequality, he shows how its hegemonic blocs played a pivotal role in the formation of U.S. and global neoliberalism. This bloc's ideology, history, traditions, and leaders have long been influential in providing a particular vision for how capitalism should develop.[7] Since at least the 1960s this regional bloc has deemed the disproportionately Black surplus labor force a threat to their political power and class interests. In turn, they have pursued a political project to reduce social expenditures for public sector employment and services and to expand the Louisiana carceral state.[8]

It is important to keep these larger political currents in mind as we consider the geography of New Orleans today. Specifically, we must be attentive to two dynamics. First we need to grapple with the extent to which social budgets at the federal level have been eviscerated over the past three decades due to the application of neoliberal policies. While some agencies, such as Housing and Urban Development (HUD), have seen their budgets slashed, others, such as FEMA, have been deeply repurposed in the wake of the events of September 11, 2001, in New York City and Washington, D.C. Regardless of the reason, the end result of deliberate structural change was a feeble and incompetent federal response to the events of 2005 in New Orleans.[9] While this response added to the vast human suffering of Black poor and working-class residents, it also reinforced neoliberal nostrums that the state itself was the problem, which, in turn, purported to justify the elite's promotion of market solutions to social and economic problems. What such claims masked, however, was the extent to which the privatization of the public sector and the consolidation of the carceral state over the past four decades had produced a disaster in Black and working-class neighborhoods well before Katrina hit.

This brings us to the second important dynamic stemming from the Katrina crisis: the event essentially became an opportunity for the reproduction of neoliberal practices, new investment possibilities for finance capital, and a chance to "remake" impacted areas in the interests of the region's hegemonic blocs. While earlier we noted Clyde's critique of the concept of disaster capitalism because it underestimates the long history of racial capitalism in places like New Orleans, this does not mean that he implied that the concept does not have any relevance for understanding capital and the state's response to the crisis. Indeed, Katrina was a conduit for billions of dollars in funding to private contractors, half of which, according to a 2006 report, was awarded without full and open competition.[10] Besides such overt forms of crisis exploitation, private profits, and public poverty were produced in a host of other ways. Kate Driscoll Derickson, for example, has shown how federal aid targeted for housing recovery in Mississippi was redirected to economic development, especially the gaming industry. Likewise, Geoffrey Whitehall and Cedric Johnson have shown how the new forms of self-governance that arose in the wake of Katrina promoted neoliberal citizen-making.[11]

Several writers have identified the various narratives that have made such diversions possible. These include treating the impacted areas as "blank spaces," insisting that Katrina was an "opportunity," and expressing a deep commitment to purportedly colorblind narratives at both the federal and local levels. While some readers may consider such terms to be euphemistic, they are anything but. The flourishing of colorblind narratives has been key to legitimating the restructuring of the political economy at different geographical scales. While, as Eric Ishiwata has argued, the Katrina crisis was a major rupture to racial formation in the United States, as it made racial and class inequalities brutally visible, many have sought—despite evidence to the contrary—to reassert a colorblind narrative in which Katrina supposedly affected people regardless of race (or economic status).[12]

Lynnell Thomas has shown how, immediately after Katrina, a new form of tourism known as disaster tourism arose. In many cases, these tours focused on Black places as sites of disaster, highlighting the hardship that thousands of Black people had to and continue to endure. Over the last several years, however, this kind of tourism has waned and was replaced by New Orleans's traditional tourism in which Black culture is celebrated and commodified but Black people and communities remain firmly subordinated. "In various ways, tourists were prompted to replace uncomfortable associations of New Orleans with black poverty, residential segregation, or African American unrest with pre-Katrina tropes of racial harmony and tourist-sanctioned performances of blackness." Thomas goes on to say, "The retreat into the sanctity of the antebellum white city from the trauma of the abandoned black city signified a retreat from the difficulty of redressing racism into the security of a white mythical past." What is important to understand is how deliberate these changes were. While New Orleans's tourism industry is central to the region's economy, it is also a microcosm of a larger racial project intent on creating a "richer, whiter, and emptier" city.[13]

Elites viewed the Katrina events as an opportunity to displace and dispossess the Black poor and working class in order to build a different New Orleans. Not only was a whiter and sanitized city thought to benefit tourism, which had become the leading industry in the wake of the 1990s oil industry collapse, but the dispossession of tens of thousands of poor Black people offered a chance to make New Orleans more amenable to the elite. This can be seen, for example, in the election of the first white mayor in decades with Democrat Mitch Landrieu, the rise of conservative Indian American Republican Bobby Jindal to the governor's mansion in Louisiana, and the gutting and privatization of public goods that were essential to African American and working-class communities, such as education, housing, religious institutions, and healthcare.[14] The deliberate nature of the effort to keep Black and working people from returning can be seen in the degree to which homeowners were privileged over renters in recovery efforts.[15] According to one guide touring the St. Bernard housing project, "The man is on TV saying, 'Come home. Come back.' To what? They can't live if they have it all fenced off. HUD and HANO arrested the people when they came back. And they had their key, they have never been evicted . . . [but] when they came back they were arrested for trespassing on their property. . . .

HANO and HUD say, 'No, that area, you can't. That's trespassing because that project is due to come down.'"[16] The fact that mass criminalization has been the immediate response on the part of the state to the dispossessed is an extension of the "neoliberal racial and security regimes" that have been operating in New Orleans for decades.[17]

These various strategies ensured that thousands of poor people, especially from the Lower Ninth Ward, would never find their way back home. In the words of law professor and attorney Bill Quigley, the destruction of habitable public housing was "a government-sanctioned Diaspora of New Orleans's poorest African American citizens."[18] Elites benefited from a demographically and economically restructured New Orleans, especially those interested in gentrification and redevelopment. While New Orleans residents across the board were forced to leave, it has been Black people, especially poor and working Black people, who have been denied their right to return and reconstruct the city. In 2000 whites constituted 26.6 percent of New Orleans's total population. As of 2013 they made up 31 percent. In contrast, African Americans dropped from 67 percent to 59 percent of the total population during that same time period. There are approximately one hundred thousand fewer Black people in New Orleans now than before Katrina.

Clyde has shown that such socio-spatial restructurings, specifically the expulsion of Black poor and working people, is nothing new to New Orleans. For example, in referring to the Great Depression he writes, "the modern 'starve the beast' strategy was historically informed by the Delta crisis of the 1930s. The local plantation bloc successfully starved African Americans out of the region using New Deal subsidies" (chapter 8). He goes on to describe the cooperation between regional and national elites and to explain how such strategies were a fundamental part of a larger restructuring process. We see a similar response to the Katrina events. Not only did the neoliberal state, at the both the federal and local levels, play a decisive role in declaring Black residential space unsalvageable. In addition, hegemonic blocs have created housing policies intended to "shrink the footprint" of New Orleans, have experimented with social policies increasingly predicated on "public-private" partnerships, and in some cases have left reconstruction entirely to the private sector.[19]

While African American workers were excluded from construction work in the wake of Katrina, the New Orleans capitalist class exploited immigrant laborers in greater numbers. The New Orleans Latina/o population increased from 3.1 percent prior to Katrina to 5.5 percent after, while Asians grew from 2.3 to 3 percent. Many Latina/o immigrants, especially Hondurans and Mexicans, migrated as laborers to the construction industry of New Orleans. It is uncertain how the new demographic realities of New Orleans will evolve, but Clyde's work suggests the importance of multiracial and working-class alliances in forging a social justice agenda in the city.[20]

Racial inequality has grown considerably in the wake of Katrina, and the geography of poverty has changed. It is important to realize that while certain sectors of the economy grew after the hurricane, namely construction and engineering, overall the entire region has suffered economically. Economic contraction was compounded by the recession that began in 2008, as well as by British Petroleum's Deepwater Oil Horizon spill in 2010, which devastated the Gulf's ecology. The overall poverty rate for New Orleans was 29 percent in 2011, a figure that had not changed since 1999. What we see instead, however, is growing poverty in the suburbs. The suburbs are now home to 56 percent of the metropolitan region's poor people. There is a connection between the changing geography of poverty and demographics. One reason suburban poverty has increased is because of the absolute decline in central, Black neighborhoods.[21]

In 2011 median household income in the New Orleans metropolitan area was $44,004. This was an 8 percent drop from 1999, including a 5 percent drop for white households and a 9 percent drop for African Americans. As of 2011, Black household income was 50 percent less than white household income. Part of this is explained by the fact that only 53 percent of working-age Black men were formally employed. In contrast, 75 percent of white men were employed in the formal economy. For women, the comparable figures were 59 percent for Black women and 65 percent for white women. To give a better sense of the racialized nature of income inequality, consider that a full 44 percent of Black families fell into the lower income quintile (earning less than $20,432), while only 18 percent of white families fell into that category. In contrast, only 5 percent of Black families were in the highest quintile ($102,158), but a whopping 29 percent of white families were.

Constituent of these economic inequalities is the fact that New Orleans renters are now spending a larger portion of their income on housing than renters nationally. Fifty-four percent of renters spend more than 35 percent of their income on rent, versus 44 percent across the country. Not only has their income decreased, but the local rents have increased. Between 2004 and 2013 New Orleans average rent (including utilities) rose from $698 to $925, a 33 percent increase.[22] Ironically, or perhaps not, New Orleans is also rapidly becoming one of the fastest-growing commercial real estate markets in the United States, as it produces luxury housing, condominiums, and hotels. Indeed, between 2012 and 2013 commercial real estate transactions increased 41 percent, from $301 million to $424.7 million. The significance of these figures can be fully appreciated only by juxtaposing them with the fact that public services have been privatized, union contracts ended, and one hundred thousand Black and poor people denied the right to return.[23]

Such polarization can be seen most starkly in the New Orleans school system. The majority of New Orleans schools are now charter schools run by nonprofits and private contractors. This was partly accomplished by firing over seven thousand public schoolteachers and staff, breaking collective bargaining agreements, and divesting the Orleans Parish School District of its authority. In 2010 Education Secretary Arne Duncan stated that Hurricane Katrina was "the best thing that happened to the education system in New Orleans."[24] It is important to realize, however, that such efforts were afoot prior to Katrina—the storm simply facilitated and hastened this transformation, what Clyde would call the enclosure of the commons. A similar story could be told about public housing. As Clyde points out in chapter 7, on the eve of Katrina, there were only fifty-one hundred public housing units left in the city.

The final point we would like to underscore about Katrina is that there was little "natural" about it. Though it is true that hurricanes have historically been endemic to the region, this should not allow us to call it a "natural disaster." The severity of Katrina was greatly deepened by the destruction of the integrity of the wetlands by the oil and gas industry. For decades the development of wells, pipes and waterways, and concomitant activities eroded the wetlands that have historically served to protect New Orleans from the full brunt of hurricanes.[25] Second, many have argued that the severity of Katrina was at least partially due to global climate change, as larger and more intense storms are one consequence of rising temperatures. Third, as Clyde has shown, engineering projects, practices, and professionals must be held accountable. Not only were many of the levees in very poor shape—problems that some engineers warned about—but other projects, such as MR-GO, were designed to ensure that more white and affluent sections of the city would be spared the worst impact of flooding, while the poor and Black would bear the heaviest cost. Finally, as Clyde goes to great lengths to demonstrate, this situation was centuries in the making. It was hardly a specific set of planning and zoning decisions that led to the residential segregation of New Orleans but a centuries-long process of white supremacy and devaluing of human life that would enable New Orleans, Louisiana, and the United States to make such decisions and consider them to be acceptable. In this way, Katrina must be seen as the logical result of such an inhumane social formation.

While it is correct that disasters have become profound opportunities to restructure the economy and the state in favor of the wealthy and powerful, Clyde Woods shows that this is nothing new for New Orleans, Louisiana, or the United States. Katrina is but the latest in a long line of disasters in which Black lives are treated as disposable. Given the reality of climate change and the ascendency of neoliberalism, we would all do well to study New Orleans and Katrina. Such an inhumane social formation will be our collective future unless we begin acting decisively to, as Clyde Woods so powerfully put it, ensure that the Reconstruction agenda is finally fulfilled.

NOTES

Introduction. The Dialectics of Bourbonism and the Blues

1. For appreciations of his work by his colleagues, see "'The Sun Never Set upon the Blues': Seven Essays Honoring Clyde Woods," Antipode Foundation, December 2012, http://antipodefoundation.org/2012/12/03/the-sun-never-set-upon-the-blues-seven-essays-honouring-clyde-woods/. See also Ingrid Banks, Gaye Theresa Johnson, George Lipsitz, Ula Taylor, Daniel Widener, and Clyde Woods, eds., *Black California Dreamin': The Crises of California's African-American Communities* (Santa Barbara: University of California, Santa Barbara, Center for Black Studies Research, 2012).

2. Clyde Woods, "'Sittin' on Top of the World': The Challenges of Blues and Hip Hop Geography," in *Black Geographies and the Politics of Place*, ed. Katherine McKittrick and Clyde Woods (Cambridge, Mass.: South End Press, 2007), 49.

3. Clyde Woods, ed., *In the Wake of Hurricane Katrina: New Paradigms and Social Visions* (Baltimore: Johns Hopkins University Press, 2010).

4. Michael Watts was the first to show that famines are not "natural," an observation that then spread into hazard studies more generally. See Watts, *Silent Violence: Food, Famine and Peasantry in Northern Nigeria* (Berkeley: University of California Press, 1983). This research ultimately led to a greater focus on vulnerability and resilience, as can be seen in Christina Finch, Christopher Emrich, and Susan Cutter, "Disaster Disparities and Differential Recovery in New Orleans," *Population and Environment* 31, no. 4 (2010): 179–202. For an excellent analysis of the ideological and political work that cloaking a disaster as "natural" does, see David Nally, *Human Encumbrances: Political Violence and the Great Irish Famine* (Notre Dame, Ind.: University of Notre Dame Press, 2011).

5. See also Barbara Lee, "A Katrina Retrospective: Structural Inequality, Environmental Justice and Our National Discourse on Race," *Huffington Post*, September 9, 2010, http://www.huffingtonpost.com/rep-barbara-lee/a-katrina-retrospective-s_b_702911.html; Robert Bullard and Beverly Wright, *Race, Place and Environmental Justice after Hurricane Katrina* (Boulder, Colo.: Westview Press, 2009).

6. Woods, "Sittin' on Top of the World," 8.

7. Clyde Woods, interview by Jordan T. Camp and Elizabeth Robinson, *No Alibis*, KCSB 91.9 FM, Santa Barbara, California, September 1, 2010. We find it symptomatic of his humility and curiosity that Clyde did not think he knew enough about the Mississippi Delta region after studying it for so many years. This speaks to both his passion for the region and his research, as well as the encyclopedic nature of his mind: he would not rest until he knew everything about a topic—which means that he did not rest much.

8. Naomi Klein, *The Shock Doctrine: The Rise of Disaster Capitalism* (New York: Picador, 2008).

9. Woods, interview.

10. Clyde Woods, *Development Arrested: The Blues and Plantation Power in the Mississippi Delta* (New York: Verso, 1998), 26.

11. Clyde Woods, "Les Misérables of New Orleans: Trap Economics and the Asset Stripping Blues, Part 1," *American Quarterly* 61, no. 3 (2009): 770, 789.

12. In this way, *Development Drowned and Reborn* can be productively read alongside the new scholarship on the history of slavery, capitalism, and imperialism. For example, Walter Johnson notes that New Orleans was "the principal channel through which Southern cotton flowed to the global economy and foreign capital came into the United States, the largest slave market in North America, and the central artery of the continent's white overseers' flirtation with the perverse attractions of global racial domination." He demonstrates how "pro-slavery globalism increasingly took the form of imperialist military action" and sought to expand on a global scale. See Walter Johnson, *River of Dark Dreams: Slavery and Empire in the Cotton Kingdom* (Cambridge, Mass.: Harvard University Press, 2013), 2, 14.

13. Daniel Fischlin, Ajay Heble, and George Lipsitz, *The Fierce Urgency of Now: Improvisation, Rights, and the Ethics of Co-creation* (Durham, N.C.: Duke University Press, 2013), 144, 160. On the ways in which the dialectics of race, class, and region exert influence on the shape of national and global political and economic developments, see, for example, Tomás Almaguer, *Racial Faultlines: The Historical Origins of White Supremacy in California* (Berkeley: University of California Press, 2008); Richard Walker, "California Rages against the Dying of the Light," *New Left Review*, no. 209 (1995): 52; Ruth Wilson Gilmore, *Golden Gulag: Prisons, Surplus, Crisis, and Opposition in Globalizing California* (Berkeley: University of California Press, 2007); David Harvey, *Rebel Cities: From the Right to the City to the Urban Revolution* (New York: Verso, 2012).

14. Woods, "Les Misérables of New Orleans," 776. On the race and class dynamics of incarceration in New Orleans and Louisiana, see Jordan T. Camp, *Incarcerating the Crisis: Freedom Struggles and the Rise of the Neoliberal State* (Oakland: University of California Press, 2016), 116–33.

15. Woods, "Les Misérables of New Orleans," 776.

16. Woods, *Development Arrested*, 289.

17. See Mary Helen Washington, *The Other Blacklist: The African American Literary and Cultural Left of the 1950s* (New York: Columbia University Press, 2014), 11, 13–14; Cedric J. Robinson, *Black Marxism: The Making of the Black Radical Tradition* (1983; repr., Chapel Hill: University of North Carolina Press, 2000), 292–93; Robin D. G. Kelley, *Hammer and Hoe: Alabama Communists during the Great Depression* (Chapel Hill: University of North Carolina Press, 1990), 23, 31, 42, 44.

18. See also Tiya Miles, *Ties That Bind: The Story of an Afro-Cherokee Family in Slavery and Freedom* (Berkeley: University of California Press, 2005).

19. Laura has countless memories of Clyde making connections between ethnic Mexicans and African Americans.

20. Woods, *Development Arrested*, 31.

21. Clyde Woods, "Katrina's World: Blues, Bourbon, and the Return to the Source," *American Quarterly* 61, no. 3 (September 2009): 429.

22. Clyde Woods, "Traps, Skid Row, and Katrina," in *Downtown Blues: A Skid Row Reader*, ed. Christina Heatherton (Los Angeles: Freedom Now Books, 2011), 51.

23. Clyde Woods, "Life after Death," *Professional Geographer* 54, no. 1 (2002): 66.

24. Jeffrey S. Lowe, Todd C. Shaw, and Clyde A. Woods, "Developing a Reconstruction Plan for the Gulf Coast Region" (paper commissioned for the Measure of America, American Human Development Report, 2008–2009).

25. Woods, "Life after Death," 66.

Chapter 1. I Thought I Heard Samba Bambara Say

1. H. F. "Pete" Gregory, "Louisiana's Native Americans: An Overview," Louisiana's Living Traditions, Louisiana Folklife Program, http://www.louisianafolklife.org/LT/Articles_Essays/creole_art_native_overview.html; Robert W. Neuman and Nancy W. Hawkins, *Louisiana Prehistory*, 2nd ed. (Baton Rouge: Louisiana Department of Culture, Recreation and Tourism, 1993), http://www.crt.state.la.us/dataprojects/archaeology/virtualbooks/LAPREHIS/lapre.htm; Heather Pringle, "Oldest Mound Complex Found at Louisiana Site," *Science* 277, no. 5333 (September 1997): 1761–62; Clarence H. Webb, "The Extent and Content of Poverty Point Culture," *American Antiquity* 33, no. 3 (July 1968): 297–321; Clarence H. Webb, *The Poverty Point Culture*, Geoscience and Man 17 (Baton Rouge: Louisiana State University School of Geoscience, 1982).

2. Vernon James Knight Jr., "The Institutional Organization of Mississippian Religion," *American Antiquity* 51, no. 4 (October 1986): 675–87; "Cahokia Mounds State Historic Site," World Heritage List, International Council on Monuments and Sites World Heritage Centre, United Nations Educational, Scientific, and Cultural Organization, http://whc.unesco.org/en/list/198.

3. Neuman and Hawkins, *Louisiana Prehistory*; Nathan Seppa, "Ancient Cahokia: Metropolitan Life on the Mississippi," *Washington Post*, March 12, 1997; Karl G. Lorenz, "The Natchez of Southwest Mississippi," in *Indians of the Greater Southeast: Historical Archaeology and Ethnohistory*, ed. Bonnie G. McEwan (Gainesville: University Press of Florida, 2000), 142–77.

4. Jerah Johnson, "Colonial New Orleans: A Fragment of the Eighteenth Century," in *Creole New Orleans: Race and Americanization*, ed. Arnold Hirsch and Joseph Logsdon (Baton Rouge: Louisiana State University Press, 1992), 18.

5. Ibid., 16.

6. Ibid., 20.

7. Ibid., 19; Caryn Cossé Bell, "Haitian Immigration to Louisiana in the Eighteenth and Nineteenth Centuries," 2005, Caribbean Migrations, Haitian Immigration: Eighteenth and Nineteenth Centuries, *In Motion: The African American Migration Experience*, Schomburg Center for Research in Black Culture, New York Public Library, http://www.inmotionaame.org/texts/?migration=5&topic=99&type=text.

8. J. Johnson, "Colonial New Orleans," 35; Gwendolyn Midlo Hall, "The Formation of Afro-Creole Culture," in Hirsch and Logsdon, *Creole New Orleans*, 61.

9. J. Johnson, "Colonial New Orleans," 37–38, 54; Light Townsend Cummins, "The Grand Marquis: Louisiana as a Stable French Colony," in *Louisiana: A History*, ed. Bennett H. Wall (Arlington Heights, Ill.: Forum Press, 1990), 43.

10. Light Townsend Cummins, "Sand as White as Silver: The Founding of French Louisiana," in Wall, *Louisiana*, 30–31.

11. J. Johnson, "Colonial New Orleans," 32–35; Hall, "The Formation of Afro-Creole Culture," 61.

12. Hall, "The Formation of Afro-Creole Culture," 62; Cummins, "Sand as White as Silver," 33–36.

13. J. Johnson, "Colonial New Orleans," 36; Hall, "The Formation of Afro-Creole Culture," 61–62; Cummins, "Sand as White as Silver," 33–36.

14. J. Johnson, "Colonial New Orleans," 36–44; Hall, "The Formation of Afro-Creole Culture," 66–69; Cummins, "Sand as White as Silver," 31.

15. Marcia Gaudet, "Bouki, the Hyena, in Louisiana and African Tales," *Journal of American Folklore* 105, no. 415 (Winter 1992): 70–71.

16. Alcee Fortier, "Louisiana Folk-Tales in French Dialect and English Translation," *Memoirs of the American Folk-Lore Society* 2 (1895): 109–10. See also William Bascom, "Perhaps Too Much to Chew?," *Western Folklore* 40, no. 4 (October 1981): 297.

17. "Bouki Goes Back Home: The Bouki Blues Festival and Conference," West African Research Association and the West African Research Center (Dakar, Senegal), call for papers circulated on H-afro-am mailing list, May 9, 2001, http://h-net.msu.edu/cgi-bin/logbrowse.pl?trx=vx&list=h-afro-am&month=0105&week=b&msg=OvsNkcb7NOF2M29kNxY12A&user=&pw.

18. On the *longue durée* as a historical category, see Marc Bloch, *The Historian's Craft* (New York: Vintage Book, 1953); Fernand Braudel and Sarah Matthews, *On History* (Chicago: University of Chicago Press, 1982); Stuart Clark, ed., *The Annales School: Critical Assessments* (New York: Routledge, 1999).

19. Jean Baptiste Bernard de La Harpe, *Historical Journal of the Establishment of the French in Louisiana* (translation of *Journal historique de l'établissement des Francais a la Louisiane*) (1831; repr. New York, 1851), 89–99, in *France in America*, Library of Congress, Rare Books and Special Collections Division, http://memory.loc.gov/cgi-bin/query/r?intldl/ascfr:@field%28DOCID+@lit%28rbfr0009_0021%29%29. The slave law of the Spanish-speaking colonies and countries was based on the Siete Partidas of 1263–65 of Alfonso X of Castile and Leon and the Spanish Slave Code of 1789.

20. Ibid.

21. Sovereign Nation of the Chitimacha, http://www.chitimacha.gov/; J. Johnson, "Colonial New Orleans," 37–38, 54; Cummins, "The Grand Marquis," 43.

22. J. Johnson, "Colonial New Orleans," 38.

23. Hall, "The Formation of Afro-Creole Culture," 76.

24. Ibid., 71–77; Patricia Galloway, "Rhetoric of Difference: Le Page du Pratz on African Slave Management in Eighteenth-Century Louisiana," *French Colonial History* 3 (2003): 10.

25. J. Johnson, "Colonial New Orleans," 40–41; Hall, "The Formation of Afro-Creole Culture," 64.

26. Ibid., 63.

27. Ibid., 62, 78–80.

28. Quoted in ibid., 78–79.

29. Galloway, "Rhetoric of Difference," 15.

30. Cummins, "The Grand Marquis," 43.

31. Laura Wolff Scanlan, "Clash of the Empires: How the French and Indian War Redrew the Map of North America," *Humanities* 26, no. 3 (May/June 2005): 18.

32. J. Johnson, "Colonial New Orleans," 45–47; Light Townsend Cummins, "By the Stroke of a Pen: Louisiana Becomes Spanish," in Wall, *Louisiana*, 56–57, 65–69.

33. J. Johnson, "Colonial New Orleans," 45–47nn60, 63; Cummins, "The Grand Marquis," 45–46; Light Townsend Cummins, "The Final Years of Colonial Louisiana," in Wall, *Louisiana*, 71–73, 82. See also John Mack Faragher, *A Great and Noble Scheme: The Tragic Story of the Expulsion of the French Acadians from Their American Homeland* (New York: W. W. Norton, 2005).

34. Cummins, "The Final Years," 74–75.

35. Robert C. Reinders, "The Churches and the Negro in New Orleans, 1850–1860," *Phylon* 22, no. 3 (1961): 243; "Colonial Louisiana: European Rulers," *The Cabildo: Two Centuries of Louisiana History*, Louisiana State Museum, http://www.crt.state.la.us/louisiana-state-museum/online-exhibits/the-cabildo/colonial-louisiana/. See also Emily Clark, *Masterless Mistresses: The New Orleans Ursulines and the Development of a New World Society, 1727–1834* (Chapel Hill: University of North Carolina Press, 2007).

36. J. Johnson, "Colonial New Orleans," 52–53.

37. Ibid., 54–56.

38. Cossé Bell, "Haitian Immigration to Louisiana."

39. Hall, "The Formation of Afro-Creole Culture," 85–87.

40. Ibid., 80–83; Gwendolyn Midlo Hall, *Africans in Colonial Louisiana: The Development of Afro-Creole Culture in the Eighteenth Century* (Baton Rouge: Louisiana State University Press, 1992), 201–36.

41. Franklin W. Knight, "The Haitian Revolution," *American Historical Review* 105, no.1 (2000): 112.

42. Anthony P. Maingot, "Haiti and the Terrified Consciousness of the Caribbean," in *Ethnicity in the Caribbean*, ed. Gert Oostindie (London: Macmillan Caribbean, 1996), 53–80; Cummins, "The Final Years," 83–85.

43. Peter Kastor, *The Nation's Crucible: The Louisiana Purchase and the Creation of America* (New Haven, Conn.: Yale University Press, 2004), 55–70.

44. Ibid., 77–79.

45. Mitch Crusto, "Blackness as Property: Sex, Race, Status, and Wealth" (Bepress Legal Series, working paper 307, July 28, 2004), 88n115, http://law.bepress.com/expresso/eps/307/; Bill Quigley and Maha Zaki, "The Significance of Race: Legislative Racial Discrimination in Louisiana," *Southern University Law Review* 24 (1997): 1803–65.

46. Kastor, *The Nation's Crucible*, 64–65.

47. Pierce F. Lewis, *New Orleans: The Making of an Urban Landscape* (Santa Fe, N.M.: Center for American Places, 2003), 42–43.

48. Kastor, *The Nation's Crucible*, 72.

49. Crusto, "Blackness as Property," 130.

50. Cossé Bell, "Haitian Immigration to Louisiana."

51. Kastor, *The Nation's Crucible*; Cossé Bell, "Haitian Immigration to Louisiana."

52. Towana Pierre, "1811 Slave Revolt," 2005, *New Orleans Unmasked*, Students at the Center Program, Xavier University of Louisiana's Center for the Advancement of Teaching, http://cat.xula.edu/unmasked/articles/430/.

53. Harvey Wish, "American Slave Insurrections before 1861," *Journal of Negro History* 22, no. 3 (1937): 319; "Antebellum Louisiana II: The 1811 Slave Revolt," *The Cabildo: Two Centuries of Louisiana History*, Louisiana State Museum, http://www.crt.state.la.us/louisiana-state-museum/online-exhibits/the-cabildo/antebellum-louisiana-agrarian-life/; Kastor, *The Nation's Crucible*, 171–73.

54. [For information on Louisiana's national rankings for 2006 and 2007, see Cowen Institute for Public Education Initiatives, Tulane University, www.coweninstitute.com.—Eds.]

55. Crusto, "Blackness as Property," 130; Wish, "American Slave Insurrections," 319.

56. Lewis, *New Orleans*, 57.

57. Ibid., 45–47.

58. Ibid., 45.

59. Ibid., 50–52.

60. Ira Berlin, *Generations of Captivity: A History of African-American Slaves* (Cambridge, Mass.: Harvard University Press, 2003), 168–79.

61. W. E. B. Du Bois, *Black Reconstruction in America, 1860–1880* (New York: Atheneum Books, 1992), 453; Berlin, *Generations of Captivity*, 181.

62. Ibid., 168–79; William W. Chenault and Robert C. Reinders, "The Northern-Born Community of New Orleans in the 1850s," *Journal of American History* 51, no. 2 (1964): 238, 243.

63. Harriet Beecher Stowe, *The Key to Uncle Tom's Cabin; Presenting the Original Facts and Documents upon Which the Story Is Founded, Together with Corroborative Statements Verifying the Truth of the Work* (Boston: John P. Jewett, 1854), 167.

64. Ibid., 168.

65. Ibid., 168.

66. Ibid., 233–35.

67. John W. Blassingame, *Black New Orleans, 1860–1880* (Chicago: University of Chicago Press, 1973), 2–3. By 1850 there were fifty-seven free Black men to every one hundred free Black women.

68. Ibid., 8–18; Walter Johnson, *Soul by Soul: Life in the Antebellum Slave Market* (Cambridge, Mass.: Harvard University Press, 1999), 113; Floyd D. Cheung, "'Les Cenelles' and Quadroon Balls: 'Hidden Transcripts' of Resistance and Domination in New Orleans," *Southern Literary Journal* 29, no. 2 (Spring 1997): 8.

69. George Lipsitz, *The Possessive Investment in Whiteness: How White People Profit from Identity Politics* (Philadelphia: Temple University Press, 2006).

70. Du Bois, *Black Reconstruction in America*, 451; Judith Kelleher Schafer, *Becoming Free, Remaining Free: Manumission and Enslavement in New Orleans, 1846–1862* (Baton Rouge: Louisiana State University Press, 2003), 8–14.

71. Schafer, *Becoming Free, Remaining Free*, 9; Blassingame, *Black New Orleans*, 9–11; W. Johnson, *Soul by Soul*, 113; Du Bois, *Black Reconstruction*, 154.

72. Blassingame, *Black New Orleans*, 3–9.

73. Hall, *Africans in Colonial Louisiana*, 35–53; Michael A. Gomez, "Muslims in Early America," *Journal of Southern History* 60, no. 4 (November 1994): 678; "Dr. Hall's

Calculations: Islamic African Names," *Afro-Louisiana History and Genealogy: 1719–1820*, http://www.ibiblio.org/laslave/calculations.php; Jonathan Curiel, "Muslim Roots of the Blues: The Music of Famous American Blues Singers Reaches Back through the South to the Culture of West Africa," *San Francisco Chronicle*, August 15, 2004; Ina J. Fandrich, "Yoruba Influences on Haitian Vodou and New Orleans Voodoo," *Journal of Black Studies* 37, no. 5 (2007): 779.

74. Cossé Bell, "Haitian Immigration to Louisiana"; see also Caryn Cossé Bell, *Revolution, Romanticism, and the Afro-Creole Protest Tradition in Louisiana, 1718–1868* (Baton Rouge: Louisiana State University Press, 2004).

75. Cossé Bell, "Haitian Immigration to Louisiana"; Cheung, "'Les Cenelles' and Quadroon Balls," 6.

76. Cossé Bell, "Haitian Immigration to Louisiana."

77. C. L. R. James, *The Black Jacobins: Toussaint L'Ouverture and the San Domingo Revolution*, 2nd ed., rev. (1963; repr., New York: Vintage Books, 1989), 87.

78. Cossé Bell, "Haitian Immigration to Louisiana." See also Hall, "The Formation of Afro-Creole Culture," 85–87; Hein Vanhee, "Central African Popular Christianity and the Making of Haitian Vodou Religion," in *Central Africans and Cultural Transformation in the American Diaspora*, ed. Linda M. Heywood (Cambridge: Cambridge University Press, 2002), 248; Susan Buck-Morss, "Hegel and Haiti," *Critical Inquiry* 26, no. 4 (Summer, 2000): 821–65. On the shifting spellings of *Vodoun*, see Fandrich, "Yoruba Influences," 779.

79. "Shotgun Houses," Greater New Orleans Community Data Center, http://www.gnocdc.org/tertiary/shotgun.html; "Shotgun Houses," *North by South: The African American Great Migration*, http://northbysouth.kenyon.edu/2002/Space/shot2.htm. Also see Robert Farris Thompson, "John Bigger's Shotguns of 1987: An American Classic," in *The Art of John Biggers: View from the Upper Room*, ed. Alva J. Wardlaw (New York: Harry N. Abrams, 1995); John Michael Vlach, *By the Work of Their Hands: Studies in African American Folklife* (Charlottesville: University Press of Virginia, 1991); Aribidesi A. Usman, "The Nineteenth-Century Black Atlantic," in *The Atlantic World, 1450–2000*, ed. Toyin Falola and Kevin David Roberts (Bloomington: Indiana University Press, 2008), 114–36.

80. "Dr. Hall's Calculations: Location of Africans of Identified Origin," *Afro-Louisiana History and Genealogy: 1719–1820*, http://www.ibiblio.org/laslave/calcs/AfOrDistrict.jpg; Joseph C. Miller, "Central Africa during the Era of the Slave Trade, c. 1490s–1850s," in Heywood, *Central Africans and Cultural Transformation*, 62–63.

81. Miller, "Central Africa," appendix 1, tables A and B, 63–66. Also see Heywood, *Central Africans and Cultural Transformation*.

82. Fandrich, "Yoruba Influences," 786; John K. Thornton, "Religious and Ceremonial Life in the Kongo and Mbundu Areas, 1500–1700," in Heywood, *Central Africans and Cultural Transformation*, 74–84.

83. Robert Farris Thompson, *Flash of the Spirit: African and Afro-American Art and Philosophy* (New York: Vintage Books, 1983), 104–31.

84. George Washington Cable, "The Dance in Place Congo," *Century Magazine* 31, no. 4 (February 1886): 517–32.

85. Blassingame, *Black New Orleans*, 3; R. Nettel, "Historical Introduction to 'La Calinda,'" *Music and Letters* 27, no. 1 (January 1946): 59–62; Gavin Jones, "Signifying Songs: The Double Meaning of Black Dialect in the Work of George Washington

Cable," *American Literary History* 9, no. 2 (Summer 1997): 250–51; Jason Berry, "African Cultural Memory in New Orleans Music," *Black Music Research Journal* 8, no. 1 (1988): 5; Samuel A. Floyd Jr., "Black Music in the Circum-Caribbean," *American Music* 17, no. 1 (Spring 1999): 5, 20; Clifton Chenier, "Calinda" (1973), *Putumayo Presents Zydeco*, 2000, PUTIJ 160–2, compact disc.

86. W. Johnson, *Soul by Soul*, 68–69.

87. Ibid., 69.

88. John Ficklen, *History of Reconstruction in Louisiana through 1868* (1910; repr., Freeport, N.Y.: Books for Libraries Press, 1971), 10–14. See also Du Bois, *Black Reconstruction*: "In 1866, Governor Wells recalled that the election in the Parishes were a cruel mockery of free government. Bands of organized desperados, immediately preceding and during an election, committed every species of outrage upon peaceful and unoffending citizens" (452–53).

89. Blassingame, *Black New Orleans*, 9.

90. Joanne Grant, *Black Protest: 350 Years of History, Documents and Analysis* (New York: Fawcett Premiere, 1991), 44; Harvey Wish, "The Slave Insurrection Panic of 1856," *Journal of Southern History* 5, no. 2 (May 1939): 206–22; Wish, "American Slave Insurrections," 299–320; Wendell G. Addington, "Slave Insurrections in Texas," *Journal of Negro History* 35, no. 4 (October 1950): 420–24.

Chapter 2. I Thought I Heard Buddy Bolden Say

1. W. E. B. Du Bois, *Black Reconstruction in America, 1860–1880* (New York: Atheneum Books, 1992), 451; John W. Blassingame, *Black New Orleans, 1860–1880* (Chicago: University of Chicago Press, 1973), 1.

2. John Ficklen, *History of Reconstruction in Louisiana through 1868* (1910; repr., Freeport, N.Y.: Books for Libraries Press, 1971), 10–14, 15.

3. Karen Battle, "New Orleans' Creoles of Color: Shattered Dreams and Broken Promises," *Loyola University Student Historical Journal* 23 (1991–92); Du Bois, *Black Reconstruction*, 157, 454; James G. Hollandsworth Jr., *An Absolute Massacre: The New Orleans Race Riot of July 30, 1866* (Baton Rouge: Louisiana State University Press, 2001), 7–8, 17; Ficklen, *History of Reconstruction in Louisiana*, 121–23. See also Brenda Marie Osbey, "Faubourg Tremé: Community in Transition," pt. 2, "Solidifying the Community," *New Orleans Tribune* 7, no. 1 (January 1991): 13, http://www.osbey.com/faubourg-trem%C3%A9.html.

4. Blassingame, *Black New Orleans*, 26; Du Bois, *Black Reconstruction*, 157, 454; Ficklen, *History of Reconstruction in Louisiana*, 121–23.

5. Blassingame, *Black New Orleans*, 28–29; *New Orleans Black Republican*, May 13, 1865.

6. Hollandsworth, *An Absolute Massacre*, 7–8, 17; Du Bois, *Black Reconstruction*, 153.

7. Du Bois, *Black Reconstruction*, 152–53; Hollandsworth, *An Absolute Massacre*, 17.

8. Battle, "New Orleans' Creoles of Color." See also Donald E. Everett, "Demands of the New Orleans Free Colored Population for Political Equality, 1862–1865," *Louisiana Historical Quarterly* (April 1955): 43.

9. Abraham Lincoln, *Selections from the Letters, Speeches, and State Papers of Abraham Lincoln*, ed. Ida B. Tarbell (Boston: Ginn, 1911), http://archive.org/stream/selectionsfromlootarbgoog/selectionsfromlootarbgoog_djvu.txt.

10. Du Bois, *Black Reconstruction*, 454.

11. Hollandsworth, *An Absolute Massacre*, 7–8, 17; Ficklen, *History of Reconstruction in Louisiana*, 121–23.

12. Du Bois, *Black Reconstruction*, 162.

13. [Abraham Lincoln, "Speech on Reconstruction," April 11, 1865, http://www.historyplace.com/lincoln/reconst.htm.—Eds.]

14. Hollandsworth, *An Absolute Massacre*, 25.

15. Ficklen, *History of Reconstruction in Louisiana*, 101; Hollandsworth, *An Absolute Massacre*, 31–32, 46.

16. Quoted in Du Bois, *Black Reconstruction*, 454–55.

17. Hollandsworth, *An Absolute Massacre*, 34–35, 64–66.

18. Ficklen, *History of Reconstruction in Louisiana*, 117–20.

19. Du Bois, *Black Reconstruction*, 455; Joanne Grant, *Black Protest: History, Documents and Analysis* (New York: Fawcett Premiere Books, 1991), 148–50.

20. Du Bois, *Black Reconstruction*, 457. See also Nina Mjagkij, ed., *Organizing Black America: An Encyclopedia of African American Associations* (New York: Routledge, 2001); Battle, "New Orleans' Creoles of Color," 20. See also Everett, "Demands of the New Orleans Free Colored Population," 59.

21. Quoted in Du Bois, *Black Reconstruction*, 457. Also see Hollandsworth, *An Absolute Massacre*, 36–42.

22. Quoted in Du Bois, *Black Reconstruction*, 458.

23. Du Bois, *Black Reconstruction*, 457; Hollandsworth, *An Absolute Massacre*, 36–42.

24. Quoted in Hollandsworth, *An Absolute Massacre*, 46.

25. Quoted in ibid., 45–47, 62.

26. Quoted in ibid., 50–52.

27. Ibid., 53–60.

28. Ibid., 92.

29. Ibid., 129.

30. "Report of the Select Committee on the New Orleans Riots," *Congressional Globe*, 39th Cong., 2nd sess., 16 (February 11, 1867), in *Mass Violence in America: New Orleans Riots of July 30, 1866*, ed. Robert M. Fogelson and Richard Rubenstein (New York: Arno Press, 1969), 16–17.

31. Ibid., 26–27.

32. Joel Gray Taylor, "Civil War and Reconstruction in Louisiana," in *Louisiana: A History*, ed. Bennett H. Wall (Arlington Heights, Ill.: Forum Press, 1990), 198–99; Roger W. Shugg, *Origins of Class Struggle in Louisiana* (Baton Rouge: Louisiana State University Press, 1972), 221; Du Bois, *Black Reconstruction*, 466.

33. Du Bois, *Black Reconstruction*, 477.

34. Taylor, "Civil War and Reconstruction," 199–201; Du Bois, *Black Reconstruction*, 477.

35. Henry Clay Warmoth, *War, Politics, and Reconstruction: Stormy Days in Louisiana* (1930; repr., Columbia: University of South Carolina Press, 2006).

36. Du Bois, *Black Reconstruction*, 522–23. On immigration policy, see *DeBow's Review, Agricultural, Commercial, Industrial Progress and Resources*, July/August 1867, 151–52, and November 1867, 575–77.

37. Du Bois, *Black Reconstruction*, 475–76. See also Warmoth, *War, Politics, and Reconstruction*, 80; Shugg, *Origins of Class Struggle in Louisiana*, 296–97.

38. Shugg, *Origins of Class Struggle in Louisiana*, 302–3.

39. Michael A. Ross, "The Commemoration of Robert E. Lee's Death and the Obstruction of Reconstruction in New Orleans," *Civil War History* 51, no. 2 (2005): 138.

40. Ficklen, *History of Reconstruction in Louisiana*, 187–88; Du Bois, *Black Reconstruction*, 470.

41. Du Bois, *Black Reconstruction*, 471.

42. Ross, "Commemoration of Robert E. Lee's Death," 135–50.

43. John Kendall, *History of New Orleans* (Chicago: Lewis, 1922), 693–94.

44. Joseph Roach, "Carnival and the Law in New Orleans," *TDR* 37, no. 3 (Autumn 1993): 63–66.

45. Eric Foner, *Reconstruction: America's Unfinished Revolution, 1863–1877* (New York: Harper and Row, 1988), 437.

46. "Reconstruction: A State Divided," *The Cabildo: Two Centuries of Louisiana History*, Louisiana State Museum, http://www.crt.state.la.U.S./museum/online_exhibits/Cabildo/11.aspx.

47. Taylor, "Civil War and Reconstruction," 202–3.

48. Du Bois, *Black Reconstruction*, 483.

49. Ibid., 482–83.

50. Kendall, *History of New Orleans*, 401–2; Roach, "Carnival and the Law," 66.

51. Taylor, "Civil War and Reconstruction," 206–8.

52. Mark T. Carleton and William Ivy Hair, "Uneasy Interlude, 1877–1892," in Wall, *Louisiana*, 218–20.

53. Ibid., 214; William Ivy Hair, *Bourbonism and Agrarian Protest: Louisiana Politics, 1877–1900* (Baton Rouge: Louisiana State University Press, 1969); William F. Holmes, review of *New Orleans in the Gilded Age: Politics and Urban Progress, 1880–1896*, by Joy J. Jackson, *American Historical Review* 75, no. 5 (June 1970): 1531–32.

54. *Constitution of the State of Louisiana: Adopted in Convention at the City of New Orleans, the Twenty-Third Day of July, A.D. 1879* (New Orleans: Jas. H. Cosgrove, 1879).

55. Mark T. Carleton, Perry H. Howard, and Joseph B. Parker, *Readings in Louisiana Politics*, 2nd ed. (Baton Rouge: Claitor's Publishing Division, 1988), 297.

56. Mark T. Carleton, *Politics and Punishment: The History of the Louisiana State Penal System* (Baton Rouge: Louisiana State University Press, 1971), 34.

57. Ibid., 35. See Hair, *Bourbonism and Agrarian Protest*, 119.

58. Kendall, *History of New Orleans*, 401–2; Roach, "Carnival and the Law," 66.

59. Carleton and Hair, "Uneasy Interlude," 215, 222–24, 314.

60. Hair, *Bourbonism and Agrarian Protest*, 185–86.

61. Carleton and Hair, "Uneasy Interlude," 216–17.

62. Pierce F. Lewis, *New Orleans: The Making of an Urban Landscape* (Santa Fe, N.M.: Center for American Places, 2003), 55–58; Shugg, *Origins of Class Struggle in Louisiana*, 298–99.

63. Robert W. Rydell, *All the World's a Fair: Visions of Empire at American International Expositions, 1876–1916* (Chicago: University of Chicago Press, 1984), 9, 77–89. A former railroad official, Burke was celebrated for delaying the arrival of federal troops during the Battle of Liberty Place in 1874. For Rydell, the southern expositions included so-called Negro departments as "instruments of social control that would keep

blacks in check by defining progress as self-improvement along industrial lines and by persuading blacks that builders of the New South would take their best interest to heart."

64. Plater Robinson, " A House Divided: A Teaching Guide on the History of Civil Rights in Louisiana," 2nd ed., 1995, Southern Institute Center for Education and Research, Tulane University, http://www.southerninstitute.info/civil_rights_education/a_house_divided.pdf.

65. Hair, *Bourbonism and Agrarian Protest*, 187.

66. Ibid., 187–88; Carleton and Hair, "Uneasy Interlude," 222–24; Michael L. Kurtz, "Reform and Race," in Wall, *Louisiana*, 314.

67. Blassingame, *Black New Orleans*, 1; Grant, *Black Protest*, 480.

68. Shugg, *Origins of Class Struggle in Louisiana*, 286, 295–97.

69. Blassingame, *Black New Orleans*, 163–65.

70. Ibid., 167–68.

71. Ibid.

72. Ibid., 145–47.

73. Danny Barker, *Buddy Bolden and the Last Days of Storyville* (New York: Continuum, 2001); Julio Finn, *The Bluesman: The Musical Heritage of Black Men and Women in the Americas* (London: Quartet Book, 1986), 97; Martha Ward, *Voodoo Queen: The Spirited Lives of Marie Laveau* (Jackson: University Press of Mississippi, 2004), 175.

74. Rydell, *All the World's a Fair*, 81–85, 95. South Carolina attorney David Straker saw the exposition as a national opportunity to bring the races together in "love, peace, unity, under equal laws, exact justice. . . . So that the antagonism of race, the hatred of creeds and parties, the prejudice of caste, and the denial of equal rights may disappear from among us forever."

75. Blassingame, *Black New Orleans*, 151.

76. George Lipsitz, "Mardi Gras Indians: Carnival and Counter-Narrative in Black New Orleans," *Cultural Critique* 10 (Autumn 1988): 99–121.

77. Roach, "Carnival and the Law," 50.

78. Hair, *Bourbonism and Agrarian Protest*, 175–76.

79. Ibid., 227; Carleton and Hair, "Uneasy Interlude," 228–30.

80. Hair, *Bourbonism and Agrarian Protest*, 172–75.

81. Ibid., 176–85.

82. Charles Barthelemy Rousseve, *The Negro in Louisiana: Aspects of His History and His Literature* (New Orleans: Xavier University Press, 1937), 130; *New Orleans Times-Democrat*, September 8, 1892, in Dale A. Somers, "Black and White New Orleans: A Study in Urban Race Relations, 1865–1900," *Journal of Southern History* 40, no. 1 (February 1974): 42. Comment overheard by the white president of Straight University in 1888: "We of the south who know the fallacy and danger of racial equality who are opposed to placing the Negro on any terms of equality, who have insisted on a separation of the races in church, hotel, car, saloon, and theater . . . are heartily opposed to any arrangement encouraging this equality, which gives Negroes false ideas and dangerous beliefs." Carleton and Hair, "Uneasy Interlude," 222–28, 314; Adam Fairclough, *Race and Democracy: The Civil Rights Struggle in Louisiana, 1915–1972* (Athens: University of Georgia Press, 1999), 6.

83. Carleton and Hair, "Uneasy Interlude," 229–30; Hair, *Bourbonism and Agrarian Protest*, 194–96.

84. Lawrence Goodwyn, *The Populist Moment: A Short History of the Agrarian Revolt in America* (Oxford: Oxford University Press, 1978).

85. Hair, *Bourbonism and Agrarian Protest*, 194–96, 225–27; Carleton and Hair, "Uneasy Interlude," 228–30.

86. Hair, *Bourbonism and Agrarian Protest*, 227, 249–57.

87. Ibid., 228–65. See "Address to the Democratic State Central Committee," *Shreveport Evening Judge*, May 6, 1896.

88. Hair, *Bourbonism and Agrarian Protest*, 260.

89. Quoted in ibid.

90. Carleton, Howard, and Parker, *Readings in Louisiana Politics*, 299; Hair, *Bourbonism and Agrarian Protest*, 261-262.

91. Perry H. Howard and T. Wayne Parent, "An Enduring Ecological Coalition in Louisiana: From Huey Long to Edwin Edwards and Beyond," in Carleton, Howard, and Parker, *Readings in Louisiana Politics*, 558–81; Grant, *Black Protest*, 111; Fairclough, *Race and Democracy*, 6.

92. Fairclough, *Race and Democracy*, 6–17; Mark Carleton and William Ivy Hair, "Bourbonism, Populism, and a Little Progressivism, 1892–1924," in Wall, *Louisiana*, 243–44.

93. Hair, *Bourbonism and Agrarian Protest*, 267–73; *Baton Rouge Daily Advocate*, February 12, 1898.

94. Hair, *Bourbonism and Agrarian Protest*, 278–79.

95. U.S. Bureau of the Census, "Population of the 100 Largest Cities and Other Urban Places in the United States: 1790 to 1990," Population Division Working Paper No. 27, Washington, D.C., June 1998, http://www.census.gov/population/www/documentation/twps0027/twps0027.html.

96. Carleton and Hair, "Bourbonism, Populism, and a Little Progressivism," 231.

97. Thomas Brothers, *Louis Armstrong's New Orleans* (New York: W. W. Norton, 2006), 134.

98. Ibid., 134–35.

99. Louis Armstrong, "'Louis Armstrong + The Jewish Family in New Orleans, La., the Year of 1907' (March 31, 1969–1970)," in *Louis Armstrong in His Own Words: Selected Writings*, ed. Thomas Brothers (Oxford: Oxford University Press, 1999), 17; italics and capitalization in original.

100. Jelly Roll Morton (Ferdinand LaMothe), "Oh! Didn't He Ramble?," *Jelly Roll Morton: The Library of Congress Recording*, vol. 1 (Kansas City Stomp), Rounder CD 1091, 1993. Baby Dodds suggests that "Didn't He Ramble" was composed by Buddy Bolden. Conversely, several other accounts suggest that the song was written and copyrighted by Bob Cole and John Rosamond Johnson under the name Will Handy in 1902, two years after the Charles affair. Johnson was the composer of "Lift Every Voice and Sing" (1900) which is also known as the "Negro National Anthem." His brother, James Weldon Johnson, wrote the lyrics for the latter song before becoming the executive secretary of the National Association for the Advancement of Colored People (NAACP) from 1920 to 1931. Also see "African American Performers on Early Sound Recordings,

1892–1916," Library of Congress, http://lcweb2.loc.gov/diglib/ihas/loc.natlib.ihas
.200038862/default.html.

101. Ida B. Wells-Barnett, *Mob Rule in New Orleans: Robert Charles and His Fight
to Death, The Story of His Life, Burning Human Beings Alive, Other Lynching Statistics*
(Chicago, September 1, 1900), Project Gutenberg, EBook #14976, http://www.gutenberg
.org/files/14976/14976-h/14976-h.htm.

102. Ibid.

103. Ibid.

104. Ibid.

105. Ibid.

106. Ibid.

107. Thomas Brothers, *Louis Armstrong's New Orleans*, 14, 283–84.

108. Derrick Ward, "Urban Race Riots in the Jim Crow Era: An Overview Essay,"
Chicken Bones: A Journal, http://www.nathanielturner.com/jimcrowriots.htm.

109. Alan Lomax, *Mister Jelly Roll: The Fortunes of Jelly Roll Morton, New Orleans
Creole and "Inventor of Jazz"* (1950; repr., New York: Pantheon Books, 1993), 70; Jeff
Hannusch, *I Hear You Knock-in': The Sound of New Orleans Rhythm and Blues* (Ville
Platte, La.: Swallow, 1989), 169.

110. William Barlow, *Looking Up at Down: The Emergence of Blues Culture* (Philadelphia: Temple University Press, 1989), 186–87. See also Lomax, *Mister Jelly Roll*, 51,
269–91.

111. Thomas Brothers, *Louis Armstrong's New Orleans*, 154, 283–84; Barlow, *Looking
Up at Down*, 191.

112. Thomas Brothers, *Louis Armstrong's New Orleans*, 11, 33, 283–84; Keith Weldon
Medley, *Dryades Street/Oretha Castle Haley Boulevard: Remembrance and Reclama-
tion* (New Orleans: New Orleans Tribune, April 2001), 19–25, http://www.writers.net/
writers/books/24622; "Central City Renaissance Alliance 'Working Toward Solutions'
Community Plan," Concordia LLC, Fall 2004, www.nolaplans.com/plans/Other%20
Plans/ccra%201.pdf.

113. Donald M. Marquis, *In Search of Buddy Bolden: The First Man of Jazz* (Baton
Rouge: Louisiana State University Press, 2005), 43–47, 99–111; Barker, *Buddy Bolden*,
91; George Abry, "Uptown Sprouted from Plantations: Streetcars Helped Link Rural
Communities," *Times-Picayune*, May 26, 2001.

114. Marquis, *In Search of Buddy Bolden*, 110–11; Barker, *Buddy Bolden*, 23.

Chapter 3. Hemispheric UNIA and the Great Flood, 1915–1928

1. John M. Barry, *Rising Tide: The Great Mississippi Flood of 1927 and How it
Changed America* (New York: Touchstone Books, 1997), 221, 355.

2. Ibid., 220–21.

3. Ibid., 220; emphasis in the original.

4. Ibid.; T. Harry Williams, "The Gentleman from Louisiana: Demagogue or Democrat," *Journal of Southern History* 26, no. 1 (February 1960): 9.

5. Kenneth T. Jackson, *The Ku Klux Klan in the City* (Chicago: Ivan R. Dee, 1992),
86–87, 239; Adam Fairclough, *Race and Democracy: The Civil Rights Struggle in Louisiana, 1915–1972* (Athens: University of Georgia Press, 1999), 9.

6. Barry, *Rising Tide*, 110–12, 148–49. On cotton in Louisiana, see James Matthew Reonas, "Planters and Plantation Culture in Louisiana's Northeast Delta: From the First World War to the Great Depression," (Ph.D. diss., Louisiana State University, 2006), 41.

7. James Weldon Johnson, "The American Occupation," *Nation* 111 (August 28, 1920). See also Wilton B. Fowler, "The Way to Withdraw Is to Withdraw," review of *The United States and the Caribbean Republics, 1921–1933*, by Dana G. Munro, *Latin American Research Review* 12, no. 3 (1977): 198–202; Hans Schmidt, *The United States Occupation of Haiti, 1915–1934* (New Brunswick, N.J.: Rutgers University Press, 1995); G. Pope Atkins and Larman C. Wilson, *The United States and the Trujillo Regime* (New Brunswick, N.J.: Rutgers University Press, 1972); and Burton I. Kaufman, "Efficiency and Expansion: Foreign Trade Organization in the Wilson Administration, 1913–1921," *Latin American Research Review* 12, no. 3 (1977): 199.

8. Marcelo Bucheli, "Good Dictator, Bad Dictator: United Fruit Company and Economic Nationalism in Central America in the Twentieth Century" (paper #06–0115, University of Illinois, College of Business, Champaign, Ill., 2006), 8–10, http://www.business.illinois.edu/Working_Papers/papers/06-0115.pdf; "New Orleans Junta Plots: City Full of Central American Revolutionaries," *New York Times*, June 12, 1911.

9. "Samuel Zemurray (1877–1961)," Biographies, United Fruit Historical Society, http://www.unitedfruit.org/zemurray.htm; Gore Vidal, "In the Lair of the Octopus (United Fruit Co., Guatemala)," *Nation* 260, no. 22 (June 5, 1995): 792–93, http://www.highbeam.com/doc/1G1-17029772.html; Pablo Neruda, "The United Fruit Co. (1950)," trans. Robert Bly, *Asheville Poetry Review* 10, no. 1 (2003), http://www.ashevillepoetry review.com/2003/issue-13/the-united-fruit-co. See also Lester D. Langley and Thomas D. Schoonover, *The Banana Men: American Mercenaries and Entrepreneurs in Central America, 1880–1930* (Lexington: University Press of Kentucky, 1995); Lester D. Langley, *The Banana Wars: United States Intervention in the Caribbean, 1898–1934* (Lanham, Md.: Rowman and Littlefield, 2001); Steve Striffler and Mark Moberg, eds., *Banana Wars: Power, Production, and History in the Americas* (Durham, N.C.: Duke University Press, 2003). On Zemurray, also see John N. Ingham, *Biographical Dictionary of American Business Leaders, V–Z* (Westport, Conn.: Greenwood Press, 1983), 1698.

10. U.S. Bureau of the Census, "Table 15. Population of the 100 Largest Urban Places: 1920," 1998, http://www.census.gov/population/www/documentation/twps0027/tab15.txt.

11. Mark Carleton and William Ivy Hair, "Bourbonism, Populism, and a Little Progressivism, 1892–1924," in *Louisiana: A History*, ed. Bennett H. Wall (Arlington Heights, Ill.: Forum Press, 1990), 249.

12. Jerrold M. Packard, *American Nightmare: The History of Jim Crow* (New York: Macmillan, 2002), 104–5; Fairclough, *Race and Democracy*, 8.

13. Buzzy Jackson, *A Bad Woman Feeling Good: Blues and the Women Who Sing Them* (New York: W. W. Norton, 2005), 5; Gerald L. Neuman, "Anomalous Zones," *Stanford Law Review* 48, no. 5 (May, 1996): 1209–11.

14. B. Jackson, *A Bad Woman Feeling Good*, 5; Alecia P. Long, *The Great Southern Babylon: Sex, Race, and Respectability in New Orleans, 1865–1920* (Baton Rouge: Louisiana State University Press, 2004), xv, 148–90.

15. Laurence Bergreen, *Louis Armstrong: An Extravagant Life* (New York: Broadway Books, 1997), 107; Thomas Brothers, *Louis Armstrong's New Orleans* (New York: W. W. Norton, 2006), 256.

16. Editorial, "Jass and Jassism," *New Orleans Times-Picayune*, June 20, 1918; Bergreen, *Louis Armstrong*, 163–64. See also "Jass and Jassism," *African American Review* 29, no. 2 (Summer 1995): 231–32.

17. *New Orleans Times-Picayune*, June 20,1918.

18. Ibid.

19. Fairclough, *Race and Democracy*, 19–24; Lee Sartain, *Invisible Activists: Women of the Louisiana NAACP and the Struggle for Civil Rights, 1915–1945* (Baton Rouge: Louisiana State University Press, 2007), 56.

20. Fairclough, *Race and Democracy*, 14–17.

21. Ibid., 10.

22. Ibid., 11.

23. Ibid., 12.

24. Barry, *Rising Tide*, 180.

25. Mahalia Jackson and Evan McLeod Wylie, *Movin' On Up* (New York: Hawthorn Books, 1966), 11–12.

26. Ibid., 24–25.

27. Danny Barker, *Buddy Bolden and the Last Days of Storyville* (New York: Continuum, 2001), 115.

28. Fairclough, *Race and Democracy*, 18; Charles E. Siler, "A Commentary: African Cultural Retentions in Louisiana," Louisiana's Living Traditions: Louisiana Folklife Festival, 2001, festival booklet, http://www.louisianafolklife.org/LT/Articles_Essays/afri_cult_retent.html.

29. Fairclough, *Race and Democracy*, 18; Siler, "A Commentary," 28; Jackson and Wylie, *Movin' On Up*, 17–36. Barker, *Buddy Bolden*, 99.

30. Jackson and Wylie, *Movin' On Up*, 17, 36.

31. Barker, *Buddy Bolden*, 99.

32. Jackson and Wylie, *Movin' On Up*, 29–30.

33. Jeff Hannusch, *I Hear You Knocking: The Sound of New Orleans' Rhythm and Blues* (Ville Platte, La.: Swallow, 1986), 3–6.

34. Ibid., 6–8.

35. William Barlow, *Looking Up at Down: The Emergence of Blues Culture* (Philadelphia: Temple University Press, 1989), 259–60.

36. Douglas Daniels, personal conversation with Clyde Woods, March 12, 2007.

37. Barlow, *Looking Up at Down*, 191. See also Martin Williams, *Jazz Masters of New Orleans* (New York: Macmillan, 1967), 162.

38. Bergreen, *Louis Armstrong*, 190–207. See also Robert G. O'Meally, *The Jazz Cadence of American Culture* (New York: Columbia University Press, 1998); "The Story of Lilian Hardin Armstrong, a History of Jazz before 1930," audio recording, *The Red Hot Jazz Archive: A History of Jazz before 1930*, http://www.redhotjazz.com/lil.html.

39. Fairclough, *Race and Democracy*, 18–20; Sartain, *Invisible Activists*, 52–56.

40. Robert Francis Engs, *Educating the Disfranchised and Disinherited: Samuel Chapman Armstrong and Hampton Institute, 1839–1893* (Knoxville: University of Ten-

nessee Press, 1999), xx, 207; Donald Spivey, *Schooling for the New Slavery* (Westport, Conn.: Greenwood Press, 1978), 152; Patti McGill Peterson, "Colonialism and Education: The Case of the Afro-American," *Comparative Education Review* 15, no. 2 (June 1971): 146–57; Edward H. Berman, "Tuskegee-in-Africa," *Journal of Negro Education* 41, no. 2 (Spring 1972): 99.

41. Mary G. Rolinson, *Grassroots Garveyism: The Universal Improvement Association in the Rural South, 1920–1927* (Chapel Hill: University of North Carolina Press, 2007), 42–43.

42. "The East St. Louis Riot," *The American Experience: Marcus Garvey: Look For Me in the Whirlwind*, PBS, 2001, http://www.pbs.org/wgbh/amex/garvey/peopleevents/e_estlouis.html. See also Charles L. Lumpkins, *American Pogrom: The East St. Louis Race Riot and Black Politics* (Athens, Ohio: Ohio University Press, 2008).

43. Marcus Garvey, "The Conspiracy of the East St. Louis Riots," speech delivered July 8, 1917, *The American Experience: Marcus Garvey: Look For Me in the Whirlwind*, PBS, 2001, http://www.pbs.org/wgbh/amex/garvey/filmmore/ps_riots.html. See also Robert A. Hill, ed., *The Marcus Garvey and Universal Negro Improvement Association Papers*, vol. 1, *1826–August 1919* (Berkeley: University of California Press, 1983).

44. Garvey, "Conspiracy of the East St. Louis Riots."

45. Ibid.

46. Ibid.

47. Ibid.

48. Quoted in "East St. Louis Riot."

49. [The Black Star Line was a shipping line run by the UNIA.—Eds.]

50. Claudrena N. Harold, *The Rise and Fall of the Garvey Movement in the Urban South, 1918–1942* (New York: Routledge, 2007), 30–31.

51. Harold, *The Rise and Fall of the Garvey Movement*, 31.

52. Ibid., 34; Rolinson, *Grassroots Garveyism*, 49.

53. Harold, *Rise and Fall of the Garvey Movement*, 1–2.

54. "Interview with Mother Audley Moore," tape no. 2 U20, 1972, Oral History of the American Left: Radical Histories Tamiment Library, New York University. See also "'Speak, Garvey, Speak': A Follower Recalls a Garvey Rally," History Matters, http://historymatters.gmu.edu/d/29/U.

55. Harold, *Rise and Fall of the Garvey Movement*, 1–2.

56. Rolinson, *Grassroots Garveyism*, 87.

57. Ibid., 20–21, 48–49, 87.

58. Ibid., 175.

59. Harold, *Rise and Fall of the Garvey Movement*, 37.

60. Ibid., 32.

61. Ibid., 36–37.

62. Ibid., 32–34.

63. Rolinson, *Grassroots Garveyism*, 83, 140–43.

64. Ibid., 143–44; "African Series: Introduction," vol. 9, "June 1921–December 1922," *The Marcus Garvey and Universal Negro Improvement Association Papers Project*, James S. Colean African Studies Center, UCLA, http://www.international.ucla.edu/africa/mgpp/intro09.asp.

65. Harold, *Rise and Fall of the Garvey Movement*, 38–39.

66. Ibid., 40–43.

67. Rolinson, *Grassroots Garveyism*, 86–87; "Primary Sources: Writing to the U.S. Attorney-General—'Garvey Must Go,'" *The American Experience: Marcus Garvey: Look For Me in the Whirlwind*, PBS, 2001, http://www.pbs.org/wgbh/amex/garvey/filmmore/ps_go.html (excerpt from Amy Jacques-Garvey, ed., *Philosophy & Opinions of Marcus Garvey* [New York: Athenaeum, 1969]).

68. Harold, *Rise and Fall of the Garvey Movement*, 43–45.

69. Ibid., 32, 44–45; Rolinson, *Grassroots Garveyism*, 49.

70. Harold, *Rise and Fall of the Garvey Movement*, 46.

71. Marcus Garvey, "Primary Sources: 'Look for Me in the Whirlwind,'" February 10, 1925, *The American Experience: Marcus Garvey: Look For Me in the Whirlwind*, PBS, 2001, http://www.pbs.org/wgbh/amex/garvey/filmmore/ps_wind.html (excerpt from Jacques-Garvey, *Philosophy & Opinions of Marcus Garvey*).

72. Pierce F. Lewis, *New Orleans: The Making of an Urban Landscape* (Santa Fe, N.M.: Center for American Places, 2003), 63.

73. Barry, *Rising Tide*, 221, 239–41.

74. Ibid., 242–48.

75. ibid., 347–58.

76. Ibid., 342, 350–51; Sartain, *Invisible Activists*, 65–66.

77. Barry, *Rising Tide*, 342, 350–51; "New Orleans Babbitry," *Memphis Commercial Appeal*, May 2, 1927.

78. Barlow, *Looking Up at Down*, 261.

Chapter 4. The Share the Wealth Plan

1. Samuel Charters, liner notes, *The Complete Blind Willie Johnson*, Columbia, C2K 52835, 1993.

2. Ibid.

3. V. O. Key Jr., *Southern Politics in State and Nation* (New York: Vintage Books, 1949), 150–61.

4. Gerald K. Smith, "How Come Huey Long? 2. Or Superman?" *New Republic*, February 13, 1935, 11–15, http://historymatters.gmu.edu/d/5107/.

5. Ibid.

6. Ibid.

7. Adam Fairclough, *Race and Democracy: The Civil Rights Struggle in Louisiana, 1915–1972* (Athens: University of Georgia Press, 1999), 23; John M. Barry, *Rising Tide: The Great Mississippi Flood of 1927 and How It Changed America* (New York: Touchstone Books, 1997), 408.

8. Fairclough, *Race and Democracy*, 33.

9. T. Harry Williams, *Huey Long: A Biography* (New York: Alfred A. Knopf, 1969), 10–15, 70, 703. See also Fairclough, *Race and Democracy*, 21–23, 36.

10. Fairclough, *Race and Democracy*, 23; Barry, *Rising Tide*, 408.

11. Fairclough, *Race and Democracy*, 22–23; Williams, *Huey Long*, 10–15.

12. Edwin Amenta, Kathleen Dunleavy, and Mary Bernstein, "Stolen Thunder? Huey Long's 'Share Our Wealth,' Political Mediation, and the Second New Deal,"

American Sociological Review 59, no. 5 (October 1994): 678–702; Williams, *Huey Long*, 702–5.

13. Senator Huey P. Long, *Statement of the Share Our Wealth Movement*, 74th Cong., 1st sess., *Congressional Record*, 79 (May 23, 1935) 8040–43, http://web.mit.edu/course/21/21h.102/www/Primary%20source%20collections/The%20New%20Deal/Long,%20Share%20Our%20Wealth.htm.

14. Ibid., 8043.

15. Huey P. Long, "Sharing Our Wealth," radio address, January 1935, *Annals of America, Encyclopedia Britannica* 15 (1968): 318–20, available at "Sage History: An American Experience," http://sageamericanhistory.net/twenties_depr_newdeal/depressionnewdeal/documents/HLongSOW.htm.

16. Ibid.

17. Williams, *Huey Long*, 8.

18. Ibid., 654–61.

19. Ibid., 661–75, 782.

20. Ibid., 837–66.

21. Fairclough, *Race and Democracy*, 34–35.

22. Key, *Southern Politics in State and Nation*, 159.

23. Amenta, Dunleavy and Bernstein, "Stolen Thunder?," 678; Williams, *Huey Long*, 702–5.

24. Williams, *Huey Long*, 10–15, 70, 703; Fairclough, *Race and Democracy*, 21–23, 36.

25. Fairclough, *Race and Democracy*, 22–23; Williams, *Huey Long*, 10–15.

26. John H. Scott and Cleo Scott Brown, *Witness to the Truth: My Struggles for Human Rights in Louisiana* (Columbia: University of South Carolina Press, 2003), 77–78. The Long machine continued to shape Louisiana politics for several more decades. His brother Earl became governor three times while his son Russell became a Bourbon-bloc icon during his service in the U.S. Senate (1948–87). Russell Long was also a staunch opponent of civil rights.

27. Pierce F. Lewis, *New Orleans: The Making of an Urban Landscape* (Santa Fe, N.M.: Center for American Places, 2003), 69.

28. Joseph Roach, "Carnival and the Law in New Orleans," *Drama Review* 37, no. 3 (Autumn 1993): 42–75; Perry Young, *Carnival and Mardi-Gras in New Orleans* (New Orleans: Harmanson's, 1939), 48.

29. "Population of the 100 Largest Urban Places: 1940," U.S. Bureau of the Census, June 15, 1998, http://www.census.gov/population/www/documentation/twps0027/tab17.txt; Charles S. Johnson, "The Negro Minority," *Annals of the American Academy of Political and Social Science* 223 (September 1942): 12; Claude F. Jacobs and Andrew J. Kaslow, *The Spiritual Churches of New Orleans: Origins, Beliefs, and Rituals of an African-American Religion* (Knoxville: University of Tennessee Press, 1991), 33.

30. Fairclough, *Race and Democracy*, 42–43; T. Lynn Smith, "Depopulation of Louisiana's Sugar Bowl," *Journal of Farm Economics* 20, no. 2 (May 1938): 503–9.

31. Jacobs and Kaslow, *Spiritual Churches of New Orleans*, 33.

32. Charles E. Grenier, "The Political Mobilization of the Black Electorate in Louisiana, 1932–1980: Black Voter Registration Trends and Correlates," in *Readings in Louisiana Politics*, 2nd ed., ed. Mark T. Carleton, Perry H. Howard, and Joseph B.

Parker (Baton Rouge: Claitor's Publishing Division, 1988), 513–29; Fairclough, *Race and Democracy*, 11, 24.

33. Fairclough, *Race and Democracy*, 24; Keith Weldon Medley, "Ernest Wright: 'People's Champion,'" *Southern Exposure* 12, no. 5 (1984): 52–55.

34. Fairclough, *Race and Democracy*, 11–14.

35. Ibid., 38–41.

36. Lee Sartain, *Invisible Activists: Women of the Louisiana NAACP and the Struggle for Civil Rights, 1915–1945* (Baton Rouge: Louisiana State University Press, 2007), 60.

37. Fairclough, *Race and Democracy*, 27–29.

38. Ibid., 30.

39. Sartain, *Invisible Activists*, 60–61; Annual Report of the NAACP, 1929 [we are unsure if this refers to the national or a local report—Eds.]; "McCrary Defense Fund," *Louisiana Weekly*, March 1, 1930.

40. Fairclough, *Race and Democracy*, 30–33.

41. Roach, "Carnival and the Law," 60.

42. Ibid., 59.

43. George Lipsitz, *Time Passages: Collective Memory and American Popular Culture* (Minneapolis: University of Minnesota Press, 1990), 233–53.

44. Shane White, "'It Was a Proud Day': African Americans, Festivals, and Parades in the North, 1741–1834," in *The New African American Urban History*, ed. Kenneth W. Goings and Raymond A. Mohl (Thousand Oaks, Calif.: Sage, 1996), 23; George Lipsitz, "Mardi Gras Indians: Carnival and Counter-Narrative in Black New Orleans," *Cultural Critique* 10 (Autumn 1988): 115.

45. Michael P. Smith, "Behind the Lines: The Black Mardi Gras Indians and the New Orleans Second Line," *Black Music Research Journal* 14, no. 1, (Spring 1994): 57.

46. Kalamu ya Salaam, *"He's the Prettiest": A Tribute to Big Chief Allison "Tootie" Montana's 50 Years of Mardi Gras Indian Suiting* (New Orleans: New Orleans Museum of Art, 1997).

47. Ibid.

48. Ibid.; Douglas Martin, "Robert Lee, Only Chief of Chiefs of Mardi Gras Indians, Is Dead at 85," *New York Times*, February 4, 2001; Roach, "Carnival and the Law," 59 (citations omitted). See also Michael P. Smith, *The Mardi Gras Indians of New Orleans* (Gretna, La.: Pelican, 2007).

49. Lipsitz, "Mardi Gras Indians," 104; Jason Berry, Jonathan Foose, and Tad Jones, *Up from the Cradle of Jazz* (Athens: University of Georgia Press, 2009), 237.

50. PBS, "Sitting Bull, Tatanka-Iyotanka (1831–1890)," *New Perspectives on the West*, 2001, http://www.pbs.org/weta/thewest/people/s_z/sittingbull.htm.

51. Salaam, *"He's the Prettiest"*; Geraldine Wyckoff, "Carnival Perspective: Bone Men Waking the Spirit," *Louisiana Weekly*, January 28, 2008; Jason Berry, Jonathan Foose, and Tad Jones, "In Search of Mardi Gras Indians," in *When Brer Rabbit Meets Coyote: African Native American Literature*, ed. Jonathan Brennan (Urbana: University of Illinois Press, 2003), 206–8. According to Salaam, "After returning from working in California shipyards during World War II, he masked with his father for several years before forming the Monogram Hunters in 1949. After Yellow Pocahontas briefly disbanded his group adopted the name. Montana was also instrumental in the movement

away 'from physical violence to aesthetic competition.' He served as Big Chief from 1956 until 1997 when he passed 'the stick' to his son Darryl 'Mutt-Mutt' Montana."

52. Berry, Foose, and Jones, "In Search of Mardi Gras Indians," 208–9.

53. Al Kennedy, "Our History: Danny Lambert: The Chief Called 'Copperwire,'" *Louisiana Weekly*, February 28, 2005. See also Martin, "Robert Lee, Only Chief of Chiefs"; Berry, Foose, and Jones, "In Search of Mardi Gras Indians," 206–8.

54. After Lambert stopped masking Indian, he became a member of the Zulu Social Aid and Pleasure Club. He died in 1981. Kennedy, "Our History: Danny Lambert."

55. Martin, "Robert Lee, Only Chief of Chiefs"; "2001 in Review: Remembering a Year We Can Never Forget," *Gambit Weekly*, December 25, 2001, http://www.bestof neworleans.com/gambit/2001-in-review/Content?oid=1239811; Geraldine Wyckoff, "BackTalk with Monk Boudreaux," Offbeat.com, February 1, 2007, http://www.offbeat .com/2007/02/01/monk-boudreaux/.

56. Salaam, *"He's the Prettiest."*

57. Kathryn VanSpanckeren, "The Mardi Gras Indian Song Cycle: A Heroic Tradition," *MELUS* 16, no. 4 (Winter 1989): 45–46; Geraldine Wyckoff, "Honoring Ike: Influential Mardi Gras Indian Isaac 'Ike' Edwards joins the Mardi Gras Indian Hall of Fame," *Gambit Weekly*, March 26, 2002, http://www.bestofneworleans.com/gambit/ honoring-ike/Content?oid=1240118.

58. Salaam, *"He's the Prettiest"*; Charles E. Siler, "A Commentary: African Cultural Retentions in Louisiana," Louisiana Folklife Festival booklet, 2001, Louisiana Folklife Program, http://www.louisianafolklife.org/LT/Articles_Essays/afri_cult_retent.html. On sewing, Siler concludes, "Louisiana's Mardi Gras Indians reflect the influence of the Plains Indians of North America in the generalized style of headpieces, also called crowns that are created. It is in the style of beadwork and suit construction where the African influence appears."

59. Lipsitz, *Time Passages*, 250–53; Siler, "A Commentary."

60. Salaam, *"He's the Prettiest."* For the lyrics of "Tu Way Packa Way," see Harold Courlander, *Negro Folk Music, U.S.A..* (New York: Columbia University Press, 1966), 173–74.

61. Richard Wright, "Blueprint for Negro Literature," 1937, in *The Black Aesthetic*, ed. Addison Gayle Jr. (Garden City, N.Y.: Doubleday, 1971).

62. Salaam, *"He's the Prettiest."* See John Miller Chernoff, "The Drums of Dagbon," in *Repercussions: A Celebration of African-American Music*, ed. Geoffrey Haydon and Dennis Marks (London: Century, 1985), 101.

63. Roach, "Carnival and the Law," 42.

64. Montana quoted in Salaam, *"He's the Prettiest."*

65. M. Smith, "Behind the Lines," 48.

66. Berry, Foose, and Jones, *Up from the Cradle of Jazz*, 237.

67. Ibid., 238.

68. Salaam, *"He's the Prettiest"*; Wyckoff, "Carnival Perspective."

69. Kennedy, "Our History: Danny Lambert"; Martin, "Robert Lee, Only Chief of Chiefs"; Berry, Foose, and Jones, *Up from the Cradle of Jazz*, 241.

70. Martin, "Robert Lee, Only Chief of Chiefs"; *Gambit Weekly*, December 25, 2001.

71. Donald Harrison, Cherice Harrison-Nelson, and Carlos Valladares, *Guardians of the Flame: A View from Within* (New Orleans: Junebug Productions, 2005), DVD.

72. Lipsitz, "Mardi Gras Indians," 114.

73. M. Smith, "Behind the Lines," 62; Salaam, *He's the Prettiest*," 20.

74. Berry, Foose, and Jones, *Up from the Cradle of Jazz*, 238; Wild Tchoupitoulas, "Indian Red," *The Wild Tchoupitoulas* (New York: Mango Records, 1976), CD 162–539 908–2.

75. Berry, Foose, and Jones, *Up from the Cradle of Jazz*, 238. For Harrison, see Harrison, Harrison-Nelson, and Valladares, *Guardians of the Flame*.

76. Jacobs and Kaslow, *Spiritual Churches of New Orleans*, 6–16, 94; Siler, "A Commentary."

77. Jacobs and Kaslow, *Spiritual Churches of New Orleans*, 3, 28–32; Zora Neale Hurston, "Hoodoo in America," *Journal of American Folklore* 44, no. 174 (1931): 319.

78. Jacobs and Kaslow, *Spiritual Churches of New Orleans*, 34–36; Judith Bettelheim, "Caribbean Espiritismo (Spiritist) Altars: The Indian and the Congo," *Art Bulletin* 87, no. 2 (June 2005).

79. Jacobs and Kaslow, *Spiritual Churches of New Orleans*, 38–40.

80. Ibid., 42–43.

81. Ibid., 149–57, 171.

82. Ibid., 98–99.

83. Ibid., 44.

84. Ibid., 44.

85. Ibid., 127.

86. Ibid., 136–47; Stephen C. Wehmeyer, "Indians at the Door: Power and Placement on New Orleans Spiritual Church Altars," *Western Folklore* (Winter 2007): 15–44.

87. Jacobs and Kaslow, *Spiritual Churches of New Orleans*, 42–43, 87.

88. Michael Tisserand, *The Kingdom of Zydeco* (New York: Avon Books, 1998), 55; Amédé Ardoin, "Les blues de la prison," *I'm Never Comin' Back*, Arhoolie Records, B004IM8K3U, 1995, compact disc.

89. Sartain, *Invisible Activists*, 57–81.

90. Fairclough, *Race and Democracy*, 17–18, 46–49.

91. Sartain, *Invisible Activists*, 59–60.

92. Ibid., 60–61.

93. Greta de Jong, "'With the Aid of God and the F.S.A.': The Louisiana Farmers' Union and the African American Freedom Struggle in the New Deal Era," *Journal of Social History* 34, no. 1 (2000): 105–6, 117.

94. Ibid., 113–21.

95. Jacobs and Kaslow, *Spiritual Churches of New Orleans*, 89. See also *Louisiana Weekly*, January 20, 1940.

Chapter 5. The Double V Generation and the Blues Agenda, 1940–1965

1. [The original title of this chapter was "The Rural Enclosure and the Double V Plan, 1940–1945." We have changed it to capture the broader geography and longer period covered here.—Eds.]

2. Adam Fairclough, *Race and Democracy: The Civil Rights Struggle in Louisiana, 1915–1972* (Athens: University of Georgia Press, 1999), 84–87.

3. Ibid., 87–92.

4. Ibid., 84–87.

5. Ibid.

6. Greta de Jong, "'With the Aid of God and the F.S.A.': The Louisiana Farmers' Union and the African American Freedom Struggle in the New Deal Era," *Journal of Social History* 34, no. 1 (Autumn 2000): 120–23.

7. Fairclough, *Race and Democracy*, 74–80. The soldiers were paroled in 1947.

8. Lee Sartain, *Invisible Activists: Women of the Louisiana NAACP and the Struggle for Civil Rights, 1915–1945* (Baton Rouge: Louisiana State University Press, 2007), 83–84.

9. Tony Scherman, *Backbeat: Earl Palmer's Story* (1999; repr., Cambridge, Mass.: Da Capo Press, 2000), 4.

10. Sartain, *Invisible Activists*, 84; Martha Mahoney, "Law and Racial Geography: Public Housing and the Economy in New Orleans," *Stanford Law Review* 42, no. 5 (May 1990): 1271.

11. Scherman, *Backbeat*, 2–6.

12. Christopher Silver and John V. Moeser, *The Separate City: Black Communities in the Urban South, 1940–1968* (Lexington: University Press of Kentucky, 1995), 21. See also Michael Jones-Correa, "The Origins and Diffusion of Racial Restrictive Covenants," *Political Science Quarterly* 115, no. 4 (Winter 2000–2001): 541–68. Jones-Correa argues that restrictive covenants were first put in use against the Chinese in California in 1892 before spreading to Louisiana by 1915.

13. Kenneth T. Jackson, *Crabgrass Frontier: The Suburbanization of the United States* (New York: Oxford University Press, 1985).

14. Mahoney, "Law and Racial Geography," 1257–59. See also Michael K. Brown, Martin Carnoy, Elliott Currie, Troy Duster, and David B. Oppenheimer, *Whitewashing Race: The Myth of a Color-Blind Society* (Berkeley: University of California Press, 2003), 77.

15. Daphne Spain, "Race Relations and Residential Segregation in New Orleans: Two Centuries of Paradox," *Annals of the American Academy of Political and Social Science* 441 (January 1979): 90; Arnold R. Hirsch, "Second Thoughts on the Second Ghetto," *Journal of Urban History* 29 (2003): 298, 304.

16. Mahoney, "Law and Racial Geography," 1269.

17. Ibid.

18. Ibid., 1253, 1271; Fairclough, *Race and Democracy*, 11, 84.

19. Fairclough, *Race and Democracy*, 79.

20. Greg Johnson, "Champion Jack Dupree," *BluesNotes*, May 1999, http://cascade blues.org/joomla/index.php/bluesnotes-online/from-the-pages-of-the-bluesnotes/ 207-champion-jack-dupree (page no longer available); Champion Jack Dupree, *Blues from the Gutter*, Atlantic, SD-8019, 1958, vinyl.

21. William Barlow, *Looking Up at Down: The Emergence of Blues Culture* (Philadelphia: Temple University Press, 1989), 282–83. See also Champion Jack Dupree quoted in *Living Blues* 32 (May–June 1977): 14.

22. Richard Wright, foreword to *Blues Fell This Morning: Meaning in the Blues*, by Paul Oliver (1960; repr., Cambridge: Cambridge University Press, 1990), xv; Larry Neal, "The Ethos of the Blues," in *Visions of a Liberated Future: Black Arts Movement*

Writings, ed. Larry Neal (New York: Thunder Mountain Press, 1989), 107–8; Richard Wright, "Blueprint for Negro Literature" (1937) in *The Black Aesthetic*, ed. Addison Gayle Jr. (Garden City, N.Y.: Doubleday, 1971), 333–34.

23. Paul Robeson, "The Negro Artist Looks Ahead," in *Paul Robeson Speaks: Writings, Speeches, Interviews, 1918–1974*, ed. Philip Sheldon Foner (Larchmont, N.Y.: Brunner/Mazel, 1978), 298–305.

24. Scherman, *Backbeat*, 47. See also Phillip McGuire, *Taps for a Jim Crow Army: Letters from Black Soldiers in World War II* (Santa Barbara, Calif.: ABC-Clio, 1983), 99, 196.

25. Fairclough, *Race and Democracy*, 74–78, 83.

26. Harlan and Logan Wilson, "Race, Cultural Groups, Social Differentiation: The Employment of Negro Women as Domestic Servants in New Orleans," *Social Forces* 22, no. 3 (March 1944): 319–23.

27. Keith Weldon Medley, "Ernest Wright: 'People's Champion,'" *Southern Exposure* 12 (1984): 53; Fairclough, *Race and Democracy*, 54–56.

28. Medley, "Ernest Wright," 54.

29. Fairclough, *Race and Democracy*, 80–81.

30. Ibid., 102–5, 123.

31. [We could not determine the source of this quotation.—Eds.]

32. Fairclough, *Race and Democracy*, 74–78.

33. Shakespeare quoted in Gore Vidal, "Guatemala '46: In the Lair of the Octopus," *Nation* 260, no. 2 (June 5, 1995): 794. Gore Vidal used this quote from *Macbeth* to describe the actions of United Fruit and the United States in the 1952 Guatemalan coup that replaced a democratically elected Arbenz government with a military dictatorship that committed numerous atrocities over the following decades.

34. Fairclough, *Race and Democracy*, 147–48.

35. Ronette King, "Shifting Landscape: African-Americans Have History of Entrepreneurship in New Orleans Dating Back to Before the Civil War," *Times-Picayune*, March 26, 2001; Mahoney, "Law and Racial Geography," 1271.

36. Brown et al., *Whitewashing Race*, 76–77.

37. Mahoney, "Law and Racial Geography," 1271; King, "Shifting Landscape"; Coleman Warner, "Jim Crow: In 1950, Lives Separated by Law," *Times-Picayune*, June 15, 1993.

38. Fairclough, *Race and Democracy*, 150–51; Mahoney, "Law and Racial Geography," 1260, 1278–79.

39. Mahoney, "Law and Racial Geography," 1260, 1278–79.

40. Fairclough, *Race and Democracy*, 150–51; Mahoney, "Law and Racial Geography," 1260, 1278–79.

41. Fairclough, *Race and Democracy*, 150–51.

42. Warner, "Jim Crow."

43. Ibid.

44. Spain, "Race Relations and Residential Segregation," 90.

45. Brown et al., *Whitewashing Race*, 78.

46. Arnold Hirsch, *Making the Second Ghetto: Race and Housing in Chicago 1940–1960* (Chicago: University of Chicago Press, 1998).

47. Mahoney, "Law and Racial Geography," 1272–74.

48. Ibid., 1272–76.

49. Fairclough, *Race and Democracy*, 113–19.

50. Ibid., 120–21.

51. Ibid., 120–22.

52. Scherman, *Backbeat*, 85, 95.

53. Fairclough, *Race and Democracy*, 168.

54. Warner, "Jim Crow."

55. The Temptations, "Psychedelic Shack," *Psychedelic Shack*, Gordy GS947, 1970, album.

56. Scherman, *Backbeat*, 63–75.

57. Scherman, *Backbeat*, 93; emphasis in original.

58. Jeff Hannusch, *I Hear you Knockin': The Sound of New Orleans Rhythm and Blues* (Ville Platte, La.: Swallow, 1985), 242, 274.

59. Grace Lichtenstein and Laura Dankner, *Musical Gumbo: The Music of New Orleans* (New York: W. W. Norton, 1993), 72–79; John Broven, *Rhythm and Blues in New Orleans* (Gretna, La.: Pelican, 1978), 105.

60. Scherman, *Backbeat*, 84–85; Broven, *Rhythm and Blues*, 19.

61. Scherman, *Backbeat*, 84; Broven, *Rhythm and Blues*, 13, 17.

62. Scherman, *Backbeat*, 69–76, 80–83; Lichtenstein and Dankner, *Musical Gumbo*, 90–91; Broven, *Rhythm and Blues*, 18–19.

63. Broven, *Rhythm and Blues*, 18, 27, 49.

64. Scherman, *Backbeat*, 84–85; Hannusch, *I Hear you Knockin'*, 240.

65. Scherman, *Backbeat*, 80–83; Broven, *Rhythm and Blues*, 43–45, 58.

66. Hannusch, *I Hear you Knockin'*, 242, 289.

67. The most common story says that some white men were angered when a white woman, the daughter of the house, lent her handkerchief to Amédé to wipe the sweat from his face. Canray Fontenot and Wade Fruge, in PBS's *American Patchwork* (see "The Death of Amedee Ardoin," https://www.youtube.com/watch?v=WyIbUD5_7Ko), explain that after Amédé left the place, he was run over by a Model A car that crushed his head and throat, damaging his vocal cords. He was found the next day, lying in a ditch. According to Canray, he "went plumb crazy" and "didn't know if he was hungry or not. Others had to feed him. He got weaker and weaker until he died." Others consider the story apocryphal. Other versions say that Amédé was poisoned, not beaten, possibly by a jealous fellow musician.

68. Nick Tosches argues that he was immediately blacklisted after he became one of the few Black performers to successfully sue a record company for unpaid royalties. After that, he more or less retired. Nick Tosches, *Unsung Heroes of Rock 'n' Roll: The Birth of Rock in the Wild Years before Elvis* (1984; repr., New York: Da Capo Press, 1999).

69. Roy Brown, "Hard Luck Blues," BMI 1950.

70. Broven, *Rhythm and Blues*, 22–24.

71. Hannusch, *I Hear you Knockin'*, 16–19.

72. Tad Jones, "Professor Longhair Interview," *Living Blues Magazine* 26 (March/April 1976).

73. Professor Longhair, "Professor Longhair Blues," *Atlantic* 906, November 1949.

74. Hannusch, *I Hear you Knockin'*, 19–23; Professor Longhair, "Mardi Gras in New Orleans," *Atlantic* 807, November 1949; Lichtenstein and Dankner, *Musical Gumbo*, 79–89; Broven, *Rhythm and Blues*, 6–7.

75. Smiley Lewis, "Gumbo Blues," *Gumbo Blues*, Imperial Records, 1952.

76. Smiley Lewis, "Dirty People," *Getting Funky: The Birth of New Orleans R&B: The Pioneers*, Proper Records, 2001 (orig.), compact disc.

77. Hannusch, *I Hear you Knockin'*, 10; Smiley Lewis, "Tee Nah Nah," *The Chronological Smiley Lewis 1947–1952*, Classics R&B, 2006 (orig.), compact disc; Broven, *Rhythm and Blues*, 34.

78. [Mahalia Jackson, "Move on Up a Little Higher," Apollo Records, 1947.—Eds.].

79. Broven, *Rhythm and Blues*, 37–39.

80. Hannusch, *I Hear you Knockin'*, 259–60.

81. Jeff Hannusch, "Back Talk with James 'Sugar Boy' Crawford," *OffBeat: Louisiana Music and Culture*, February 2002, http://www.offbeat.com/2002/02/01/james-sugar-boy-crawford/.

82. Sugar Boy and His Cane Cutters, "Jock-A-Mo," Checker 787, 1954, vinyl.

83. Ray Charles and David Ritz, *Brother Ray: Ray Charles' Own Story* (1978; repr., Cambridge, Mass.: Da Capo Press, 2004), 137.

84. Broven, *Rhythm and Blues*, 54.

85. Hannusch, *I Hear you Knockin'*, 242, 289.

86. Broven, *Rhythm and Blues*, 33.

87. Ibid.

88. [Linton Kwesi Johnson, "Bass Culture," *Bass Culture*, Island Records, 1980.—Eds.]

89. Fairclough, *Race and Democracy*, 123–30.

90. Ibid., 123–32.

91. Warner, "Jim Crow"; Fairclough, *Race and Democracy*, 108–9.

92. Fairclough, *Race and Democracy*, 156.

93. Warner, "Jim Crow"; Fairclough, *Race and Democracy*, 106, 152–56.

94. Scherman, *Backbeat*, 94.

95. "The Baton Rouge Bus Boycott of 1953: A Recaptured Past," Louisiana State University Library, http://www.lib.lsu.edu/sites/all/files/sc/exhibits/e-exhibits/boycott/index.html.

96. Ibid. See also Debbie Elliott, "The First Civil Rights Bus Boycott 50 Years Ago, Baton Rouge Jim Crow Protest Made History," *All Things Considered*, NPR, June 19, 2003; John Toorean, *Signpost to Freedom: The 1953 Baton Rouge Bus Boycott*, Louisiana Public Broadcasting, September 15, 2009, http://beta.lpb.org/index.php?/site/programs/signpost_to_freedom_the_1953_baton_rouge_bus_boycott/signpost_to_freedom_the_1953_baton_rouge_bus_boycott.

97. Fairclough, *Race and Democracy*, 99–103.

98. Warner, "Jim Crow"; Fairclough, *Race and Democracy*, 108.

99. Fairclough, *Race and Democracy*, 108–9.

100. Ibid., 137–40. See also Joe M. Richardson, "Edgar B. Stern: A White New Orleans Philanthropist Helps Build a Black University," *Journal of Negro History* 82, no. 3 (Summer 1997): 328–42.

101. Gerald Horne, *Black and Red: W. E. B. Du Bois and the Afro-American Response to the Cold War 1944–1963* (Albany, N.Y.: SUNY Press, 1986), 2.

102. Fairclough, *Race and Democracy*, 140–47.

103. Fairclough *Race and Democracy*, 135–36.

104. Justin D. Poche, *Religion, Race and Rights in Catholic Louisiana, 1938–1970* (Ann Arbor, Mich.: ProQuest, 2007), 100–101.

105. Fairclough, *Race and Democracy*, 154–55; 167.

Chapter 6. The Second Reconstruction, 1965–1977

1. [Woods lists the conservative intellectuals Nicholas Lehmann and Charles Murray as architects of the demonology he discusses, but we could not be sure of the exact sources.—Eds.]

2. Associated Press, "Hurricane Pounds at New Orleans; 185,000 Flee in Southern Louisiana," *New York Times*, September 10, 1965; Constance Adler, "Neither Wind nor Rain," *Gambit Weekly*, May 5, 2001; Associated Press, "Hurricane Flood Raises Toll to 50," *New York Times*, September 12, 1965.

3. "Lower Ninth Ward Neighborhood Snapshot," Greater New Orleans Community Data Center, http://www.gnocdc.org/orleans/8/22/snapshot.html.

4. Associated Press, "Hurricane Flood Raises Toll to 50"; Associated Press, "Hurricane Pounds at New Orleans"; Richard Eder, "Johnson Directs Relief," *New York Times*, September 13, 1965; "Profiteering Reported in New Orleans; Storm Refugees Growing Restive," *New York Times*, September 13, 1965.

5. Todd A. Shallat, "Holding Louisiana," *Technology and Culture* 47, no. 1 (January 2006): 105; Roy Reed, "Louisiana Counts Rising Death Toll," *New York Times*, September 14, 1965; "$1 Billion Damage Seen in Louisiana," *New York Times*, September 15, 1965; "New Orleans: Up from the Deluge," *Time*, September 24, 1965.

6. Eder, "Johnson Directs Relief."

7. *New York Times*, "Profiteering Reported in New Orleans."

8. Eder, "Johnson Directs Relief"; *New York Times,*, "Profiteering Reported in New Orleans."

9. "Pumping Started by New Orleans," *New York Times*, September 16, 1965; "New Orleans Mayor Wins Second Term," *New York Times*, November 7, 1965; Craig E. Colten, "The Rusting of the Chemical Corridor," *Technology and Culture* 47, no. 1 (January 2006): 95–101.

10. Shallat, "Holding Louisiana," 105–6.

11. "Environmental Justice Professor Robert Bullard on How Race Affected the Federal Government's Response to Katrina," interview by Amy Goodman, *Democracy Now: The War and Peace Report*, broadcast October 24, 2005, http://www.democracynow .org/2005/10/24/environmental_justice_professor_robert_bullard_on.

12. Quoted in Frank Etheridge, "Last of the Ninth," *Gambit Weekly*, November 11, 2005 (from Salon.com, September 13, 2005).

13. Goodman, "Environmental Justice Professor Robert Bullard."

14. Shallat, "Holding Louisiana," 107.

15. Reverend Dr. Martin Luther King, "The Other America," speech, Stanford University, April 14, 1967, in Aurora Forum at Stanford University, "Martin Luther King and Economic Justice: The Fortieth Anniversary Commemoration of Dr. King's 'The Other America' Speech at Stanford," April 15, 2007, transcript, http://auroraforum .stanford.edu/files/transcripts/Aurora_Forum_Transcript_Martin_Luther_King_The _Other_America_Speech_at_Stanford_04.15.07.pdf.

16. Adam Fairclough, *Race and Democracy: The Civil Rights Struggle in Louisiana, 1915–1972* (Athens: University of Georgia Press, 1999), 374–76.

17. Ibid., 374–76.

18. Lance Hill, *The Deacons for Defense: Armed Resistance and the Civil Rights Movement* (Chapel Hill: University of North Carolina Press, 2004), 252.

19. Ibid., 252–53.

20. Fairclough, *Race and Democracy*, 379–80, 413.

21. Ibid., 411.

22. Quoted in ibid., 429–33.

23. Quoted in ibid., 459.

24. Ibid.

25. Charles M. Payne, "'The Whole United States Is Southern!': *Brown v. Board* and the Mystification of Race," *Journal of American History* 91, no. 1 (June 2004): 90.

26. Fairclough, *Race and Democracy*, 459–60. The tragic deaths of Denver Smith and Leonard Brown are remembered daily on campus by the central place given the Smith-Brown Memorial Student Union.

27. Justin D. Poche, *Religion, Race and Rights in Catholic Louisiana 1938–1970* (Ann Arbor, Mich.: ProQuest, 2007), 320.

28. Ibid., 321. Brown quoted in *Louisiana Weekly*, May 24, 1968.

29. Clyde Woods, *Development Arrested: The Blues and Plantation Power in the Mississippi Delta* (New York: Verso, 1998).

30. Thomas J. Sugrue, "Revisiting the Second Ghetto," *Journal of Urban History* 29, no. 3 (March 2003): 281–90.

31. The Black Panther Party, "Ten Point Platform and Program," October 1966, *It's About Time*, http://www.itsabouttimebpp.com/home/bpp_program_platform.html.

32. Ibid; "Hoover and the F.B.I.," *A Huey P. Newton Story*, PBS, http://www.pbs.org/hueypnewton/people/people_hoover.html.

33. Black Panther Party Legacy and Alumni, "Programs of Survival," *It's About Time*, http://www.itsabouttimebpp.com/Survival_Programs/survival_programs.html.

34. Fairclough, *Race and Democracy*, 424–25.

35. Ibid.; PBS, "Hoover and the F.B.I."

36. Kent B. Germany, *New Orleans after the Promises: Poverty, Citizenship, and the Search for the Great Society* (Athens: University of Georgia Press, 2007), 274–75.

37. "Why Twenty-Four Panthers Are Political Prisoners in Louisiana," The Black Panther: Intercommunal News Service, June 12, 1971, *It's About Time*, http://www.itsabouttimebpp.com/chapter_history/pdf/new_orleans/neworleans24.pdf.

38. Martha Mahoney, "Law and Racial Geography: Public Housing and the Economy in New Orleans," *Stanford Law Review* 42, no. 5 (May 1990): 1277.

39. Germany, *New Orleans after the Promises*, 276.

40. Warren Brown, "Residents Defend Panthers," *It's About Time*, September 15, 1970, http://www.itsabouttimebpp.com/Chapter_History/pdf/New_Orleans/New_Orleans_Panther_office_raid.pdf.

41. Germany, *New Orleans after the Promises*, 277; Black Panther: Intercommunal News Service, "Why Twenty-Four Panthers Are Political Prisoners."

42. Orissa Arend, *Showdown in Desire: People, Panthers, Piety, and Police; The Story of the Black Panthers in New Orleans, 1970* (New Orleans: Self-published, 2003), 36.

43. Plater Robinson, "Chronology of the Modern Civil Rights Movement in New Orleans, 1961–Present," in *A House Divided: A Study Guide on the History of Civil Rights in Louisiana*, Southern Institute for Education and Research, http://www.southerninstitute .info/civil_rights_education/divided12.html.

44. Arnold R. Hirsch, "Simply a Matter of Black and White: The Transformation of Race and Politics in Twentieth-Century New Orleans," in *Creole New Orleans: Race and Americanization*, ed. Arnold R. Hirsch and Joseph Logsdon (Baton Rouge: Louisiana State University Press, 1992), 277–81, 291–94.

45. Ronette King, "Shifting Landscape: African-Americans Have a History of Entrepreneurship in New Orleans Dating Back to Before the Civil War," *Times-Picayune*, March 26, 2001.

46. Fairclough, *Race and Democracy*, 428.

47. Orissa Arend, "Trio Ignited Controlled Revolution in the '70's," *Louisiana Weekly*, May 26, 2003.

48. Pierce F. Lewis, *New Orleans: The Making of an Urban Landscape* (Santa Fe, N.M.: Center for American Places, 2003), 96.

49. Ibid., 89–91.

50. King, "Shifting Landscape."

51. Ibid.

52. Lewis, *New Orleans*, 92–99.

53. Ibid., 144–46.

54. Ibid., 78–80.

55. "St. Bernard Parish: History," St. Bernard Parish website, http://www.saint bernardparish.net/about%20us.html. On the Chalmette aluminum refinery, see George J. Binczewski, "The Energy Crisis and the Aluminum Industry: Can We Learn from History?," *JOM: The Journal of the Minerals, Metals & Materials Society* (February 2002), http://www.tms.org/pubs/journals/JOM/0202/Binczewski-0202.html. On bauxite and Jamaica, see "Battling over Bauxite," *Time*, July 8, 1974; and "Seaga under Siege," *Multinational Monitor* 6, no. 6 (May 31, 1985). For a discussion of the thousands of Louisiana workers displaced by Hurricane Katrina who were living in trailer parks set up by employers such as Domino Sugar, see Anne Hull, "A Company Town on the Mississippi," *Washington Post*, January 22, 2006.

56. For a general discussion, see Kenneth T. Jackson, *Crabgrass Frontier: The Suburbanization of the United States* (New York: Oxford University Press, 1987); and Douglas Massey and Nancy Denton, *American Apartheid: Segregation and the Making of the Underclass* (Cambridge, Mass.: Harvard University Press, 1998).

57. "The World's Longest Bridge," Louisiana's Northshore website, http://www .louisiananorthshore.com/cms/d/fun_facts.php.

58. Fairclough, *Race and Democracy*, 447–48.

59. Ibid., 457.

60. Ibid., 435, 442–44.

61. Mark T. Carleton, "The Louisiana Constitution of 1974," in *Readings in Louisiana Politics*, 2nd ed., ed. Mark T. Carleton, Perry H. Howard, and Joseph B. Barker (Baton Rouge: Claitor's Publishing Division, 1988), 487–512.

62. Errol Laborde, "Louisiana Politics," *PS* 18, no. 3 (Summer 1985): 599–600.

63. Fairclough, *Race and Democracy*, 417–22.

64. Mahoney, "Law and Racial Geography," 1253.

65. King, "Shifting Landscape."

66. Lewis, *New Orleans*, 71–76.

67. Matthew Brown, "MR-GO Goes from Hero to Villain: Some Want Channel to Stay Open," *Times-Picayune*, January 8, 2006.

68. Ibid.

69. "F. Edward Hebert, Oral History Interview I," by Dorothy Pierce McSweeny, transcript, July 15, 1969, Lyndon Baines Johnson Library, Austin, Texas, http://www.lbjlib.utexas.edu/johnson/archives.hom/oralhistory.hom/Hebert/Hebert.pdf.

70. Thomas A. Becnel, *Senator Allen Ellender of Louisiana: A Biography* (Baton Rouge: Louisiana State University Press, 1995), 252.

71. Laborde, "Louisiana Politics," 598.

72. Hirsch, "Simply a Matter of Black and White," 289.

73. Fairclough, *Race and Democracy*, 391.

74. Gill, *Lords of Misrule*, 213; Rodgers, *Righteous Lives*, 59–60; Hirsch, "Simply a Matter of Black and White," 278–80.

75. Hirsch, "Simply a Matter of Black and White," 280; James Gill, *Lords of Misrule: Mardi Gras and the Politics of Race in New Orleans* (Jackson: University Press of Mississippi, 1997), 213; Kim Lacy Rodgers, *Righteous Lives: Narratives of the New Orleans Civil Rights Movement* (New York: New York University Press, 1993), 59–60.

76. Robert K. Whelan, Alma H. Young, and Mickey Lauria, "Urban Regimes and Racial Politics in New Orleans," *Journal of Urban Affairs* 16, no. 1 (March 1994): 5; Hirsch, "Simply a Matter of Black and White," 297–98.

77. Fairclough, *Race and Democracy*, 388–94; Perry H. Howard and T. Wayne Parent, "An Enduring Ecological Coalition in Louisiana: From Huey Long to Edwin Edwards and Beyond," in Carleton, Howard, and Parker, *Readings in Louisiana Politics*, 560–61.

78. Fairclough, *Race and Democracy*, 388–94, 464; Howard and Parent, "Enduring Ecological Coalition in Louisiana," 560–61.

79. Laborde, "Louisiana Politics," 593–600.

80. Fairclough, *Race and Democracy*, 464.

81. Joseph G. Dawson III, ed., *The Louisiana Governors: From Iberville to Edwards* (Baton Rouge: Louisiana State University Press, 1990), 271–76.

82. Quoted in Germany, *New Orleans after the Promises*, 43.

Chapter 7. The Disaster before the Disaster

1. [Both epigraphs come from interviews conducted by Clyde Woods. We could not ascertain the names of the activists.—Eds.]

2. Robert K. Whelan, Alma H. Young, and Mickey Lauria, "Urban Regimes and Racial Politics in New Orleans," *Journal of Urban Affairs* 16, no. 1 (March 1994): 5; Arnold R. Hirsch, "Simply a Matter of Black and White: The Transformation of Race and Politics in Twentieth Century New Orleans," in *Creole New Orleans: Race and Americanization*, ed. Arnold R. Hirsch and Joseph Logsdon (Baton Rouge: Louisiana State University Press, 1992), 291–93.

3. Hirsch, "Simply a Matter of Black and White," 293–94, 310.

4. Ibid., 291–94, 313.

5. Whelan, Young, and Lauria, "Urban Regimes and Racial Politics," 6.

6. Ibid. Federal and state funds were also used toward expanding manufacturing in the Almonaster-Michoud Industrial District.

7. Joseph G. Dawson III, *The Louisiana Governors: From Iberville to Edwards* (Baton Rouge: Louisiana State University Press, 1990), 279.

8. "Guy Banister, Leander Perez and Jim Garrison," Jerry P. Shinley Archive, http://www.jfk-online.com/jpsgblpjg.html; Perry H. Howard and T. Wayne Parent, "An Enduring Ecological Coalition in Louisiana: From Huey Long to Edwin Edwards and Beyond," in *Readings in Louisiana Politics*, 2nd ed., ed. Mark T. Carleton, Perry H. Howard and Joseph B. Parker (Baton Rouge: Claitor's Publishing Division, 1988), 561–62; Dawson, *Louisiana Governors*, 278; Glen Jeansonne, *Leander Perez: Boss of the Delta*, 2nd ed. (Baton Rouge: Louisiana State University Press, 1995), 318; "Gerryduck in Louisiana" (editorial), *New York Times*, October 1, 1983, 26.

9. Dawson, *Louisiana Governors*, 278–79; Clyde Woods, "Sittin' on Top of the World: The Challenges of Blues and Hip Hop Geography," in *Black Geographies and the Politics of Place*, ed. Katherine McKittrick and Clyde Woods (Cambridge, Mass.: South End Press, 2007), 46–81. See also David Harvey, *A Brief History of Neoliberalism* (New York: Oxford University Press, 2005).

10. Whelan, Young, and Lauria, "Urban Regimes and Racial Politics," 7.

11. Frances Frank Marcus, "New Orleans Weighs Anti-bias Law on Carnival," *New York Times*, December 7, 1991; Larry Rohter, "Bias Law Casts Pall over New Orleans Mardi Gras," *New York Times*, February 2, 1992.

12. [David Duke, a former grand wizard of the Ku Klux Klan, became a professional right-wing politician. In 1991 he ran for governor of Louisiana. He lost to Edwin Edwards but received 55 percent of the white vote.—Eds.]

13. Rohter, "Bias Law Casts Pall"; Marcus, "New Orleans Weighs Anti-bias Law"; Frances Frank Marcus, "New Orleans Outlaws Bias by Mardi Gras Parade Clubs," *New York Times*, December 21, 1991.

14. Frances Frank Marcus, "New Orleans Journal: A Sulky Undercurrent at Mardi Gras," *New York Times*, February 14, 1993.

15. Rohter, "Bias Law Casts Pall"; Marcus, "New Orleans Weighs Anti-bias Law."

16. Frances Frank Marcus, "Law Is Softened to Quell Furor over Mardi Gras," *New York Times*, February 8, 1992.

17. Frances Frank Marcus, "Council Eases Anti-bias Law on Mardi Gras," *New York Times*, May 10, 1992.

18. Marcus, "New Orleans Journal."

19. Susan Finch, "Men's Clubs Win in Ruling," *Times-Picayune*, March 11, 1994.

20. Adam Fairclough, *Race and Democracy: The Civil Rights Struggle in Louisiana, 1915–1972* (Athens: University of Georgia Press, 1999), 284–85.

21. Fairclough, *Race and Democracy*, 1–2; James R. Bobo, *The New Orleans Economy: Pro Bono Publico?*, Research Study No. 19 (New Orleans: Division of Business and Economic Research, College of Business Administration, University of New Orleans, 1975); J. Mark Souther, "Into the Big League: Conventions, Football, and the Color Line

in New Orleans," *Journal of Urban History* 29, no. 6 (September 2003); Joseph Luders, "The Economics of Movement Success: Business Responses to Civil Rights Mobilization," *American Journal of Sociology* 111, no. 4 (January 2006).

22. Social movement leader social service provider, interview by Clyde Woods, 2007.

23. Terry Lynn Karl, "Oil-Led Development: Social, Political and Economic Consequences" (working paper, Center for Democracy Development and the Rule of Law, Freeman Spogli Institute for International Studies, Stanford University, January 2007), 1–2.

24. Pierce F. Lewis, *New Orleans: The Making of an Urban Landscape* (Santa Fe, N.M.: Center for American Places, 2003), 121–22.

25. Ibid., 107–8.

26. Karl, "Oil-Led Development," 3.

27. Josh Harkinson, "5 Ways the Chamber Shills for BP," *Mother Jones*, June 30, 2010.

28. Craig E. Colten, "The Rusting of the Chemical Corridor," *Technology and Culture* 47, no. 1 (January 2006): 95–96.

29. Karl, "Oil-Led Development," 2, 25.

30. [Woods is referring to the Deepwater Horizon oil spill.—Eds.]

31. Karl, "Oil-Led Development," 26. See also Steve Lerner, *Diamond: A Struggle for Environmental Justice in Louisiana's Chemical Corridor* (Cambridge, Mass.: MIT Press, 2006).

32. Lerner, *Diamond*; National Council of Churches, "African American Church Leaders Pledge Their Support to the Struggle against Environmental Racism," news release, National Council of Churches, March 1998, http://www.ncccusa.org/news/news21.html; Juanita Marie Holland, "Touring Cancer Alley," Africana.com, June 21, 2001, http://www.hartford-hwp.com/archives/45/295.html.

33. Karl, "Oil-Led Development," 21.

34. Karl, "Oil-Led Development," 21–23. In her study of modern oil-exporting countries, Karl argues that the degree of elite stability in oil regimes is unmatched, even by plantation-dominated states and regions. "Regimes have even used their largess to prevent the formation of social groups independent from the state that might someday prove to be political challengers or to rid themselves of already existing challengers. . . . Thus oil wealth is robustly associated with more durable regimes, and oil dependence is a positive predictor of greater regime durability. Even though authoritarian regimes in general are more likely to fall during economic crises, oil based authoritarian regimes have some cushion from this general rule."

35. Lewis, *New Orleans*, 122; Roberto Suro, "Economic Pulse: The Oil States—A Special Report: 3 States, Once Fat on Oil, Try to Break with Past," *New York Times*, January 14, 1990.

36. Fairclough, *Race and Democracy*, 472. See also Suro, "Economic Pulse"; Frances Frank Marcus, "Focus: New Orleans, Toe-to-Toe Riverside Space Race," *New York Times*, June 8, 1986.

37. Lyle Kenneth Perkins, "Failing the Race: A Historical Assessment of New Orleans Mayor Sidney Barthelemy, 1986–1994" (master's thesis, Louisiana State University, 2005), 17. See also C. C. Campbell, "Hard Work and Miracles on Mayor Barthelemy's Agenda," *Louisiana Weekly*, May 10, 1986.

38. Lewis, *New Orleans*, 123.

39. Suro, "Economic Pulse."

40. Ibid.

41. Tyler Bridges, "Revitalized and Shifted Right, Ex-governor Says He Wants to Listen, Lead," *Times-Picayune*, September 20, 1995; John Pope, "Carlos Marcello (1910–1993) Mafia Chief Dies in Sleep," *Times-Picayune*, March 3, 1993; Dawson, *Louisiana Governors*, 36; "Rice Growing in Louisiana: A New Source of Wealth Developed since the War," *New York Times*, August 29, 1893.

42. Burk Foster, "Louisiana Corrections in the 1980s: In Search of Alternatives," July 1988, www.burkfoster.com/1980sAlternatives.doc (site no longer available).

43. Bridges, "Revitalized and Shifted Right"; Pope, "Carlos Marcello"; Thomas L. Jones, "Carlos Marcello: Big Daddy in the Big Easy," *TruTV: Crime Library*, http://www.trutv.com/library/crime/gangsters_outlaws/family_epics/marcello/16.html (page no longer available); *New York Times*, "Rice Growing in Louisiana."

44. [Quoted in Clyde Woods, "Do You Know What It Means to Miss New Orleans?: Katrina, Trap Economics, and the Rebirth of the Blues," in *American Studies: An Anthology*, ed. J. Radway, K. Gaines, B. Shank and P. von Eschen (Malden, Mass.: Wiley-Blackwell, 2009), 510.—Eds.]

45. People for the American Way and the National Association for the Advancement of Colored People, *The Long Shadow of Jim Crow: Voter Intimidation and Suppression in America Today* (Washington, D.C.: People for the American Way, 2004), 12, http://www.pfaw.org/sites/default/files/thelongshadowofjimcrow.pdf; Fairclough, *Race and Democracy*, 472.

46. Chandler Davidson, Tanya Dunlap, Gale Kenny, and Benjamin Wise, *Republican Ballot Security Programs: Vote Protection or Minority Vote Suppression—or Both?* (Washington, D.C.: Center for Voting Rights and Protection, September 2004), 60, www.votelaw.com/blog/blogdocs/GOP_Ballot_Security_Programs.pdf.

47. Ibid., 60–61.

48. Ibid., 61.

49. "Louisiana Forced to Change Spendthrift Tune," *New York Times*, January 24, 1983.

50. Ibid.

51. Fairclough, *Race and Democracy*, 473.

52. Perkins, "Failing the Race," 28.

53. Ibid., 18.

54. Ibid., 19–21.

55. Whelan, Young, and Lauria, "Urban Regimes and Racial Politics," 8–9.

56. Perkins, "Failing the Race," 29–30.

57. Joe C. Ireland, "Poem Found Scratched into a Cell Wall at Orleans Parish Prison," in *From a Bend in the River: 100 New Orleans Poets*, ed. Kalamu ya Salaam (New Orleans: Runagate Press, 1998), 100.

58. "New Orleans: Recent History," in *Shielded from Justice: Police Brutality and Accountability in the United States*, Human Rights Watch, June 1998, http://www.hrw.org/reports98/police/usp093.htm.

59. Reginald Stuart, "Shootings by Police Roil New Orleans," *New York Times*, April 21, 1981.

60. Perkins, "Failing the Race," 38.

61. Human Rights Watch, "New Orleans: Recent History."

62. Ibid.; Paul Keegan, "The Thinnest Blue Line," *New York Times Magazine*, March 31, 1996, 32–35; Perkins, "Failing the Race," 39; Karl, "Oil-Led Development," 22–23.

63. Perkins, "Failing the Race," 38, 85.

64. Foster, "Louisiana Corrections in the 1980s."

65. Human Rights Watch, "New Orleans: Recent History."

66. Ibid. Comments of U.S. attorney for the Eastern District of Louisiana on National Public Radio program, February 4, 1998. When the attorney reviewed IAD's files covering 1987 to March 1990, she found that approximately 8 percent of the officers were the subject of 38 percent of all complaints.

67. Human Rights Watch, "New Orleans: Recent History."

68. Human Rights Watch, "Incarcerated America: Human Rights Watch Backgrounder," April 2003, www.hrw.org/backgrounder/usa/incarceration; "Sentencing of Youth to Life Without Parole," in Human Rights Watch, *The Rest of Their Lives: Life without Parole for Child Offenders in the United States*, 2005, hrw.org/reports/2005/us1005/5.htm#_Toc114638398.

69. Michael A. Mohammed, "Will Natural Gas Prices Turn off Louisiana's Chemical Industry?" *Times-Picayune*, August 1, 2004; Todd Billiot, "Report: State Has Highest Incarceration Rate per Capita," *Lafayette Daily Advertiser*, August 5, 2003.

70. Fairclough, *Race and Democracy*, 471. See Coramae Richey Mann, *Unequal Justice: A Question of Color* (Bloomington: University of Indiana Press, 1993).

71. William Oakland, Peter Dangerfield, and J. Kelley Terry, *Chronic Poverty in New Orleans: Pro Bono Publico Revisited* (New Orleans: Total Community Action, 2006); Total Community Action, *Poverty Reduction Proposal* (New Orleans: Total Community Action, 2006), 17–19.

72. Ed Anderson, "Alexander's Prayer Jabs Gov. Foster," *Times-Picayune*, March 25, 1996.

73. Oakland, Dangerfield, and Terry, "Chronic Poverty in New Orleans," 16–17, 20–21; Fairclough, *Race & Democracy*.

74. Emma Dixon, "New Orleans' Racial Divide: An Unnatural Disaster," CommonDreams.org, November 16, 2005, http://www.commondreams.org/views05/1116-34.htm (page no longer available).

75. Harry Holzer and Robert I. Lerman, *Employment Issues and Challenges in Post-Katrina New Orleans* (Washington D.C.: Urban Institute, February 10, 2006), http://www.urban.org/url.cfm?ID=900921.

76. Harry J. Holzer, *Back to Work in New Orleans* (Washington, D.C.: Metropolitan Policy Program, Brookings Institution, October 2005), http://www.brookings.edu/metro/pubs/200510_backtowork.pdf.

77. Carol DeVita, Kelvin Pollard, and Robert McIntire, *Kids Count Data Book 1995: State Profiles of Child Well-Being* (Baltimore: Annie E. Casey Foundation, 1995), 69, 81, http://www.aecf.org/KnowledgeCenter/Publications.aspx?pubguid=%7BE69859E4-A0E1-4F6C-9E00-B034B24E5351%7D (page no longer available); Fairclough, *Race and Democracy*, 469.

78. Sheila R. Zedlewski, "Building a Better Safety Net for the *New* New Orleans," in *After Katrina: Rebuilding Opportunity and Equity into the New New Orleans*, ed. Margery Austin Turner and Sheila R. Zedlewski (Washington, D.C.: Urban Institute, 2006), 66–67, http://www.urban.org/uploadedpdf/311406_after_katrina.pdf.

79. Leslie Williams, "Americans Don't Grasp the Extent of Poverty," *Times-Picayune*, January 13, 2004.

80. Governor of Louisiana, *Louisiana Solutions to Poverty: Engaging Ideas, Empowering People, Enhancing Lives, Governor's Summit on Solutions to Poverty Summary Report and the First Annual Solutions to Poverty Initiative Roadmap and Action Plan* (Baton Rouge: State of Louisiana, May 2005), http://www.ifedgbr.com/files/poverty/governorsummit.pdf; William P. O'Hare and Megan Reynolds, *Kids Count Date Book 2003: State Profiles of Child Well-Being* (Baltimore: Annie E. Casey Foundation, 2003); Arloc Sherman and Isaac Shapiro, *Essential Facts about the Victims of Hurricane Katrina*, (Washington, D.C.: Center on Budget and Policy Priorities, September 19, 2005), http://www.cbpp.org/cms/?fa=view&id=658.

81. Zedlewski, "Building a Better Safety Net," 64.

82. O'Hare and Reynolds, *Kids Count Data Book 2003*.

83. Zedlewski, "Building a Better Safety Net," 67.

84. Mathematica Policy Research, Inc., and Feeding America (formerly America's Second Harvest), *Hunger in America 2006: Local Report Prepared for the Second Harvest Food Bank of Greater New Orleans and Acadiana*, February 1, 2006, 2–4; "LFBA Seeking State Help to Stave Off Looming Hunger Crisis," *Louisiana Weekly*, April 23, 2007.

85. Zedlewski, "Building a Better Safety Net," 67.

86. Unity for the Homeless, *2004 Annual Report*, 20, http://unitygno.org/newsUploads/37_1.pdf.

87. Katy Reckdahl, "Walking While Homeless," *Gambit Weekly*, September 24, 2002.

88. Governor of Louisiana, *Louisiana Solutions to Poverty*, 9.

89. Center for Disease Control and Prevention and U.S. Department of Health and Human Services, "Table 4. Persons Living with HIV/AIDS, by Ryan White CARE Act Eligible Metropolitan Area of Residence, as of December 2004—Areas with Confidential Name-Based HIV Infection Reporting," *HIV/AIDS Surveillance Supplemental Report*, 12, no. 3, http://www.cdc.gov/hiv/surveillance/resources/reports/2006supp_vol12no3/.

90. Louisiana Office of Public Health, "Infectious Disease Epidemiology Section," Annual Report 2004, http://dhh.louisiana.gov/.

91. Barbour Griffith & Rogers, "Client List," http://www.bgrdc.com/clients.html (page no longer available); Kevin Bogardus, "K Street Lobbyists Carry Water for OPEC," *Center for Public Integrity*, September 22, 2004, http://www.publicintegrity.org/2004/09/22/5955/k-street-lobbyists-carry-water-opec; The Delta Pine and Land Company, "About US," http://www.deltapine.com/Pages/home.aspx (page no longer available).

92. Craig Flournoy, "Housing Plans Go Against Neighborhood's Wishes: HUD Says Site Remains Viable for Rebuilding," *Dallas Morning News*, October 2, 2000; J. Timmons Roberts and Melissa M. Toffolon-Weiss, *Chronicles from the Environmental Justice Frontline* (Cambridge: Cambridge University Press, 2001); Alicia Lyttle, "Agriculture Street Landfill: Environmental Justice Case Study," University of Michigan, December 2000, http://www.umich.edu/~snre492/Jones/agstreet.htm.

93. Flournoy, "Housing Plans"; Melissa M. Toffolon-Weiss and J. Timmons Roberts, "Toxic Torts, Public Interest Law, and Environmental Justice: Evidence from Louisiana," *Law & Policy* 26, no. 2 (April 2004): 259–87.

94. Flournoy, "Housing Plans."

95. Ibid.

96. Holland, "Touring Cancer Alley."

97. National Council of Churches, "African American Church Leaders Pledge Their Support."

98. Holland, "Touring Cancer Alley"; Lerner, *Diamond*.

99. Ibid.

100. Ibid.

101. Ibid.

102. Paul Hill and Jane Hannaway, *The Future of Public Education in New Orleans* (Washington, D.C.: Urban Institute, January 2006), http://urban.org/uploadedpdf/900913_public_education.pdf.

103. Mavis Staples, "Down in Mississippi" (orig. by J. B. Lenoir), *We'll Never Turn Back*, Anti, ASIN:B000MR8SZU, 2007, compact disc.

104. Barbour Griffith & Rogers, "Client List"; Bogardus, "K Street Lobbyists Carry Water"; Delta Pine and Land Company, "About US."

105. "Democrats Hope to Trump Republicans in Texas; What Will Help Democrats Win Back White House?," transcript, *Judy Woodruff's Inside Politics*, CNN, May 13, 2003, http://transcripts.cnn.com/TRANSCRIPTS/0305/13/ip.00.html; Eric Stringfellow, "Barbour Links Himself to CCC by Not Acting," *Jackson Clarion-Ledger*, October 21, 2003; PBS, "NOW with Bill Moyers," archive transcript, July 16, 2004, http://www.pbs.org/now/transcript/transcript329_full.html.

106. PBS, "NOW with Bill Moyers." See also Governor Haley Barbour, "Leaving No PLAD Behind," *Jackson Free Press*, July 2, 2004.

107. Erik Eckholm, "In Turnabout, Infant Deaths Climb in the South," *New York Times*, April 22, 2007.

108. Ibid.

109. Ibid.

110. Bob Herbert, "Gross Neglect," *New York Times*, March 13, 2006.

111. PBS, "NOW with Bill Moyers."

Chapter 8. The New Urban Crisis

1. The Legendary K.O., "George Bush Doesn't Care about Black People," 2005, http://www.rappersiknow.com/2005/09/06/day-24-myone-hands-up-featuring-kay-produced-by-symbolyc-one-bw-the-legendary-ko-george-bush-doesnt-care-about-black-people-produced-by-kanye-west/.

2. Alexis de Tocqueville, *Democracy in America*, ed. J. P. Mayer (Garden City, N.Y.: Doubleday, 1975), 358.

3. Amin Sharif, "Big Easy Blues," *Chicken Bones: A Journal*, September 8, 2005, http://www.nathanielturner.com/bigeasybluesaminsharif.htm.

4. Claire Carew, "It Ain't about Race," *Chicken Bones: A Journal*, http://www.nathanielturner.com/itaintaboutrace.htm.

5. Household (nongroup quarters) population estimates by parish, 2000–2006, Census Population Estimates 2000–2006 for New Orleans Metropolitan Statistical Area, U.S. Census Bureau, Population Division; county total population and estimated components of population change, April 1, 2000–July 1, 2006, from a compilation by

the Greater New Orleans Community Data Center (now the Data Center), http://www
.gnocdc.org. 2000 figures are from the U.S. Census Bureau, Census 2000 Full-Count
Characteristics (COSF1); January 2006 figures are from the U.S. Census Bureau, Special
Population Estimates for Impacted Countries in the Gulf Coast Area. See also Division
of Business and Economic Research, University of New Orleans, *Metropolitan Report:
Economic Indicators for the New Orleans Area*, 18, no. 1 (August 2007), http://www.uno
.edu/coba/DBER/docs/MetroAug07.pdf.

6. Amy Liu and Allison Plyer, "A Review of Key Indicators of Recovery Two Years
after Katrina," *The New Orleans Index: Second Anniversary Special Edition*, data
tables (Brookings Institution Metropolitan Policy Program and Greater New Orleans
Community Data Center, August 2007) https://www.brookings.edu/research/
a-review-of-key-indicators-of-recovery-two-years-after-katrina-second-anniversary
-special-edition/; Carrie Kahn, "Population in Flux Redefines New Orleans," *National
Public Radio*, August 26, 2007, http://www.npr.org/templates/story/story.php?storyId
=13878477.

7. Allison Plyer, "How Many New Orleanians Are Still Displaced?," Greater New
Orleans Community Data Center, http://www.gnocdc.org/FAQ/index.html (page no
longer available).

8. Division of Business and Economic Research, University of New Orleans, *Metropolitan Report*.

9. Alan Sayre, "New Orleans Economic Recovery Stalls," Associated Press, August 29,
2007, http://www.abcmoney.co.uk/news/292007125895.htm (page no longer available).

10. Division of Business and Economic Research, University of New Orleans, *Metropolitan Report*, 4.

11. Harry Holzer and Robert I. Lerman, *Employment Issues and Challenges in Post-
Katrina New Orleans* (Washington, D.C.: Urban Institute, February 10, 2006), 1–2,
http://www.urban.org/url.cfm?ID=900921; Liu and Plyer, "Review of Key Indicators."

12. Paul Krugman, "The Tax-Cut Con," *New York Times*, September 14, 2003.

13. Ibid.

14. See Clyde Woods, *Development Arrested: Race, Power, and the Blues in the
Mississippi Delta* (New York: Verso, 1998), chapter 6, note 30; Russell Kirk, *The Attack
on Leviathan: Donald Davidson and Southern Conservatism*, Heritage Lectures, 206
(Washington, D.C.: Heritage Foundation, 1989); Krugman, "Tax-Cut Con."

15. [We think that Woods did not finish elaborating the connection he was making
between the New Deal and Reagan's "starve the beast" policies.—Eds.]

16. Krugman, "Tax-Cut Con." This isn't just speculation. Krugman writes, "Irving
Kristol, in his role as coeditor of the *Public Interest*, was arguably the single most important proponent of supply-side economics. But years later he suggested that he himself wasn't all that persuaded by the doctrine: 'I was not certain of its economic merits
but quickly saw its political possibilities.' Writing in 1995, he explained that his real aim
was to shrink the government and the tax cuts were a means to that end: 'The task, as
I saw it, was to create a new majority, which evidently would mean a conservative majority, which came to mean, in turn, a Republican majority—so political effectiveness
was the priority, not the accounting deficiencies of government.'"

17. Ibid.

18. Ibid.

19. Lawrence J. McAndrews, "Beyond Busing: George H. W. Bush and School Desegregation," *Educational Foundations* 15, no. 4 (Fall 2001): 41–56.

20. "The Texecutioner," Canadian Coalition Against the Death Penalty, http://www.ccadp.org/serialpresident.htm (site no longer available); U.S. Commission on Civil Rights, *Voting Irregularities in Florida during the 2000 Presidential Election*, June 2001, www.usccr.gov/pubs/vote2000/report/main.htm; Gregory Palast, "Vanishing Votes," *Nation*, May 17, 2004; Dan Eggen, "Justice Staff Saw Texas Districting as Illegal," *Washington Post*, December 2, 2005; Dan Eggen, "Civil Rights Focus Shift Roils Staff at Justice: Veterans Exit Division as Traditional Cases Decline," *Washington Post*, November 13, 2005; Bill Minutaglio, *First Son: George W. Bush and the Bush Family Dynasty* (New York: Three Rivers Press, 1999).

21. Meghan Clyne, "Rangel's Jibe at President Draws Support from Democrats," *New York Sun*, September 27, 2005.

22. Krugman, "Tax-Cut Con."

23. Ed Kilgore, "Starving the Beast: If President Bush Keeps Listening to Grover Norquist, Republicans Won't Have a Government to Kick around Anymore," *Blueprint Magazine* (Democratic Leadership Council), June 30, 2003, http://www.dlc.org/ndol_cic92b.html?kaid=127&subid=170&contentid=251788.

24. Meghan Gordon and Mark Schleifstein, "Corps Issue Call to Close MR-GO: Economic, not Storm Threat, Cited in Report," *Times-Picayune*, December 16, 2006. Although its own December 2006 preliminary report concluded that the channel should be closed, the corps refused to make a final decision on its fate until December 2007. At the behest of the hegemonic bloc and the firms that occasionally use the channel, the corps has decided to place the city on the precipice of another apocalypse while providing additional support for the redlining policy of major insurers who will be abandoning the city for years to come. See Andrew Martin and Andrew Zajac, "Flood-Control Funds Short of Requests," *Chicago Tribune*, September 1, 2005.

25. Federal Emergency Management Agency, "About the Agency," http://www.fema.gov/about.

26. Jessica Azulay, "FEMA Planned to Leave New Orleans Poor Behind," *New Standard*, September 4, 2005, http://newstandardnews.net/content/index.cfm/items/2322; Mark Schleifstein, "In Case of Emergency: Officials Hope Eight Days of Intense Training for a Catastrophic Hurricane Will Aid Recovery Efforts if the Real Thing Ever Hits," *Times-Picayune*, July 20, 2004; Mark Schleifstein, "Have Evacuation Plan, Will Travel— Survey Offers Insight on Locals' Attitudes," *Times-Picayune*, December 1, 2004.

27. Jan Moller, "Hurricane Scenario Tests Officials' Disaster Readiness; 'Pam' Helps Prepare Them for Severe Storm," *Times-Picayune*, July 24, 2004.

28. Testimony of Johnny B. Bradberry, secretary, Louisiana Department of Transportation and Development Secretary, U.S. Senate Committee on Homeland Security and Governmental Affairs, *Challenges in a Catastrophe: Evacuating New Orleans in Advance of Hurricane Katrina*, hearing, January 31, 2006, http://www.hsgac.senate.gov/hearings/evacuating-new-orleans-hurricane-katrina; Douglas Brinkley, *The Great Deluge: Hurricane Katrina, New Orleans, and the Mississippi Gulf Coast* (New York: William Morrow, 2006), 35.

29. Bruce Nolan, "In Storm, N.O. Wants No One Left Behind; Number of People without Cars Makes Evacuation Difficult," *Times-Picayune*, July 24, 2005.

30. Ann O'Neill, "Grim Signs of Katrina's Staggering Toll: 25,000 Body Bags Arrive in New Orleans," CNN, September 9, 2005.

31. Michael Brown, "Select Bipartisan Committee to Investigate Preparation for and Response to Hurricane Katrina," deposition, U.S. House of Representatives, Washington, D.C., February 11, 2006.

32. Chris Kromm, "Gulf Watch: Gingrich at CPAC: New Orleans Destroyed by Lack of Education, 'Citizenship,'" Institute for Southern Studies, March 5, 2007, http://www.southernstudies.org/2007/03/gulf-watch-gingrich-at-cpac-new-orleans-destroyed-by-lack-of-education-citizenship.html.

33. Gordon Russell, "Nagin Denies Racial Intent in His Speech: He Says Stories Misinterpreted Him," *Times-Picayune*, March 20, 2007; WDSU, New Orleans, "Nagin's Headline-Making Speech in D.C.," video, http://www.wdsu.com/ (page no longer available).

34. George W. Bush, "Bush: 'We will do what it takes,'" CNN, transcript of September 15, 2005 speech, http://www.cnn.com/2005/POLITICS/09/15/bush.transcript/index.html.

35. [The page with this footnote was missing from the original manuscript, and the information could not be located.—Eds.]

36. [The page with this footnote was missing from the original manuscript, and the information could not be located.—Eds.]

37. [The page with this footnote was missing from the original manuscript, and the information could not be located.—Eds.]

38. [The source of this quote could not be determined.—Eds.]

39. Clyde Woods, "Sittin' on Top of the World: The Challenges of Blues and Hip Hop Geography," in *Black Geographies and the Politics of Place*, ed. Katherine Mc-Kittrick and Clyde Woods (Cambridge, Mass.: South End Press, 2007), 46–81. Special thanks to Susan Ruddick of the University of Toronto for suggesting a closer investigation into the relationship between the plantation and neoliberal traditions.

40. Robert Dreyfuss, "How the DLC Does It," *American Prospect* 12, no. 7 (December 19, 2001); Democratic Leadership Council, "New Dem of the Week: Mary Landrieu, U.S. Senator, Louisiana," December 16, 2002, http://www.dlc.org/ndol_cid24a.html?contentid=251108&kaid=103&subid=110 (site no longer available); Democratic Leadership Council, "New Dem of the Week: Kathleen Blanco, Governor, Louisiana," October 18, 2004, http://www.dlc.org/ndol_ci28fb.html?kaid=104&subid=116&contentid=252958 (site no longer available); Democratic Leadership Council, "New Dem of the Week: Ray Nagin, Mayor, New Orleans," March 15, 2004, http://www.dlc.org/ndol_ci4999.html?kaid=104&subid=117&contentid=252452 (site no longer available); Democratic Leadership Council, "New Dem of the Week: Karen Carter, State Representative, Louisiana," December 19, 2004; "Membership," New Democrat Coalition, http://newdemocratcoalition-kind.house.gov/membership (page no longer available); Charlie Melancon, "Statement by Charlie Melancon: President and General Manager, American Sugar Cane League," http://www.ussugar.com/news/trade/archives_trade/2004/melancon_statement.html (page no longer available); "Caucus

Members," Congressional Progressive Caucus, http://cpc.grijalva.house.gov/caucus -members/; "Congressman Bennie Thompson, Representing the Second District of Mississippi," http://benniethompson.house.gov/.

41. Jayne Cortez and the Firespitters, "U.S./Nigerian Relations," *There It Is* (audio), Bola Press, 1982.

42. "History of the Yellow Dog Democrat," Yellow Dog History, www.yellowdog democrat.com/history.htm (site no longer available); The Blue Dogs, "Mike Ross (AR-04)," The Club for Growth, http://www.clubforgrowth.org/bluedogs/?id=822 (page no longer available).

43. Southern Auto Corridor, http://www.southernautocorridor.com/; David Firestone, "Black Families Resist Mississippi Land Push," *New York Times*, September 10, 2001; U.S. Department of Transportation, Federal Highway Administration, "Study of U.S. 43 and U.S. 80 Corridor Potential to Attract New Automotive Suppliers Based on Highway Improvements," November 2003, http://www.fhwa.dot.gov/planning/ economic_development/technical_and_analytical/alcor.cfm.

44. Samuel R. Schubert, "Revisiting the Oil Curse," *Development* 49, no. 3 (September 2006): 64–67.

45. Frederic T. Billings III, "Cancer Corridors and Toxic Terrors—Is It Safe to Eat and Drink?," *Transactions of the American Clinical and Climatological Association* 116 (2005): 116; John McQuaid, "'Cancer Alley': Myth or Fact?," *Times-Picayune*, May 23, 2000; Robert D. Bullard, *Dumping in Dixie: Race, Class and Environmental Quality*, 3rd ed. (Boulder, Colo.: Westview Press, 2000); Ben Greenberg, "Katrina Hits Cancer Alley: An Interview with Environmental Justice Activist Monique Harden," *Dollars & Sense Newsletter* 264 (Thomson Gale), March 1, 2006, 34; Steve Lerner, *Diamond: A Struggle for Environmental Justice in Louisiana's Chemical Corridor* (Cambridge, Mass.: MIT Press, 2005).

46. U.S. Department of the Interior, Minerals Management Service, Gulf of Mexico OCS Region, *Gulf of Mexico OCS Oil and Gas Scenario Examination: Pipeline Landfalls* (New Orleans: U.S. Department of the Interior, August 2007), 3, http://www.boem.gov/ BOEM-Newsroom/Library/Publications/2007/2007-053.aspx.

47. Michael A. Mohammed, "Will Natural Gas Prices Turn Off Louisiana's Chemical Industry?," *Times-Picayune*, July 31, 2004; Todd Billiot, "Report: State Has Highest Incarceration Rate per Capita," *Lafayette Daily Advertiser*, August 5, 2003.

48. Deon Roberts, "Protestors to Take on Road Home, La. Recovery Authority," *New Orleans City Business*, November 15, 2006; U.S. Department of Housing and Urban Development, "Jackson Approves Louisiana's $4.6 billion 'Road Home Program,'" HUD news release, May 30, 2006.

49. [We believe this quotation came from an interview Woods conducted, but we could not locate the interview.—Eds.]

50. [The source of this quotation could not be determined.—Eds.]

51. Greater New Orleans Community Data Center, "Public School Enrollment 2000–2007," http://www.gnocdc.org/school_enrollment.html (page no longer available). Data compiled from Louisiana Department of Education.

52. Steve Ritea, "N.O. Teachers Union Loses Its Force in Storm's Wake," *Times-Picayune*, March 5, 2006; Bill Quigley, "Fighting for the Right to Learn: The Public Ed-

ucation Experiment in New Orleans Two Years after Katrina," *San Francisco Bay View*, August 15, 2007; American Federation of Teachers, Louisiana Federation of Teachers, and United Teachers of New Orleans, Louisiana, *No Experience Necessary: How the New Orleans School Takeover Experiment Devalues Experienced Teachers*, June 1, 2007; Brookings Institution, *The New Orleans Index: Second Anniversary Special Edition*, data tables (Brookings Institution Metropolitan Policy Program and Greater New Orleans Community Data Center, August 2007); Associated Press, "Louisiana to Receive $23.9 Million Charter School Grant," *USA Today*, June 12, 2006; Governor of Louisiana, Executive Department, "Emergency Suspension to Assist in Meeting Educational Needs of Louisiana Students Regarding Type 3 Charter Schools," Executive Order No. KBB 2005–79, October 28, 2005, http://www.blancogovernor.com/assets/docs/Executive_Orders/79Type3CharterSchool.pdf.

53. Cultural and educational activist, interview by Clyde Woods, July 2007.

54. [We believe this quotation came from an interview Woods conducted, but we could not locate the interview.—Eds.]

55. Leader of women's organizations, interview by Clyde Woods, July 2007.

56. Urban Land Institute, "Proposal to House More Than 300,000 New Orleans Residents Announced by ULI and New Orleans Housing Officials," March 21, 2006.

57. Policy Link, "Louisiana: Analysis of Development Trends," August 2007, http://www.policylink.org/Communities/Louisiana/NewOrleans.html#Analysis (page no longer available).

58. Institute for Southern Studies, "Lack of Shelter Imperils New Orleans' Homeless," *Facing South*, November 2006, http://www.southernstudies.org/2006/11/lack-of-shelter-imperils-new-orleans-homeless.html.

59. [We believe this quotation came from an interview with a youth cultural worker, but we could not locate the interview.—Eds.]

60. Sharon L. Crenson, "New Orleans, Ravaged by Katrina, Hit Again by Subprime Crisis," Bloomberg.Com, May 10, 2007.

61. [This very compelling quote advances the argument, but we have been unable to verify the source.—Eds.]

62. American Civil Liberties Union, *Broken Promises: Two Years after Katrina*, August 2007.

63. Ibid.

64. [We believe this quotation comes from an interview with a senior service provider, but we could not locate the interview.—Eds.]

65. *Crime in the United States: Preliminary Annual Uniform Crime Report* (Washington, D.C.: Federal Bureau of Investigation, 2006); Brendan McCarthy, "Study: Murder Rate Is Even Higher: Figures Make N.O. the Deadliest City," *Times-Picayune*, March 12, 2007.

66. [We believe this quotation comes from an interview with a cultural leader, but we could not locate the interview.—Eds.]

67. [We believe this quotation came from an interview with a social movement leader, but we could not locate the interview.—Eds.]

68. Mathematica Policy Research, Inc., and Feeding America (formerly America's Second Harvest), *Hunger in America 2006 Local Report Prepared for the Second Harvest*

Food Bank of Greater New Orleans and Acadiana, February 1, 2006, 2–4; "LFBA Seeking State Help to Stave Off Looming Hunger Crisis," *Louisiana Weekly*, April 23, 2007.

69. Clancy DuBos, "Blanco's Legacy," *Gambit Weekly*, May 8, 2007; Bill Barrow, "Marchers Demand Blanco's Attention," *Times-Picayune*, June 15, 2007.

70. Bill Barrow, "All Road Home Money Has Been Committed," *Times-Picayune*, June 11, 2007.

71. The Road Home, "Program Statistics as of September 17, 2007," no. 36, September 20, 2007, http://www.roadcommunications.com/index.cfm?md=emaillist&tmp =viewcampaign&nowrap=1&msgid=287&uid=hW (site no longer available); Miguel Bustillo, "New Orleans: Two years Later: Half Empty, Half Full after Katrina," *Los Angeles Times*, August 25, 2007; Michelle Krupa, "LRA Shifts $557.5 Million in Federal Aid to Road Home Program," *Times-Picayune*, June 25, 2007; David Hammer, "Road Home Shortfall $1 Billion Higher," *Times-Picayune*, September 21, 2007.

72. [We believe this quotation came from an interview with a senior social service provider, but we could not locate the interview.—Eds.]

73. U.S. Department of Housing and Urban Development, Office of Public Affairs, "Conference Call: Housing Assistance for Residents Affected by Gulf Coast Hurricanes," transcript, April 26, 2007, Washington, D.C.: Federal Emergency Management Administration, 2007, 30–31, http://www.fema.gov/txt/media/2007/hud_fema_presser.txt.

74. Mary Foster, "Katrina Victims Feel Trapped by Trailers: With No Replacement Housing, Those Displaced by Katrina Feel Trapped in FEMA Trailers," Associated Press, August 4, 2007, http://www.ccdiobr.org/news/74-mary-foster.

75. [We believe this quotation came from an interview with a social service provider, but we could not locate the interview.—Eds.]

76. *Hurricane Katrina Evacuees in Texas* (Austin: Texas Health and Human Services Commission, August 2006).

77. Mark J. Schafer and Joachim Singelmann, *Louisiana FEMA Park Survey: Interim Report* (Louisiana Recovery Authority, April 2007); Davey D, "Breakdown FM: Fighting for the Soul of the City: Meet New Orleans Rapper," session 4–5, September 6, 2007, http://katrinareader.org/toc/620 [This interview by Davey D has been widely cited on the Internet, but we could not locate a working audio link.—Eds.]

78. [We believe that this quotation came from an interview conducted with a New Orleans community leader, but we could not locate the interview.—Eds.]

79. David Harvey, "Neoliberalism as Creative Destruction," *Annals of the American Academy of Political and Social Science* 610 (March 2007): 39–43.

Conclusion. The Cornerstone of a Third Reconstruction

1. Paul Ortiz, "The New Battle for New Orleans," in *Hurricane Katrina: Response and Responsibilities*, ed. John Brown Childs (Santa Cruz, Calif.: New Pacific Press, 2005), 1–9.

2. See Anjali Kamat's film *Baltimore Rising*, Al Jazeera America, June 7, 2015; and Kamat, "The Baltimore Uprising," in *Policing the Planet: Why the Policing Crisis Led to Black Lives Matter*, ed. Jordan T. Camp and Christina Heatherton (New York: Verso, 2016), 73–82.

3. Clyde A. Woods, "Life after Death," *Professional Geographer* 54, no. 1 (2002): 62.

4. Ibid., 64–65. For a documentation of the movement for social justice in post-Katrina New Orleans, see Jordan Flaherty, *Floodlines: Community and Resistance from Katrina to the Jena Six* (Chicago: Haymarket Books, 2010).

5. Clyde A. Woods, "Katrina's World: Blues, Bourbon, and the Return to the Source," *American Quarterly* 61, no. 3 (2009): 429.

6. On the connection between the South and U.S. neoliberalism, see Nancy Mac-Lean, "Southern Dominance in Borrowed Language: The Regional Origins of American Neoliberalism," in *New Landscapes of Inequality: Neoliberalism and the Erosion of Democracy in America*, ed. J. Collins, M. di Leonardo, and B. Williams (Santa Fe, N.M.: School for Advanced Research Press, 2008), 21–37.

7. On the extreme influence of the South, especially large planters, in the nineteenth century, see Bruce Levine, *The Fall of the House of Dixie: The Civil War and the Social Revolution That Transformed the South* (New York: Random House, 2013).

8. Mike Davis, foreword to *New Orleans under Reconstruction: The Crises of Planning*, by Anthony Fontenot, Carol McMichael Reese, and Michael Sorkin (New York: Verso, 2014), xi.

9. On direct housing assistance, see Cushing Dolbeare and Sheila Crowley, *Changing Priorities: The Federal Budget and Housing Assistance, 1976–2007*, (Washington, D.C.: National Low Income Housing Coalition, August 2002), http://nlihc.org/library/other/periodic/changing-priorities-1976-2007. On HUD's budget more generally, see Western Regional Advocacy Project (WRAP), *Without Housing: Decades of Federal Housing Cutbacks, Massive Homelessness, and Policy Failures* (San Francisco: WRAP, n.d.); WRAP, "2012 HUD Budget Fact Sheet," wraphome.org. For a detailed examination of FEMA's role, see Rita King, "Post-Katrina Profiteering: The New Big Easy," in *Race, Place, and Environmental Justice after Hurricane Katrina*, ed. R. Bullard and B. Wright (Boulder, Colo.: Westview Press, 2009), 169–82.

10. King, "Post-Katrina Profiteering," 170.

11. Naomi Klein, *The Shock Doctrine: The Rise of Disaster Capitalism* (New York: Picador, 2007); Kate Driscoll Derickson, "The Racial Politics of Neoliberal Regulation in Post-Katrina Mississippi," *Annals of the Association of American Geographers* 104, no. 4 (2014): 889–902; Geoffrey Whitehall and Cedric Johnson, "Making Citizens in Magnaville: Katrina Refugees and Neoliberal Self-Governance," in *The Neoliberal Deluge: Hurricane Katrina, Late Capitalism, and the Remaking of New Orleans*, ed. Cedric Johnson (Minneapolis: University of Minnesota Press, 2011), 60–84.

12. Derickson, "Racial Politics of Neoliberal Regulation"; Eric Ishiwata, "We Are Seeing People We Didn't Know Exist: Katrina and the Neoliberal Erasure of Race," in C. Johnson, *Neoliberal Deluge*, 32–59; Eric Mann, *Katrina's Legacy: White Racism and Black Reconstruction in New Orleans and the Gulf Coast* (Los Angeles: Frontlines Press, 2006).

13. Lynnell Thomas, *Desire and Disaster in New Orleans: Tourism, Race, and Historical Memory* (Durham, N.C.: Duke University Press, 2014), esp. chapter 5. Quotes from pp. 128, 149, and 161, respectively.

14. On schools, see Kristen L. Buras with Jim Randels, Kalamu ya Salaam, and Students at the Center, *Pedagogy, Policy, and the Privatized City: Stories of Dispossession and Defiance from New Orleans* (New York: Teachers College Press, 2010);

Catherine Michna, "Stories at the Center: Story Circles, Educational Organizing, and Fate of Neighborhood Public Schools in New Orleans" *American Quarterly* 61, no. 3 (2009): 529–55; Adrienne Dixon, "Whose Choice? A Critical Race Perspective on Charter Schools," in C. Johnson, *Neoliberal Deluge*, 130–51. On churches, see Trushna Parekh, "Of Armed Guards and Kente Cloth: Afro-Creole Catholics and the Battle for St. Augustine Parish in Post-Katrina New Orleans," *American Quarterly* 61, no. 3 (2009): 557–81. On housing, see Lisa Bates and Rebekah Green, "Housing Recovery in the Ninth Ward: Disparities in Policy, Process and Prospects," in Bullard and Wright, *Race, Place, and Environmental Justice*, 229–45; Elizabeth Fusell and Elizabeth Harris, "Homeownership and Housing Displacement after Hurricane Katrina among Low-Income African-American Mothers in New Orleans," *Social Science Quarterly* 95, no. 4 (2014): 1086–1110; Cedric Johnson, "Charming Accommodations: Progressive Urbanism Meets Privatization in Brad Pitt's Make It Right Foundation," in C. Johnson, *Neoliberal Deluge*, 187–224; Whitehall and Johnson, "Making Citizens in Magnaville"; John Arena, "Black and White, Unite and Fight: Identity Politics and New Orleans's Post-Katrina Public Housing Movement," in C. Johnson, *Neoliberal Deluge*, 152–83. On the rightward drift in Louisiana politics, see Vijay Prashad, "Bobby Jindal Is the Republican's Obama," *Progressive*, January 16, 2008, http:// progressive.org/.

15. Fusell and Harris, "Homeownership and Housing Displacement."

16. Thomas, *Desire and Disaster*, 135.

17. Jordan T. Camp, *Incarcerating the Crisis: Freedom Struggles and the Rise of the Neoliberal State* (Oakland: University of California Press, 2016), 116-132.

18. Quoted in Parekh, "Of Armed Guards and Kente Cloth," 559.

19. On privatized housing, see C. Johnson, "Charming Accommodations"; Whitehall and Johnson, "Making Citizens in Magnaville."

20. On Latino workers in New Orleans, see Nicole Trujillo-Pagan, "Hazardous Constructions: Mexican Immigrant Masculinity and the Rebuilding of New Orleans" in C. Johnson, *Neoliberal Deluge*, 327–53. On the Vietnamese community, see Eric Tang, "A Gulf Unites Us: The Vietnamese Americans of Black New Orleans East," *American Quarterly* 63, no. 1 (March 2011): 117–49. On the evolving state of the U.S. racial formation, see Eduardo Bonilla-Silva, "From Bi-racial to Tri-racial: Towards a New System of Racial Stratification in the USA," *Ethnic and Racial Studies* 27 (2004): 931–50; Andrew Sluyter, Case Watkins, James Chaney, and Annie Gibson, *Hispanic and Latino New Orleans* (Baton Rouge: Louisiana State University Press, 2015).

21. John Logan, "Unnatural Disaster: Social Impacts and Policy Choices after Katrina," in Bullard and Wright, *Race, Place, and Environmental Justice*, 249–64.

22. Nihal Shrinath, Vicki Mack, and Allison Plyer, *Who Lives in New Orleans and Metro Parishes Now?* (Data Center Research.org, October 2014), https://gnocdc.s3 .amazonaws.com/reports/TheDataCenter_WhoLivesInNewOrleansAndMetroParishes Now.pdf.

23. John Arena, *Driven from New Orleans: How Nonprofits Betray Public Housing and Promote Privatization* (Minneapolis: University of Minnesota Press, 2012).

24. Mary Bruce, "Duncan: Katrina Was the 'Best Thing' for New Orleans School System," January 29, 2010,ABCNews.com, http://blogs.abcnews.com/politicalpunch/

2010/01/duncan-katrina-was-the-best-thing-for-new-orleans-schools.html. On public
schools more generally, see Michna, "Stories at the Center"; Dixon, "Whose Choice?"

25. On the history of Caribbean hurricanes, see Stuart Schwartz, *Sea of Storms: A
History of Hurricanes in the Greater Caribbean from Columbus to Katrina* (Princeton,
N.J.: Princeton University Press, 2015). On the destruction of the bayou, see Mike Tid-
well, *Bayou Farewell: The Rich Life and Tragic Death of Louisiana's Cajun Coast* (New
York: Vintage, 2003).

CREDITS

The University of Georgia Press and the editors gratefully acknowledge the permission to reprint the following poems and song lyrics:

INDEX

abandonment: of New Orleans, xxv, 268–70, 285–86; policies of, xxii, 11

Abbott, Robert S., 105

abolition movement, 38

ACLU (American Civil Liberties Union), 282–83

Adams, John Quincy, 19

affirmative action, 148, 272; elimination of, 241–42, 264

African Americans: class divisions among, 187; demonization of, 79, 115, 237, 262, 264, 268, 270; disenfranchisement of, xxiv, 30, 55, 57–58, 70–71, 76, 114, 121, 124, 165, 233, 234; disposability of, 74, 187, 267, 269, 297; and electoral politics, 211–12; enclosure of, xxii–xxiii, 180, 274; Great Migration of, xxvii; impoverishment of, 274; incarceration rates of, 238–39; political power of, 124

African Communities League, 96

Agricultural Adjustment Act (1935), 147; enclosure policies of, 123, 159

Agriculture Street landfill, 186, 201, 247

Aid to Families with Dependent Children, 272

Alexander, Avery, 241

Alexander, Texas, 93

Allen, Lee, 165, 168

Allen, Oscar Kelly, Sr., 118

American Zulu Social and Pleasure Club, 65–66, 221

Anderson, Leafy, 138, 140

Anderson, Thomas W., 101

Annie E. Casey Foundation, 242, 243

anticommunism, 119, 149; and Catholicism, 178

antimiscegenation laws, 71

antiracism, xxi, 1–2, 155, 288; and blues development tradition, 94; and communism, xxvii; working class, xxvii. See also racism

anti-Semitism, 119

Archie, Adolph, 237

Ardoin, Amédé, 142–43, 169, 322n67

Armstrong, Louis, xxviii, 72, 73, 77, 93, 131; and New Orleans Renaissance, 94; "The Saints," version of, 122

Army Corps of Engineers, 109, 182–84, 186, 210, 266, 282, 335n44

assimilation, 63, 195, 200; and colonization, 4, 6–7, 9, 12, 29; and uplift, 188

Atlanta Exposition, 64

Atwater, Lee, 264

authoritarianism, xxiii, 55, 84; and Bourbonism, xxiv–xxv, 57, 66; and oil dependency, 222–23, 238, 329n34; and plantation bloc, 55

Badger, Algernon Sidney, 51–52

Bambara, 9; knowledge system of, 31

Bambara, Samba, 12, 14

Bambara Conspiracy, 12, 14

Banana Republic, origin of term, 83

Banks, Nathaniel, 40

Baptiste-Colbert, Jean, 4

Barbour, Haley, 251–54; Medicaid cuts under, 252–53

Barker, Danny, 77, 91, 92

Barthelemy, Sidney, 200, 213–14, 221, 229, 237; budgets cuts of, 235–36

Bartholomew, Dave, 167–68, 170, 174

Batiste, Alvin, 168

Batiste, Becate, 65, 128, 130

Battiste, Harold, 168

Battle of Liberty Place, 54, 56, 112, 308n63

Beauregard, P. G. T., 57

Be Bop, 154, 168. See also Jazz

Bechet, Sidney, 78

CPSIA information can be obtained
at www.ICGtesting.com
Printed in the USA
LVHW092304031222
734541LV00017B/1158

9 780820 350929